The Shi'i World

Pathways in Tradition and Modernity

CW01499484

Edited by
Farhad Daftary,
Amyn B. Sajoo and
Shainool Jiwa

I.B.Tauris *Publishers*
LONDON · NEW YORK
in association with
The Institute of Ismaili Studies
LONDON

Published in 2015 by
I.B.Tauris & Co. Ltd
London • New York
www.ibtauris.com

in association with The Institute of Ismaili Studies
210 Euston Road, London NW1 2DA
www.iis.ac.uk

Every attempt has been made to gain permission for the use of the images in this
book. Any omissions will be rectified in future editions.

References to websites were correct at the time of writing.

ISBN: 978 1 78453 477 6
eISBN: 978 0 85772 967 5

A full CIP record for this book is available from the British Library
A full CIP record is available from the Library of Congress

Library of Congress Catalog Card Number: available

Typeset in Minion Pro for The Institute of Ismaili Studies

Printed and bound by in Great Britain by T.J. International, Padstow, Cornwall

The Shi'i World

The Institute of Ismaili Studies

MUSLIM HERITAGE SERIES, 4

General Editor: Amyn B. Sajoo

This series explores vital themes in the civilisations of Islam – including the nature of religious authority, ethics and law, social justice and civil society, the arts and sciences, and the interplay of spiritual and secular lifeworlds. In keeping with the Institute's mandate, the series is informed by the plurality of communities and interpretations of Islam, as well as their locus in modernity and tradition.

Previously published titles:
1. *A Companion to the Muslim World*, ed. Amyn B. Sajoo (2009)
2. *A Companion to Muslim Ethics*, ed. Amyn B. Sajoo (2010)
3. *A Companion to Muslim Cultures*, ed. Amyn B. Sajoo (2013)

The Institute of Ismaili Studies

The Institute of Ismaili Studies was established in 1977 with the object of promoting scholarship and learning on Islam, in the historical as well as contemporary contexts, and a better understanding of its relationship with other societies and faiths.

The Institute's programmes encourage a perspective which is not confined to the theological and religious heritage of Islam, but seeks to explore the relationship of religious ideas to broader dimensions of society and culture. The programmes thus encourage an interdisciplinary approach to the materials of Islamic history and thought. Particular attention is also given to issues of modernity that arise as Muslims seek to relate their heritage to the contemporary situation.

Within the Islamic tradition, the Institute's programmes promote research on those areas which have, to date, received relatively little attention from scholars. These include the intellectual and literary expressions of Shi'ism in general, and Ismailism in particular.

In the context of Islamic societies, the Institute's programmes are informed by the full range and diversity of cultures in which Islam is practised today, from the Middle East, South and Central Asia, and Africa to the industrialised societies of the West, thus taking into consideration the variety of contexts which shape the ideals, beliefs and practices of the faith.

These objectives are realised through concrete programmes and activities organised and implemented by various departments of the Institute. The Institute also collaborates periodically, on a programme-specific basis, with other institutions of learning in the United Kingdom and abroad.

The Institute's academic publications fall into a number of inter-related categories:

1. Occasional papers or essays addressing broad themes of the relationship between religion and society, with special reference to Islam.
2. Monographs exploring specific aspects of Islamic faith and culture, or the contributions of individual Muslim thinkers or writers.
3. Editions or translations of significant primary or secondary texts.
4. Translations of poetic or literary texts which illustrate the rich heritage of spiritual, devotional and symbolic expressions in Muslim history.
5. Works on Ismaili history and thought, and the relationship of the Ismailis to other traditions, communities and schools of thought in Islam.
6. Proceedings of conferences and seminars sponsored by the Institute.
7. Bibliographical works and catalogues which document manuscripts, printed texts and other source materials.

This book falls into category 2 listed above.

In facilitating these and other publications, the Institute's sole aim is to encourage original research and analysis of relevant issues. While every effort is made to ensure that the publications are of a high academic standard, there is naturally bound to be a diversity of views, ideas and interpretations. As such, the opinions expressed in these publications must be understood as belonging to their authors alone.

Contents

List of Illustrations

Chapter 11

Chapter 13

Chapter 14

Chapter 16

About the Contributors

Rula J. Abisaab is an Associate Professor and former Acting Director at McGill University's Institute of Islamic Studies (Montreal), where she teaches diverse areas of Islamic and Shi'i history. Her research is focused on two aspects of Shi'i studies: the juristic tradition and its historical transformation, with particular regard to the relations of religion and power; and on modern clerical leadership, including the role of Marxism and secularism in postcolonial Shi'i thought. Her publications include *Converting Persia: Religion and Power in Safavid Iran* (London, 2004) and *The Shi'ites of Lebanon: Modernism, Communism and Hizbullah's Islamists* (Syracuse, 2014; co-author with Malek Abisaab). She is also a poet, and her collection *Ghilaf al-qalb* (*The Heart's Peel*) (2014) is being translated into English and French.

Ali S. Asani is Professor of Indo-Muslim and Islamic Religion and Cultures at Harvard and Director of the university's Prince Al-Waleed bin Talal Program in Islamic Studies. His research focuses on Ismaili and Sufi devotional traditions in South Asia. Asani's books include *The Bujh Niranjan: An Ismaili Mystical Poem* (Cambridge, MA, 1992); *The Harvard Collection of Ismaili Literature in Indic Languages: A Descriptive Catalog and Finding Aid* (Boston, 1992); *Celebrating Muhammad: Images of the Prophet in Muslim Devotional Poetry* (Columbia, SC, 1995; co-author); and *Ecstasy and Enlightenment: The Ismaili Devotional Literature of South Asia* (London, 2002). In 2002 he was awarded the Harvard Foundation medal for outstanding contributions to intercultural and race relations at Harvard and in the nation, and he is a recipient of Harvard's Petra Shattuck Excellence in Teaching Award.

Bridget Blomfield is the Director of the Islamic Studies programme at the University of Nebraska at Omaha, where she is Associate Professor of Religious Studies. She has contributed extensively to academic volumes and journals on issues concerning Shi'i diasporic women, the symbolism of Fatima, *adab*, and teaching about Islam, and she is the author of *The Language of Tears: My Five Year Journey into the World of*

Shi'i Women (Ashland, OR, 2015). Blomfield's current research interests are Iraqi Shi'i refugees living in Lincoln, Nebraska, and narrating voices from Palestinian villages.

Jonathan M. Bloom shares the Norma Jean Calderwood University Professorship of Islamic and Asian Art at Boston College, and the Hamad bin Khalifa Endowed Chair of Islamic Art at Virginia Commonwealth University with his wife and colleague, Sheila Blair. His latest publication, *The Minaret* (Edinburgh, 2013), is a revised version of his 1989 book on this quintessential architectural form. His *Arts of the City Victorious: Islamic Art and Architecture in Fatimid North Africa and Egypt* (New Haven, 2007) is the first book-length study on the art patronised by this Shi'i Ismaili dynasty. Bloom's *Paper before Print: The History and Impact of Paper in the Islamic Lands* (New Haven, 2001) won the 2003 Morey Prize in art history. With Sheila Blair he edited *God is Beautiful and Loves Beauty: The Object in Islamic Art and Civilization* (New Haven, 2013), and the *Grove Encyclopedia of Islamic Art and Architecture* (New York, 2009), which won the 2010 World Book of the Year Prize in the Islamic Republic of Iran.

Karim Douglas Crow is Principal Fellow at the International Institute of Advanced Islamic Studies (IAIS) in Kuala Lumpur, Malaysia. He has taught at Columbia University, the University of Virginia, New York University and the Rajaratnam School of International Studies, Singapore. He also serves as curriculum advisor for peace organisations in the Middle East, Indonesia and the Caucasus. Crow's books include *Shi'ah Islam* (Singapore, 2005); he has also edited *Islam, Cultural Transformation, and the Re-Emergence of Falsafah* (Tehran, 2009).

Farhad Daftary is the Co-Director of The Institute of Ismaili Studies, London (IIS), where he also heads (since 1992) the Department of Academic Research and Publications. He is a consulting-editor of *Encyclopaedia Iranica*, co-editor of *Encyclopaedia Islamica*, a member of the advisory board of the *Encyclopaedia of Islam* (3rd ed.), and general editor of the IIS's Ismaili Heritage Series, Ismaili Texts and Translations Series and Shi'i Heritage Series. An authority on Ismaili studies, Daftary has written more than 150 articles and written and edited more than a dozen acclaimed books in this field, including *The Isma'ilis: Their History and Doctrines* (Cambridge, 1990, 2nd ed., 2007), *The Assassin Legends: Myths of the Isma'ilis* (London, 1994), *Mediaeval Isma'ili History and Thought* (Cambridge, 1996), *Ismaili Literature* (London, 2004), *The Ismailis: An Illustrated History* (London, 2008; co-author with Z. Hirji), *A Modern History of the Ismailis* (London, 2011), *Historical Dictionary* *of the Ismailis* (Lanham, MD and Toronto, 2012) and *A History of Shi'i Islam* (London, 2013). Most recently, he has edited W. Ivanow's memoirs, entitled *Fifty Years in the East* (London, 2015). His books have been translated into Arabic, Persian, Turkish, Urdu, Gujarati, Chinese and numerous European languages.

Zulfikar Hirji is an Associate Professor and Graduate Program Director in anthropology at York University. He is the co-author of *The Ismailis: An Illustrated History* (London, 2008), editor of *Diversity and Pluralism in Muslim Contexts* (London, 2010), and author of *Between Empires* (London, 2012), an illustrated biography of Sheikh Mbarak al-Hinawy (d. 1959) set within the context of colonial East Africa, and editor of *The Qur'an in Sub-Saharan Africa* (Oxford, forthcoming). His research focuses on the social and cultural expressions of Muslims in a variety of historical and contemporary contexts, particularly in the western Indian Ocean and other diasporic arenas.

Shainool Jiwa is the head of the Constituency Studies Unit at The Institute of Ismaili Studies, where she specialises in Fatimid history. Previously, she was the co-ordinator of the Institute's Quranic Studies Unit. Dr Jiwa is on the Board of Governors of Edinburgh Napier University, and serves as a chief examiner in Islamic history for the International Baccalaureate Organization. Her latest publication is *The Founder of Cairo: The Fatimid Imam-Caliph al-Muizz and his Era* (London, 2013), which complements her earlier work, *Towards a Shi'i Mediterranean Empire* (London, 2009). She is currently working on a monograph on the life and times of the Fatimid Imam-caliph al-'Aziz bi'llah.

Zayn Kassam is the John Knox McLean Professor of Religious Studies at Pomona College in Claremont, California. Honoured with three Wig Awards for Distinguished Teaching, as well as an Excellence in Teaching Award from the American Academy of Religion, she has lectured widely on both sides of the Atlantic. Kassam is the author of *Introduction to the World's Major Religions: Islam* (Westport, CN, 2006), and editor of *Women and Islam* (Santa Barbara, CA, 2010). She has published articles on a range of issues relating to the status of women, mysticism and ecology in Islam, as well as on the teaching of Islam in diverse settings.

Andrew J. Newman is Reader in Islamic Studies and Persian at the University of Edinburgh. His *Twelver Shi'ism: Unity and Diversity in the Life of Islam, 632 to 1722* (Edinburgh, 2013) is the basis of his chapter here. He is also the author of *Safavid Iran: Rebirth of a Persian Empire* (London, 2006), *The Formative Period of Shi'i Law: Hadith as Discourse Between Qum and Baghdad* (Richmond, 2000) and numerous articles and chapters in books on Twelver Shiʿism and on Shiʿism in Safawid Iran. He is the founder of the 'Shiʿi News' listserve, 'Chercheur associé' of the CNRS (UMR 7528 Mondes Iranien et Indien) and section editor, History of Iran, for *The Encyclopedia of Islam* (3rd ed.).

Eric Ormsby was a Senior Research Associate at The Institute of Ismaili Studies from 2005 until his retirement in 2013. He was previously the Director of McGill University's Institute of Islamic Studies, Montreal, and earlier, Curator of Islamic Manuscripts at Princeton University, New Jersey. His most recent publication was a translation of Nasir-i Khusraw's last known work, *Jamiʿ al-hikmatayn* under the title *Between Reason and Revelation* (London, 2012). Ormsby is the author of *Ghazali: The Revival of Islam* (Oxford, 2007), and of numerous articles on Islamic philosophy, theology and mysticism, including chapters in the IIS's Muslim Heritage Series. He is a frequent contributor to *The New York Times Book Review*, the *Times Literary Supplement*, *The New Criterion* and the *Wall Street Journal*.

Nacim Pak-Shiraz is Head of Persian Studies and Senior Lecturer in Persian and Film Studies at the University of Edinburgh. She was previously a lecturer at The Institute of Ismaili Studies and has written extensively on Iranian cinema, including on genre and comedy. Her chapter here draws on and adds to material from her book *Shiʿi Islam in Iranian Cinema: Religion and Spirituality in Film* (London, 2011). Her current research focuses on religious epics, and constructions of masculinity in Iranian cinema.

Karen Ruffle is an Associate Professor in the Department of Historical Studies and the Department for the Study of Religion at the University of Toronto. She is a scholar of Indo-Persian Shiʿism, focusing on devotional texts, ritual practice, and material practices in South Asia. She is the author of *Gender, Sainthood, and Everyday Practice in South Asian Shiʿism* (Chapel Hill, NC, 2011). Her current research and publications focus on issues of Shiʿi material practices and ritual performance, as well as on broader comparative religious material practices in the Indian Ocean World.

Omid Safi is the Director of Islamic Studies at Duke University, and has been 'Study of Islam' chair of the American Academy of Religion. He was recognised in 2009 and again in 2010 for outstanding contributions to teaching at the University of North Carolina. His scholarship focuses on modernity and religion, including the interface with liberationist thought, as well as on Islamic mysticism. Safi is the editor of several books including *Progressive Muslims: On Justice, Gender, and*

Pluralism (Oxford, 2003), *Politics of Knowledge in Premodern Islam* (Chapel Hill, NC, 2006), *Voices of Islam: Voices of Change* (Westport, CT, 2006), *The Cambridge Companion to American Islam* (with Julianne Hammer, Cambridge, 2013), and the author of *Memories of Muhammad* (New York, 2009), on which his present chapter is based, with appreciation to his publisher, HarperCollins. He is a regular contributor to international news media, and blogs regularly at OnBeing (www.onbeing.org).

Amyn B. Sajoo is Scholar-in-Residence at Simon Fraser University's Centre for the Comparative Study of Muslim Societies and Cultures (Vancouver). He has held visiting appointments at Cambridge and McGill Universities, the Institute of Southeast Asian Studies in Singapore, and The Institute of Ismaili Studies in London, where he was founding editor of the Muslim Heritage Series. His books include *Civil Society in the Muslim World* (London, 2002), *Muslim Ethics* (London, 2004), *Muslim Modernities* (London, 2008) and *A Companion to Muslim Cultures* (London, 2012). He is a frequent contributor to the news media, including the *Guardian*, *Christian Science Monitor*, *Globe and Mail*, and *Asian Wall Street Journal*. Sajoo was the Canadian Department of Foreign Affairs' 2010 Middle East Visiting Academic (in Egypt, Jordan and Syria), having earlier served as an advisor to the Justice Department in Ottawa.

Reza Shah-Kazemi is a Research Associate at The Institute of Ismaili Studies, where he also serves as managing editor of *Encyclopaedia Islamica*. He has lectured internationally in the areas of Quranic studies, Sufism, Shi'ism and Comparative Mysticism. Shah-Kazemi's publications include *Paths to Transcendence: According to Shankara, Ibn Arabi and Meister Eckhart* (Bloomington, IN, 2006), *Justice and Remembrance: An Introduction to the Spirituality of Imam Ali* (London, 2006), *The Other in the Light of the One: The Universality of the Qur'an and Interfaith Dialogue* (Cambridge, 2006), *Common Ground between Islam and Buddhism* (Louisville, KY, 2010), *Spiritual Quest: Reflections on Quranic Prayer according to the Teachings of Imam Ali* (London, 2011) and *The Spirit of Tolerance in Islam* (London, 2012).

William Sumits is an ethnomusicologist and music historian who specialises in the music of Central Asia and the greater Middle East, and has been a Research Fellow at the University of Central Asia in Tajikistan. His research has explored the comparative history of *maqam* traditions, innovation within tradition, and historical sound recordings. He has collaborated in a variety of capacities with the Aga Khan Music Initiative (AKMI) on music education programmes in Central Asia, working with traditional musicians and music educators to explore new models in traditional music performance, education and innovation. AKMI director Fairouz Nishanova, Senior Project Consultant Theodore Levin and Consultant Anna Senerslan also contributed to this chapter.

Paul E. Walker is the Deputy Director for academic programmes at the University of Chicago's Center for Middle Eastern Studies, having served as Director of the American Research Center in Cairo (1976–86). His current research focuses on popular ritual, governing institutions and Ismaili doctrine in the Fatimid period. As a specialist in the history of Islamic thought, Walker has published numerous articles and 12 books, among them *Early Philosophical Shiism: The Ismaili Neoplatonism of Abu Ya'qub al-Sijistani* (Cambridge, 1993), *The Advent of the Fatimids: A Contemporary Shi'i Witness* (London, 2000; co-author with Wilferd Madelung); *Exploring an Islamic Empire: Fatimid History and its Sources* (London, 2002), *Orations of the Fatimid Caliphs: Festival Sermons of the Ismaili Imams* (London, 2009), and *Caliph of Cairo: al-Hakim bi-Amr Allah, 996–1021* (Cairo, 2009). His most recent work is *A Code of Conduct* (London, 2011; co-author with Verena Klemm), an edition of the Arabic text and English translation of al-Naysaburi's *al-Risala al-mujaza al-kafiya*.

Introduction

Farhad Daftary, Amyn B. Sajoo and Shainool Jiwa

The burgeoning process of the recovery of Shiʻi texts over the past few decades has kindled scholarly interest in the study of Shiʻi Islam, establishing it as a fertile area within the field of Islamic studies and related disciplines. This dedicated attention to the many expressions of Shiʻi Islam that have appeared over the course of the centuries is long overdue: for most of its existence Shiʻi Islam has been described by its detractors as the other, and sometimes inherently inimical, face of Islam. Constituting over 15 per cent of the global Muslim population, the Shiʻi communities include Twelver Shiʻis (Ithnaʻasharis), Ismailis, Zaydis and Alawis, not counting others who have Shiʻi origins, such as the Druze, and the Turkish Alevis. In addition to their significant numbers (around 200 million), Shiʻi Muslims have, both historically and in contemporary times, played a crucial role in furthering the intellectual and cultural efflorescence of the Muslim world, adding to its richness and diversity.

Yet Sunni authors, who represent a different strand of literary and intellectual tradition, and who are the mainstay of Muslim historiography and tradition as it has reached us today, were not generally speaking interested in collecting accurate information on Shiʻi Islam and its internal divisions. Medieval Europeans had an even more deficient knowledge of Shiʻi Islam, since their overall understanding of Islam was in any case extremely limited. With the establishment of Twelver Shiʻism as the official religion of Safawid Persia in 1501, the ground was prepared for the better availability of information on Shiʻi Islam to visiting Westerners. However, European scholars, although trained in theological and philological disciplines, had not yet found a means of access to the texts of Islamic traditions that could have led to a breakthrough in their study of Islam. This was a development that had to await the commencement of scientific orientalism in the 19th century.

However, the availability of Islamic texts to the orientalists, in and of itself, did not significantly ameliorate the state of Shiʻi studies, as the bulk of such texts available in Europe were by Sunni authors and, as such, they generally reflected their variegated anti-Shiʻi biases. Indeed, few Shiʻi texts were to be found in European libraries before the middle of the 20th century. Consequently, until more recent times, the orientalists also studied Islam on the basis of the Sunni perspectives of their sources. And a Sunni-centric approach to the study of Islam has continued to dominate, to varying degrees, the state of Western scholarship in the field. In sum, Shiʻi studies of any genre have been a marginal subject in Western scholarship.

In Muslim countries, with the exception of Iran, Iraq and Lebanon, Shiʻi studies either have not received any particular attention, or have been ignored completely. In Iran and Iraq in particular, where Twelver Shiʻis are predominant, matters have been quite different. These countries also possess thriving religious seminaries, as well as extensive collections of manuscripts on Shiʻi subjects. In Iran, Islamic studies generally imply Shiʻi, and more specifically Twelver Shiʻi, studies, with consideration given to the disciplines of theology, jurisprudence and philosophy, as well as to the Shiʻi contributions to Quranic and *hadith* studies.

A new interest in the study of Shiʻi Islam was sparked by the Islamic Revolution in Iran in 1979. This important event in the modern history of Islam has also served as a turning point by emphasising the popularity of Twelver Shiʻism and its theological underpinning of the leadership of a politically powerful class of clerics. As a result, in the last few decades attention has been increasingly devoted to a series of new scholarly investigations in the field. The political and ideological aftermath of the Islamic Revolution, allied with the rise of Sunni Salafi movements, and encouraged by the scourge of Sunni-Shiʻi sectarian strife in the aftermath of the events of 9/11, has led to a heightened interest in the role played by Shiʻi Islam in government and policy.

Building on the need for scholarship on various aspects of Shiʻi history, beliefs and practices, the study of Shiʻi Islam has also been augmented by the increasing availability of primary texts on all the major branches of the Shiʻa. As a result, one of the trends in Shiʻi studies is an impetus to develop an informed understanding of how the Shiʻi communities of interpretation view themselves, through examining their history and lived experience across the centuries in varied geographic and cultural landscapes. The resultant revisionist views of Shiʻi history, doctrine and heritage are beginning to make their mark.

This Volume

A multifaceted dynamic is reflected in the structure of *The Shiʻi World*. Ranging from the historical and conceptual foundations and formative figures, to the intellectual, legal, literary and moral traditions, this volume also highlights devotional practices and artistic expressions, as well as expressions and experiences of modernity. Benefitting from the collaborative efforts of scholars with expertise in a range of disciplines, this volume aims to contribute to a better understanding of Shi'i Islam and the multiplicity of ways in which it is expressed.

Among the themes found in the volume are the historical narratives that illuminate the origins and evolution of the Shi'a, their articulations of authority, leadership and governance, explorations of spirituality, theology and cultural expression, as well as the ways in which diverse communities of interpretation and identity have met the challenge of modernity.

The first three chapters of the volume cover the foundational narratives of Shi'i Islam. Drawing upon the 'historical Muhammad' as well as the 'Muhammad of grace', Omid Safi examines how Muhammad's legacy has unfolded in the collective memories and experiences of all the Muslim communities. Delineating the Prophet Muhammad (ca. 570–632) and his message within the larger Abrahamic family of monotheism, Safi recalls the 'theological sisterhood of the monotheisms', with the twin aims of developing a deeper appreciation of that complex relationship as well as shedding light on the modern context of interfaith and communal relations. Underscoring the various readings to which both scripture and history lend themselves, Safi recognises that the ideal of what he terms 'theological pluralism' has often proved elusive for Sunni and Shi'i Muslims, whose different understandings of prophethood have led them to take distinct and, at times, divergent paths. It is therefore all the more pertinent when contextualising the relationship between Shi'i and Sunni Muslims, past and present, to achieve an understanding of these paths. Safi concludes that the memory of Muhammad 'is most fully honoured beyond ownership'.

Reza Shah-Kazemi begins the chapter on the foundations of Shi'i Islam by noting that to speak about Shi'i Islam is quintessentially to speak of Imam Ali b. Abi Talib (ca. 600–661). In his exposition of the historical and theological developments that have led to the formation of the *Shi'at 'Ali*, Shah-Kazemi focuses on *walaya* in which he discerns two complementary principles: the first being 'spiritual authority or guardianship, which derives from proximity to God, love, intimacy or friendship with Him'; and the second being 'fidelity, devotion, and affiliation manifested by the follower' to the *wali Allah*, the friend of God. *Walaya* to the Prophet and his progeny, which came to be varyingly interpreted by the many Shi'i denominations, is the central principle of Shi'i Islam. It is therefore variously articulated in several chapters of this volume.

Highlighting the 'charismatic lineage' of Imam Ja'far al-Sadiq (ca. 702–765), on his paternal as well as maternal side, that is, from Imam Ali b. Abi Talib and Abu Bakr (ca. 573–634) respectively, Karim Douglas Crow traces Ja'far al-Sadiq's legacy as a unifying figure for Muslims of various persuasions, which has led to his being acknowledged as an authority by most legal schools. Crow notes al-Sadiq's unrivalled status in articulating the creedal basis of the imamate in the intellectually vibrant, yet politically tumultuous, times in which he lived, and illustrates how this came to shape the incipient communal identity of the Imami Shiʻa. Following Jaʻfar al-Sadiq's demise, this community eventually coalesced into the two major branches of Shiʻi Islam – the Ismailis and the Ithnaʻasharis. Crow notes that, drawing upon the teachings of his father Imam Muhammad al-Baqir (d. 733) as well as those of his forefathers, al-Sadiq portrayed the imams as 'divinely designated initiatic guides and authoritative exponents of salvific knowledge'. This was a perspective which came to permeate the Sufi understanding of figures of inspired authority whom they designated as *shaykh*s or *pir*s. Thus, the Shiʻi and the Sufi approaches to concepts of charismatic leadership developed into a coherent alternative to the *Weltanschauung* of Sunni doctors of law, for whom al-Sadiq's paramount authority in relaying traditions from the Prophet remained contested.

The next two chapters shed light on the distinctive features and processes that have informed the shaping of Shiʻi legal and intellectual traditions. In recounting the historical developments that have led to the formulations of the Ithnaʻashari legal tradition, Andrew J. Newman notes that what has come to distinguish Shiʻi law from Sunni law is, 'the former's derivation from the practices of, and narratives attributed to, the imams, as well as its recourse to a distinctly Shiʻi form of *ijma* (consensus) and *ijtihad* (independent legal judgment)'. He also highlights the point that among the Shiʻa, there is a 'shared discursive pluralism' of legal opinion about key facets of theology and daily practice that have engendered varying pathways. While each Shiʻi group traces the origins of its doctrines and practices back to a 'normative' past, each of these individual paths has been marked by 'internal debate and external challenges'.

In the chapter on the intellectual traditions in Shiʻi Islam, Paul E. Walker argues that, while Shiʻi Islam revolves around a specific doctrine of the imamate which deems the succession to the Prophet to belong to Imam Ali and his descendants, it does this not only on the basis of faith and inherited tradition but also by establishing intellectual proofs, that is, by means of 'rationally determined judgement'. Walker poses the question as to whether the succession of Ali can be defended as an essential result, while all others, including those accepted by non-Shiʻi Muslims, fail the test of reason. He explores the contours of Shiʻi intellectual traditions through the works of five seminal Shiʻi intellectuals: Abu Yaʻqub al-Sijistani (ca. 934 to ca. 971), Hamid al-Din al-Kirmani (d. ca. 1021), Abu Abd Allah Muhammad, known as al-Shaykh al-Mufid (948–1022), Muhammad al-Tusi (1201–1274) and Muhammad b. Ibrahim al-Shirazi, known as Mulla Sadra (1572–1640). In so doing, he highlights the role of philosophy and its use as a means of articulating the Shiʻi worldview.

Farhad Daftary, in his chapter on Shi'i communities in history, provides an overview of the historical origins and conceptual developments that have shaped the course of the major branches of Shi'i Islam, including the Ithna'asharis, the Ismailis and the Zaydis. While charting the commonalities as well as the distinctions that have led to the crystallisation of each of these major Shi'i denominations, Daftary also draws upon current scholarship in Shi'i studies to elucidate the process of their formation and efflorescence, while also presenting the challenges they faced. In conclusion he notes, 'Shi'i Muslims have contributed significantly over the entire course of Islamic history to the richness and diversity of Islamic traditions, enabling Islam to evolve not merely as a religion, but also as a major world civilisation.'

Daftary's chapter provides an instructive backdrop for two other chapters in particular. These two chapters examine specific periods of Shi'i history and governance – the Fatimids in 10th-century North Africa and Egypt, and the Safawids in 16th-century Iran.

In the chapter on Fatimid governance and pluralism, Shainool Jiwa analyses a number of early Fatimid texts in order to discern the theoretical constructs that underpinned what has often been termed an inclusive and accommodative model of governance over the ethnically and religiously diverse populations of the Mediterranean littoral of the time. She examines the extent to which Fatimid policy was, 'the result of the interplay between doctrinal commitments and their lived experience, tempered by local conditions and communal dynamics'. In reviewing these developments, Jiwa reiterates the symbiotic relationship between doctrine and history. Her discussion of this reiterates the charismatic religious and temporal authority which the Fatimid Imam-caliphs asserted as their designated inheritance from the Prophet, which thus accorded them the distinction of being the supreme source of law and doctrine.

Rula J. Abisaab in her chapter on moral authority in the Safawid state examines the ethical tropes and dilemmas with which jurists in the service of the Safawids had to grapple in order to arrive at their rulings. Delving into the writings of two eminent Ithna'ashari Usuli scholars, Ali b. Abd al-Ali al-Karaki (ca. 1465–1534), known as al-Muhaqqiq al-Thani, and Zayn al-Din al-Juba'i known as al-Shahid al-Thani (1506–1558), she demonstrates how these jurists implemented the *shari'a*'s legal-ethical principles in the emerging Shi'i society of the Safawid empire. Yet 'the methods, which they used to derive the law, and the new connections that emerged between legal authority and Safawid state patronage, had critical ethical consequences', and had an impact on the state of legal scholarship in Iran. Abisaab elucidates the dynamics of the Shi'i ethical-legal nexus through a review of the status of the Friday prayer, which also reflected issues related to the scope of authority of the Ithna'ashari *ulama* in the Safawid state.

The following few chapters focus on the expression of faith in Shiʻi Islam, which reflects various facets of human experience and endeavour, through devotional practices, art and architecture, literature, music and cinema.

Reverence for the *ahl al-bayt*, the family of the Prophet, which is a recurring theme throughout the volume, forms the focus of the chapter on devotional practices by Ali S. Asani. He notes that while veneration for Ali and other members of the Prophet's family is a quintessential marker of Shiʻi piety, it is not unique to the Shiʻa. Imam Ali is also regarded as the progenitor of most Sufi orders, and a founding father and sage of Islam. Shrines built in Imam Ali's memory continue to be loci of visitation by Sunnis, Sufis and the Shiʻa alike, leading them to be considered 'as a continuum in which these figures [the imams] play a variety of roles across the devotional practices of Muslims'. Asani concludes that it is the doctrine of *walaya*, and the theological and cosmological frameworks that it engenders as regards the Shiʻi imams, that distinguishes Shiʻi practices from those of other Muslim groups. He illustrates this point by describing various Shiʻi practices, including the commemoration of the martyrdom of Imam Husayn at Karbala which is observed wherever the Shiʻa have settled across the globe.

The definition of Shiʻi art is a question which Jonathan M. Bloom addresses in his chapter on art and architecture. In exploring Shiʻi art from various angles and in various eras, Bloom provides a discursive survey of some of the memorable architecture commissioned by Shiʻi rulers, including al-Azhar mosque, built in Cairo under the Fatimids, and the Imam Reza shrine in Mashhad. In his survey, Bloom identifies certain characteristics that designate a piece of art or indeed a building as having a Shiʻi provenance, through its inscriptions, its functions and its patronage. In noting the veneration for the family of the Prophet, found not only among the Shiʻa but among most Muslims, Bloom surmises that, 'the Family of the Prophet represented intercession, hope of salvation, a rallying point for public opinion, and consistently the most visible icon in the daily religion of the great bulk of Muslims everywhere'.

In posing a similar question regarding literature, Eric Ormsby explores in his chapter what distinguishes Shiʻi literature from that of other Muslim literary traditions. Ormsby examines several examples of Shiʻi literature including *The Path of Eloquence* (*Nahj al-balagha*) of Imam Ali, the *Epistles* of the Ikhwan al-Safa and the writings of Nasir-i Khusraw and Farid al-Din Attar, in search of an answer. From each of these works, Ormsby extrapolates the key strands of thought that are central to the rich repertoire of Shiʻi literature. One of the features that he identifies is a profound reverence for the Imams, with Imam Ali being 'at once the model and the mainspring of Shiʻi literature'. He also notes that there is 'an abiding sense of the contrast between outer and inner truth, the *zahir* and the *batin*' which characterises most Shiʻi works, and which it shares with Sufi mystical traditions. Shiʻi literature is infused with what the great Andalusian mystic Ibn Arabi described as 'the breath of the Merciful'; in Ormsby's words, 'a living breath beneath the fixed form of words'.

An exploration through music of the dialectic between the spiritual and the secular, the sectarian and the universal, and the traditional and the contemporary is the focus of the chapter by William Sumits. Sumits presents the musical diversity of the Shiʻi world through time and across regions, using selected genres and master musicians as examples. When highlighting the vital role of music in the rhythms of life of each community, in giving voice to its social, cultural, ethical and spiritual mores, Sumits considers the role of musicians to be 'bearers of tradition and transmitters of cultural patrimony'. It is the preservation of this invaluable yet endangered musical patrimony in today's globalised world that forms the remit of the Aga Khan Music Initiative, which nurtures a 'cosmopolitan musical family' where there is a confluence of the traditional and the contemporary.

In her chapter on Shiʻism in Iranian cinema, Nacim Pak-Shiraz endeavours to examine how films share and engage with Shiʻi expressions of Islam. Through a socio-historical review of the representations of Shiʻi Islam in Iranian cinema, Pak-Shiraz illustrates a complexity which ranges from legalistic and formalistic approaches to the more popular and personal interpretations. She lists a rich range of views, academic, religious and practitioner, on how film should engage with religion and spirituality in the Iranian context. She concludes by noting: 'These filmic discourses constitute a new addition to the rich corpus of Shiʻi religious expressions in literature, poetry, art and architecture.'

Zayn Kassam and Bridget Blomfield explore gender perspectives in Shiʻi narratives in the chapter titled 'Remembering Fatima and Zaynab'. The Prophet's daughter and Imam Ali's wife, Fatima takes on special significance for the Shiʻa as the figure that connects the lineage of the imams to that of the Prophet. The chapter reviews the role of seminal female figures in the Prophet's progeny including Fatima and her daughter Zaynab, as well as their descendant Nafisa, and other female figures, including those who were at Karbala and those from later periods of Shiʻi history. They became examples for the Shiʻi faithful of their time, as well as serving as models of valour, piety and agency for Shiʻi women in particular. Drawing upon the recurring notion of *walaya*, Kassam and Blomfield trace how the figure of Fatima acquired a spiritual significance that over the centuries has become central to the Shiʻi worldview. Reflecting upon the events of Karbala, the authors note that these are, '"refracted through a woman's universe because women survived the battle", and offer an occasion for a memorial, signifying the centrality of Fatima and Zaynab to the Shiʿi sacred narrative'.

Shiʿi diasporas are the focus of the chapter by Zulfikar Hirji and Karen Ruffle which surveys the histories, social forms and cultural expressions of selected Shiʿi settlements in Asia, Sub-Saharan Africa, Western Europe and North America. Among the features which they delineate are: the views of these communities on authority and identity, spaces of worship and gathering, rituals, gender, engagement with the state, transnational formations and relations with other Muslim groups. On the basis of material gathered from various parts of Asia, Africa, Europe, North and South America, the authors illustrate how, despite the dislocation engendered by migration, many Shiʿi communities have flourished in the global age: 'Drawing on the opportunities provided by new forms of communication and transnational networks, they navigate expertly between the far-flung localities in which their members live, and today constitute globalised communities.'

In the final chapter on modernity, Amyn B. Sajoo probes the ethics of identity. Along with the current rise of sectarianism where the definition of a Muslim is hotly and at times violently contested, Sajoo reassesses the perennial question in Islamic history: 'Who are the Shiʿa?' juxtaposing it against the pluralistic ethic which Muslims civilisations and communities have long valued as part of their heritage. Sajoo examines the pressures that 'modernity and its social imaginaries' make on the particulars of communal identity for the Shiʿa in their varied social environments today, including the many diasporas. He finds that while the Twelvers, Ismailis and Zaydis are generally recognised, other groups such as the Turkish Alevis have been regarded as less amendable to any categorisation as Shiʿi. These categorisations have acquired a greater intensity in political as well as scholarly quarters. In framing these issues of identity-building and bridging in modern settings where cosmopolitanism has so often thrived, Sajoo concludes: 'The notion that identities can or ought to flourish in splendid isolation rests on a conflation of the "distinctive" and the "exclusive"; while the former may be laudable in favouring a positive sense of selfhood, the latter will most likely favour chauvinism.'

The growing recognition of Shiʿi studies as an academic discipline is itself a significant marker of the coming of age of the multifaceted study of Shiʿi Islam. The momentum generated in the field of Shiʿi studies through the confluence of factors discussed above is likely to continue in the decades to come. While the historical and conceptual mapping of the contours of most Shiʿi groups has progressed apace, anthropological and sociological studies related to the Shiʿi world are, despite significant progress in recent years, still in their infancy. Furthermore, the study of Shiʿi appropriations and contestations of the debates on politics of identity and their link to religious beliefs and ethnic origins is likely to elicit a growing interest in academic as well as in social policy circles. In developing approaches that can generate a healthy regard for each other among Sunnis and Shi'a, His Highness the Aga Khan proffers some salutary counsel:

> Perhaps the most important area of incomprehension, outside the Ummah, is the conflict between Sunni and Shi'i interpretations of Islam and the consequences for the Sunni and Shi'i peoples. This powerful tension is sometimes even more profound than conflicts between Muslims and other faiths ... It is important, therefore, for non-Muslims who are dealing with the Ummah to communicate with both Sunni and Shi'i voices. To be oblivious to this reality would be like ignoring over many centuries that there were differences between Catholics and Protestants, or trying to resolve the civil war in Northern Ireland without engaging both Christian communities. What would have been the consequences if the Protestant-Catholic struggle in Ireland had spread throughout the Christian world, as is happening today between Shi'i and Sunni Muslims in more than nine countries? It is of the highest priority that these dangerous trends be well understood and resisted, and that the fundamental legitimacy of pluralistic outlooks be honoured in all aspects of our lives together — including matters of faith.[1]

*   *   *

In the inaugural volume of the Muslim Heritage Series, *A Companion to the Muslim World*, the editor observed that in the aftermath of the events of 11 September 2001, journalists and academics alike quickly embraced 'generalizations and stereotypes that ... heightened prejudice, as well as fear' about Islam and Muslims, sentiments that were 'often tied to ignorance'.[2] Surely that is no less true today of views about Shi'i Islam and Shi'i Muslims, amid the sectarian conflicts that plague the Muslim world. This state of affairs also has roots in the longer history of Islamic studies, as noted at the outset of this introduction. But recent events, in

---

[1] Address by His Highness the Aga Khan to both Houses of the Parliament of Canada, House of Commons Chamber, Ottawa, 27 February 2014: full text at http://www.akdn.org/Content/1253/Address-of-His-Highness-the-Aga-Khan-to-both-Houses-of-the-Parliament-of-Canada-in-the-House-of-Commons-Chamber-Ottawa.

[2] *A Companion to the Muslim World*, ed. Amyn B. Sajoo (London, 2009), p. 3.

which a number of Western governments has either directly or obliquely become a party to militant conflict within and between Muslim societies, have significantly enlarged the distorting prism through which these complexities are seen. One need only glance at the plethora of titles now available about the politics, history and theology of the Shiʿa, virtually none of which offers a comprehensive picture of the richly textured narratives that have shaped the social and moral universe of diverse and often far-flung communities of the Muslim world. There is remarkably little appreciation of the current realities of Shiʿi communities as upholders of a minority faith in the Muslim world and beyond; yet the 'hidden transcripts' of traditions and communities in contexts dominated by others are vital to that appreciation.[3] This fourth volume in the Muslim Heritage Series aims to fill that sizable gap for lay and specialist readers alike.

---

[3]   James C. Scott, *Domination and the Arts of Resistance: Hidden Transcripts* (New Haven and London, 1990).

Remembering Muhammad

Omid Safi

Muslims traditionally invoke the name of the Prophet with a blessing. Whereas one may in Western languages casually mention 'Muhammad', the etiquette in an Islamic context acknowledges 'the one in whom we sense the Presence of God – Muhammad, may the peace and blessings of God be upon him'. This might sound overly ornate or pious to some; for others it is a matter of basic spiritual, as well as social, conduct. All the more so when the act is enjoined by the Quran itself in imitation of the divine blessing bestowed on the Prophet (33:56). As with any prophetic figure, it is not only about rising to an unusual level of spiritual grace, but also about being 'sent', willingly, to share the revelation. One thinks, for example, of a *bodhisattva* who, in the Buddhist tradition, postpones his own entry into *nirvana* for the sake of the community. The idea is a key facet of Muslim life: to live in full the life of the ordinary, from family to work and social interaction, yet to be constantly mindful of the eternal.

The claim that a religious figure *should* be remembered surely raises the question as to whose memory is being privileged. There was one Abraham, one Moses, one Siddhartha Gautama Buddha, one Jesus Christ, and one Muhammad. Yet there are countless imaginings of them in the course of history. In the past, there have been attempts to capture this reality as the inevitable difference between say, the Jesus of history and the Christ of faith. Today, we complicate matters by saying that even when trying to tell the story of Muhammad 'as it really was', it is hard if not impossible to get away from a particular understanding of him. To grasp the significance and centrality of the Prophet in Islam, one must step in and out of the narratives his life and see how Muslims have recalled and interpreted these episodes – that is, the mode of interpretation moves between looking at the 'historical Muhammad' and the 'Muhammad of grace'. One then encounters not only multiple varieties of the Prophet in Muslim traditions, but also, especially today, in what Western and other non-Muslim sources say about him and in what Muslims, in turn, make of these perspectives.

Of the biographical details of the Prophet's life, there are many fine accounts available.[1] This chapter is about how Muhammad's legacy has unfolded in the collective memories of Muslim communities, Shi'i and Sunni alike. As we shall see, the Shi'a have accorded a special reverence to the Prophet's family (*ahl al-bayt*) in their reading of scripture and its afterlife. At the same time, since the man and the message are firmly located in the larger Abrahamic family of monotheistic religions, it seems proper that we begin there – in the 'universal' setting of his journey. The Quran engages at length not only with the pagan past of the *jahiliyya* (pre-Islamic polytheistic Arabia), but also with the Judaeo-Christian traditions as the outcome of prior revelations. What is the nature of the relationship between Muhammad and his message on the one hand and those traditions and communities on the other? A deeper appreciation of this complex relationship may shed some light on the modern context of interfaith and communal relations, which have often been captive to postcolonial narratives. It certainly helps to recall the theological sisterhood of the monotheisms, which finds such robust expression in the Quran. As a reminder of the plural readings to which both scripture and history lend themselves, this is just as pertinent to the relationship between Shi'i and Sunni Muslims, as followers of Muhammad past and present.

In the Abrahamic Tradition

Is the message that Muhammad brought a reaffirmation of the earlier Judaeo-Christian revelations, or does it set out to supersede them? This tension has been preserved through the centuries, with Muslims of different persuasions gravitating now to this, now to that, perspective. The tension is not fundamentally different from how Christians have grappled with the problem of whether the statement in the Gospel of Matthew (5:17) that Christ 'completes the Law' means that Jesus reaffirms the Jewish tradition, or supersedes it. Here is what can be stated with certainty: the Quran views itself as the latest revelation from the same One God who had earlier sent guidance to humanity through prophets like Noah, Abraham, Moses, David, Solomon and Jesus. We frequently find passages in the Quran such as, 'Verily, all of this has indeed been said in the earlier revelations – the revelations of Abraham and Moses' (87:18–19). What is significant about the revelation is not

---

[1]   These include Martin Lings, *Muhammad: His Life Based on the Earliest Sources* (Kuala Lumpur, 1983); Tariq Ramadan, *In the Footsteps of the Prophet* (Oxford, 2006); and Karen Armstrong, *Muhammad: A Biography of the Prophet* (London, 1991).

that it is new, but rather it reveals the truth that humanity needs to be reminded of – again and again.

In fact, the cycle of revelation described in the Quran is seen as encompassing the whole of humanity. Muhammad himself is described as having been sent as a universal messenger in both the Quran and in his earliest surviving biography:

> *And We sent you as a messenger to all humanity.* (34:28)

And,

> When Muhammad the Messenger of God reached the age of forty, God sent him in compassion to humanity, *as a messenger to all humanity.* (Ibn Ishaq, *Life of the Messenger of God*)[2]

The God who reveals the Quran is not a tribal God, but rather the universal God of the whole of humanity. At times the list of messengers in the Quran seems biblical in the most familiar way:

> *We have sent the inspiration to you, as We sent it to Noah and the prophets after him.*
> *We sent the inspiration to Abraham, Ishmael, Isaac, Jacob, and the Tribes*
> *And to Jesus, Job, Jonah, Aaron, and Solomon.*
> *And to David we gave the Psalms.* (4:163)

This litany of biblical prophets is not an isolated example in the Quran. Aside from the narratives of individual prophets, we often find similar lists that emphasise the commonality of all prophetic revelations:

> *Say ye: 'We have faith in God, and in what has been revealed to us,*
> *And what was revealed to Abraham, and Ishmael, and Isaac, and Jacob, and the Tribes.*
> *And [to the scriptures] given to Moses and Jesus,*
> *And that which was given to all the prophets from their Lord.'*
> (2:136)

The Quran repeatedly emphasises the point since all the prophets bring the same divine message, one should not differentiate among them or

---

The Life of Muhammad: A Translation of Ibn Ishaq's Sirat Rasul Allah, trans. A. Guillaume (Oxford, 1955), p. 104.

favour one over another. Indeed, the faithful are commanded to say: *We make no difference between one and another of them, we submit ourselves to God* (2:136). Some 28 prophetic figures are named in the Quran specifically, and the list encompasses familiar figures like Adam, Noah, Abraham, David, Solomon, Moses and Jesus. In practice, a key part of Islamic piety is to connect honorifics with each of them. Adam is often called *Safi Allah* (the one purified and chosen by God), Noah is *Naji Allah* (the one saved by God), Abraham is *Khalil Allah* (the intimate friend of God) and Moses is *Kalim Allah* (the one with whom God spoke). Jesus receives special mention as *Kalimat Allah* (the Word of God) and *Ruh Allah* (the spirit of God). At the end of Muhammad's ascension or *miraj* in the famous Night Journey recounted in the Quran (17:1, 53:1–18), he too receives his own honorifics as the *Mustafa* (Purified and Chosen by God), the *Habib Allah* (Beloved of God), and *Rasul Allah* (Messenger of God). A common Muslim practice is to invoke blessings and salutations upon *all* the different prophets.

If God is the Lord of the whole universe, and if all prophetic guidance is traced back to the same divine source, then the number of prophets has to be drastically expanded beyond the familiar biblical scope. In addition to the figures who are named in the Quran, the total number of prophets is put by tradition at 124,000 (a number equivalent to our notion of 'a zillion') in order to indicate the fact that God has sent a prophet to every community.[3] According to the text, the scope of prophetic guidance is so vast that some of the prophets remain unnamed and unknown even to Muhammad:

> *We did send messengers before you. Of them there are some whose story we have told you [Muhammad], and some whose story we have not told you.* (40:78)

The mention of prophets sent by God and who are nevertheless not explicitly named in the Quran allowed later Muslims to incorporate other theistic traditions (such as Zoroastrianism in Iran, and some metaphysical forms of the Hindu traditions) into a Quranic worldview without much difficulty. More recently, pluralistically oriented Muslims have pondered the possibility of venturing further beyond an explicitly theistic realm by recognising the teachings of Tibetan Buddhism as part of sacred guidance.[4]

---

[3]   This is according to a *hadith* of the Prophet, recorded by Ibn Hanbal. The number of messengers (prophets with a scripture) is put at 315.

[4]   There was an historic meeting in this regard between His Holiness the Dalai Lama and many Muslim leaders in San Francisco in April 2006.

Islam and the People of the Book

Like any religious community, the early Muslims also had to establish their own particularity. That is to say, they could not simply be generic 'Abrahamics'. They would have their own distinct practices and beliefs that demarcated them from Jews, Christians and other monotheistic communities. This type of demarcation is one that is commonly found in the various faith traditions. Thus, in the book of Genesis we find the assertion of a specific covenant with Abraham that sets him and his descendants apart from the rest of God's creation, favouring them above the rest of humanity (Genesis 17). In readings of the early Christian tradition, we see an effort (notably through the teachings of St Paul) to delineate the nascent Christian community as distinct from the surrounding Jewish and Hellenistic communities. The teachings of the Buddha likewise differentiated his path from more severe forms of Hindu asceticism. The case of Islam, then, is not all that different. Demarcations in religious history are felt to be important precisely in relation to earlier communities that are theologically similar, not to ones that already proclaim a very different ethos.

Significantly, though, in the context of the Quran there is no move to negate the earlier revelations. In fact, a common criticism of the Jewish and Christian communities around Muhammad is that they had become too exclusivist, denying the truth of other revelations. The response of the Quran seems to be to connect the example of Muhammad to that of Abraham, the archetypal Prophet and monotheist:

> *They say: 'Become Jews or Christians if you wish to be guided.'*
> *Say you: 'No! I would rather be part of the tradition of Abraham,*
> *the true one, who did not associate partners with God.'* (2:135)

In this vein, the teachings of the Prophet himself harkened back to the Abrahamic notion of primordial monotheism. In other verses, the Quran positions itself vis-à-vis the polemical attacks by Jews and Christians towards one another:

> *Jews say: 'The Christians have nothing to stand on.'*
> *Christians say: 'Jews have nothing to stand on.'*
> *Yet they both profess to study the same Book!*

In a typical Quranic pattern, the ultimate evaluation is relegated back to God:

> *But God will judge between them in their quarrel on the Day of Judgement.* (2:113)

Some of the most emphatic Quranic dismissals are against claims that any one religious community can claim salvation is exclusively theirs.

> *And they say: 'None shall enter Paradise unless he be a Jew*
> *Or unless he be a Christian.'*
> *Those are their vain desires.*
> *Say: 'Produce your proof if you are truthful.'*

In the worldview of the Quran, the gates of salvation are open to all religious communities, and no single group – including Muslims – can claim exclusive salvation:

> *No, whoever submits his core being to God*
> *and is good and beautiful shall have a reward with his Lord.*
> *On such a soul shall be no fear,*
> *And grief.* (2:111–112)

In this vein, 'Islam' is evidently not so much the name of a new religious tradition, as it is the quality of having submitted oneself to God wholeheartedly. In the verse above, for example, the reference is to submitting one's 'core being' (*wajh*, literally 'face') to the divine. The characteristic Quranic refrain for salvation is that the one who shall receive it is one 'on whom shall be no fear, no grief'. The door of salvation will remain open to one who has submitted wholeheartedly to God, and is good and beautiful (*muhsin*). To put it differently, for the most part, in the Quran the word 'Islam' is a verb, not a noun. Different individuals are talked about as having 'Islam-ed' (*aslama*), that is to say, submitted themselves wholeheartedly to God.

There is another Quranic idea, a radical notion that would later surface here and there in Islamic thought. Muslims, as much as other devout human beings, tend to speak in terms of Absolute Truth. Yet, as articulated in the Quran and more fully teased out in the context of Islamic mysticism, Truth as such can be identified not with a religious tradition but only with God. The word Truth (*al-haqq*) is in fact a name of God: when we come across a reference to Truth in Islamic texts, the referent is always God. This is how these Muslims read the Quranic verse about the divine being revealed in three sites: in scripture, in the natural realm and in the very souls of humanity. As such, the study of scripture leads one to God. Scientific study of the natural realm can lead one to marvel at its majesty and intricacy as part of the divine order. For these readers of the Quran, both the mystical and the ethical are pathways in a holistic appreciation of 'reality'. That is how these Muslims have read the verse:

We shall show them Our Signs (ayat)
on the furthest horizons,
and inside their own souls,
until it becomes manifest to them that God is al-Haqq. (41:53)

This is one of the ways in which the word 'sign' (*aya*) functions in the Quran. The same word that is used for each verse of the Quran (*aya*) also means sign or symbol. A sign is something that points to a meaning beyond itself as does each verse of the Quran. Each verse is also seen as an invitation to meditate and ponder. And yet the Signs of God are not only in scripture, but also in the natural domain, and in humanity. This is a religious worldview in which reading scripture, meditation, study of the natural domain and mysticism all complement each other in leading humanity back to the Divine.

From this perspective, Islam is a path that leads one to Truth, but it is not the Truth itself. Truth can only be equated with the Origin and the Destination, only with God. That which comes from God may be true, and Muslims undoubtedly hold the Quranic revelation and Islam to be true, but religion cannot be considered Truth in the same way that God is Truth. This, too, is part of the radical monotheism of Islam.

Yet not all Muslims would be pluralists; just as some Jews and some Christians have come to see their own tradition as the zenith of God's engagement with humanity, so have some Muslims. These Muslims tend to focus on other passages in the Quran, specifically those where the word Islam is employed in terms of the act of surrendering to God. Here it might be useful to distinguish between more generic and more particular usages of the terms Islam and Muslim in the context of the Quran.

For the most part, the Quran does not conceive of 'Judaism', 'Christianity' and 'Islam' per se, but simply of the notion of One God and one guidance being sent through multiple messengers to address the multiplicity of humanity. The majority of occasions when words that derive from the root word 'Islam' are used, have to do not with the revelation of the Prophet as such, but simply with submitting oneself fully to God. Prophetic figures prior to Muhammad also identify themselves as 'muslim' in the Quran. Abraham is identified as a pure one who submits wholeheartedly to God:

Abraham was neither Jewish nor Christian, but he was a pure
monotheist (hanif) submitting himself wholeheartedly to God
(muslim). (3:67)

Likewise, Joseph, the young son of Jacob, who is also considered a prophet, offers this prayer to God in the Quran:

O my Lord!
You have indeed bestowed on me power,
and taught me the hidden meaning of events.
O You, the Creator of the heavens and earth!
You are my protector in this world, and in the Hereafter.
Take my soul as one who submits wholeheartedly to you [literally, a *'muslim'*]
And unite me with the righteous ones. (12:101)

In engaging with – and occasionally being confronted by – the People of the Book (*ahl al-kitab*, including Jews and Christians), Muslims are instructed to not engage in endless disputations:

And dispute not with the People of the Book, except in a way that
is lovely, unless it is with those who are oppressing you.
Say to them: 'We have faith in the revelation that has come to us,
and in that which has come down to you.
Our God and your God is One.
We submit wholeheartedly to him.' (29:46)

It is worth recalling in this context that the disciples of Jesus tell him that they will be his helpers in the path of God (*ansar Allah*), that they have faith in God. Significantly, they ask Jesus to bear witness that they have 'surrendered ourselves unto' God – and wish to join with all those who bear witness to the Divine (for instance, in 3:52). So what does it mean if figures like Abraham, Joseph, and the disciples of Jesus are identified as 'muslim'? They cannot in any historical sense be conceived of as having followed the particular practices of a later Arabian Prophet. While the Arabic language does not distinguish between terms in this exact way, it is good to think of a distinction between 'Muslim' as a particular identity referring to one who follows Muhammad's tradition of Islam, and 'muslim' as a broader category of those who submit fully to God, regardless of which prophet they follow. Likewise, one may distinguish between 'Islam' as Muhammad's tradition and 'islam' as a universal and primordial pattern of complete submission to God. It is in this latter sense that the Quran refers to the figures who lived prior to the era of Muhammad.

Yet any tradition – especially an emerging tradition – will eventually need to define its boundaries. On a few occasions, 'Islam' is mentioned as something closer to our notion of a religious system. This is particularly the case in a famous verse that is often taken to have been the last verse ever revealed to Muhammad:

Today, those who are bent on denying the truth have lost all hope
of [your ever forsaking] your religion:
Do not, then, hold them in awe, but stand in awe of Me!
Today have I perfected your religious law (din) for you, and have
bestowed upon you the full measure of my blessings, and willed
that self-surrender unto Me (islam) shall be your religion (din).
(5:3)[5]

The word *din* comes closest to our idea of religion, though it implies a host of meanings ranging from humanity's debt to God to what we think of as religion. Those who wish to see Islam as a completed (and even perfect) body will read the notion of a whole system of laws, practices and beliefs back into this verse, which they believe has already been guaranteed perfection. This reading has become popular with many Muslims who have experienced colonialism and Christian missionary activity, and who have responded by stating that Islam indeed supersedes earlier revelations. Hence, it is common to find a counter-missionary polemic against Christianity that originated in South Asia, and is found in many other places today. In these interpretations, God has chosen 'Islam' as humanity's religion. At this point, Muslims themselves differ over the relation of these verses to the more pluralistic approaches found in scripture. More inclusive Muslims adopt the same criticism of this narrower interpretation as the Quran seems to have made of exclusivist Jewish and Christian claims in the Prophet's time, that the door of salvation was open only to them. That both pluralistic and exclusivist Muslims seek to justify their positions by resorting to the Quran is a reminder of the fluidity of meanings that can and have been extracted – and projected – onto it.

The majority of the references to the People of the Book in the Quran are positive, stressing the commonality of revelation and guidance. Historically, this theological pluralism sanctioned in the very verses of scripture was of profound social importance for Muslims: it allowed them to live in peace with those who did not share their faith, to conduct trade with them, eat with them, and even to conduct that most crucial of human interactions, marriage, with the People of the Book.

---

[5]   The translation is from Muhammad Asad's classic work *The Message of the Quran* (Gibraltar, 1984). The word *din* is used twice in this verse, yet Asad translates the first occasion as 'religious law' to narrow its scope. Many other translations simply translate the first part of the verse as 'Today I have perfected your religion for you.'

This day all things good and pure are made lawful unto you.
The food of the People of the Book is lawful unto you, and yours
lawful unto them.
Lawful unto you in marriage are chaste women who are believers
(Muslims), and chaste women from the People of the Book. (5:5)

There would be of course restrictions and clarifications. While male Muslims were generally free to marry non-Muslim women from the People of the Book, the same liberty was not extended to Muslim women marrying men from the People of the Book. This is something that many Muslim women, particularly in the West, question today.

Yet commonality and identity should not be confused. After all, if the Quran merely repeated what Christianity holds about Jesus, then Muslims would be called Christians. There are a few verses in the Quran about the People of the Book that have a definite polemical edge to them. Of Christians, the criticism is theological, mainly about the claim that the nature of Christ is equal to that of God:

Christ, son of Mary, was not more than a messenger [of God].
[Many were the messengers that passed away before him.]
His mother was a woman of truth.
They both had to eat their daily bread.
See how God makes his Signs clear to them, yet see in what ways
they are deluded away from truth. (5:75)

and

They do blaspheme who say: 'God is Christ the son of Mary.'
But Christ said: 'O children of Israel!
Worship God, who is my Lord and your Lord.'
Whoever associates deities with God, then God will forbid him
entry to Paradise, and Hellfire will be his abode …
They do blaspheme who say that God is one of three in a Trinity,
For there is no deity except the One God.
If they desist not from their words of blasphemy, indeed a
grievous penalty will befall the blasphemers among them.
Why turn not to God and seek God's forgiveness?
For God is most-Forgiving, Full of compassionate mercy. (5:72–74)

Many Christians also see the above notions of God as 'one of three in a Trinity' as referring to a heretical understanding that might be properly characterised not as monotheistic but rather tri-theistic. It is worth remembering that in Muhammad's age, Arabia was filled with Christian movements that the orthodoxy espoused in Constantinople deemed heretical.

The above criticism, combined with the ambiguous passages in the Quran that seem to counter the claims of Jesus' crucifixion – or at least one Jewish group's boast of having crucified Jesus – do present something of a theological impasse between Islam and Christianity. Here is the opaque verse, directed against an unnamed Jewish group:

> *And so, [We punished them] for the breaking of their pledge, and their refusal to acknowledge God's messages, and their slaying of prophets against all right, and their boast: 'Our hearts are already full of knowledge.'*
>
> *Nay, but God has sealed their hearts in result of their denial of the truth, and [now] they believe in but few things – and for their refusal to acknowledge the truth, and the awesome calumny which they utter against Mary and their boast, 'Behold, we have slain the Christ Jesus, son of Mary, [who claimed to be] an apostle of God!'*
>
> *However, they did not slay him, and neither did they crucify him, but it only seemed to them [as if it had been] so; and verily, those who hold conflicting views thereon are indeed confused, having no [real] knowledge thereof, and following mere conjecture.*
>
> *For, of a certainty, they did not slay him: nay, God exalted him unto Himself, and God is indeed almighty, wise.* (4:155–158)

Knowing that Jesus' crucifixion took place at the hands of the Romans – and not Jews – the above verse surely is open to a great deal of debate and controversy and has been interpreted in multiple ways in Quranic commentaries. Some Muslims have taken the phrase 'they did not slay him' to mean that Jesus was in fact not crucified, whereas others have taken the phrase 'but it only seemed to them' to mean that a look-alike was sacrificed in the place of Christ. Perhaps the most charitable reading is that the verses are addressed more to the haughty claims of this unknown Jewish group, rather than the historicity of the crucifixion itself.[6]

The above verses do point to some theological demarcations between Islam and Christianity, yet it is important to read these verses in the light of the long and detailed passages in the Quran that provide a strong reverential stance towards Christ and Mary. Muslims are fond of pointing out that Mary is treated in a much more extended fashion

---

6   See Neal Robinson, *Christ in Islam and Christianity* (Albany, NY, 1991), and Jane D. McAuliffe, *Quranic Christians: An Analysis of Classical and Modern Exegesis* (Cambridge, 1991) for a survey of these debates.

in the Quran than she is in the Christian Testament. There are long and beautiful passages in the Quran describing the Nativity of Jesus. Mary herself is described in the same glowing fashion as Muhammad, purified and chosen:

> *And Lo! The angels said: 'O Mary! Behold, God has elected thee and made thee pure, and raised thee above all the women of the world.*

> *'O Mary! Remain thou truly devout unto thy Sustainer, and prostrate thyself in worship, and bow down with those who bow down [before Him].'* (3:42–43)

The Annunciation of the coming Christ child is celebrated in the Quran in most reverential terms, including the Virgin Birth:

> *Lo! The angels said: 'O Mary! Behold, God sends thee the glad tidings, through a word from Him, [of a son] who shall become known as the Christ Jesus, son of Mary, of great honour in this world and in the life to come, and shall be of those who are drawn near to God.'* (3:45)

Mary expresses her astonishment, for she has had no sexual relations with any man up to that point: *'O my Sustainer! How can I have a son when no man has ever touched me?'* The response comes:

> *Thus it is: God creates what He wills. When He wills a thing to be, He but says unto it, 'Be' – and it is. And He will impart unto thy son revelation, and wisdom, and the Torah, and the Gospel, and make him an apostle unto the children of Israel.* (3:47–49)

In the beginning of the narrative, the angels address Mary. She, on the other hand, addresses God directly, and receives a response back from God. The fact that she communicates with God directly led some pre-modern Muslims (such as the followers of the Zahiri school) to recognise her as a prophet. Other Muslims insisted that maleness was a necessary qualification of prophethood. Here is another indication of the ways in which gender norms have shaped the ways in which Muslims have read some of the most sublime verses of scripture.

Returning to the Quranic narrative, we see that after the birth of Christ, some of his miracles are commemorated:

'I have come unto you with a message from your Sustainer, I shall create for you out of clay, as it were, the shape of a bird, and then breathe into it, so that it flies by God's permission.

And I shall heal the blind and the leper, and bring the dead back to life by God's permission. And I shall let you know what you may eat and what you should store up in your houses. Behold, in all this there is indeed a message for you, if you are truly faithful.' (3:49)

In one of these miracles, which are also attested to in some of the apocryphal gospels such as the Infancy Gospel of Thomas, Jesus re-enacts (by God's explicit permission) the divine process of creation by taking a piece of clay and breathing into it. It is the breath/spirit that God has also breathed into humanity. Jesus' miracles include the familiar healing and bringing back to life, of bringing dead hearts to life which for Muslims was both metaphorical as well as literal. After all, the Quran repeatedly reminds humanity that the Earth was dead, and God brought it back to life. In these types of narratives, yet again, we see Jesus both as a historical prophet and also as what might be called a prophetic mode of consciousness. Thus mystics like Rumi wondered who, or what, was the Jesus within our own souls.

In his proclamation to the Children of Israel in the Quran, Jesus ends by stating:

'I have come to confirm the truth of the Torah before me, and to make lawful unto you some of the things which were forbidden to you.

And I have come unto you with a message from your Sustainer: remain, then, conscious of God, and pay heed unto me. Verily, God is my Sustainer as well as your Sustainer, so worship Him alone. This is a straight way.' (3:50–51)

The Quran and People of the Book Today

Jesus' remarks in addressing his own community, the Children of Israel, bring us to the intricate place of the Jewish community in the Quranic text. This remains important in influencing contemporary relations between Muslims and Jews, in all their complexity.

Both share traditions with a core of revelation, scripture and a strong legal ethos. True, mystical life is more extensive and popular in the Islamic tradition, often rivaling and occasionally equaling the legal ethos. While the Jewish *Kabbalah* is highly esoteric and has had a tangential presence in the wider Jewish community, Sufism has been intellectually pervasive, politically patronised and often populist. In societies such as Egypt and Senegal, historically the majority of people have been initiated into Sufi orders.

Yet these two monotheisms work in a similar fashion, and the perceived tensions are sometimes overstated. One could argue that many of the tensions stem from the overlapping ways of seeing things, not unlike sibling rivalry. Muslims and Jews have lived side-by-side through much of their history, if not always in mutual love then at least in coexistence. From the 8th through to the 10th century, somewhere between 85 and 90 per cent of all Jews lived among Muslims.[7] Certainly, Muslims have a far superior record of coexistence alongside Jews than Christians can claim, with a millennia-old tradition of anti-Semitism that is frequently tied to readings of Christian theology. Yet there are also very deep tensions between Muslims and Jews in both the Quran and in episodes of Muhammad's life. These have tended to be magnified in the 20th century beyond anything in their shared histories, in the context of the establishment of the state of Israel and the displacement of the indigenous Palestinian people. This makes it particularly urgent that issues in the Quranic narrative be handled in a thoughtful and dispassionate manner.

In the case of Christians, we have witnessed that there is a theological criticism of some views of Christ vis-à-vis the understanding of the Trinity and the crucifixion. Yet paradoxically, in the biography of the Prophet Muhammad, Christians are by and large viewed with favour. An outstanding instance is the shelter given to the nascent Muslim community through the intervention of the Abyssinian Christian king. Jews on the other hand, or one should clarify this by stating that *some* Jews, are the subject of ethical criticism in the Quran. The polemic is most often directed against those Jewish clans and political groups in Medina which formed open or clandestine alliances against Muhammad and his vulnerable early community. It often charges these Jewish opponents with breaking the covenant and with arrogance, themes as old as the Hebrew Bible and probably familiar to the Quran's contemporaries. In some passages, certain Jews are depicted as having boasted to Muhammad that they would escape divine retribution:

> *'Hell-fire will most certainly not touch us for more than a limited*
> *number of days.'*
> *Say [to them]: 'Have you taken a promise from God, for God*
> *never breaks His promise?*
> *Or is it that you say of God that which you know not?' (2:80)*

---

7   Jane S. Gerber, 'Judaism in the Middle East and North Africa since 1492', *Encyclopedia of Religion*, vol. 8, p. 158; cited in Steven Wasserstrom, *Between Muslim and Jew: The Problem of Symbiosis under Early Islam* (Princeton, NJ, 2004), p. 18.

Another offence which the Quran ascribes to Jews is having attributed to God that which was not originally part of the revelation given to them. At times the Quran describes this literally:

> *Woe, then, unto those who write down, with their own hands, something which they claim to be divine writ, and then they say: 'This is from God', in order to acquire a trifling gain thereby. Woe, then, unto them for what their hands have written, and woe unto them for all that they may have gained.* (2:79)

At other times, the Quran speaks more metaphorically about such actions as ones that making religion hard for people, and it describes Jesus as having come back to the Children of Israel to facilitate matters of faith for them. Some Jews are also criticised for having rejected the message of the Quran even though it originates from the same God and confirms much of their own teaching:

> *And when there comes to them a scripture from God, confirming what is with them – even though from of old they had prayed for victory against those without faith – when there comes to them that which they should have recognised, they refuse to believe it.* (2:89)

Like many of the passages in the Bible that some Christians have used over the centuries to justify animosity towards Jews, these types of verses can readily be, and are, taken outside the historical context in which they were revealed. In Muhammad's own time, leaders of some Jewish clans in Medina at various points conspired with the polytheists of Mecca to oppose Muhammad's fragile community. As a result, such clans were viewed with suspicion – on occasion with dire results, as in the well-known cases of the Banu Nadir and the Banu Qurayza.

Perhaps the corollary example about the need to read verses in their historical context will make the point in a slightly different fashion. When speaking in a contemporary setting with Christians, Muslims often privilege those verses that emphasise the commonality and affection between Muslims and Christians:

> *You find that the closest to the [Muslim] faithful are those who say:*
> *'We are Christians.'*
> *This is because among them are those devoted to learning, and those who have renounced worldliness, and they are not arrogant.* (5:82)

Yet in these same pluralistically-inclined gatherings, Muslims rarely cite the beginning words of that same verse:

> *You find that the most hostile to the believers are Jews and the polytheists.*
> *You will find that the closest to the [Muslim] faithful are those who say:*
> *'We are Christians.'* (5:82)

Muslims today praise the second part of the verse, especially in Western settings where Muslims live in largely Christian (or post-Christian) societies. It is as if these verses stand above time and place, pointing to an archetypal affection that Muslims and Christians are to have for one another. Yet when confronted with the first part of these verses, Muslims often quickly turn to the answer that 'one must read things in their proper historical context'. The truth of the matter, however, is more complicated. In order to have an intellectually honest reading of any scripture, including the Quran, it is surely vital to be consistent about matters of historicity and context. Either all of these verses should be read in the light of their immediate historical context, or they all should be read in a transhistorical fashion. Intellectually and spiritually honest readings of scripture demand that we take a more sensible approach – all the more so in the light of the stakes today, when these types of verses can be taken as license to justify perpetual animosity between Muslims and Jews.

All of our scriptures contain these multiple possibilities. There are passages in both the Quran and the Bible (as in the teachings of other faiths) that teach mutual respect and coexistence, alongside passages that appear to justify chauvinism and even violence. The question for us is how to approach any scripture in a way that is both historically informed and intellectually honest. This is a harder challenge than most faithful are willing to admit, at least publicly.

In today's globalised world, no religious community lives in isolation. Muslims live as neighbours to Jews and Christians in numerous settings, including the places where all three have lived for over 1,000 years (such as in the Middle East), and newer locations in Europe and North America as well. One challenge for Muslims is whether they can recreate the sense of Muhammad as a *biblical* prophet, which is present in traditional sources like 'Tales of the Prophets' by Kisa'i and in illuminated miniatures. A similar challenge is for Jews and Christians to come to terms with the fact that God's communication with humanity includes Abraham's descendants through both Isaac and Ishmael, which is to say Jews, Christians and Muslims. The challenge for those who aspire to worship Abraham's God is to recall that this God blessed all the offspring of Abraham.

The children of Abraham often find themselves at odds today, yet it is a mistaken reading of history to insist they have always lived in tension with one another. It also betrays a poverty of imagination and compassion to say that the children of Abraham are somehow destined to live in conflict, and to enact a 'clash of civilisations'. The tensions of the 20th and 21st centuries are in many ways historically unprecedented, and more often than not related to the traumas and aftershocks of colonialism.

Indeed, over the course of Islam's 14 centuries of history, the most important clashes involving Muslims have not been against Jews or Christians, but rather between Muslims. If the Umma as the mother-community of faith remains the ideal for all those who commemorate Muhammad, then Muslims have fallen short of that reality just as frequently as other members of humanity have failed their own faith traditions. The ideal of pluralism espoused by the Quran and the Prophet has often proved elusive – not the least when it comes to the Sunni and Shi'i followers of Muhammad, communities whose attachment to Muhammad led them to take distinct and at times divergent paths.

After Muhammad

There are some events whose significance outstrips their mere historicity. A 1st-century Palestinian Jew, son of a carpenter, is hung between two thieves at the behest of Roman authorities, and today over a billion Christians see the crucifixion as the ultimate symbol of their belief in God's deliverance of humanity. Six centuries before Christ, an Indian prince sat under a tree, vowing not to move until he had transcended the cycles of birth and rebirth. Today hundreds of millions of Buddhists look at the enlightenment of Siddhartha Gautama as the model of how to rise above attachment and ignorance. Muhammad's fateful journey to Medina under persecution in Mecca in 622 CE – the *hijra* – is such an event. It heralded a fresh start in his prophetic career, and has come to mark the beginning of the Muslim calendar. Then there is the martyrdom of Muhammad's grandson, Husayn by which is intended in fact the massacre of 72 individuals on the plains of Karbala in Iraq at the behest of a corrupt and violent ruler. For many Muslims, especially those who call themselves the Shi'a, the martyrdom of Imam Husayn is an event whose symbolism is far weightier than a slaughter of innocents in 680 CE.[8]

---

[8] For detailed accounts of Husayn's historical role and status, see Wilferd Madelung, *The Succession to Muhammad* (Cambridge, 1997), and S. H. M. Jafri, *The Origins and Early Development of Shi'a Islam* (Oxford, 2003).

Such events – Christ's crucifixion, the Buddha's awakening, Muhammad's migration, Husayn's martyrdom – become symbols of something fundamental about the human condition. Christians do not simply look back to the crucifixion, but see it as an act of redemption that shapes their lives here and now. For Buddhists, the key is less about retracing the awakening of the prince than about how we are to be enlightened. Muslims not so much recount the details of Muhammad's epic *hijra*, but cherish it for the potent renewal which it represents. At stake for Shi'i Muslims is less the chronicle of how Husayn died on that tenth day (Ashura) of the Islamic month of Muharram, but rather its moral import in contemporary spiritual life.

Much of the contention among Muslims relates to passionate claims upon the Prophet, an irony perhaps captured best by the philosopher of religion, Frithjof Schuon. Those who became the Sunnis esteemed the Prophet to the point that they could not imagine anyone else laying claim to his authority. So they demarcated the example of Muhammad from all others and invested the bulk of authority in his sayings (the *hadith* narratives), which acquired a singular place in Sunni tradition. Those who became the Shi'a cherished the Prophet to the point that they could not imagine living without those who reminded them of him. They came to see his legacy as being preserved primarily in the imams, the physical and spiritual descendants of Muhammad.[9] Among the final attestations of the Prophet was that he would leave his community two weighty gifts: Sunnis and Shi'is remember these slightly differently. Both take the Quran as the first of the gifts, but for the Sunni, the second is the example of Muhammad (*sunna*, hence the Sunni) as guide and commentary upon the scripture. The Shi'a remember the Prophet's Family as guides and living commentators as the other gift.

Yet this distinction is not quite as clear-cut as it may appear. The Shi'a also value the transmission of *hadith*s from the Prophet, but significantly through the Prophet's Family (*ahl al-bayt*). In the Sunni spiritual cosmos, it is often the mystics (Sufis) who perform a similar task of transmitting the spiritual grace and power (*baraka*) of the Prophet, generally via Ali b. Abi Talib, the Prophet's cousin and close companion. Again, one witnesses a great deal of attachment and devotion among many Sunnis to the Prophet's Family. Thus the martyrdom of Imam Husayn is commemorated with great tenderness every year in Turkey, and one of the holiest shrines in overwhelmingly Sunni Cairo is devoted to him.

---

[9]   F. Schuon, 'Images of Islam', *Studies in Comparative Religion*, 8 (1974), p. 4; reprinted in F. Schuon, *Christianity/Islam: Perspectives on Esoteric Ecumenism* (Bloomington, IN, 2008), pp. 125–126, available online at: http://www.studiesincomparativereligion.com/public/articles/Seeds_of_a_Divergence-by_Frithjof_Schuon.aspx.

Indeed, many of the earliest commemorative narratives, including the famed *Garden of Martyrs* (*Rawdat al-shuhada*), were composed by Sunni scholars. Yet over time, Sunni and Shi'i memory respectively has tended to harden. This is particularly so with regard to the events that surround the passing of Muhammad and the choice of a successor. Since the early communities each had their own loyalties, there are conflicting narratives that can readily be traced back to the various individuals involved at the time of the Prophet's death. In this respect, it seems more useful to understand *how* that history is remembered, as is so often the case in appreciating not only religious but also secular legacies.

Idealisations, Sunni and Shi'i

The turbulent era of transition, after the era of Muhammad's prophethood, of the early succession disputes and then Husayn's martyrdom, has had an immense impact on the way Muslims have viewed the relationship between historical time and the realm of the spirit. In much of the Sunni tradition, the notion emerged that, with the passage of time, the spiritual state of the cosmos gradually declines. The most perfect of days were deemed to be those of the Prophet and the age of Revelation, then the age of the Righteous Forefathers (*al-salaf al-salih*), and finally of those who came after, the Followers. This model was modified slightly by allowing for a *mujaddid* (renewer) figure each century to reinvigorate the faith. Integral to the model was an idealisation of the founding era, particularly that of the first four caliphs who were cast as 'Rightly-Guided' (*rashidun*). Muslims could not realistically seek to recreate the age of the Prophet, given his special relationship with God. But the age of the first four caliphs held a promise as a paradigm in which it is said the Muslim community lived in accordance with the teachings of scripture and the Prophet.

It would be rather hard for the Shi'a to retrospectively participate in the same romantic idealisation of the 'Righteous Forefathers'. The period of *al-salaf al-salih* and the subsequent generation of the Followers was when Ali b. Abi Talib – the Prophet's cousin, son-in-law and closest of Companions – was denied what the Shi'a regard as the rightful succession to leadership which Muhammad himself had designated. And then the Prophet's grandson, Husayn, and other members of his family were massacred. Hence, the Shi'i and Sunni perspectives on history differ not just as to who should have been the leader of the Muslim *umma* or what the roles and responsibilities of this figure should be; the differences extend to the very worldview of each tradition. These particularities of each tradition are of paramount importance as Muslims today seek to take dialogue among Sunnis and Shi'is as seriously as they have taken interfaith dialogue. Today we see many Muslims, in what is surely a welcome exercise, speaking in ecumenical voices with the aim of bringing together the Sunni and Shiʻi perspectives. At the same time, it is vital that mutual respect and coexistence should not be used as a license for eradicating real historical particularities and the grievances that they express. Not surprisingly, this is all the more important for the minority Shiʻi tradition, seeking to maintain their identity in the face of a larger and dominant Sunni tradition.

Pluralising Remembrance

Christianity saw the splintering off of the Protestants from the Catholic Church; while Judaism later saw the emergence of the Reformed and the Conservative traditions out of the Orthodox. In contrast, in Islam the Sunni and the Shiʻi traditions emerged simultaneously. The frequent association of 'orthodoxy' with Sunni interpretations of Islam is misplaced; neither side has an exclusive claim to being designated as orthodox. There are, of course, voices within both traditions that wish to stake such an exclusive claim for themselves, and to portray all others as (in varying degrees) outside the fold. Yet the historical record, even if it is confined only to shared narratives, hardly allows for such exclusivity. In their origins, Shiʻis and Sunnis alike reached back to the revelatory grace of the Quran and the spiritual being of the Prophet. While one may privilege the sayings-legacy of the Prophet, and the other the family-legacy of the Prophet, both traditions represent 'orthodox' understandings of Islam, if the concern here is about seeking pathways to the divine. And this, within Islam or any other theistic tradition, is and has always been the task of religion.

The later Sunni and Shiʻi traditions contain profound internal diversity, and one can find strands of each that stand closer to one another than to other perspectives within each tradition. Still, each offers a vital set of fundamental truths. One is reminded here of the story, so dear to Muslims (as well as Hindus, Buddhists and others), of the elephant wandering into the city of the blind. The citizens of the town came up to the creature, trying to identify it by feeling it. Each person felt a portion of the elephant, and sought to match what they felt to what they knew. One who felt the belly thought that the creature was rough like a wool carpet, another who felt the tusk thought it smooth, yet another who felt the tail imagined it as a snake, and one who grabbed the legs thought of a massive pillar. All the experiences were valid, but none alone was total.

So it is with Islam, where the totality transcends the key emphasis in each tradition. Among the Sunnis, public order and the rule of law have tended to attract the keenest concern. Rebellion is feared because lawlessness can easily descend into chaos and disorder, which in turn is often seen as paving the way towards heresy. There is also the conviction that history more or less unfolds according to divine will. Here and there we may have a mystery, but something as fundamental as the succession to the last Messenger of God is deemed too precious as to have gone askew.

In the Shiʻi tradition, however, the concern is essentially with justice, and the need to stand up for justice even against one's own community. Here, there is something redemptive about the very process of rising up against injustice, even if one does not achieve immediate success. Traditions with an emancipatory message come to oppose what they perceive as injustice and tyranny even when they lack political power; the very act of resistance is of the essence. The Quran reminds Muslims that the Truth it reveals stands out against falsehood, a proclamation that is not conditioned on an immediate balance of material odds. Karbala is not a single closed historical episode but a spiritual event that echoes here and now – just as Islam as a whole has ebbs and flows that call for spiritual revitalisation.

Whether it is a matter of keeping alive the legacy of the Prophet as faithfully conveyed through the Companions of Muhammad, as for the Sunnis, or of keeping alive the memory of Muhammad through the teachings of the Family of the Prophet, as for the Shiʻis, each side has looked for regenerative inspiration. Surely the same reality extends outside Islam, to the Abrahamic traditions, and beyond. One may ask, for example, which of Christ's utterances one would choose to recall today. Would it be the voice that says, 'No one shall come to the father except through me' (John 14:6)? Or this one, which echoes some of the most assertive verses in the Old Testament?

> *Do not think that I have come to bring peace to the earth;*
> *I have not come to bring peace but a sword.*
> *For I have come to set a man against his father,*
> *And a daughter against her mother.* (Matthew 10:34–36)

Might it be the Christ of the downtrodden whose suffering he sought to redeem?

> *He has anointed me preach the Gospel to the poor, heal the brokenhearted, set the captives free, offer sight to the blind and liberate those who are oppressed.* (Luke 4:18)

One may reasonably insist that these diverse voices be placed in their proper context, and that Christians are free to determine how to honour both tradition and the sensibilities of our time. This stance is open today in accounting for the no less varied voices of the Buddhist, Hindu and Jewish traditions during the course of their different experiences.

For Muslims – Shiʻi and Sunni alike – the Prophet clearly was and still is many things; yet the Quran has the last word in affirming that Muhammad is *rahma liʼl-alamin*, 'a mercy to all the universes' (21:107). His memory is most fully honoured beyond ownership.

Further Reading

Armstrong, Karen. *Muhammad: A Prophet for Our Time.* London, 2006.

Asani, Ali and Kamal Abdel-Malek. *Celebrating Muhammad: Images of the Prophet in Popular Muslim Poetry.* Columbia, SC, 1995.

Donner, Fred. *Muhammad and the Believers: At the Origins of Islam.* Cambridge, MA, 2010.

Ernst, Carl W. *Following Muhammad: Rethinking Islam in the Contemporary World.* Chapel Hill, NC, 2003.

Hazleton, Lesley. *The First Muslim: The Story of Muhammad.* New York, 2013.

Hirji, Zulfikar, ed. *Diversity and Pluralism in Islam: Historical and Contemporary Discourses.* London, 2010.

Hussain, Amir. 'Islam in the Plural', in Amyn B. Sajoo, ed., *A Companion to the Muslim World.* London, 2009, pp. 87–105.

Jafri, S. H. M. *The Origins and Early Development of Shiʻa Islam.* Oxford, 2003.

Lecker, Michael. *Muslims, Jews, and Pagans: Studies in Early Islamic Medina.* Leiden, 1995.

Ramadan, Tariq. *The Messenger: The Meanings of the Life of Muhammad.* London, 2007.

Safi, Omid. *Memories of Muhammad.* New York, 2009.

Schimmel, Annemarie. *And Muhammad Is His Messenger: The Veneration of the Prophet in Islamic Piety.* Chapel Hill, NC, 1985.

2

Imam Ali

Reza Shah-Kazemi

To speak of the Shi'a or Shi'i Islam is to speak inescapably of Ali b. Abi Talib, for the term *Shi'a* is an abbreviation of the designation *Shi'at 'Ali*, the 'supporters', 'followers' or 'partisans' of Ali. He is, therefore, regarded in the Shi'i tradition not simply as the first in a line of hereditary imams, but rather as the archetypal figure embodying all the qualities which would later be formally articulated within the doctrine of the imamate (*al-imama*). The spiritual essence of the imamate is *walaya*, a notoriously difficult word to translate. It comprises the following meanings, among others: authority, mastership, guardianship, friendship, love, affiliation, sanctity – this latter quality deriving from the idea of intimate 'nearness' to God: the root *w-l-y*, literally meaning 'being close to'. The deepest connotations of the term are brought out in the succinct definition of *walaya* found in the mystical traditions of Islam: 'the inner dimension of prophethood' (*batin al-nubuwwa*).

In addition to being the first imam of the Shi'a – and, in the Ismaili branch of Shi'i Islam, the 'foundation' (*asas*) of the imamate – Ali has always been regarded within Muslim cultures across the globe as a figure of exceptional sanctity, the 'beloved friend of God' (*wali Allah*). It would be blinkered, therefore, to see Ali's role within Islam as somehow confined within a confessional box labelled 'Shi'ism'. Rather, he should be seen as a symbol or manifestation of the sanctifying power of Islam, beyond confessional, theological and juridical distinctions. For the spiritual traditions of both branches of Islam – that is, broadly speaking, Sufism within Sunni Islam,[1] and *irfan* within Shi'i Islam – are dominated by the quest for that *walaya* which Ali is deemed to have realised in all its plenitude.

---

[1] There are also Shi'i orders in Sufism. For an overview of the connections between Shi'ism and Sufism, see Seyyed Hossein Nasr, 'Sufism and Shi'ism: Their Relationship in Essence and in History', in his *Sufi Essays* (London, 1972), pp. 104–120.

In this light, it is not suprising to find that Ali stands at the pinnacle of all the chains of transmission (*salasil*, sing. *silsila*) by which the mystical orders trace their spiritual masters back to the Prophet. In the words of Sayyid Ali Hujwiri (990–1071), author of one of the most authoritative texts of early Sufism, *Kashf al-mahjub*, Ali is 'the leader of the saints and the pure (*muqtada-yi awliya wa asfiya*)'.[2] From the point of view of Islamic spirituality, the fact that Ali was the fourth of the so-called 'rightly-guided' caliphs (*al-khulafa al-rashidun*) is of secondary importance; for, given the spiritual preeminence of his *walaya*, it is asserted that by becoming caliph, it was not Ali who was elevated by the office, but the office that was elevated by Ali.

In this chapter we introduce this seminal figure of nascent Islam under the following three headings:

1. Proximity to the Prophet.
2. The Caliphate – both his own, and that of his three predecessors.
3. The *Shi'at Ali* and the principle of *walaya*.

Proximity to the Prophet

One of the clearest ways of revealing the extraordinarily close relationship between the Prophet and Ali is to reflect upon the numerous sayings of the Prophet relating to Ali. In purely literary terms, it is this corpus of sayings which, together with Ali's own aphorisms, sermons and letters as compiled in the *Nahj al-balagha*,[3] help to explain the depth of veneration accorded to Ali throughout the Muslim world. It is because Ali was so close to the Prophet Muhammad, not simply in familial terms (*qaraba*) but more importantly in spiritual kinship, that veneration accorded to Ali has been seen traditionally as a concomitant of the veneration due to the Prophet. The following saying of the Prophet is a key to appreciating this principle: 'I am the city of knowledge, and Ali is its gate.'[4] This prin-

---

[2] Sayyid Ali Hujwiri, *Kashf al-mahjub*, ed. V. A. Zhukovskiï (Tehran, 1376 Sh./1997; reprint of St. Petersburg, 1899 ed.), p. 84.

[3] The authenticity of the sermons, letters and aphorisms compiled in the *Nahj* by al-Sharif al-Radi, has been challenged in certain circles. After his extensive review of the sources, Moktar Djebli concludes with a compelling argument in favour of the *Nahj*'s authenticity; see his 'Encore à propos de l'authenticité du Nahj al-Balagha!', *Studia Islamica*, 75 (1992), pp. 33–56. See also 'Nahdj al-Balagha', *EI2*, vol. 7, p. 904.

[4] Al-Hakim al-Nisaburi, *al-Mustadrak ala'l-sahihayn* (Beirut, 2002), p. 929, no. 4694. In their effort to trace the roots of their particular specialisation, philosophers, theologians, grammarians, calligraphers, etc. – and not just mystics – traced their disciplines back to the Prophet through Ali, who can thus indeed be regarded as a 'gate' to prophetic knowledge for successive generations of Muslims.

ciple also explains why Ali so indignantly rejected the epithet 'religion of Ali' (*din Ali*) used by his opponents to discredit him. The religion of Ali, he asserted, was the religion of Muhammad.[5]

The Prophet ascribed to Ali a range of virtues (*fada'il*) and titles of honour (*manaqib*) in sayings which are granted a high degree of authenticity in both Sunni and Shi'i sources. Ahmad b. Hanbal (780–855), prominent Sunni traditionist and founder of one of the four Sunni schools of law, stated boldly: 'No Companion of the Prophet has had such virtues ascribed to him as those which have been ascribed to Ali b. Abi Talib.'[6] Many compendiums of these sayings, which often include verses of the Quran that are deemed to refer to Ali, have been compiled by traditionists.

The following sayings of the Prophet are found, with minor variations, in standard Shi'i compilations of *hadith*; most of them can also be found in such authoritative Sunni sources as the *Musnad* of Ahmad b. Hanbal, the *Mustadrak* of al-Hakim al-Nisaburi, Ahmad b. Shu'ayb al-Nasa'i's *Khasa'is amir al-mu'minin Ali b. Abi Talib*, and Abu Bakr al-Mardawayh's *Manaqib Ali b. Abi Talib*.

- 'Truly, Ali is from me and I am from him, and he is the *wali* of every believer after me.'
- 'Ali is with the Quran and the Quran is with Ali. They will not separate from each other until they return to me at the [paradisal] pool (*al-hawd*).'
- 'Looking at Ali is an act of worship.'
- The Prophet said that Ali was 'as my own soul' (*ka-nafsi*).
- '… whoever obeys Ali obeys me, and whoever disobeys him disobeys me.'
- 'There is one amongst you who will fight for the *ta'wil* [spiritual interpretation] of the Quran as I have fought for its *tanzil* [literal revelation].' The Prophet then made an allusion to Ali.
- Ali himself relates that the Prophet said to him that none but a believer will love him, (Ali), and none but a hypocrite will hate him.
- The Prophet said to Ali: 'Are you not happy that you should have in relation to me the rank of Aaron in relation to Moses, except that there is no prophet after me?'
- The most celebrated of all the Prophet's sayings regarding Ali, perhaps, is the Ghadir Khumm tradition. On his return to Medina after his final Hajj, on 18 Dhu'l-Hijja 10/16 March 632, at a pool

---

[5] See Wilferd Madelung, *The Succession to Muhammad* (Cambridge, 1997), p. 178.
[6] Nisaburi, *Mustadrak*, p. 916.

midway between Mecca and Medina, known as Ghadir Khumm, the Prophet assembled all the returning pilgrims. He had a pulpit erected and delivered an address to the congregation, which numbered in the thousands. The address culminated in the statement: 'For whomever I am the *mawla* [a synonym of *wali*], Ali is his *mawla* (*man kuntu mawlahu fa-Ali mawlahu*).'

We shall explore further the implications of the last saying both in the following section on the caliphate, and later with regard to the principle of *walaya*. Turning now to some historical aspects of this proximity, it should be noted that just as Abu Talib had been a father figure to Muhammad – having taken charge of his orphaned nephew from an early age – so in turn, Muhammad was to be the father figure to his young cousin, Ali. For, when the latter was about five years old, he was taken into the household of Muhammad, who was at that time in his mid-30s; in other words, this event took place about five years before the commencement of the prophetic mission. From this time onwards, Ali was constantly at the Prophet's side, the relationship between the two being akin to that of father and son. In one of his sermons Ali looks back at this period of his upbringing by the Prophet as follows:

> When I was but a child he took me under his wing ... I would follow him [the Prophet] as a baby camel follows the footsteps of its mother. Every day he would raise up for me a sign of his noble character, enjoining me to follow it.
> ...
> He [the Prophet] would go each year into seclusion at [the mountain of] Hira. I saw him and nobody else saw him ... I saw the light of the revelation and the message, and I smelt the fragrance of prophecy.[7]

Soon after the commencement of his prophetic mission, the Prophet told Ali about the revelations he had received, and, as a result, Ali immediately embraced the new faith. He was the first male to enter the religion of Islam, at the tender age of about ten years.[8] When it was revealed to the Prophet that he was to warn his near kin (26:214), he asked Ali to invite the leading members of his clan to a feast; once they were assembled, he asked who among them would be his 'brother', his *wasi* ('executor'), and

---

[7]   Ibn Abi'l-Hadid, *Sharh Nahj al-balagha* (Beirut, 1965), vol. 13, p. 197.
[8]   Ibn Ishaq, *The Life of Muhammad*, tr. A. Guillaume (London, 1968), p. 114. Abu Bakr was the first adult male to embrace the new faith, and Khadija, the wife of the Prophet, was the first woman to enter Islam.

his *khalifa* ('deputy', 'lieutenant' or 'successor'). Ali, now about 13 years old, was the only one who replied, and the Prophet affirmed him in all three respects, adding 'Hearken to him and obey him'.[9] The result was ridicule on the part of the clan towards the Prophet, Ali and Abu Talib, mocking the latter by saying that he now had to be subservient to his own teenage son.

In Medina, the Prophet instituted a pact of brotherhood between the 'emigrants' (*muhajirun*) from Mecca and the 'helpers' (*ansar*), the Muslims of Medina; as for himself, he most significantly 'adopted' Ali as his 'brother'. Ali distinguished himself on the field of battle, such that his martial skill and fearless courage became proverbial. He remained undefeated in all of the single combat duels with which the battles usually began. There are numerous reports indicating that, during the battle of Khaybar in 629, he used as a shield a gate which could only be lifted, after the battle, by several men. The many reports of such feats, in conjunction with his moral and spiritual qualities – particularly his forgiving of his enemies, and his defence of the weak and the oppressed – have meant that Ali was adopted as the patron saint of chivalry (*futuwwa*) across the Islamic world.

Ali was also a scribe of the Prophet. He wrote down, not only the verses of the Quranic revelation at the Prophet's dictation, but also several of his letters and treaties. The Prophet gave Ali the honour of marrying his daughter, Fatima, considered, with her mother, Muhammad's first wife, Khadija, as the epitome of feminine sanctity in Islam. The Prophet's *ahl al-bayt* ('People of the House') – to whom the Quran refers to in 33:33 as being 'purified of all defilement' – was indicated by the Prophet as consisting of himself, Ali, Fatima, and their two sons, Hasan and Husayn. After the Prophet himself, then, it was Ali who was regarded as the head of the *ahl al-bayt*. Ali and Fatima are therefore the progenitors of all of the Prophet's surviving offspring, known as the *shurafa* (sing. *sharif*) or *sadat* (sing. *sayyid*) who are held in the highest esteem in all traditional Muslim societies.

The Caliphate

One of the key historical questions at issue in the Sunni-Shi'i discourse is Ali's relationship with the first three caliphs. The historical sources make it difficult for the historian to arrive at hard and fast conclusions. For, on the whole, Sunni authors tend to overlook or downplay the disagreements between Ali and the first three caliphs in an effort to present as harmonious a picture as possible of what later was to be referred to as

---

9   Ibn Ishaq, *Life of Muhammad*, pp. 117–118.

the period of the four orthodox caliphs. By contrast, Shi'i works high-light, and occasionally exaggerate, the differences of opinion between Ali and his predecessors. However, the incontrovertible point here is that Ali pledged allegiance to each of the caliphs in turn, and remained faithful to his pledge. Indeed, he served as a valued advisor, even if his advice was not always followed, and even if he disagreed with particular decisions or policies adopted by them. From his pledge of allegiance one can infer that Ali did accept, in differing degrees, the formal legitimacy – moral, political as well as religious – of the rule of his predecessors.

According to the majority of the Shi'a, Ali's belief that he had the greatest right to rule was derived from his certainty that he had been appointed by the Prophet to be his successor and his *wasi* (legatee) not just at Ghadir Khumm, but on several other occasions; and that this prophetic designation was the expression of the will of God. From this standpoint, Ali's political authority was seen as one of the concomitants of his status as the divinely appointed imam of the Muslims, whether he exercised the prerogative to rule or not. This is an important qualifi-cation from the point of view of the relationship between the imamate and the caliphate, such as it was later elaborated and crystallised in Shi'i doctrine: the imam has the right to rule, in principle, but whether he rules in fact is contingent on outward circumstances. He always remains imam in the full sense, his imamate being constituted by spiritual authority – an authority which is not compromised or diluted if he does not exercise his political prerogatives. This precedence of spiritual guid-ance over political authority was made explicit in Imam Jafar al-Sadiq's doctrine of the imamate. He articulated the three essential functions of the imamate – spiritual guidance on the basis of inspired knowledge (*ilm*); exegesis of the Quran and its application in law and society; and political rule – on the basis of the sayings, actions and attitudes of Ali. Hence, leadership within Shi'i Islam acquired its particular texture and emphases – intellectual, moral and spiritual guidance taking priority over political authority – from the precedents and principles implicit in the conduct of Ali.[10]

Turning to the historical context, let us briefly outline Ali's relation-ship with his predecessors in the caliphate before turning to his own period of rule. As regards the first caliph, it is stated in a few pro-Sunni sources that Ali immediately proferred his pledge of allegiance (*baya*) to Abu Bakr. But according to the majority of the sources this pledge took place six months after Abu Bakr's assumption of the caliphate. The pledge followed the death of Fatima, who had a serious dispute with Abu

---

[10] See S. Husain M. Jafri, *Origins and Early Development of Shi'a Islam* (London and New York, 1979), pp. 58–76.

Bakr over her claim to have inherited the oasis of Fadak from her father. Abu Bakr had refused to accept this claim, stating that the Prophet himself had said that the prophets do not leave any inheritance.

Be that as it may, the fact that Ali did pledge his allegiance to Abu Bakr as the leader of the Muslim community is indisputable. While Sunni historians point to the pledge as evidence of Ali's acceptance of the legitimacy of Abu Bakr's caliphate, Shi'i historians on the whole argue that the pledge was made out of expediency: Ali was prepared to sacrifice his own right to rule for the sake of maintaining the unity of the Muslim community. However, one may regard Ali's allegiance to Abu Bakr as having been proferred *both* for the sake of Muslim unity, *and* as an act of recognition of the legitimacy of Abu Bakr's rule. Ali's acceptance of Abu Bakr's authority need not imply that Ali did not believe in his own right to rule (whether this right be seen as deriving from divine appointment and prophetic designation; or simply on the basis of greater merits and closer kinship with the Prophet). Ali's pledge of allegiance can be viewed as an implicit acceptance of the distinction between temporal and spiritual authority.[11] This distinction was underlined in the doctrine of the imamate as expounded by Imam Jafar al-Sadiq. From this point of view, the two functions, spiritual and political, may come together, as they did during Ali's caliphate; or they may not, without this de facto separation of powers necessarily implying that the political power thus constituted is devoid of legitimacy.

The same situation prevailed during the rule of the second caliph, Umar (r. 634–644). Ali's posture was one of loyalty and passive acquiescence in political affairs, combined with the imparting of advice on all matters relating to religious doctrine and the application of legal rulings and judgments. Ali was regarded as being among the most knowledgeable of the Companions in respect of the Quran and legal applications of Quranic principles, and was thus consulted frequently on such matters. One revealing instance is provided by the case brought before Umar of a woman accused of adultery by her husband. He made the accusation because his wife had given birth to a baby only six months after their marriage. Umar ordered that she receive the penalty for adultery. Ali objected, arguing that according to the Quran, the period covering conception to birth can be as little as six months. According to 46:15, 'the bearing of the baby to his weaning is thirty months'; and according to 31:14, 'in two years is his weaning'. If the weaning period of two years

---

[11] 'Certainly, one can speak of the *authority* of the Imams', writes Henry Corbin, 'but what is in question here is a purely *spiritual* authority, not a power competing, under a different name, with the powers of this world' (emphases in the original). *En Islam iranien: Aspects spirituels et philosophiques* (Paris, 1971), vol. 1, 'Le Shî'isme duodécimain', p. 170.

is deducted from the 30 months covering the duration of bearing and weaning, then six months are left as a possible period from conception to birth. After hearing this irrefutable argument, Umar famously declared: 'Were it not for Ali, Umar would indeed have been destroyed.'[12]

Ali's atttitude to all three of his predecessors is well expressed in his statements made during the deliberations of the council (*shura*) which Umar established shortly before his death in 644, to determine who was best qualified to succeed him. This council of six, which included both Ali and Uthman, decided in favour of the latter. Ali's response is recorded in the *Nahj al-balagha*:

> You are all well aware that I am the most entitled to this [the caliphate]. But by God, I shall resign myself [to this situation] for as long as the affairs of the Muslims are being soundly governed (*ma salimat umur al-Muslimin*), and for as long as there be no unfairness except in relation to me alone. I do this, seeking the reward and the bounty of such a course of action, being detached from that to which you people aspire: the adornments and trappings [of power].[13]

The logic of Ali's statement here can be applied, retrospectively, to the rule of the previous caliphs as well as to the coming caliphate of Uthman: that he had resigned himself to the rule of the first two caliphs because the affairs of the Muslims were indeed being 'soundly governed', with no fundamental oppression or injustice on the part of the rulers such as would have elicited Ali's opposition. Even if he regarded himself as more 'entitled' (*ahaqqu*) to the caliphate than them, Ali was prepared to forego his right, insofar as the character of caliphal governance was based on sound Islamic principles.

It should be noted, however, that Ali refused to be bound by the precedents established by the first two caliphs. This was in fact the main reason why the council decided to offer the caliphate to Uthman. Upon being asked by Abd al-Rahman b. Awf, the head of the council, whether he was willing to assume the caliphate on the basis of the Quran, the *sunna* (conduct), of the Prophet and the precedent of Abu Bakr and Umar, Ali replied by saying he would rule solely on the basis of the Quran and the *sunna* of the Prophet. When Uthman was asked the same question he replied unconditionally in the affirmative and was duly appointed caliph. Again, Ali's insistence on being bound only by

---

[12] Abu Ja'far Muhammad Ibn Shahrashub, *Manaqib Al Abi Talib* (Qumm, 1421/2000), vol. 2, p. 407.
[13] Ibn Abi'l-Hadid, *Sharh*, sermon no. 73, vol. 6, p. 166.

the Quran and the prophetic *sunna* was to set a historic precedent and particular tonality for the conception of leadership in Shi'i Islam.

Unlike those of Abu Bakr and Umar, the caliphate of Uthman (r. 644–656) was increasingly characterised by the corruption and nepotism of his governors, nearly all of whom were from the same clan as Uthman, the Umayyads. Towards the end of Uthman's caliphate, the consequences of this corruption were destabilising both state and society. Rebellions erupted in various provinces, and Ali felt duty-bound to intervene in the political domain in a manner not deemed necessary during the rule of the first two caliphs. He served as mediator between the malcontents and the caliph, while indicating to the latter the just nature of many of the grievances being presented to him, and doing his utmost to ensure that the expression of grievances remained peaceful. But his mediation was undermined by the machinations of various factions, and in the end the rebels killed Uthman, despite Ali's best efforts to protect him (Hasan and Husayn were posted by their father to secure the gates of the caliph's palace). Ali was then prevailed upon by popular pressure to assume power.

The Caliphate of Ali (656–661)

There are two aspects of Ali's caliphate to be noted: the outer, political chronicle of events, and the inner, spiritual ideals determining his policies. The political chronicle is dominated by three tragic civil wars, initiated by those who rebelled against Ali's rule; while the key spiritual principle which moulded his policies in all domains – ethical, legal, socio-economic and political – was justice.

The political expression of his adamantine sense of justice became apparent at the very inception of his caliphate. His cousin and close confidant, Ibn Abbas, advised him to temporarily confirm in power all of Uthman's governors, and then replace them later with his own appointees when his power was consolidated. Ali's response was: 'I do not doubt that this would be best for the sake of reconciliation in this world. But there is my obligation to the Truth, and my knowledge of Uthman's governors – so, by God, I shall never appoint one of them.'[14]

This decisive act at the outset of his caliphate has been characterised by certain historians as naivety on Ali's part, a sign of his inability to deal with the worldly exigencies of *realpolitik*. It has also been viewed as the only possible course of action open to him. According to this view, Ali could hardly have acted in any other way without ruining his own

---

[14] Abu Ja'far Muhammad b. Jarir al-Tabari, *Ta'rikh al-rusul wa'l-muluk* (Leiden, 1964), vol. 6, p. 3084.

credibility, and being seen by his own supporters as having sacrificed the imperatives of justice for political gain. His own power-base in Medina would have been undermined if he had overlooked the glaringly obvious injustices and corruption of most of the governors appointed by the previous caliph.

The first challenge to Ali's rule arose from two senior companions of the Prophet, Talha b. Ubayd Allah and al-Zubayr b. al-Awwam, together with A'isha, one of the widows of the Prophet, and some of the governors ousted by Ali. They accused Ali of failing to punish the murderers of Uthman and mounted a revolt against him in the name of vengeance for the murdered caliph. Ali reminded Talha and al-Zubayr that they had pledged allegiance to him and were now breaking their oath, and he insisted that he would bring the murderers to justice as soon as he could find them. But to no avail: the ensuing battle, which took place near Basra in December 656, was the first civil conflict in Islam. It was named al-Jamal ('the Camel') after the camel litter of A'isha which became the focus of the fighting. It resulted in the victory of Ali's army, the death of Talha and al-Zubayr, and the surrender of A'isha. Far from engaging in any acts of recrimination against A'isha, Ali treated her with magnanimity and with all the respect due to her status as a wife of the Prophet and thus, according to the Quran, as one of the 'mothers' of the believers (33:6).

The next rebellion against Ali's rule was far more challenging. It was mounted by the governor of Syria, Mu'awiya b. Abi Sufyan, who refused to accept Ali's order to step down as governor and accept Ali's appointee. Mu'awiya instead called for Ali to be deposed, alleging that he had not brought the killers of Uthman to justice. The battle of Siffin began on 26 July 657. When, after much bloodshed, Ali's army was on the point of victory, Mu'awiya was advised by his cunning ally, Amr b. al-As, to hoist copies of the Quran on spears and call for arbitration according to the Quran. Though clearly a trick, the majority of Ali's army laid down their arms and refused to fight, thereby leaving him no choice but to accept the arbitration proposal.

The text of the arbitration agreement was drawn up on 2 August 657. It called merely for the arbitrators – Abu Musa al-Ash'ari representing Ali and Amr b. al-As representing Mu'awiya – to use the Quran and, if necessary, the *sunna*, to arrive at a settlement of the dispute which would be binding on all parties. While discussions were being held at a place called Dumat al-Jandal, there was increasing discontent within the ranks of Ali's army. Many of those who had initially been enthusiastic about arbitration now felt remorse for what they considered to be a sin. Their slogan was: 'no judgement but that of God' (*la hukm illa li'llah*). They called on all parties to abandon the arbitration, and to repent for their sin of making men the arbitrators of what must be resolved only through the will of God. Many started to 'secede' (*kharaja*, whence the designation *khariji*) from Ali's army, and the stage was set for the third civil war in Ali's caliphate. Through dialogue, a large number of the 'seceders' were reconciled, but the hard core resisted and resolved to fight to the finish. This core consisted of about 1,500 men, who were led by Abd Allah b. Wahb. The battle, at Nahrawan in 658, resulted in their defeat and dispersal.

The final stage of the arbitration which was held at Adhruh, in 659, was brought to an end, as it had been initiated in the first place, by one of Amr's ruses: he proposed to Abu Musa that they both depose their respective masters, and then set up a council to appoint the new caliph. Abu Musa agreed, and duly 'deposed' Ali, upon which Amr immediately declared Mu'awiya as the sole caliph. This declaration was of course rejected by Ali, who had no choice but to prepare once again for a resumption of hostilities. However, before he was able to regroup his forces, he was attacked and mortally wounded by Ibn Muljam, one of the Kharijites, in the congregational mosque of Kufa, on 26 January 661, dying two days later.

Social and Spiritual Justice

Some instances of Ali's unflinching adherence to justice in the political and legal domains have been noted above. His rulings, sayings and attitudes establish clear principles also for policies in the domain of religious tolerance. For example, in what was to become one of the most important treatises on good governance in the Islamic tradition – his letter to Malik al-Ashtar, appointing him governor of Egypt – he writes:

> Infuse your heart with mercy for the subjects, love for them and kindness towards them. Be not like a ravenous beast of prey over them, seeking to devour them. For they are of two types: either your brother in religion or your like in creation. Mistakes slip from them, defects emerge from them, deliberately or accidentally. So bestow upon them your forgiveness and your pardon, just as you would have God bestow upon you His forgiveness and pardon; for you are over them, and the one who appointed you as governor is over you, and God is over him who appointed you … and through them He tests you.[15]

---

[15] For references to this and the following sayings in this section, see R. Shah-Kazemi, *Justice and Remembrance: Introducing the Spirituality of Imam Ali* (London, 2006), ch. 2: 'A Sacred Conception of Justice in Imam Ali's Letter to Malik al-Ashtar', pp. 73–133.

The theme of justice to all – of whatever religion – is here intertwined
with the principle of compassion. This passage from the letter remains
to this day one of the most important and explicit articulations of the
principle of the essential unity of the human race, and the consequent
equality of all human beings. It is a powerful antidote against the poison
of religious prejudice; and upholds the centrality of mercy to any articulation of the meaning of justice, and, still more, to the implementation
of justice. In this context, one should note such sayings of Ali's as the
following:

- The dispensing of mercy brings down [divine] mercy.
- As you grant mercy, so will you be granted mercy.
- I am astounded by the person who hopes for mercy from one above
  him, while he is not merciful to those beneath him.

However, Ali's espousal of the principle of mercy and compassion did
not prevent him from meting out appropriate punishment to officials
found guilty of corruption whenever it was necessary. In his letter to
Malik he tells him to inflict severe punishment upon any official found
guilty of misappropriation of public funds. In a letter to Ziyad b. Abihi,
deputy to the governor of Basra, he issues this stern warning:

> I swear by God an oath in all sincerity: if news reaches me that
> you have misappropriated the revenue of the Muslims, whether
> a small or large amount, I shall inflict a severe punishment
> upon you, one which will lighten your wealth, burden your
> back, and degrade your condition.

It was Ali's fiscal policy that signified most clearly his desire to restore
economic justice by eliminating the vast inequalities that had become
entrenched in Muslim society as a result, chiefly, of the policies of his
predecessor in the caliphate. In enforcing an equal distribution of
wealth to all Muslims – whether freed slaves of Persian origin or Arab
tribal chieftains – Ali was returning to the Prophet's policy (which was
followed also by Abu Bakr, but not by Umar or Uthman), which recognised no hierarchy or stratification in distributing the wealth of the
community. Ali took this policy so seriously that, even when confronted
by the aggressive opposition of the Kharijites – who had begun to
insult him, disrupt public prayers which he was leading in the mosque
of Kufa, calling him a *kafir* and so forth – he continued to pay them
their stipends from the public treasury. When urged by his supporters
to punish the Kharijites for their behaviour, he replied by saying that for
as long as they attacked him with their tongues, he would defend himself
with his tongue; if they resorted to violence with their hands, he would

defend himself with his hand; and only if they took up arms against him would he draw his sword in defence. In other words, he allowed them to give vent to their grievances, so long as their opposition to him was expressed only verbally. In modern parlance, the inviolability of the principle of freedom of expression is clearly being upheld here, together with that of proportionate retaliation within the framework of legitimate self-defence.

Another act of great significance, from the point of view of establishing a precedent in the domains of both redistributive justice and religious non-discrimination, is Ali's encounter with an old, blind beggar in Kufa. He made some inquiries about the beggar and was told that he was a Christian. He remonstrated with the people in the vicinity: 'You have employed him to the point where he is old and infirm, and now you refuse to help him. Give him a regular stipend from the public funds (*bayt al-mal*).'

Such an attitude expresses clearly the principle underlying the institution of the *dhimma*, that is, the protection – understanding this 'protection' in the widest possible sense, including protection against the worst consequences of disability, old age and poverty – of religious minorities by the Muslim state in return for the payment of a poll-tax (*jizya*). This principle is expressed as follows by Ali: 'Those who have contracted the agreement of *dhimma* … their lives and their properties should be as inviolable as our own.'

Finally, let us note this important saying of Ali, underlining the principle of non-discrimination between Muslims and non-Muslims. He distributed a certain amount of state revenue equally to two women, one an Arab, the other a Jew; but the Arab woman complained: 'By God, I am an Arab and this one a non-Arab.' Ali replied: 'By God I find no grounds for favouring the descendants of Ismail over those of Isaac in respect of distributing this revenue.'[16]

Shi'at Ali and the Principle of Walaya

As noted at the outset, the term *Shi'a* is an abbreviation of *Shi'at Ali*, 'the supporters/group/ partisans of Ali'. The vital point is that this designation is not derived from post-prophetic theological or political developments and controversies. The term may have acquired distinctive theological and political connotations as the nascent Islamic state and society developed in the subsequent generations, but reference to the 'Shi'a' of Ali was made in the prophetic period. Even during Muhammad's lifetime, a group was already known for their particular love for, and attachment

---

16   Ali Muhammad al-Sallabi, *Ali b. Abi Talib* (Cairo, 2004), vol. 1, pp. 279–280.

to, Ali. According to Shi'i and Sunni sources alike, it is to this group of companions that the Prophet referred in his answer to a question about the Quranic verse 98:7: 'Those who have faith and do righteous deeds – they are the best of created beings (*khayr al-bariyya*).' In his encyclopaedic Quran commentary, the Sunni exegete and historian al-Tabari (d. 923) refers to the report recounting that the Prophet was asked who was meant by the term 'best of created beings'. He answered by referring to Ali and 'his *Shi'a*'.[17]

Similarly, in his comment on 98:7, the later Sunni authority and Quran commentator, Jalal al-Din al-Suyuti (d. 1505) refers to the report that the Prophet recited this verse and then addressed Ali: 'That is, you and your followers (*shi'atuk*) on the Day of Judgment, pleased and well-pleasing.'[18] According to the Companion Jabir b. Abd Allah, the Prophet, upon seeing Ali, said, 'By Him in whose hand is my soul, truly he and his *Shi'a* are triumphant on the Day of Judgment', after which 98:7 was revealed. The narration continues: 'So the Companions of the Prophet used to say, when meeting Ali, "the best of created beings (*khayr al-bariyya*) has come".'[19] It should be pointed out here that these references to the Shi'a of Ali need not be interpreted in a triumphalist or even exclusivist sense. Rather, in line with so many of Ali's own sayings encouraging his Shi'a to go from the outward form of things to their inner reality, and from specific personalities to universal principles,[20] these references to the Shi'a can be read in a pluralist and supra-confessional sense to include all those souls – of whatever religion – who orient themselves to the realisation of *walaya*, loving the person or persons in their religion who have themselves realised this sanctity, the heart of the spiritual quest.

The members of this group of Companions who were known for their particular devotion to the person of Ali were Salman al-Farisi, Abu Dharr al-Ghiffari, Ammar b. Yasir and Miqdad b. Amr. As Husain Jafri notes: 'Historically it cannot be denied … that these men formed the nucleus of the first Alid party, or the Shi'a.' These four persons are therefore regarded in later Shi'i tradition as 'the four pillars' of Shi'i Islam.[21] At the historical origin and the spiritual heart of Shi'ism, then, is the notion of fidelity to Ali, or more deeply, fidelity to the spiritual principle that he is deemed to embody, *walaya*. In this context, *walaya* denotes two

---

[17] Abu Jarir al-Tabari, *Jami al-bayan* (Cairo, n.d.), vol. 30, p. 320.

[18] Jalal al-Din al-Suyuti, *al-Durr al-manthur* (Beirut, 1314/1896), vol. 6, p. 379.

[19] Abu Bakr Ahmad b. Mardawayh, *Manaqib Ali b. Abi Talib* (Qumm, 2001), p. 347.

[20] For example: 'Know the Truth, and you will know those who belong to it as its people (*ahl*)'; 'do not look at who said it, but at what was said', etc. See *Justice and Remembrance*, pp. 1–10, for discussion of this and similar sayings.

[21] Jafri, *Origins and Early Development*, p. 53.

complementary principles, the first being spiritual authority or guardianship, deriving from proximity to God, love, intimacy or friendship with Him, as noted above; and the second being fidelity, devotion, affiliation manifested by the follower towards the one qualified by *walaya*, the *wali Allah*, 'friend of God'.

It is important to note that neither personal devotion to Ali, nor the spiritual orientation towards the *walaya* he is deemed to embody, is confined within Shi'i Islam; it extends to all the schools of Islam, for veneration of Ali as head of the *ahl al-bayt* ('People of the Household') of the Prophet is found throughout the length and breadth of the Muslim world, from the inception of Islam to the present. A fine example is the poem in which al-Shafi'i, founder of one of the four schools of Sunni jurisprudence, claims to have befriended 'the best imam, the best guide' (*khayra imam wa khayra hadi*), this love for Ali going hand in hand with his love for the first three caliphs.[22]

The orientation towards *walaya*, understood as sanctity, lies at the heart of the spiritual quest in Islam, as it does in every revealed religion. This point is strongly stressed in Shi'i sources: both prophecy and sanctity are universal principles, and as such are found at the heart of every religion revealed by God. Whereas the outward dimension of the message of Islam, the *zahir*, is immediately accessible to all, its inner dimension, the *batin*, requires initiation into the spiritual life by a guide (*murshid*, *shaykh* or, in Persian, *pir*), who has himself (or herself) been initiated into this inner dimension of the prophetic message. *Walaya*, as we have seen, has been defined in terms of this inner dimension of prophecy (*al-walaya batin al-nubuwwa*). Whilst the Prophet is regarded as combining both sanctity and prophethood in all their fullness, Ali is deemed to be an embodiment of *walaya*, and not of prophethood, *nubuwwa*. The latter is identified with the formal revelation (*tanzil*) of the Quran, while from *walaya* there emerges that which unveils the inner dimension of revelation, that is, the disclosures that emerge from spiritual exegesis (*ta'wil*). Similarly, it is through the principle of *walaya* that the moral-religious law (*shari'a*) is rendered transparent, revealing its inner spiritual reality (*haqiqa*). Ali's role as an embodiment of *walaya* is to make manifest the esoteric significance of the Word of God, on the one hand; and the spirit infusing the letter of the Law, on the other. The spiritual guidance imparted by Ali is based essentially upon these twin foundations.

The status of Ali is all too often presented as a point of divergence between Sunni and Shi'i in both theology and ideology. This makes all the more significant his unifying role in the ethical, spiritual, mystical

---

[22] Muhammad b. Idris al-Shafi'i, *Diwan* (Beirut, 1996), p. 27.

and metaphysical traditions of Islam.[23] One of the most important figures in this regard is Sayyid Haydar Amuli (d. 1385), whose writings can be seen as building a bridge between Sunni Sufism and Shi'i spirituality, or *irfan*. He asserts that despite the formal, juridical differences between Sunni and Shi'i, when it comes to spirituality, the terms *Sufi* and *Shi'i* are different names of one and the same orientation towards ultimate reality (*haqiqa*), the inner dimension of Islam. Here, Ali is seen as an ideal personification of this *haqiqa* and, after the Prophet, the chief spiritual guide leading mystical aspirants along the path to the *haqiqa*. It is for this reason that Amuli says that if one needed to find, among the sayings of the saints, means by which the *haqiqa* of *tawhid* can be dislosed, the sayings of Ali suffice, for he is 'the most tremendous among them and the most complete among them'.[24]

In his monumental work, *al-Futuhat al-Makkiyya*, the Sufi master known in the tradition as 'the greatest shaykh' (*al-shaykh al-akbar*), Muhyi al-Din Ibn al-Arabi (1165–1240) maintains that Ali was the closest of all human spirits to the Prophet in the primordial 'cloud' which foreshadowed all manifested creation, referring to Ali as 'imam of the world and secret of all the prophets'.[25] This view of Ali's *walaya* is close to that found within Shi'i sources. For example, regarding the 'proximity' between the Prophet and Ali in the spiritual realm prior to the creation of the world, we find the Prophet addressing Ali thus: 'O Ali, God was and nothing was with Him, whereupon He created me and created you as two spirits from the light of His majesty ... you and I are of a single light and a single clay.' Similarly, as regards Ali constituting the 'secret' of all the prophets: 'The *walaya* of Ali is inscribed in all the books of the prophets; every other messenger was only sent to proclaim the prophethood of Muhammad and the *walaya* of Ali.'[26] In the Shi'i tradition one finds interpretations of this kind of saying which range from the most literal and exclusivist – identifying the principle of *walaya* exclusively with the personhood of Ali – to the most mystical and metaphysical: viewing Ali as an embodiment of the universal principle of *walaya*.

---

[23] See the article 'Ali' in *Encyclopaedia Islamica*, vol. 3, pp. 532–547, section 6, entitled 'Mysticism', by M. R. Jozi and R. Shah-Kazemi, for elaboration on the points being made here, together with bibliographical references of the citations in the following paragraphs.

[24] Sayyid Haydar Amuli, *Jami al-asrar*, ed. H. Corbin and O. Yahya, in *La philosophie shi'ite* (Tehran and Paris, 1969), p. 301.

[25] Muhyi al-Din Ibn al-Arabi, *al-Futuhat al-Makkiyya* (Cairo, 1269/1853), vol. 1, p. 132.

[26] Al-Saffar al-Qummi, *Basa'ir al-darajat* (Tabriz, n.d.), p. 72.

The principle of *walaya* is so tightly woven into the fabric of spiritual realisation in Shi'i Islam that the Shi'a refer to themselves frequently as 'the people of *walaya*' (*ahl al-walaya*).[27] The *ahl al-walaya* are thus identical to the *Shi'at Ali*, and this leads us to pose the question: how could there have arisen a group of the Prophet's Companions who manifested such a degree of veneration for Ali that they could be designated as his *Shi'a*, a designation legitimated and ratified by the Prophet himself? Answering this question helps us to appreciate the spirit motivating Shi'i Muslims, and to dispel various misconceptions, such as the absurd notion that the Shi'a are more devoted to Ali and the imams than to the Prophet. What is clear about this early group of supporters of Ali is that they did not in any way consider their devotion to him as a distraction from, or dilution of, their devotion to the Prophet. Rather, their devotion to Ali can be seen as an overflow of their devotion to the Prophet, and served only to bring them closer to his spiritual presence.

A conventional theological answer to the question why a group of followers of Ali should have formed in the lifetime of the Prophet is this: this group of Companions recognised Ali's authority as an imam, a spiritual leader, possessing an authority bestowed upon him by God and the Prophet. But a more nuanced answer emerges as a result of what Ali himself said, implicitly, about the difference of degrees of spiritual knowledge within this very group of his close companions: 'If Abu Dharr knew what was in the heart of Salman, he would kill him.' Whereas Abu Dharr's devotion to Ali was based upon fundamentally exoteric notions of faith, Salman's was fed by an intuition of the esoteric mysteries which were not only disclosed by Ali, but also rendered spiritually accessible by him, thus, realisable by others. Those who 'had ears to hear', those who could 'read between the lines' of the many allusions to the esoteric depths of the faith made by Ali, responded to his teachings and his presence according to the depth of their own intuition of the mysteries alluded to in those teachings. It was thanks to his depth of understanding that Salman was referred to by Ali (and, according to some sources, by the Prophet) as being 'one amongst us, the *ahl al-bayt*'.[28]

However, both Salman and Abu Dharr, representing archetypes along a spectrum of devotion ranging from the most formal and outward (*zahir*) dimensions to the most subtle and inward (*batin*), would have appreciated their devotion to Ali as deriving from, and therefore subordinated to, their devotion to the Prophet. As noted earlier, it was the

---

[27] M. A. Amir-Moezzi, *The Spirituality of Shi'i Islam: Beliefs and Practices* (London, 2011), p. 231.

[28] See Corbin, *En Islam iranien*, vol. 1, p. 264 ff. for a profound discussion of the implications of this 'adoption' of Salman into the prophetic 'household'.

Prophet himself who fostered, cultivated and clearly approved of this devotion to Ali, knowing that it served only to enhance devotion to the Prophet himself and to God, and to deepen receptivity to the inner graces transmitted through his *nubuwwa*.

Addressing now the spiritual quality, *walaya*, upon which the whole idea of devotion to Ali is founded, let us return to the key prophetic saying referring to Ali's *walaya*, the Ghadir Khumm declaration. In some versions of the tradition, the Prophet makes this declaration after first asking the congregation: 'Am I not closer (*awla*) to the believers than their own selves?'[29] This is understood as an evocation of the following Quranic verse: 'The Prophet is closer to the believers than their selves, and his wives are [as] their mothers. And the owners of kinship are closer to one another in the ordinance of God than [other] believers and emigrants …' (33:6). All Shiʻi, and some Sunni, sources have mentioned the relevance of this verse to the Ghadir declaration, as the verse was revealed just prior to it: 'O Messenger! Convey that which has been revealed unto you from your Lord. If you do it not, you would not have conveyed His Message. And God will defend you against the people' (5:67). Similarly, great stress is placed by the Shiʻa on the fact that 5:3 was revealed during the Prophet's final Hajj, that is, just a matter of days before Ghadir. The key part of this verse reads as follows: 'This day I have perfected for you your religion, and completed my favour upon you, and have chosen for you *islam* as religion.' The conveying of the Message in all its completeness mentioned in 5:67 is explicitly identified with the Ghadir declaration of Ali's *walaya*; and the latter, in turn, is identified by Shiʻi theologians with the 'perfection' and 'completion' of the religion of Islam.[30] This assertion is underlined by the fact that in one version of the sermon given by the Prophet at Ghadir there is the famous saying: 'I leave behind me two weighty things (*thaqalayn*): the Book of God and my *ahl al-bayt*.'

In order to appreciate the spiritual significance of the principle of *walaya*, both in itself and in relation to Ali, one should take careful note of 5:55: 'Your *Wali* is only God and His Messenger, and the believers – those who establish the prayer and pay *zakat* while they are bowing at prayer.' Quranic commentators – Shiʻi and Sunni alike – agree that the referent of 'believers' is Ali. For it was well known that a beggar had entered the mosque while the worshippers were at prayer, asking for alms, and that Ali, in the bowing position, pointed to his ring; the

---

[29] Shaykh al-Mufid, *Kitab al-Irshad: The Book of Guidance*, tr. I. K. A. Howard (London, 1981), pp. 3–4; see also Maria Massi Dakake, *The Charismatic Community: Shiʻite Identity in Early Islam* (Albany, NY, 2007), pp. 34–35.
[30] See Amir-Moezzi, *Spirituality*, pp. 237–239, and Badr Shahin, *Verses of Ghadir* (Qumm, 2000), p. 20.

beggar understood the sign, and removed the ring from Ali's finger. This identification of the broad category of 'believers' with a single believer, Ali, is inclusively interpreted to mean that Ali is the perfect exemplar, after the Prophet, of that degree of faith which opens out into the spiritual knowledge, unitive power and divine presence which pertain to *walaya*.

The mystical aspects of *walaya* are alluded to in the utterance in which God 'declares war' against whomever opposes one of His *awliya*, and proceeds to describe the two stages by which the servant of God becomes a *wali* of God:

> My servant draws near to Me through nothing I love more than that which I have made obligatory for him. My servant never ceases to draw near to Me through supererogatory acts until I love him. And when I love him, I am his hearing by which he hears, his sight by which he sees, his hand by which he strikes, and his foot by which he walks.

The mysterious penetration of the human *wali* by the divine quality of *walaya* is one of the richest sources of mystical speculation within the spiritual traditions of Islam. It helps to explain the otherwise baffling statement of the Prophet in regard to Ali, noted above: 'Looking at Ali is an act of worship.' It helps us to make the following analogy: insofar as the *wali* is a perfectly polished mirror reflecting the divine nature, looking at the *wali*, with the right intention, and through the eye of the heart, is tantamount to contemplating the Qualities of God. Such contemplation can be designated as a form of worship. The acts of the *wali*, likewise, are assimilable to the acts of God, as attested not only by the *hadith* just cited, but also by the words addressed to the Prophet by God in the Quran: 'And you (Muhammad) did not throw when you threw, but God it was who threw' (78:17).

Jalal al-Din Rumi gives us a sublime commentary on this verse in relation to a famous act of Ali on the battlefield – one of many for which he became known as the *fata*, or chivalrous knight par excellence. At the battle of *Khandaq* ('the Trench') in 627, Ali defeated the Qurayshi champion Amr b. Abd Wudd in single combat, but was seen to hesitate, as if in fear. When asked by the Prophet about this, he replied: 'He had reviled my mother and spat in my face. I feared that if I struck then, it would have been out of personal anger.'[31] Rumi immortalised this incident in his *Mathnawi*, using Ali's attitude as an exemplification of the

---

[31] Muhammad Rayshahri, ed., *Mawsu'at al-Imam Ali b. Abi Talib* (Qumm, 1421/2000), vol. 1, pp. 218–219.

principle expressed in 78:17, thereby evoking the 'pearls of union' which reside at the heart of the mystery of *walaya*. He puts the following words in the mouth of Ali as a reply to the defeated warrior who asks why he has been spared:

> He said, 'I am wielding the sword for God's sake, I am the servant of God, I am not under the command of the body.
> I am the Lion of God, I am not the lion of my passion: my deed bears witness to my religion.
> In war I am (manifesting the truth of) *thou didst not throw when thou threwest* (78:17):
> I am (but) as the sword, and the wielder is the (Divine) Sun.
> I have removed the baggage of self out of the way, I have deemed (what is) other than
> God to be non-existence.'
>
> (*Mathnawi*, 1: 3787–3792)

The removal of the 'baggage' of the ego, and realising that what is other than God is 'non-existence': such is only possible, in Ali's perspective, through what we might call the operative aspect of *walaya*, namely, the 'remembrance of God' (*dhikr Allah*). On the one hand, according to Ali, God Himself has made this remembrance 'a polish for the hearts, by means of which they see after being blind, hear after being deaf'; and, on the other, the remembrance of God only attains its ultimate reality (*haqiqa*) through the 'forgetting' of the self. In other words, through that self-effacement, or *fana*, which renders the human *wali* transparent to the light of God's *walaya*.

However, for Ali, the power – at once extinctive and unitive – of the remembrance of God is inoperative without intellectual contemplation and moral purification, and these two principles in turn are inseparable from divine revelation. It is through God's revelation that the intellect is able to attain perfection, and attain victory in 'the greatest struggle' (*al-jihad al-akbar*), the battle for authentic virtue and spiritual rectitude, to which Ali, echoing the Prophet, refers in numerous sayings. The cultivation of the intellect, the attainment of perfect virtue in the soul, the vision of God by the heart, the remembrance of God with self-effacement – such are the points of reference in Ali's discourses for the realisation of that *walaya* which is the 'inner dimension' of prophethood.

Human Nature and the Principle of Tawhid

The realisation of sanctity as the inner dimension of prophethood is prefaced by the rediscovery of the hidden treasures buried in the depths of the intellect.[32] For, on the one hand, Ali asserts that 'the messenger (*rasul*) of a man is the translator of his own intellect'; and on the other, he tells us, in Sermon 1 of the *Nahj al-balagha*, that among the reasons why God sent to mankind 'His Messengers', was that through these Messengers, God might 'unearth for humanity the buried treasures of the intellects'. These 'buried treasures' of the intellect can be understood as the seeds of consciousness embedded by God in the primordial nature of the human being, the *fitra*, referred to in the Quran in the following verse:

> So turn your face towards religion as one ever oriented to the truth: the primordial nature of [created by] God, according to which He created humankind. There is no changing the creation of God. That is the perpetually upright religion, but most people know not. (30:30)

Ali's teachings on *walaya*, together with his own exemplification of the principle, constitute reminders of what it means to be fully human, to be fully in accord with the *fitra*. As Ali says in one of the poems of his *Diwan*:

> Although you see yourself as an insignificant speck, within you the entire universe is contained;
> You are thus yourself 'the meaningful book' [*kitab mubin*; 43:2 *et passim*] whose letters make clear that which was concealed.

Reflecting on these remarkable lines of poetry helps us to integrate Ali's mystical vision of humanity within the principle of *walaya*: for Ali, the process of discovering the essence of the human being is analogous to plumbing the depths of divine revelation. Both the revelation of Scripture – the 'clear Book' – and the creation of the human being are seen by Ali as means or processes by which God discloses or unveils Himself (which is what Ali calls *tajalli*). On the one hand: 'God has disclosed Himself to His creatures through His creatures'; and on the other, 'He has disclosed Himself to His creatures in His Book'.

Throughout the entire realm of creation, then, there is nothing but divine revelation, whence Ali's famous dictum: 'I never saw anything without seeing God', a dictum which can be read as a comment on the Quranic verse: 'Unto God belong the East and the West; so wherever you turn, there is the Face of God' (2:115). Whether one looks at the

---

[32] This final section summarises some of the main points made in R. Shah-Kazemi, *Justice and Remembrance*, Ch. 3; and in *Spiritual Quest: Reflections on Qur'anic Prayer According to the Teachings of Imam Ali* (London, 2011), especially pp. 1–14.

human soul (the microcosm), or the entire creation (the macrocosm), or the scriptural revelations – it is always the self-disclosure of God that one perceives. The mystical sayings of Ali concerning the ultimate nature of God – so many of which are akin to Zen-style koans – are intended not so much to inform as to *transform*: they are intended to be catalysts which precipitate fundamental shifts of perception, evoking realities which can be 'tasted' spiritually rather than articulated verbally or conceptually, transforming our modes of awareness, reflection, and contemplation, such that we are better equipped to interiorise the esoteric mysteries of divine unity. These mysteries transcend conceptual and logical categories of thought in the very measure that the esoteric transcends the exoteric. It is only through an intuition fashioned, to some degree at least, by the spiritual essence of *walaya* that such descriptions of *tawhid* as the following will make any sense at all: '[God is] with everything, but not through association; and other than everything, but not through separation.'[33]

* * *

In terms of Ali's legacy, one must refer first and foremost to the *Nahj al-balagha*. In addition to providing profound formulations which served as seeds for the theological elaboration of such central doctrines of *tawhid* and *tanzih* (the transcendence of God), it became established in all schools of thought as the very model of Arabic eloquence (*balagha*) expressing the highest wisdom in the most eloquent terms. The great emphasis in the *Nahj* upon the importance of the intellect served to deepen the receptivity of Shi'i Muslims to philosophical speculation and theosophical meditation. In terms of Arabic literature, few texts have exerted a greater influence than the *Nahj*. Several moving supplications are also attributed to Ali; these have come to play a major role in the devotional life of Shi'i Islam, the most famous supplication being the *Du'a Kumayl*. Finally, it is important to stress the foundational role played by Ali in the genesis of a wide variety of disciplines within Islamic culture, the later elaborators of which most often elevated Ali to be a major point of reference for their particular discipline. He is deemed to have provided impetus and content for such sciences as Quran exegesis (*tafsir*), theology (*kalam*), philosophy (*falsafa*), jurisprudence (*fiqh*), rhetoric (*balagha*) and grammar (*nahw*), and calligraphy (*khatt*); as well as for the mystical traditions of Islam, as noted above, and various arcane sciences such as numerology (*jafr*) and alchemy (*kimiya*).

---

[33] Sermon 1 of the *Nahj al-balagha*. For an annotated translation of this sermon, see Appendix 1 of *Justice and Remembrance*, pp. 208–218.

Further Reading

Amir-Moezzi, Mohammad Ali. *The Divine Guide in Early Shi'ism: The Sources of Esotericism in Islam*, tr. David Streight. New York, 1994.

—— *The Spirituality of Shi'i Islam: Beliefs and Practices*. London, 2011.

Chirri, Mohammad Jawad. *The Brother of the Prophet Mohammad*, 2 vols. Detroit, 1982.

Corbin, Henry. *En Islam iranien: Aspects spirituels et philosophiques*. Paris, 1971–1972.

Dakake, Maria Massi. *The Charismatic Community: Shi'ite Identity in Early Islam*. Albany, NY, 2007.

Djebli, Moktar. 'Encore à propos de l'authenticité du Nahj al-Balagha!', *Studia Islamica*, 75 (1992), pp. 33–56.

Jafri, S. Husain M. *Origins and Early Development of Shi'a Islam*. London and New York, 1979.

Lakhani, Ali M., ed. *The Sacred Foundations of Justice in Islam: The Teachings of Ali ibn Abi Talib*. Bloomington, IN, 2006.

Landolt, Hermann. 'Walayah', *Encyclopedia of Religion*, vol. 15, pp. 316–323.

Madelung, Wilferd. *The Succession to Muhammad*. Cambridge, 1997.

al-Mufid, al-Shaykh (Muhammad al-Harithi al-Baghdadi), *Kitab al-Irshad: The Book of Guidance*, trans. I. K. A. Howard. London, 1981.

Mutahhari, Murtada. *Glimpses of the Nahj al-Balagha*. Qumm, 1997.

Nasr, Seyyed Hossein. 'Sufism and Shi'ism: Their Relationship in Essence and in History', in his *Sufi Essays*. London, 1972, pp. 104–120.

Qutbuddin, Tahera. *A Treasury of Virtues: Sayings, Sermons, and Teachings of Ali*. New York and London, 2013.

Shah-Kazemi, Reza. *Justice and Remembrance: Introducing the Spirituality of Imam Ali*. London, 2006.

—— *Spiritual Quest: Reflections on Quranic Prayer According to the Teachings of Imam Ali*. London, 2011.

—— et al. 'Ali b. Abi Talib', *Encylopaedia Islamica*, vol. 3, pp. 477–583.

Sobhani, Ja'far. *Doctrines of Shi'i Islam: A Compendium of Imami Beliefs and Practices*, tr. and ed. R. Shah-Kazemi. London, 2001.

Tabataba'i, Sayyid Muhammad Husayn. *Kernel of the Kernel: Concerning the Wayfaring and Spiritual Journey of the People of Intellect*, tr. Mohammad H. Faghfoory. Albany, NY, 2003.

3

Imam Ja'far al-Sadiq and the Elaboration of Shi'ism

Karim Douglas Crow

Ja'far al-Sadiq (d. 765) was a prominent spokesman in Medina of the Banu Hashim, and the descendants of the *ahl al-bayt* (the Family of Muhammad), at a remarkably intense time in the foundational history of Islam. During his lifetime, the Umayyad dynasty was vanquished by the Abbasid revolution in 750, and non-Arab Muslim participation in religious and intellectual activities grew significantly. It is likely that Ja'far received his honorific title '*sadiq*' (truthsayer) for veracity in narrating traditions, or possibly due to predictions reportedly verified by subsequent events. He enjoyed double maternal descent from the first caliph, Abu Bakr al-Siddiq, through his mother Umm Farwa bint al-Qasim b. Muhammad b. Abi Bakr, and through her mother, Asma bint Abd al-Rahman b. Abi Bakr – affirming '*Abu Bakr bore me twice*'. Al-Sadiq was widely esteemed among Sunni Muslims as a model of wisdom, and particularly by the Sufis for his reputation in spiritual initiation as well as esoteric elucidation (*ta'wil*) of the Quran.

As the direct descendant of the Prophet Muhammad through Ali and Fatima's younger son al-Husayn, al-Sadiq is venerated as the sixth Imam or spiritual leader of the Imamiyya (later Twelver Shi'a), and the fifth Imam of the Ismaili Shi'a. The Ja'fari legal school of the Imamiyya is named after him; while the Isma'iliyya trace their imamate through al-Sadiq's eldest son Isma'il b. Ja'far and Isma'il's son Muhammad. These two major Shi'i communities sprang from one root: Ja'far's articulation of the doctrine of the imamate, grounded in his advocating the spiritual authority (*walaya*) of the imam whose unique functions and qualities exemplify the prolongation of divine guidance after the death of the Prophet Muhammad. Nevertheless, Sunni authorities were anxious to establish that al-Sadiq upheld the legitimacy of Abu Bakr's succession to the Prophet as the first caliph, mindful of his maternal lineage.

Al-Sadiq was intimately involved in the rival religious, intellectual and political trends of his era, interacting directly with leading personalities from a wide ideological spectrum. He was visited in his home by the great Kufan *faqih* Abu Hanifa (d. 767), who championed rationalist techniques for deriving legal rulings (*qiyas* and *ra'y*); by the prominent Medinan scholar Malik b. Anas (d. 795), who praised his religious probity; and by Amr b. Ubayd and Wasil b. Ata, the founders of the Mu'tazili movement in Basra. Al-Sadiq was summoned to Iraq repeatedly for audiences at the court of the Abbasid caliphs al-Saffah (r. 749–754) and al-Mansur (r. 754–775) – yet he had strained relations with the latter, who monitored Ja'far for suspected political ambitions and whose ambivalent dealings with him became legendary. Al-Sadiq is further linked with the disciplines of letter numerology (*ilm al-huruf* or *jafr*), prognostication (*fal*), and alchemy as the reputed master of Jabir b. Hayyan [in Latin translations called Geber], the founder of Islamic alchemy. He served over the centuries as a symbol of unity for Muslims of differing persuasions, respected and invoked by most doctrinal schools, and deemed 'unparalleled among his peers'.

Many controversial questions obstruct a proper understanding of his historical role and have obscured his position on important issues. Conflicting images of al-Sadiq were built up over time – Sunni, Shi'i, Sufi – each reflecting a selective portrait of his activities and teachings. 'It is the manner in which his contribution has been recast and, at times, re-invented that enables him to be employed by writers in the different Islamic sciences as integral to their development', observes Robert Gleave.[1]

To fully appreciate the significance of Ja'far al-Sadiq's life and thought, this chapter surveys the distinctive role of the *ahl al-bayt*, together with a glance at the contributions of his grandfather and father in fostering his family's teaching tradition. Al-Sadiq's achievement in articulating the creedal and intellectual basis of the imamate, as well as his function as a salvific and initiatic guide in consolidating a nascent communal identity and promoting Imami Shi'i doctrinal cohesiveness is the core of our survey here. In this regard, representative dimensions of his theological, ethical and spiritual instructions are noted – in an historical context of tumult, in which numerous apocalyptic Shi'i movements were active.

Ahl al-Bayt

From the earliest period, certain descendants of the Prophet's family played a significant role in the elaboration of Islamic religious disciplines, theological doctrines and spirituality. To better grasp the attitude of al-Sadiq towards the early unfolding of the community, the

---

[1]   Robert Gleave, 'Ja'far al-Sadeq', *Encyclopaedia Iranica*, vol. 14, pp. 349–366, available online at: http://www.iranicaonline.org/.

history of his family should be borne in mind. With the slaying in Kufa of the Prophet's first cousin and son-in-law, the fourth caliph Ali b. Abi Talib, in 661, and six months later the abdication of Ali's eldest son al-Hasan, dynastic power was transferred to Syria by Mu'awiya b. Abi Sufyan. He was the victor of the bitter conflict over the caliphal succession, which now passed to the Umayyad family that had come to prominence when Uthman b. Affan became the third caliph (r. 644–656). Devoted supporters of the *ahl al-bayt* associated with Ali in Iraq were hunted down and severely persecuted by the Umayyads, who instituted the public cursing of Ali from pulpits across the empire. Hasan b. Ali adopted a policy of accommodation towards Umayyad rule – which facilitated Mu'awiya's appointment of his own son Yazid to succeed him in Damascus.

Ali's younger son al-Husayn now pursued an activist stance by seeking support against Yazid, but his small band of relatives and devoted retainers were massacred by Umayyad troops in Karbala in 680. Karbala marked the schism between Umayyad despotism and Alid legitimacy. Husayn's death and the intercessory function he was held to provide for faithful partisans of his family dramatically shaped the unfolding Shi'i image of the 'imam' as saviour. He also offered a model of resistance to oppression and the rendering of conscious sacrifice – and is an enduring presence for the Shi'a, animating the idea of witnessing to the truth, whatever the odds.

Era of Zayn al-Abidin and al-Baqir

Husayn's single surviving son was Ja'far al-Sadiq's grandfather, Ali Zayn al-Abidin (d. 712), who maintained the accommodationist stance of Hasan towards Umayyad power, as did al-Sadiq's father Muhammad al-Baqir (d. 733). Zayn al-Abidin was also known as al-Sajjad for his exemplary devotions, and avoided entanglement with the political schemes against Syrian rule spearheaded by Abd Allah b. al-Zubayr in Mecca and al-Mukhtar al-Thaqafi in Kufa. Zayn al-Abidin's restraint allowed him to safely weather the stormy reigns of the Umayyad caliphs, Abd al-Malik and Sulayman, while maintaining his preeminent moral authority intact. His spiritual invocations and supplications are recorded in the beautiful collection *al-Sahifat al-Sajjadiyya*, which his sons preserved and handed down to posterity – and his social ideals are expressed in his epistle on rights and obligations, *Risalat al-huquq*.

In his final decades, Zayn al-Abidin assembled a select circle of followers who looked to him as their guide in religious and spiritual affairs. They included Abu Hamza al-Thumali and Aban b. Taghlib, who became devoted supporters of Zayn al-Abidin's son Muhammad al-Baqir, and of his grandson Ja'far al-Sadiq. Al-Baqir also attracted a growing number of devoted pupils during his 20 years as chief of his family, sublimating any political ambition. The Husaynid Alids were marked by their concern to develop and articulate a distinct body of legal knowledge, and to cultivate the egalitarian moral and social principles enunciated by Ali. Al-Baqir succeeded in spreading his teaching – which included his elucidations of the Quran (*tafsir*) – into Iraq through his leading disciples in Kufa, such as Muhammad b. Muslim, Abu Basir al-Asadi, and Jabir b. Yazid al-Jufi.

Apocalyptic Revolt

During the era of al-Sadiq's grandfather Zayn al-Abidin, and then his father al-Baqir, many partisans of the *ahl al-bayt* embraced an apocalyptic ideology that combined messianism with concrete political expectations, first spread by the Kaysaniyya movement.[2] Partisans of Ali's third son Muhammad Ibn al-Hanafiyya, and his son Abu Hashim, the Kaysaniyya even succeeded in setting up a short-lived state in Kufa. For them, Ali was a deathless Redeemer (*mahdi*) whose return from concealment would restore the just rule of the Prophet's family. Their vision integrated widespread apocalyptic ideals cultivated in Jewish, Christian and Zoroastrian traditions, and internalised by Arab tribesmen from Yemen who had been transplanted to lower Iraq by the early Muslim conquests.[3]

Messianic Shi'i tendencies were vivified by the catalytic impact of persecution and socio-political marginalisation by the Umayyads. Various individuals capitalised on this sense of deprivation in the name of one or other figure from the Prophet's family; these zealous groupings are commonly termed *ghulat* (exaggerators). Their extremist leanings were marked by a debased 'prophetism' with claims to secret knowledge, the cursing of the first two caliphs Abu Bakr and Umar, and the divinising of their chosen imam. These beliefs only survived later in exclusivist pockets of adherents in the Near East.

Al-Sadiq and the Advent of Abbasid Rule

Upon al-Baqir's death in Medina, al-Sadiq's younger brother from the same mother, Umm Farwah, was interrogated by the Umayyad governor of Medina; he was accused of inciting people to follow his brother Ja'far

---

[2] Farhad Daftary, *A History of Shi'i Islam* (London, 2013), pp. 36–42.
[3] Sean W. Anthony, *The Caliph and the Heretic: Ibn Saba and the Origins of Shi'ism* (Leiden, 2012), and Wadad al-Qadi, *al-Kaysaniyya fi'l-ta'rikh wa'l-adab* (Beirut, 1974).

as the imam, and slain. It may have been around this time that al-Sadiq arranged the marriage of his favoured eldest son Isma'il to Umm Ibrahim al-Makhzumiyya, the daughter of the next Umayyad governor of Medina, probably to smooth relations with the ruling power.

Activist groups opposed to the Umayyad dynasty sought to channel the energy and direction of religio-political opposition, including the various wings of the Shi'i movement. Al-Sadiq's paternal uncle, Zayd b. Ali, led an uprising in Iraq (739–740) which widely garnered sympathy yet was ruthlessly crushed, followed by another failed revolt by Zayd's son Yahya in the east. The Abbasids engineered an underground revolution in the name of the Prophet's family, which succeeded in toppling the despised Umayyad regime. During the tumultuous events in the transition from Umayyad to Abbasid rule, al-Sadiq received at least three letters appealing to him to emerge from Medina and assume leadership over the nascent revolutionary regime; two came from Shi'i partisans in Iraq, and one from the renegade Abbasid war leader Bassam b. Ibrahim. Al-Sadiq spurned all such appeals and managed to avoid imprisonment or execution. The advent of Abbasid power offered him a greater opportunity to expand his teaching activities and guide his growing circles of students until his death 16 years later in 765 at his home in Medina. During these final years al-Sadiq intensified his work in consolidating his followers and disseminating his ideas, under the menacing scrutiny of Abbasid rule. Towards the end of his life, al-Sadiq was frail in health and had several physical mishaps, including a fall from his mount in Mecca while on pilgrimage.

Hasanid Rivalry

The prominent Hasanid, Abd Allah al-Mahd (grandson of Hasan b. Ali, and the paternal cousin of al-Sadiq), prepared his eldest son Muhammad to serve as the Mahdi, claiming the aura of the 'the pure soul' (*al-nafs al-zakiyya*) who would inaugurate just rule. At the famous assembly convened by the Banu Hashim at al-Abwa between Medina and Mecca just six years before the fall of the Umayyads, al-Mahd elicited support from key leaders of the Banu Hashim for the leadership of his son in the opposition to Umayyad rule, including from the prominent Abbasids Ibrahim b. Muhammad 'al-Imam' and his brother (the future caliph) Abu Ja'far al-Mansur. Al-Sadiq initially boycotted this meeting, and when pressured to attend by his relatives he refused to render allegiance to al-Mahd's son. Evidently cognisant of organised Abbasid political activity, he appeared to have foreseen their immanent success in grasping the reins of government. At al-Abwa, al-Sadiq is reported to have uttered his prediction that the self-proclaimed Mahdi, al-Nafs al-Zakiyya, would be *'slain at the oiled stones'* at the behest of Mansur

– which event indeed occurred at the shiny lava outcrop on the outskirts of Medina in 762, during al-Nafs al-Zakiyya's failed rebellion against Abbasid rule.

Al-Mahd and al-Sadiq were rivals in bidding for the allegiance of the Batri Zaydiyya – activist partisans of the *ahl al-bayt* stemming from Zayd b. Ali's revolt against the Umayyads. More broadly, al-Mahd accused al-Sadiq of envying the Hasanid leadership, and of inability to be a military leader by labelling him a bookworm (*rajulun suhufi*) due to his preoccupation with learning. Once the Abbasids seized power in 750 they resented their former allegiance to the Hasanids, and sought to seize Muhammad al-Nafs al-Zakiyya who had gone into hiding. The caliph Mansur imprisoned al-Mahd along with over a dozen members of his family to force them to surrender al-Nafs al-Zakiyya; almost all of these Hasanid nobles died in detention in Iraq after severe abuse by their captors, their properties being confiscated by al-Mansur.

Articulation of Imami Shiʿism

The waning appeal of apocalyptic projects, coupled with the persistent persecution of the Shiʿa by the Umayyad authorities continued under the early Abbasids, and brought soul-searching and re-thinking within the leadership of the *ahl al-bayt*. This presented al-Sadiq with the opportunity to redirect the energies of activist partisans towards a more inwardly-oriented religious, legal and ethical praxis. It was matched by a deeper speculative thought alive to broader religious and intellectual currents in society – without forsaking the utopian ideals for political reversal and communal Shiʿi self-definition that were incommensurable with the majority community. Al-Sadiq worked through the informal circles of his associates and disciples to form the nucleus of an organisational structure that served the social and spiritual needs of an emerging community (the Imami Shiʿa), and to lay the foundation of its legal, religious and intellectual superstructure. Of all the leaders of the Husaynid line, he played an outstanding role in this formative process – evidenced by the sheer number of key individuals through whom he passed on his ideas, the discipline and guidance he exercised for his followers, and the mass of his narrations recorded in the extant literature.

Walaya

Once developed, the Imami and Ismaili schools assigned primary responsibility to both al-Baqir and especially his son al-Sadiq for elaborating the doctrine of *walaya* (spiritual allegiance) to their imams. This portrayed the imams as divinely designated initiatic guides and authoritative exponents of salvific knowledge,[4] a perspective which developed into a coherent alternative to the dominant Sunni worldview. The principle of *walaya* served as the necessary prerequisite of faith, affirming bonds of devotion with the community's designated leaders and solidarity with community members subject to their initiatic and worldly authority. The necessary corollary of *walaya* is 'dissociation' (*bara'a*) from those viewed as opponents of the Prophet's family. The embracing of *walaya* led to the consolidation of a distinctive inner communal self-definition – an identity forged primarily among communities in lower Iraq, notably around Kufa and Baghdad, which had significant links to other groups in central Iran, Khurasan, Yemen, Syria (Aleppo) and Armenia.

Imamate

Normative Sunni Islam understood community guidance after the Prophet to be vouchsafed in the Quran and by the authoritative religious-legal consensus of religious experts. Neither the Umayyad rulers nor the Abbasid caliphs could make any claim to the spiritual guidance of the faithful, nor could they project a comprehensive theological or legal doctrine. Al-Sadiq's articulation of the imamate did just that, and formed the bedrock of the Imami Shi'a (both Twelver and Ismaili) ideals of moral and political authority. The Shi'a generally upheld the conviction that valid guidance requires the presence of a divinely favoured imam from the Prophet's family, who authoritatively interprets the Quran for his followers as the *hujja* 'decisive-proof'. In this respect, the function of the imam anticipated or perhaps prompted the Sufi notion of the *shaykh* or *pir* whose individual initiatic guidance (*walaya*) is derived from the wisdom of the Prophet. For many Sufi orders (sing. *tariqa*) – Sunni and Shi'a alike – the chain of spiritual initiation names al-Sadiq as transmitting authoritative praxis, from the Prophet Muhammad via Ali. A prominent example is the Naqshbandi *tariqa*, a major Sunni order with adherents across the Middle East, South and Central Asia, and Southeast Asia.

The issue, frequently disputed by Sunni Muslims, was whether al-Sadiq himself upheld the conviction that Ali had been explicitly designated as successor to the Prophet, although his leadership was thwarted by senior Companions, and that the *ahl al-bayt* (in the Husaynid hereditary line) alone could exercise legitimate temporal and spiritual leadership. This is reflected in the general tendency of Sunni authorities from an

---

[4] See the discussion of *walaya* in Chapter 2 of this volume, and in Maria M. Dakake, *The Charismatic Community* (Albany, NY, 2007).

early period to reject the validity of most narrations assigned to al-Sadiq in Shi'i *hadith*. It raises the question of the status of Ja'far's narrations, with specific regard to their literary recording and transmission over generations.

Literary Transmission

Major bio-bibliographic catalogues of the classical period by Ibn al-Nadim, Shaykh al-Tusi and al-Najashi (10th–11th century), show that the preponderance of numerous Imami writings attributed to associates of al-Sadiq, and to pupils of his associates, dealt with the full range of legal praxis and ritual observances. They engaged with major doctrinal and theological topics, from the imamate to Quranic exegesis, as well as disputations and polemics with rival or opposing groups.[5] The overwhelming majority of their narrations (perhaps 70 per cent) cite al-Sadiq, transmitting through the chain of his forefathers back to Ali and/or Muhammad. Later the Imami school maintained that no less than 4,000 transmitters, Shi'i and Sunni, reported al-Sadiq's utterances or instruction.[6] This tradition also attests to the existence of hundreds of 'source-books', where the teachings of Husaynid leaders were recorded and/or elaborated upon by associates of the imams.[7] Although few of those original source-books are extant today, much of their content was sifted and topically rearranged in early compilations – notably by al-Barqi, al-Kulayni, and Ibn Babawayh al-Qummi.

Al-Sadiq also transmitted a number of narrations on the authority of earlier successors who were not his forebears (such as Muhammad b. al-Munkadar, Ubayd Allah b. Abi Rafi, Ata b. Abi Rabah, and Nafi the *mawla* of Abd Allah ibn Umar); this is evidenced in Sunni and occasionally even Shi'i *hadith*s. His most often cited prophetic *hadith* is the famous 'long narration of the Pilgrimage', on a transmission chain (*isnad*) which includes al-Sadiq and his father, cited in five of the six Sunni canonical *hadith* collections. Basra's eminent 8th-century Sunni traditionist critic Yahya b. Sa'id al-Qattan transmitted this narration directly on the authority of al-Sadiq, whom he personally deemed reliable. Yet on the whole, canonical Sunni *hadith* citations of al-Sadiq's

---

5   Hossein Modarressi, *Tradition and Survival* (Oxford, 2003), vol. 1.
6   Abu Ja'far al-Tusi, *Rijal*, ed. Jawad al-Qayyumi (Qumm, 1994; repr. 2009), pp. 155–328 (lists over 3,225 names); and Abd al-Husayn al-Shabastari, *al-Fa'iq fi ruwat wa ashab al-Imam al-Sadiq* (Qumm, 1997), 3 vols (lists 3,759 names of known transmitters from al-Sadiq). One may add over a hundred further names, gleaned from a wide variety of sources.
7   Etan Kohlberg, 'al-Usul al-arba'umi'a', *Jerusalem Studies in Arabic and Islam*, 10 (1987), pp. 128–166.

narrations are sparse, reflecting their cautious attitude to his reporting. Thus, al-Bukhari entirely excluded any narrations from al-Sadiq in his *Sahih* (though al-Sadiq is cited several times in al-Bukhari's ethical compilation *al-Adab al-mufrad*); on the other hand, Muslim's *Sahih* cites 26 *isnad*s narrated through al-Sadiq.[8]

During the 8th century Sunni scholars of traditions debated al-Sadiq's probity in the field of *hadith* in view of the very large number of reports circulating under his authority, many purveyed by rival Iraqi Shi'i scholars. Ishaq Ibn Rahawayh, a leading traditionist of Nishapur, debated with the famous jurist al-Shafi'i (d. 820) over whether al-Sadiq was to be deemed 'trustworthy' (*thiqa*) rather than 'weak' (*da'if*). Al-Shafi'i was known to be sympathetic to the *ahl al-bayt*, being himself a descendant of the Muttalibi clan of Quraysh, which the Prophet had regarded as part of his own clan of Banu Hashim. Al-Shafi'i deemed al-Sadiq to be trustworthy, and his school drew on narrations by al-Sadiq and al-Baqir notably from the large *Sunan* work by al-Hafiz al-Bayhaqi.[9] Early Maliki and Hanafi jurispruden-tial works also contain occasional narrations transmitted on the authority of al-Sadiq. However, major Sunni critics often maintained that narrations through al-Sadiq's family *isnad* contained defective links in the chain from the Prophet and were therefore better avoided. This was clearly intended to discredit and dispense with the mass of Shi'i *hadith*s where the doctrine of the imamate and the portrayal of the motives and deeds of certain leading Companions were anathema to Sunni Muslims, and which invested the imams with a miraculous aura they found unpalatable.

A revealing statement explaining a general Sunni antipathy to narra-tions assigned to al-Sadiq was reported by the Kufan traditionist Yahya b. Abd al-Hamid al-Himmani. Yahya questioned his teacher and mentor, the Kufan magistrate Sharik b. Abd Allah al-Nakha'i, about why unspecified groups deemed al-Sadiq to be 'weak' in his narrations, thus marginalising or even boycotting his *hadith*s. Sharik was an accom-plished traditionist and jurist who served as judge under the Abbasids, but was later removed by the caliph al-Mahdi (r. 775–785) for allegedly pro-Alid sympathies.[10] Yahya probably consulted Sharik about al-Sadiq's

---

8   See Yasir Battikh, *al-Imam Ja'far al-Sadiq wa marwiyatuhu al-hadithiyya* (Alexandria, 2008).

9   Al-Shafi'i in his *Kitab al-umm* cited a fair number of narrations from al-Sadiq, and more so in his *qadim* corpus. The latter citations are partly recoverable through al-Hafiz al-Bayhaqi's massive *al-Sunan al-kubra* (see indices to the 1936 Hyderabad edition, *s.v.* Ja'far b. Muhammad).

10   Ibn Hajar al-Asqalani, *Tahdhib al-tahdhib* (Hyderabad, 1907–1909), vol. 4, §577, pp. 333–337. Sharik was reported to have preferred Ali over Uthman in merit, while upholding the surpassing merit of Abu Bakr and Umar. Imami Shi'i critics deemed him a Sunni.

status as a traditionist about 20 to 30 years after the latter's demise; clearly he was aware that Sharik had known al-Sadiq personally.[11]

I asked Sharik: '(Why is it that) groups of people maintain Jaʿfar b. Muhammad is weak in hadith?' Sharik replied:

'I will tell you about the situation. Jaʿfar b. Muhammad was a righteous man and a God-fearing Muslim. Then a group of foolishly ignorant persons [*qawm juhhal*] surrounded him frequenting his home and leaving his presence, and saying "Jaʿfar b. Muhammad informed us." They narrated traditions all of them objectionable [*munkarat*] – lies, forgeries imputed to Jaʿfar – in order to exploit people to their own advantage and take their dirhams, and to this end they produced all kinds of objectionable traditions. Thereupon the public [*al-awamm*] heard these from them, and some were brought to ruin (by accepting them), while others disclaimed them.

These (ignorami) were the likes of al-Mufaddal b. Umar and Bayan [b. Samʿan] and Amr al-Nabati [*sic*, correct to Ammar al-Sabati] and others. They stated that Jaʿfar narrated to them that recognition of the imam suffices to spare one from fasting and prayer; and that he narrated to them from his father [al-Baqir], from his grandfather [Ali] who informed them about (events that will occur) before the Resurrection; and that Ali is in the clouds flying with the wind, and that he used to speak after his death, and moved as he was being washed (for burial); and that (Ali) is god in heaven while god on earth is the imam[12] – so these errant fools appointed a partner for God!

By God, Jaʿfar never said anything like this at all! Jaʿfar was more God-mindful and God-revering than that. So when the people (narrating traditions) heard these things, they deemed him 'weak' (and forsook transmitting his narrations). If you had seen Jaʿfar, you would have known that he was truly unparalleled among his peers [*wahid al-nas*].'

---

[11] This conversation is from al-Kashshi, *Rijal* [recension by al-Shaykh al-Tusi], ed. Hasan al-Mustafawi (Mashhad, 1970), §588, pp. 324–325.
[12] Implying that Ali subsisted in a supranatural mode of existence and would return as the eschatological redeemer. Some Imami reports state that when his sons were preparing to bury Ali's body, unseen forces lifted him to assist in the washing of his corpse. The messianic motif of Ali borne up on the clouds emerged after his assassination (c.f. *sahabiyya* 'cloud-riders'). On the Quranic 'god on earth' see al-Kashshi, *Rijal*, §538, p. 300, §547, p. 304.

Sharik's explanation for the mistrust by many proto-Sunni traditionists of narrations attributed to al-Sadiq circles of Iraqi Shi'a claiming
to receive teachings, spiritual guidance and legal rulings directly from
al-Sadiq is persuasive at one level. It points to the well-attested role of
'exaggerators' in his entourage, who ascribed all manner of supernatural abilities to their imam. Sharik's insistence that al-Sadiq himself
had nothing at all to do with such views raises a pertinent question. Did
al-Sadiq teach the bulk of his Imami partisans their theological, ethical
and legal ideas and practices – or are the many narrations which they
ascribed to al-Sadiq also to be rejected as 'lies and forgeries'? Sharik's
statement implies that there were in fact sound, properly transmitted
*hadith*s from Ja'far that were valid narrations; rejecting the validity of
this large body of narrations would therefore be unwarranted.

Esoteric Cells

Sharik's mention of al-Mufaddal b. Umar al-Ju'fi is instructive.
Al-Mufaddal was a Kufan who served as an important financial agent for
al-Sadiq in Iraq – and then served Ja'far's younger son Musa al-Kazim
(d. 799), the seventh Imam of the Twelver Shi'a; and became the figure-
head of an influential stream of esoteric (*batini*) teaching. Several texts
of a rationalist genre attributed to al-Mufaddal remain popular among
the Imami Shi'a today, including the work *al-Tawhid* wherein al-Sadiq
disputes with a sceptical free-thinker regarding divine Providence and
Oneness; and the *Kitab al-ihlilija* where Ja'far is portrayed as debating
with an Indian physician on monotheism.[13] Al-Mufaddal was at one
time associated with Abu'l-Khattab al-Asadi, who was killed during
al-Sadiq's life, in 756 while leading his band of disciples in an uprising at
the mosque of Kufa. His adherents, the Khattabiyya, reportedly viewed
Abu'l-Khattab as a prophet and divinised al-Sadiq – who denounced
their leader as an idolater and strongly disavowed them. Al-Mufaddal
then severed his ties with the Khattabiyya and reconciled with al-Sadiq,
remaining close to him and to Musa al-Kazim for the rest of his life.

Apocalyptic notions and esoteric writings cast in dialogue format
and magnifying the person of the imam and/or the Prophet were also
ascribed to a disciple of al-Baqir and then of al-Sadiq, Jabir b. Yazid
al-Ju'fi, certain of whose narrations were accepted into Sunni *hadith*.

---

[13] Nine works attributed to al-Mufaddal are published both as separate texts and
as part of larger Imami writings; most are in the form of dialogues between this
disciple and his master al-Sadiq. But the majority of the writings are likely to
be later compositions assigned to al-Mufaddal; see Mushegh Asatryan, 'Mofazzal
al-Jo'fi', *Encyclopaedia Iranica* (2012), available online at: http://www.iranicaon-
line.org/articles/mofazzal-al-jofi.

During the 8th and 9th centuries there developed several distinct groups of esoteric cells which paid allegiance to al-Baqir and al-Sadiq and their descendants, and whose figureheads served as mouthpieces for radical ideas elevating the figure of the imam. These cells coexisted under the umbrella of the wider Shi'i community, and were mainly active in lower Iraq and central Iran.[14] Various ontological and soteriological themes propounded in these esoteric circles were echoed among a significant wing of the early Imami Shi'a known as the Mufawwida or Delegationists, whose impact continues to be contested.[15] They taught that the Muhammadan light preceded the creation, and that God had delegated to the Prophet and his descendants, the imams, the power to provide living creatures with worldly sustenance. The Mufawwida were actively opposed by legally and theologically oriented circles whom the Delegationists labelled as the Muqassira or Deficients – those who 'fall short' of properly comprehending the true supernatural status of the imam. After the 10th century, the rationalist trajectory prevailed, streamlining the Imami community's social and doctrinal engagement with Sunni Islam as a coherent self-contained alternative. It is this latter trajectory which has shaped the religious and intellectual expressions of the Shi'i Ja'fari school to this day. Yet there remained a continuous undercurrent of tension within Twelver Shi'i religious and theosophic conceptions which echoed the earlier divergence, and eventually fed into the contrasting Akhbari and Usuli schools of thought of the Safawid era (1501–1722).

Another persistent association is the linking of al-Sadiq with Jabir, the father of Islamic alchemy. The large number of early alchemical writings attributed to Jabir b. Hayyan attracted the serious attention of a number of researchers into the history of Islamic science in the 20th century. The historical relation between al-Sadiq and Jabir remains controversial, involving unresolved questions over the dating, composition and authorship of texts attributed to Jabir. Various scholars (J. Ruska, P. Kraus, P. Lory) view al-Sadiq's involvement in the transmission of alchemical knowledge as nothing but literary fiction. However, others

---

[14] For the role of such factions within the early Imami Shi'a, see Sayyed Muhammad Hadi Gurami, *Nakhustin manasibat-i fikri-yi tashayyu'* (Tehran, 2012).

[15] See Hossein Modarressi, *Crisis and Consolidation in the Formative Period of Shi'ite Islam* (Princeton, NJ, 1993), pp. 19–51. See also M. A. Amir-Moezzi, *The Spirituality of Shi'i Islam* (London, 2011), as well as the informative exchange between K. D. Crow, 'Shi'i Spirituality: A Response to Amir-Moezzi', *Journal of Shi'a Islamic Studies*, 5 (2012), pp. 295–315, and M. A. Amir-Moezzi, 'On Spirituality of Shi'i Islam: A Reply to Prof. Karim Douglas Crow', *Studia Islamica*, 108 (2013), pp. 108–115.

(F. Sezgin, T. Fahd, Nomanul Haq) accept the likelihood of alchemical activity in Medina during Jaʻfar's lifetime, while remaining uncertain over the authenticity of the Jabirian corpus and the attribution of certain alchemical works to al-Sadiq. The 13th-century scholar Ibn Khallikan echoed a view widespread among many Muslims when he remarked of al-Sadiq: 'His pupil, Abu Musa Jabir b. Hayyan al-Sufi, wrote a book of one thousand folios containing the researches of al-Sadiq, in five hundred books.' Suffice it to observe that the underlying basis of Jabir's alchemical system (his 'Science of the Balance' or *ilm al-mizan*) relies on the numerologic values assigned to Arabic letters, while the divinatory technique of *jafr* was commonly associated in Islam with al-Sadiq.

Teaching

During Jaʻfar's life, the Muslim society experienced the proliferation and creative elaboration of major disciplines of learning ranging from *hadith* collection, jurisprudence (emerging regional legal schools in Mecca, Medina, Kufa, Cairo and Damascus), and Quranic exegesis (*tafsir*) to linguistics and grammar, ethics, ascetic-mystical praxis and theological speculations. Many of these disciplines were not always distinct at first, and could be combined in varying degrees as the expertise of a single individual. Thus, the leading Kufan traditionist Sufyan al-Thawri (d. 778) was a jurist who established his own body of legal praxis, published a compilation of reliable narrations entitled *al-Jami*, and was a practitioner of asceticism who never married or lived in a home of his own. Sufyan's interactions with al-Sadiq became widely cited, as when he chided Jaʻfar for wearing fine robes and costly perfume in contrast to Sufyan's own ragged clothing advertising his renunciation of worldly affairs. Al-Sadiq in turn admonished Sufyan for his ostentatious display of self-denial, reminding him that fine apparel was entirely appropriate at their age. A similar tale is related of the Basran renunciant (*zahid*) Abbad b. Kathir and al-Sadiq. A feature of the juridical practice of al-Sadiq was the rejection of analogical reasoning (*qiyas*) in rulings, mindful of the scope of knowledge of the Husaynid Imams. His disputations with the prominent Kufan rationalist-jurist Abu Hanifa centred on this.

The centre of gravity of al-Sadiq's religious and intellectual activity integrated legal instruction, ethical praxis, theological principles and individual spiritual guidance. Al-Sadiq built upon his father's work by inheriting a number of the senior disciples in the circle of al-Baqir, including his close associates Muhammad b. Muslim, Aban b. Taghlib, Amr b. Abi'l-Miqdam and Abu Basir al-Asadi. Jaʻfar further consolidated important circles of younger pupils through whom he spread his own distinctive legal, theological and spiritual teachings. They were overwhelmingly Iraqi partisans, many of whom attached themselves afterwards to al-Sadiq's younger son Musa al-Kazim. A significant role was exercised by a number of leading families in Iraq over successive generations who enjoyed special trust and responsibility as close associates of al-Baqir, al-Sadiq and al-Kazim, and whose forefathers had been partisans of Ali b. Abi Talib. This intimate familial aspect of al-Sadiq's role as imam is not well known. The majority of al-Sadiq's associates were non-Arab clients (*mawali*) of petty craftsmen, tradesmen, shopkeepers and, towards the end of his life, a number of wealthy bankers or money-changers. He evidently understood that these professions were vital to the future of Muslim society, and encouraged their increased religious observance and intellectual engagement with the majority of the community.

Among al-Sadiq's many prominent close associates was Zurara b. A'yan, a leading rationalist-jurist and theologian of Kufa, along with several of his brothers, descendants of a former monk. Hisham b. Salim al-Jawaliqi combined theological and legal competency; while Ammar b. Musa al-Sabati was an esoteric initiate with clear legal and theological interests. There are definite indications that al-Sadiq sought out and recruited specific individuals to his personal following, presumably in expectation of their capacity to fortify and extend his circle of associates and advance the mission of his family. An outstanding example was the leading theologian Hisham b. al-Hakam (d. 795), who spearheaded the rationalist defence of the doctrine of the imamate in famous disputations with Mu'tazili opponents before the fifth Abbasid caliph, Harun al-Rashid (r. 786–809). Al-Sadiq also succeeded in attracting important individuals among Sunni traditionists and jurists, grammarian-linguists and poets – as well as several government administrators and governors. His intellectual exchanges involved not only representatives of diverse Muslim intellectual and doctrinal tendencies, but reputedly extended to Gnostics, Manichaeans and pagan philosophers.

Nurturing a Community

The voluminous Imami legal literature represents the largest extant body of narrations from al-Sadiq. These narrations provide important insights into how he guided the religious and material lives of his followers, disciplined his close associates and corrected doctrinal distortions, counselled and oversaw their individual and communal practices and worldly enterprises, and inspired and exhorted them to achieve a deeper understanding of essential Islamic tenets. When seeking to understand how al-Sadiq nurtured and strengthened his expanding community of followers, and to better appreciate the manner and methods he employed, one cannot ignore this mass of narrations. To focus primarily upon specific doctrinal and initiatic ideas without coupling them to his legal and ethical teachings, would amount to walking on one leg. Fundamental aspects of al-Sadiq's social, communal and ethical undertakings are outlined here.

Al-Sadiq sought to inspire conscientious adherence to the Prophet's *sunna* and implant permanent awareness of the necessity of observing and maintaining it. He often invoked the precedents of his father al-Baqir as well as his great-great-grandfather Ali, with the clear implication that their practices and explanations correctly exemplified the authentic precedents of the Prophet Muhammad. On occasion, he indicated that common majority practices with regard to specific religious tenets – for example, on paying the *zakat* and *khums*, temporary marriage, or *jihad* – may have ignored or diverged from authentic Prophetic *sunna* as understood and implemented by his family, the Husaynids.

Al-Sadiq strongly emphasised the need to exercise 'protective precaution' (*taqiyya*) in awareness of prevailing expectations and attitudes upheld by the dominant community and governing class. He encouraged his close associates to shield from public view specific practices or doctrines he espoused which might provoke negative reactions, thus advocating outer conformity to commonly approved observances in vogue among the majority. Core Shiʻi convictions undoubtedly undermined and threatened the majoritarian self-image, since distrust had been ingrained by decades of Umayyad propaganda with public vilification of Ali and his family (this only ceased under the caliph Umar b. Abd al-Aziz when al-Sadiq was 16 years old). The majority community rejected the validity of the Imami claims to sole authoritative knowledge and correct practice, and scorned their advocacy of the exclusive *walaya* of the Prophet's family. Al-Sadiq's insistence that his followers observe precaution had a double motive: to safeguard them from censure and punitive measures and to deflect suspicion and baneful consequences directed towards himself and his extended family. At times his directive to outwardly adopt certain observances might have been designed for the welfare of certain individuals or neighbourhoods facing special circumstances. He counselled his associates to:

> Conduct yourselves with the people in accordance with their characters, while differing from them in their deeds; for truly each man gets what he earns, and on the Resurrection Day he shall be in the company of the one he loved. Do not induce people against yourselves nor against us, and join in with the populace! Truly, we [the *ahl al-bayt*] have a time and a rule which God shall bring about when He wills.[16]

---

16 Muhammad b. al-Nuʻman al-Mufid, *al-Amali* (Najaf, 1947–1948).

Al-Sadiq made a definite distinction between an ideal 'true polity' versus conditions in place under the reigning 'false polity' (*dawlat al-haqq* vs. *dawlat al-batil*), or a hoped for 'just order' versus the prevailing conditions of 'temporary-truce' (*dawlat al-adl* vs. *dawlat al-hudna*). He deemed the reigning false polity to be 'the abode of precaution' (*dar al-taqiyya*) for his partisans, which obviated the duty of armed struggle:

> *Jihad* is binding upon all under a Just Leader [namely, the imam]; while whomever is slain defending his personal property is a martyr. It is impermissible to slay anyone of the unbelievers and despisers within the 'abode of precaution' (*fi dari'l-taqiyya*), save for a murderer or one who spreads sinful-corruption – which applies only when you and your companions are well aware of his deed. Employing protective-precaution within the 'abode of precaution' is binding, and there is no perjury accrued nor atonement incumbent upon one forced to swear an oath by means of which he averts an injustice from himself.[17]

Al-Sadiq exhibited compassionate flexibility and lenient concern for the varied personal circumstances of individuals who confided to him their private conditions, and confessed individual limitations or shortcomings in fulfilling religious and ritual obligations. Nevertheless, when in recognition of human frailty he suggested less demanding alternatives, or waived the strict fulfilment of religious requirements, he always underscored the preferred ideal of discharging one's obligations. His followers were encouraged not to lose sight of this in their own daily practice as far as humanly possible.

At the same time, al-Sadiq demonstrated a lively concern for practical ethical concerns over the outward performance of religious requirements.[18] Weightiest above all for one's personal salvation was attentive service to fellow believers (*hajat al-ikhwan/al-mu'min* or meeting the

---

[17]   Ibn Babawayh, *al-Khisal*, ed. Ali Akbar al-Ghaffari (Tehran, 1389/1969–1970) at p. 607, from al-Sadiq's creedal instruction to al-Amash. He specified that this 'abode of precaution' is the same as *dar al-islam* – neither an 'abode of faith' (*iman*) nor an 'abode of unfaith' (*kufr*), but an intermediate domain. Al-Sadiq's nuanced position on the legality of jihad and on *dawlat al-hudna* is found in al-Kulayni, *al-Kafi*, ed. Ali Akbar al-Ghaffari (Tehran, 1375–1381/1955–1961), vol. 5, 'Kitab al-jihad'.

[18]   For this and what follows in this section, see al-Kulayni, *al-Kafi*, vols 2, 4 and 5; and Liakat Takim, '*Maqasid al-Shari'a* in Contemporary Shi'i Jurisprudence', in Adis Duderija, ed., *Maqasid al-Shari'a and Contemporary Reformist Muslim Thought* (New York, 2014), Chapter 4.

needs of one's faithful brethren) by placing the welfare of others above
one's own, providing for the necessities of one's immediate family and
kin, and heeding the directives and counsel of the imam-guide. These
priorities deserved unfailing attention and amounted to conforming to
the higher imperatives of faith itself – namely, the promotion of human
wellbeing by means of compassionate and equitable conduct towards all.

Al-Sadiq manifested a vital personal interest and cognisance of the
particular circumstances of individual followers and their brethren – at
times questioning them about private or intimate situations which they
assumed were unknown save to themselves or to their closest companions. These matters could involve health and well-being, financial or
business situations, relations with neighbours and the wider community, or the latest events or issues that might have an impact on individual or family security. An important feature of his interaction with
followers was imparting specific invocations and supplications for alle-
viating trying circumstances, or ensuring favourable outcomes; many
of al-Sadiq's prayerful entreaties achieved widespread fame and are still
recited today.

Followers might be questioned by al-Sadiq about their views and attitudes, and the reactions of their opponents with regard to specific ideas,
doctrines or practices – and then offered his own authoritative understanding of these matters. He kept abreast of shifting intellectual and
political conditions in distant areas by means of actively engaging his
followers to inform him of their concerns and anxieties, and providing
counsel and direction on how to best to react to their problems. These
varied social, communal and situational concerns are manifestly evident
in the legal corpus of Imami narrations, and minutely detailed in the
particular contexts of the various religious topics that they treat with.
The particular ethical core of al-Sadiq's teaching activity and personal
guidance may be sought here, serving as a benchmark by which to
measure enigmatic features of many other narrations assigned to him.

Doctrine and Theology

In his instructions to the Kufan traditionist, Sulayman b. Mihran
al-Amash, on the fundamental ritual and creedal obligations of Islam,
al-Sadiq listed six primary components of proper faith-practice: Purity
(ablution acts are properly repeated once or twice, never thrice), Prayer,
zakat, Fasting, Pilgrimage, and then *jihad*.[19] Next, he strongly emphasised *walaya* or love and devotion to the *ahl al-bayt*, matched by active
dissociation (*baraʾa*) from their opponents. Repeated mention is made of

---

[19]   Ibn Babawayh, *al-Khisal*, ed. al-Ghaffari, pp. 603–610.

protective precaution and the 'abode of *taqiyya*', the impeccable nature
of prophets and their legatees, and of temporary-marriage (*mut'at
al-hajj* and *mut'at al-nisa*). Basic doctrinal convictions are also given.
Human deeds are accomplished through divine grace. Faith or *iman* is
superior to *islam*, and may increase or diminish by means of virtuous or
bad deeds; it comprises acknowledgement in the heart, confession by the
tongue and deeds of the limbs. Sinners remain *muslim* or even immoral
(*fasiq*); those with a preponderance of demerit (*mustadif*) might yet be
saved, depending on God's grace or by intercession. The Quran is 'God's
Speech, neither Creator nor created'.[20] Al-Sadiq completes his creedal
affirmation by listing major and minor sins. The cardinal ones are idol-
atry, slaying the innocent soul, breaking the bonds of blood kinship
with our parents, fleeing after the advance (of one's army), sequestering
the property of orphans, consuming interest in financial transactions
and slandering married women. There follow the more conventional
sins, such as adultery and pederasty; and finally, blameworthy deeds
including extravagant indulgence and wasteful consumption.

Perhaps the best-known theological teaching was on the 'mid-most
position' between the divine constraint of determinism and the self-
empowerment of free will ('*la jabr wa la tafwid*'). This allowed for a latitude in human action while acknowledging divine foreknowledge in the
awarding of reward and punishment – a hotly debated topic in al-Sadiq's
day. Wilferd Madelung observes that the Imami position on *jabr* and
tafwid was 'an intermediate position between the Jahmite position of
constraint (*jabr*) and the Mu'tazilite thesis of empowerment (*tafwid*)'.[21]
Al-Sadiq's recorded utterances on this controversy appear at times to be
contradictory or open to divergent interpretations; his circles of associates, who held varying views, invoked various utterances in support of
their own positions.

Al-Sadiq devoted considerable attention to expounding on the role
of faith in human experience, with its hierarchical degrees and its
subtle function in higher cognition. A significant aspect of his teaching
stressed the centrality of intelligence (*aql*) for faith. He conveyed seminal
insights into aspects of divine names and attributes, the supernal throne

---

[20] Certain doctrinal convictions were subjected to nuanced discussion within
the circle of his associates, and al-Sadiq's actual position regarding the status of
deeds with respect to human capability (*istita'a*) or about the increate Quran were
debated. Thus, al-Sadiq is also cited as affirming the Quran to be *muhdath* or
'temporally created'. On the stance of one of his associates, Zurara b. A'yan, with
regard to *istita'a*, see Josef Van Ess, *Theologie und Gesellschaft* (Berlin, 1991–1997),
vol. 1, pp. 321–322.
[21] Wilferd Madelung, 'Kharijite Contributions to pre-Ash'arite *Kalam*', in Parviz
Morewedge, ed., *Islamic Philosophical Theology* (Albany, NY, 1979), p. 124.

realm, the cosmic role of angels, the Prophet's bodily ascension, the reality of the Muhammadan light (*nur Muhammad*), and presence of the 'great angel' of the sanctified spirit (*al-ruh al-qudus*). On the inner dynamics of prophecy and revelation, al-Sadiq specified a hierarchy of inspiration: this ranged from veridical (non-illusory) dream, to clair-voyant audition, to conscious eye-witnessing by the Prophet. The puri-fied consciousness of God's intimate (*wali*, pl. *awliya*) is receptive to inner promptings vouchsafed through auditory disclosures of angelic inspiration (*muhaddath*) without eyewitnessing, with innermost reali-sations continually replenished, and yielding deepened understanding. This evidently reflects his own experience of mystical realisation, and became influential for an emerging mystical doctrine of the hierarchy of saints.[22]

Throughout his varied pronouncements, al-Sadiq unfailingly invoked relevant Quranic verses which illuminated his meaning and intent. His abundant explanatory citations were offered when elucidating major topics, and constitute the closest expression of his own inner compre-hension of the Quran preserved mainly in Imami *hadith*s. Later, there appeared several major strands of exegesis assigned to him in Iraqi Sufi circles purporting to convey a *tafsir* transmitted from Jaʻfar, yet their connections to him are quite uncertain.[23] Whether or not it is actually derived from him, this corpus of teaching retains great significance for apprehending Muslim 'interior appropriation' of the Quran.

Ethical and Spiritual Instruction

Al-Sadiq made a clear distinction between two essential states of the human condition which stem from a primordial partition (*fi asliʼl-khalq*): those who pertain to 'the state of truth' (*dawlat al-haqq*), and those in the grip of 'the state of falsehood' (*dawlat al-batil*). Prophets and their legatees (*awsiya*, the imams) sprang from the former, while kings and tyrants belonged to the latter. Individual allegiance to one or the other reflects an original inclination within one's innate consti-tution, kneaded into the primal substance (*tina* or 'clay') of one's very being. The seminal Quranic description of the moment of the primor-dial covenant (*yawm al-mithaq*) between the Creator and Adam's future progeny (7:172) relates to this division with far-reaching implications for human experience.

---

[22] Notably in the teaching of the 9th-century Central Asian mystic al-Hakim al-Tirmidhi on the 'seal of sainthood', elaborated further by the great Andalusian mystic-saint Ibn al-Arabi (1165–1240).

[23] Such as with the exegetical remarks ascribed to al-Sadiq in the large *Haqaʼiq al-tafsir* by Abd al-Rahman al-Sulami (d. 1021).

Throughout human history the struggle between these two competing trajectories is mirrored in the external realm of the governing of the polity and society, and within the inner psycho-spiritual realm of individual moral and religious existence. Al-Sadiq thereby elaborated a grand narrative of sacred history, centred on the successive transmission of the prophetic legacy (*wasiya*) from Adam down to Muhammad and beyond to his family. He consciously linked this to the role of his family within the Muslim community, beginning with Ali who served as designated legatee (*wasi*) for the Prophet, and continuing with the special knowledge that the Husaynid Imams inherited, enabling them to serve as authoritative religious and salvific guides for their followers. For the Twelver Shi'a in particular, the progression of sacred history inexorably moves towards its divinely ordained culmination, when the redeeming saviour (*mahdi* or *qa'im* from the Prophetic family) will manifest himself in order to inaugurate the awaited rule of the just, and usher in universal abundance at the end of Time.

A significant example of this outer and inner historico-psychic process is evidenced in al-Sadiq's transformation of the widespread early Muslim teaching which described God's creation and testing of the human faculty of innate intelligence (*aql*). This teaching was expressed as narrative theology in narrations depicting the function of human intelligence in terms of moral obligation with implications for the human ability to perform acts of obedience or of disobedience, thereby meriting either divine reward or divine punishment. These archaic *aql*-creation narratives among both proto-Sunni and Shi'i Muslims were central to intense early debates over determinism or empowerment (*qadar*). Al-Sadiq's distinctive re-alignment of this tradition highlights the polarity between *aql* ('reason-wisdom') and *jahl* ('ignorance-folly'), by expounding on the conflict between Adam and Iblis wherein both are empowered by God with 75 psychic traits (or 'troops').[24] Al-Sadiq portrays *aql* here as 'the first creature created among the immaterial-spiritual-beings', engendered from God's light on the right side of the divine throne; its adversary *jahl* derives from the salty ocean depths of darkness. In this cosmic setting of conflict between these two forces, the centrality of the nexus of *aql* and the innate trait of human intelligence is always present. This is evidenced by the listing of *aql*'s 75 virtuous human character-traits. Al-Sadiq's creative Islamic religio-ethical notion of *aql* understood the divinely provisioned trait of innate intelligence as crucial to the religious enterprise, actively contributing to faith-certainty, inner purification, salvation and spiritual insight.

---

[24] Al-Kulayni, *al-Kafi*, ed. al-Ghaffari, vol. 1, 'Kitab al-aql', §14, pp. 20–23.

The context of Jaʻfar's *aql*-creation narrative is best grasped within the ancient tradition of religious meditation upon the divine throne as the locus of first-born Wisdom (Hebrew *Hokhmah*, Greek *Sophia*, Pahlavi *Xrad*). Biblical as well as Zoroastrian teachings portrayed pre-existing Wisdom as light deriving from the supernal realm. In this rarefied domain the immateriality or spirituality of *aql* is uppermost, with its creation preceding its presence in the human constitution. Al-Sadiq was probably combatting Manichaean ethical dualism when he joined personifications of Intelligence and Ignorance (or Wisdom and Folly) to the prototypes of Adam and Iblis. Their combat mirrors the psychic tension within the human breast, whose innate faculties and energies evoke a cosmic drama which sets out the parameters of spiritual experience. This expanded narrative creatively forged by al-Sadiq from teachings drawn from his environment is not what preceding Hellenic Neoplatonists, or later Muslim philosophers, intended by the 'First Intellect'. Yet this primordial drama of innate faculties set in the throne realm propelled al-Sadiq's narrative towards its eventual coalescence with Hellenic thought – so that by the 9th century, the doctrine of First Intellect was naturalised into Islamic thought. Al-Sadiq's seminal teaching on Intelligence and Ignorance was to have important repercussions among Ismaili thinkers and Sufi circles, with entire systems of thought built upon its foundation (such as those of the Druze faith); and major thinkers devoting detailed commentaries on it until the 20th century.

The impact of Jaʻfar al-Sadiq upon Islamic civilisation is extensive and multifaceted. His teachings were pressed into service by a variety of doctrinal schools and intellectual disciplines which sought to profit from his imposing reputation for acumen and profound insight. Al-Sadiq's intimate association with an astonishing breadth of disciplines has rarely been surpassed – while the fact that he was embraced by opposing schools is an acutely relevant lesson in tolerance for our era of intra-Muslim bloodshed.

Al-Sadiq's most evident legacy may be found in his detailed juridical instructions that underlie the Jaʻfari legal school. Further, there is the wealth of his ethico-theological guidance on the transformative realisation of human possibilities, in the stream of prophetic consciousness to which humans are heir. The quality and import of al-Sadiq's ideas is often highly demanding, as he himself acknowledged.[25] He was known to pose responses to questions in riddles or paradoxical statements, thereby

---

[25] 'Our discourse is difficult and painful to comprehend; none may endure it save for a dispatched prophet, or an angel brought nigh, or a believer whose heart God has tested for sincere-faith.' See al-Saffar al-Qummi, *Basaʼir al-darajat* (Tabriz, 1380/2001), pp. 21–28; and al-Kulayni, *al-Kafi*, vol. 1, 'Kitab al-hujja', pp. 401–402.

offering an initiatory discipline for his pupils and communicating the solution by means of perplexing utterances through hints or implications. In such oracular statements al-Sadiq adopted a middle course, offering the seeds of solutions to the discriminating hearer. His esoteric ideas about the universe and man were not aimed at filling his pupils with ideas that were merely fascinating – but rather with providing key principles for making these ideas real in a person's lived experience, which over time may enable him to answer questions for himself.

Despite the extensive literary records attesting to his life and teachings with their challenging complexity, and the legendary accretions clouding his historical actuality, an irreducible aura of elusiveness still clings to Imam Jaʿfar al-Sadiq which it is difficult to ignore.

Further Reading

Böwering, Gerhard. 'Isnad, Ambiguity and the Quran Commentary of Jaʿfar al-Sadiq', in Lynda Clarke, ed., *Shiʿite Heritage: Essays on Classical and Modern Traditions*. Binghamton, NY, 2001.

Buckley, Ronald Paul. 'The Imam Jaʿfar al-Sadiq, Abu'l-Khattab and the Abbasids', *Der Islam*, 79 (2002), pp. 118–140.

Daftary, Farhad. *A History of Shiʿi Islam*. London, 2013.

Dakake, Maria M. *The Charismatic Community*. Albany, NY, 2007.

Encyclopaedia Iranica. 'Jaʿfar al-Sadeq, Abu ʿAbd-Allah': 1) 'Life' – R. Gleave; 2) 'Teachings' – R. Gleave; 3) 'Sufism' – H. Algar; 4) 'Esoteric Sciences' – D. De Smet; 5) 'Herbal Medicine' – A. K. Moussavi; 6) 'Shiʿite jurisprudence' [forthcoming], vol. 14, pp. 349–366; available online at: http://www.iranicaonline.org/.

Fahd, Toufic. *La divination arabe: Etudes religieuses, sociologiques et folkloriques sur le milieu natif de l'islam*. Leiden, 1966.

Gleave, Robert. 'Between *Hadith* and *Fiqh*: The "Canonical" Imami Collections of Akhbar', *Islamic Law and Society*, 8 (2001), pp. 350–382.

Jafri, S. H. M. *The Origins and Early Development of Shiʿa Islam*. Oxford, 2011.

Lalani, Arzina R. *Early Shiʿi Thought: The Teachings of Imam Muhammad al-Baqir*. London, 2000.

Loebenstein, Judith. 'Miracles in Šhiʿi Thought: A Case Study of the Miracles Attributed to Imam Jaʿfar al-Sadiq', *Arabica*, 50 (2003), pp. 199–244.

Modarressi, Hossein. *Tradition and Survival: A Bibliographical Survey of Early Shiʿite Literature*. Oxford, 2003.

Nwyia, Paul. 'Le Tafsir mystique attribué à Ǧaʿfar Sadiq: edition critique', *Mélanges de l'Université St.-Joseph*, 43 (1967), pp. 179–230.

Takim, Liyakat N. *The Heirs of the Prophet: Charisma and Religious Authority in Shiʿite Islam*. Albany, NY, 2006.

4

Legal Traditions

Andrew J. Newman

What distinguishes Shi'i law from Sunni law is the former's derivation from the practices of, and narratives attributed to, the imams, as well as its recourse to a distinctly Shi'i form of *ijma* (consensus) and *ijtihad* (independent legal judgement). Today there are a handful of distinctive Shi'i groups extant – of which the Twelver, Ismaili and Zaydi are the major ones – compared with more than 20 different Shi'i groups in the 10th century. More are noted in earlier times, each seemingly and primarily distinguished from others by support for different male descendants of Ali (d. 661), cousin and son-in-law of the Prophet Muhammad (d. 632).

Although information on the beliefs and practices of the Shi'a of the pre-modern period is much more limited, careful reading of the works composed by selected scholars across these centuries reveals considerable 'pluralism' in the legal doctrines and practices of the three main surviving groups. The views of the authors of these texts – most well known among today's faithful as well as academics – were often in the minority in their own time. In fact, many of the salient formulations of theological and legal doctrine and legal practice laid down by these scholars that are recognisable in present-day doctrine and practice were initially offered precisely in rejoinder to internal disagreement.

Several periods in pre-modern Shi'i history illustrate this dynamic. These are the pre-Buyid (to 945) and Buyid periods (945–1055), the Mongol/Timurid period (1258–1501), and the early Safawid period (1501–1640s). Such were the disagreements over these matters across these periods that, coupled with a myriad of external challenges, the survival of the above-named three groups with the bodies of legal doctrine and legal practices with which each is identified today was no foregone conclusion.

While these historical phases highlight the legal traditions of the Twelver Shi'a, they also harken to aspects of the Zaydi and Ismaili experience, especially in the formative period. There is a shared discursive pluralism of legal opinion about key facets of theology and daily practice – the results of which engendered varying pathways. Among the

Zaydis of Yemen (by far the largest regional setting for the community), the proximity to Sunni approaches to law became prominent from the 13th century onwards.[1] In contrast, the Ismaili Shi'a came to codify a vast body of legal doctrine and practice under the Fatimids in the 10th century through the efforts of al-Qadi al-Nu'man (d. 974), completed on behalf of the reigning Imam-Caliph al-Mu'izz (r. 953–975).[2] Although this opus, the *Da'a'im al-Islam* (The Pillars of Islam), privileges the theological and legal role of the imam, it draws upon diverse sources, including Zaydi, Twelver and Sunni Maliki.

Our focus in this chapter, however, is on salient aspects of Twelver legal traditions. This not only reflects their relatively dominant place in the wider Shi'i context, but also more practically, the constraints of access to detailed historical records. At the same time, there are numerous cross-references to Zaydi and Ismaili legal traditions in this volume.

The Pre-Buyid Years

From their base in Gilan in the north of modern-day Iran, the Zaydi Buyids captured Baghdad in 945, having already taken territory as far east as Kirman and Bam, and south to the Persian Gulf. While the Buyids held the military balance of power, the Abbasid caliphs enjoyed the spiritual-political support of Sunni traditionists, especially in Baghdad. As Shi'i Iranians, the Buyid amirs cultivated a Mu'tazili rationalist discourse over the next century – with a thriving of Shi'i discourse at large, and rationalist Shi'i discourse in particular.

For the Twelver community, the occultation of their twelfth Imam soon after his birth (ca. 870) had already generated interest in the traditions ascribed to the imams; but this was with the assumption that the imam would soon return to the community. Of the several collections of the imams' *hadith*s assembled in these years, the most notable was *al-Kafi* (The Sufficient), a collection of some 16,000 of the imams' traditions assembled by Muhammad b. Ya'qub al-Kulayni (d. 941) in Baghdad, where he resided in the final decades of his life.

Al-Kulayni organised these traditions into two volumes of texts on theology, five volumes on *furu* (covering acts of devotion, transactions, personal status and penal law) and one of miscellaneous texts. He divided the nearly 12,000 *furu* traditions into chapters of *fiqh* quite

---

[1]   Najam Haider, *The Origins of the Shi'a* (Cambridge, 2011); S. Al-Wazir, 'The Theory of *Mal* Among the Zaydis', in F. Daftary and G. Miskinzoda, ed., *The Study of Shi'i Islam* (London, 2014), pp. 353–370.
[2]   I. K. Poonawala, 'The Evolution of al-Qadi al-Nu'man's Theory of Ismaili Jurisprudence as Reflected in the Chronology of his Works on Jurisprudence', in Daftary and Miskinzoda, ed., *The Study of Shi'i Islam*, pp. 295–351.

similar to those used by such earlier compilers of the Sunni collections of prophetic *hadith*s as Muhammad al-Bukhari (810–870) and Muslim b. Hajjaj (ca. 815–875). As such, *al-Kafi* was an explicit rejoinder to these Sunni works, intended to underline the existence of a body of traditions from the imams on as wide-ranging and comprehensive a series of issues as those available in Sunni compilations. It was the traditionists of Qumm in Iran, where al-Kulayni had previously resided, who were the preponderant source of *al-Kafi*'s traditions. So *al-Kafi* was also a Qummi response to certain rationalist (anti-traditionist) tendencies that al-Kulayni observed among some Twelvers in Abbasid Baghdad.

The theological pronouncements of the imams in *al-Kafi* highlighted their own authority in *furu* matters. The imams identified themselves variously as the *hujaj* (proofs), the *khulafa* (successors), the *nur* (light) and the *ayat* (signs) offered by God to humankind. As such they were the repositories of *ilm* (knowledge), which included all documents and sources previously revealed by God to His creation, and the authentic version of the Quran. The imams eschewed all forms of rationalist jurisprudential principles and analysis.

Hence, the source of legal doctrine and practice was the imams' traditions. For al-Kulayni and his contemporaries living in the immediate aftermath of the twelfth Imam's occultation, *al-Kafi*'s *furu* traditions documented the manner in which successive imams had maintained links with the faithful via networks of *wakil*s (agents) and offered bases for legal practices distinctive from those emerging among their Sunni contemporaries.

Yet there is no evidence of the institutionalisation of a system for appointing these agents, nor are the imams seen as designating any individual as the sole representative to perform community activities or, for the future development of legal doctrine and practice, to legislate during their absence, let alone during the forthcoming occultation(s). *Al-Kafi*'s traditions on the numbers and length of these occultations were contradictory; al-Kulayni made no effort to reconcile these or other apparent contradictions on matters of legal doctrine and practice.

The famous tradition on *qada* (judicial arbitration) narrated via Umar b. Hanzala from the sixth Imam Ja'far al-Sadiq (d. 765) did make provisions for short-term absences of the imam. There, the imam referred to a believer who was knowledgeable in the traditions of the imams and their *ahkam* (precepts) as an appointed *hakim* (judge). However, the imam ultimately advised waiting – 'hesitation at points of doubt is better than leaping into destruction' – until a question of doctrine or practice could be put to the imam himself. In fact, some texts in *al-Kafi*'s final volume referred to signs that, if read as references to events in al-Kulayni's time, seemed to portend the imam's imminent return, when he would still have been of 'normal' human age. Perhaps the chance to query the imam was not so far off. Indeed, the imam's return would in any case signal the onset of the final days.

The Early Buyid Period: al-Hayra and Beyond

When the imam did not return in the years immediately after al-Kulayni's death many believers questioned if he were dead and some left the faith. These years, in the mid-10th century, were known as 'al-Hayra' (the [period of] uncertainty). Over the century, again by referring to the traditions, elements of the Twelver community both addressed and overcame these doubts and continued the process of evolving legal doctrine and practice.

Buyid interest in rationalist Mu'tazili thought allowed them to reach out to both Sunni and Shi'i rationalist elements who broadly speaking rejected the concept of fate. These rationalists believed that intellect, to a greater or lesser extent than revealed texts, was the means to understanding the Divine and to distinguishing between right and wrong. For them, the Quran was created rather than timeless, and references to God as 'Seeing' or 'Knowing' were not about such attributes as humans commonly understood them. Among the Twelvers, these tendencies only attracted a minority in the early and middle years of the 10th century.

In the early years of the century, concern with the issues and problems of 'al-Hayra' was of far greater import than the further evolution of matters of legal doctrine and practice. Indeed, a student of al-Kulayni, Ibn Abi Zaynab al-Nu'mani, assembled a collection of traditions, some from *al-Kafi*, that suggest there were concerns about the legitimacy of the Husaynid line of the imams, the number of the imams as 12, the nature and length of the imam's absences, and the imam reappearing as a young man. In the process, al-Nu'mani referred to the presence of *sufara* (intermediaries) between the people and the imam during the first, shorter absence and to the imam's prolonged absence as a test of resolve. A Qummi student of al-Kulayni, Ibn Qulawayh, assembled a collection of the narrations by the imams on *ziyarat* (visitations) to the imams' burial places, especially Karbala (the site of Imam Husayn's tomb), including texts that privileged such visitations over the hajj itself. His delineation of such practices as distinctive to the community suggests some individuals were overcoming elements of the self-doubt that characterised 'al-Hayra'.

In these same years the Qummi Muhammad b. Ali (d. 991), known as al-Shaykh al-Saduq or Ibn Babawayh, offered a series of tradition-based contributions to Twelver doctrine and practice. The *Kamal al-din*, perhaps an early compilation, referred to a variety of alternative visions of the imamate extant at the time. These included the ideas that the imam had died and that the number of imams was not 12. Ibn Babawayh's theological work, *al-I'tiqadat*, also suggests the surmounting of self-doubt. The early portions of the work highlight the compatibility of Twelver and Sunni theology and even some aspects of Mu'tazili thought as favoured by the Buyid political elite with whom Ibn Babawayh had contacts. However, the work's latter portions stress the unique role of the 12 imams and rely on the imam's traditions as proof thereof. He also refers to certain tools of analysis, on offer in the works of both Sunni and Shi'i rationalist scholars, to be applied to these texts.

Ibn Babawayh's privileging of the imams' traditions extended to the law; he compiled a collection of texts on *furu* that, like corresponding portions of *al-Kafi*, addressed matters of legal doctrine and, especially, practice. Often referred to by its short title *al-Faqih,* it became known as the second of 'the four books' of the imams' traditions completed before the Saljuq capture of Baghdad in 1055. Although *al-Faqih*, with some 6,000 traditions, contained fewer texts than *al-Kafi's furu* sections, these did break new ground in Twelver law. The imams, for example, are seen to delegate matters of judicial arbitration and interpretation, though stressing that this was based on the traditions. The legal obligation of attending Friday congregational prayers was stressed; provisions for leading these in the imam's absence were cited as were the qualities of those leading. A Twelver *qadi* (judge) was also given more legal leeway to associate with the secular political establishment than in *al-Kafi*. And judges could implement the *hudud* (the legal punishments).

Ibn Babawayh's work marks the acceptance, at least in some quarters of the Twelver community, of the imam's extended absence. Thence, the scope for human intervention was relatively greater, and certain human-derived tools of legal analysis were deemed useful. A contemporary of Ibn Babawayh, the Baghdadi Ibn Abi'l-Junayd al-Iskafi, favoured recourse to rationalist tools of analysis in the formulation of theology and the law. He approved the use of *qiyas* (analogy) and was said to be especially proficient in *dhann* (speculative opinion); both of these were integral to Sunni jurisprudence. But overall, non-tradition based approaches to the law that bespoke association with elements of Sunni legal theory seem to have been in the minority.

The Later Buyid Period

In subsequent years, by contrast, non-traditionist approaches to legal interpretation found favour among some of the community's Baghdad-based scholars who are well known today. These did not prove widely popular, however, and required considerable defence. Accounts of life in contemporary Baghdad, to the west of the plateau where Ibn Babawayh was based, are based on later Sunni sources. These suggest that Buyid support for distinctly Shi'i practices – such as the commemoration of

Ghadir Khumm and the killing of Imam Husayn at Karbala,[3] as well as the refurbishment of the tombs of Imams Ali and Husayn at Najaf and Karbala respectively – exacerbated tensions with Sunnis. These sources cite repeated rioting by Sunni and Shi'i 'popular' elements over the period.

Yet some leading Shi'i scholars engaged not only with Sunni criticisms of their faith, but also with others among the Twelver faithful on matters of both theology and legal practice (efforts that were often received with much hostility). Illustrious examples are at Shaykh al-Mufid (948–1022), al-Sharif al-Murtada (965–1044), and their student Muhammad b. al-Hasan al-Tusi (996–1067). Al-Mufid was critical of the traditionists – including his teacher Ibn Babawayh – for using unreliable texts, and upheld the authority of those skilled in the use of *aql* (intellect) in the delineation of doctrine and practice. He also rejected Ibn Abi'l-Junayd's reference to *qiyas*. For al-Mufid, Imam Ja'far's injunction concerning hesitation meant that the layman should put the matter in question to 'someone more learned than himself'. Al-Mufid cited himself as such a person.

His *ahkam/furu* work, *al-Muqnia fi'l-fiqh*, offers evidence for the authority of senior clerics in matters of daily legal practice during the occultation, but also of divisions within the community on these issues and of the minority status of his interpretations. During the imam's absence, al-Mufid ruled that the believers should deliver the *zakat* revenues to 'the trustworthy *fuqaha* (sing. *faqih*)', as they are 'more knowledgeable' on its disposition. He also suggested that the imams had entrusted the *fuqaha* with convening various prayers and rendering judgments. As to *khums* monies, his view was that these should be entrusted to someone whose *aql* (wisdom) and *diyanatihi* (his faith) was but one. He stopped short of naming that person as the *faqih*, and also noted competing opinions (such as that the obligation to pay *khums* had lapsed, or that the funds should be buried in the ground until the imam's return). Al-Mufid sought to downplay contemporary sectarianism: he rejected Shi'i questioning of the Uthmanic Quran, for example, as well as claims that all the imams had been poisoned.

Al-Murtada shared many of al-Shaykh al-Mufid's opinions, such as the one on the dynamic role of the scholarly elite in the absence of the imam; he also regarded many of the received traditions as unreliable. Al-Murtada himself enjoyed a prestigious lineage, being a descendant of Imam Ali and Imam Musa (d. 799), the seventh Imam. He owned villages, built a school, supported many students, and had an enormous library. That he and al-Mufid maintained that the 'trustworthy *faqih*'

---

[3] See Chapters 1 and 2 of this volume.

should receive the *zakat* in the absence of the imam suggests the view was not universally accepted. In a separate essay that al-Murtada dedicated to a Twelver government official, he ruled that believers might hold office under the *zalimun* (oppressors). That he addressed certain of the imams' traditions censuring such service in the essay suggests that the opponents of such service had marshalled traditions in support of their arguments.

As a student of al-Mufid and al-Murtada, and a recipient of the caliph's favour, al-Tusi was clearly aware both of the capital's sectarian tensions and the challenges within the Twelver community to his teachers' methodology and rulings. His first great work, the compilation of traditions entitled *Tahdhib al-ahkam* (The Rectification of Rulings), comprising some 13,600 texts, was a commentary on al-Mufid's *al-Muqniʿa* in which al-Tusi cited traditions in support of his teacher's rulings. He discussed at the outset the means by which he would work with the traditions in order to achieve clarity. In his second compilation, *al-Istibsar* (The Seeking of Insight), he offered a more developed system for the categorisation of the traditions.[4] In *Uddat al-usul* (The Instrument of the *Usul*), an essay on jurisprudence, al-Tusi cited various exegetical principles, non-Twelver in origin, to be applied in order to achieve proper understanding of the revelation.

Al-Tusi also held that it was 'permissible' for the 'ordinary believer' to follow (using the term *taqlid*) the *ulama*, in keeping with longstanding Imami practice. Likewise, the judge was authorised by the imams to exercise full legal authority. On *khums*, al-Tusi, like al-Mufid, acknowledged various views within the community over what to do with the revenues during the imam's absence. His own view was that some could be handed out directly but that the 'trustworthy' individual should receive the rest to distribute.

The works of al-Tusi covered the widest range of religious sciences by any Twelver scholar, with recourse both to rationalist argumentation as well as to the imams' traditions. In effect, al-Tusi endowed the occultation of the imam with a semi-permanent status. Hence, in accommodation with an 'unjust' world, senior scholarly figures trained in and using extra-traditionist tools of legal analyses were to have a role as leaders of the community.

---

4   Al-Tusi's two compilations were the third and fourth of 'the four books' of traditions, completed before the Saljuq seizure of Baghdad in 1055.

From the Saljuqs to the Safawids

The centuries between the rise of the Saljuqs and the appearance of the Safawids witnessed a series of severe, existential challenges to Shi'ism. The Saljuqs, who were converts to the Hanafi legal school of Islam, seized Baghdad in the mid-11th century, which resulted in the destruction of Twelver Shi'i libraries and other resources, and the flight of many Shi'a from the city. In these years pockets of the faithful were found on the Iranian plateau as well as among the Arab regions of modern-day Iraq, Syria and Lebanon.

Extant scholarly literature from this period suggests that some *ulama* among the latter were initially beholden to al-Tusi's rationalist theological and jurisprudential legacy. At the same time, the destruction of the Shi'i libraries of Baghdad certainly contributed to a notable dearth of copies of earlier texts across a range of religious sciences. In later years there is evidence of the continued strength of traditionism, especially among Baghdad's 'popular' classes. Nearby Hilla witnessed the questioning of uncritical adherence to al-Tusi's legal methodology and *ahkam* – though not his rationalist theology and jurisprudence generally, nor the position of authority on doctrine and legal practice to which his work had elevated the senior *ulama*.

On the Iranian plateau, *Kitab al-naqd* (The Book of Criticism), a work written between 1164 and 1171 as a rebuttal to an attack on the faith, contains information on the faith and its adherents among the urban 'popular' classes. That the author of *al-Naqd* repudiated allegations of widespread adherence to traditionism, something the Saljuqs opposed, among the Shi'a suggests its popularity among those classes. The work also points to the blurring of lines between Sunni and Shi'i discourse among such elements, notably in visitations to Imam al-Rida's tomb in Tus and to that of the Imam's sister Fatima in Qumm, as well as in the veneration of the Prophet's family more generally. 'Imamism' was also widespread among Saljuq Turkish levies and the region's Sufi-style popular movements. Even the discourse of some of the region's Shi'i scholars reflected this. It included critiques of rationalism and philosophy, if not the practical authority of the clerical class, in favour of traditionism.

The Mongol capture of Baghdad in 1258 ended the Abbasid caliphate and resulted in further losses of Shi'i infrastructure and texts. Hilla was saved by direct appeals by key Shi'i scholars to the approaching Mongol forces and the town's timely surrender. Thereafter, Twelver Shi'ism is often discussed mainly, if not solely, with reference to two scholars of Hilla, Ja'far b. al-Hasan al-Muhaqqiq (ca. 1205–1277), and his nephew, al-Hasan b. Yusuf al-Allama (1250–1325). Both had connections at the Mongol court of the Il Khans in Iran where there was interest in Shi'ism generally. Al-Allama dedicated a number of works on the faith to the Ilkhanid Sultan Uljaitu (1280–1316), and Twelver sources credit him with Uljaitu's conversion to the faith.

Both Hillis were noted for their rationalist formulations of doctrine and legal practice, and the associated arguments for a hierarchical structure of authority within the community during the imam's continued absence. Their works on jurisprudence reprised and progressed some of al-Tusi's arguments and legal rulings. Al-Allama divided the believers into *mujtahid* ('the one who endeavours', or the legist) and *muqallid* ('follower', or lay believer), and maintained that the latter was to follow the former even if the *mujtahid* made an error. Following even a mistaken ruling absolved the lay believer of any sin and a mistaken *mujtahid* would suffer no penalties for his mistake. Al-Allama expounded on the knowledge and skill-base to be possessed by the *mujtahid*, and stated that such a person could have skills to exercise *ijtihad* (independent legal reasoning) in some areas of the law but not others.

On matters of daily practice, their rulings endow the *faqih/mujtahid* with authority but display some caution and equivocation that, together with the references to the traditions and alternative interpretations, attest to dissent within the community. Indeed, the works are not entirely consistent on matters such as the role of the *faqih* in the Friday prayer, and on the collection and distribution of *zakat*. Thus, al-Allama in several works made no formal provision for the prayer's performance during the occultation: in one, he stated that the *fuqaha* could assemble the people for all the prayers except the Friday prayer, while elsewhere he allowed it to be conducted by the *fuqaha*. On *zakat* he deemed it 'desirable' that the *faqih* receive these revenues so that donor could gain *ijza* (reward), but elsewhere held that reward could be gained by direct distribution of the funds to the recipients.

These centuries witnessed no great recovery of pre-Saljuq texts. Moreover, many of al-Allama's works were lost and copies of his and al-Muhaqqiq's works on various disciplines, including the *furu*, appear not to have been widely available across the communities in greater Syria, Iraq, the Hijaz, the Persian Gulf and the Iranian plateau. The Lebanese Muhammad b. Makki al-Amili, Ibn Makki (1334–1384), later called *al-Shahid al-Awwal* (the First Martyr), had studied in Hilla and was generally faithful to the Hillis' basic rationalist theology and jurisprudence. Well travelled in the western Arab communities, his trial and execution were less down to any personal overt, extreme anti-Sunnism than to broader anti-Shi'i currents in these communities at the time.

A potentially greater challenge was offered by the rise of Shi'i-Sufi style millenarian movements across the region and, especially, on the Iranian plateau from the early decades of the 14th century. These were only encouraged by Timur's invasion of the region later that century, his push into Iraq and Syria and defeat of the Ottoman sultan. These movements included both quietist and militantly pantheistic, messianic and egalitarian Sufi orders and other 'heterodox' spiritual movements whose polemics displayed Shi'i, anti-establishment tones. Such discourse was at the base of movements such as the Hurufis, influential from Khurasan to Anatolia and Syria, the Nurbakhshis in southwestern Iran and the Mushasha in southern Iraq. These highly messianic Shi'i-Sufi discourses threatened to subsume distinctive features of Twelver Shi'ism as these had developed up to this time. In such a milieu some Iran-based Shi'i clerics explored more esoteric forms of inquiry, while others relocated to sites further west. Arab scholars continued to study in the Iraqi sites but there was movement between these and sites to the east, even as far as the Indian subcontinent.

Interest in and attention to the law and legal practice among the communities of believers scattered across the region is hard to trace in these years. The legacy of Hilla, let alone that of the pre-Saljuq Twelver scholarly community, was at best quite limited among them.

The First Safawid Century

The Safawids were originally a quietist Sunni Sufi order 'founded' by one Shaykh Safi al-Din (1252–1334) and based in Ardabil. From the 15th century onwards, the order's discourse increasingly reflected and was attractive to the region's Turkish tribal forces beholden to the region's widespread Shi'i-Sufi messianism. Some of these had provided the military backbone of earlier Turkish polities that succeeded to power in the region after Timur's death in 1405. In opposition to these polities, such elements and others were attracted by the heterodoxy of Safawid spiritual discourse. In 1501, Safawid forces under the first Shah Isma'il took Tabriz, and he declared Twelver Shi'ism to be his realm's established faith. Within a decade the Safawids had taken control of most of the Iranian plateau.

There was no strong presence at the centre, or across the plateau, of senior Twelver scholarly figures in the early years of the Safawid state. These were based and remained mainly in urban centres in Sunni-Ottoman controlled Arab territories to the west, the Hijaz and the Persian Gulf. Indeed, the continued viability of the Safawid project and its commitment to the faith, however limited, was problematic throughout the century. The centre's discourse stayed heterodox, and Safawid forces suffered defeat by the Ottomans at Chaldiran in 1514. A ten-year long civil war followed Isma'il's death, with a second civil war after the death of Isma'il's son and successor, Tahmasp, in 1576. Amid the steady loss of Safawid territories to Ottoman and Uzbeg forces to the west and northeast, there was a brief effort to re-establish Sunnism.

Several Iranian scholars in fact left Safawid territory for the west, while others travelled between these Arab centres and sites in India, avoiding Iran.

The Lebanese scholar Ali al-Karaki (1464–1534) did come to court early during the reign of Isma'il. His open association with the Safawids generated opposition from Twelver scholars in Iran and, especially, in the Arab west. Al-Karaki offered his key legal formulation, that the *faqih* stood as *na'ib-i amm* (general deputy) of the Hidden Imam, to rebut criticism of his service to and acceptance of remuneration from Isma'il. He also used the formulation to allow the *faqih* to perform the Friday prayer during the imam's continued absence. In 1532, in the midst of the civil war that followed Isma'il's death and accompanying Ottoman and Uzbeg incursions, the shah issued a *firman* designating al-Karaki as the *na'ib* of the Hidden Imam.

Following al-Karaki's death two years later, however, his several projects to establish the faith in Safawid territories were abandoned. Further, the Lebanese Shaykh Zayn al-Din Amili (1506–1558), later called *al-Shahid al-Thani*, and his student and associate Shaykh al-Husayn al-Amili – both of whom had secured teaching positions in Ottoman Lebanon, after having presented themselves as Shafi'i scholars – criticised al-Karaki's legacy. Still, Zayn al-Din did equate the *na'ib-i amm* with the *faqih* in the collection and distribution of *zakat*. As well, al-Karaki's son and grandson were honoured at the court and adhered to scholarly and legal positions similar to al-Karaki's.

During the century, however, court elites, after nominal conversions to the new faith, knew little of its distinctive doctrines and practices. Among the rural majority and urban elements, the earlier Shi'i-Sufi messianism continued to be popular. By contrast, the faith's Arab centres, in Iraq, Lebanon, the Hijaz and the Persian Gulf, remained active. In this century also, Twelver Shi'ism became the established faith in three of the five 'Deccan' states in southern India, as political elites sought to attract Safawid favour and thereby counter the growing power of the Mughal empire in the north. However, as in Iran, the faith enjoyed limited popular support. Some Arab Twelver scholars maintained links with the Deccan elites, in preference to Iran. The period also witnessed no great recovery in the availability of any key, early texts.

The Second Safawid Century

Only in the course of the 17th century was the Twelver faith finally established in the Safawid polity, and this was a product of a series of important challenges both to the realm and to spiritual discourses within the community itself. The second Safawid civil war brought Abbas I (r. 1588–1629) to power, sponsored by a coalition of Qizilbash and Tajik elements. Abbas' reign was marked by Ottoman and Uzbeg incursions and further internal challenges. In response, over these years, the Qizilbash were reorganised in order to incorporate new tribes, to eliminate some whose loyalty was problematic, and to give the *ghulam* (crown servants) greater administrative and military roles. The capital was also moved to Isfahan, far from the Ottoman and Uzbeg borders. There, the shah's new *maydan* (square), with major new 'secular' and commercial infrastructure, spoke of Safawid power and longevity to domestic and foreign audiences. Abbas' reign was also marked by continued, widespread urban and rural affection for the sort of Shi'i-Sufi messianism that had brought Isma'il I to power.

Just as the centre responded to internal and external challenges on the political and military fronts, so it responded to spiritual challenges. In line with the expansion of the city's secular and commercial buildings, there was also a marked expansion in its religious infrastructure – and in efforts to identify with the faith and to reach out to the Twelver scholarly class. Arab and Iran-based Twelver clerics were also encouraged to become close associates of the court. For both of Lutf Allah al-Maysi al-Amili and Abd Allah al-Shushtari, Arab émigrés in these years, the shah built a school in the capital. He also visited the tomb of Imam al-Rida and made many endowments to it and other important religious sites. The court's clerical entourage also included the Iran-born Mir Damad, descendant of al-Karaki, and Shaykh Baha'i, son of Shaykh Zayn al-Din's associate Shaykh al-Husayn, who had come to Iran as a boy with his father.

The implications of these events and trends for Twelver law were important. All of these figures were proponents of the rationalist tendencies within the faith, upholding the authority of the senior clerics both in interpreting doctrine and legal practice and in their leading role in that practice. Mir Damad, Shaykh Baha'i and such of their students as Muhammad Taqi al-Majlisi composed Persian-language religious primers on the faith. Court-designated scholars were dispatched to monitor the activities at the capital's coffee houses, preach sermons or lead prayers along acceptable lines.

Indeed, the second decade in Isfahan in particular witnessed increasing veneration of Abu Muslim (d. 755), the Iranian Alid agent of the Abbasid movement in Khurasan. Essays attacking Abu Muslim written by a small number of clerics attest to such veneration in the previous century, associated with the messianism widespread across the plateau. The many essays attacking Abu Muslim's popularity from the 1620s suggest that it had resurfaced in the expanding capital. There was also a growing interest in Sufi doctrine and practices among Isfahan's 'popular' classes and this generated a raft of essays in opposition to it. The Abu Muslim and anti-Sufi polemics, and the revived debate over Friday prayer, illustrate both the extent of disagreement among believers in Iran, especially in the capital Isfahan, and how scholars made increasing use of the imams' traditions and other, previously relatively unavailable, pre-Safavid texts.

Of most of the essays attacking the veneration of Abu Muslim, only their titles remain. The earliest of the very few extant essays date from about 1631 and cite very few traditions from a very narrow range of sources. However, by the later 1640s, this polemic had evolved into denunciations of Sufism and the alleged unorthodox practices it was said were followed by named Sufi orders. Of essays in both polemics, a large number were composed in Persian, which points to the 'popular classes' as the target audience.

Such authors of the later anti-Sufi essays as Muhammad Tahir al-Shirazi made much greater use of the imams' traditions. In his attacks on singing as a Sufi practice, Shaykh Ali al-Amili, a descendant of Shaykh Zayn al-Din who came to Iran around 1632, also cited many traditions. Muhammad Baqir al-Sabziwari wrote an Arabic-language response to an unnamed opponent of singing that is replete with traditions, cited mainly via *al-Kafi*. In his *al-Ithna'ashariyya fi al-radd ala al-Sufiyya* (The Twelve, on the Refutation of the Sufis), Muhammad b. al-Hasan, al-Hurr al-Amili, a Lebanese émigré who arrived in Iran in the 1660s, cited traditions from a wide range of Ibn Babawayh's works and al-Tusi's *Tahdhib*. He also cited statements condemning Sufi doctrine and practice from a range of well-known earlier and Safawid period Twelvers, including al-Mufid, al-Murtada, al-Tusi, al-Allama and Ali al-Karaki. As such, his was the widest range of pre-Safavid sources cited in the polemic up to this date. Al-Hurr also compiled *Wasa'il al-Shi'a*, a multi-volume collection of the imams' traditions.

The Friday prayer debates, which produced some 90 separate essays, 80 of them in the 17th century, followed a similar trajectory. In the 16th century, Ali al-Karaki, Shaykh al-Husayn al-Amili and his teacher Shaykh Zayn al-Din, as well as Sayyid al-Husayn al-Amili, all wrote on the matter. Al-Karaki supported the *takhyiri* (optional) position, ruling that the prayer could be held if the imam or his deputy were present to lead it. Zayn al-Din and Shaykh al-Husayn maintained the *ayni* position, that it should be held regardless because it had been performed when the imams were present. Their essays were composed in Arabic, suggesting a mainly scholarly audience. In the 17th century, the performance of the prayer was part of the court's programme to establish the faith firmly throughout the realm. Most of those contributing to the debate in this century backed the *ayni* position. As with essays written in the anti-Sufi polemic, so with the debate on the prayer, Persian was becoming the language of choice and authors made increasing reference to the imams' traditions as well.

The *ayni* supporters were notable for their criticism of the pro-*takhyiri* authors for maintaining that performance of the prayer required the presence of a *faqih/mujtahid* in his capacity as the *na'ib* of the Hidden Imam. Al-Sabziwari authored an essay in Arabic for his scholarly colleagues, and in Persian for 'mass' consumption, in favour of the *ayni* position. He drew heavily on Ibn Babawayh's collections and works by al-Mufid and al-Tusi. Muhammad Tahir also offered tradition-based support for the *ayni* position and against the need for a *mujtahid*, based on the Four Books and works by Ibn Babawayh, al-Murtada, al-Mufid, al-Tusi and al-Allama.

Arguing for the importance of reference to the imams' traditions and against the validity of recourse to *ijtihad* and use of the rationalist religious sciences is often identified as being the hallmark of the Akhbari school of Twelver jurisprudence. In opposition to the Usuli rationalism and its engendering of such legal tools as *ijtihad*, the Akhbari school is often held to have been 'founded' by the 17th-century Iranian scholar Muhammad Amin al-Astarabadi. To be sure, al-Astarabadi did censure al-Allama for having divided the community into *mujtahid* and *muqallid*, and such scholars as Ibn Makki, Ali al-Karaki, Shaykh Zayn al-Din and Shaykh Baha'i for adopting Sunni Muʻtazila principles and ignoring the traditions. But the favouring of the traditions did not entail a critique of clerical authority per se. Muhsin Fayd al-Kashani, Mulla Sadra's son-in-law, argued for the *ayni* position on Friday prayer, and criticised proponents of *ijtihad* for their insistence both on the presence of the *faqih* in his capacity as *na'ib* and on the concept of *al-idhn al-amm* (the general permission). Appointed as the capital's Friday prayer leader by Abbas II (r. 1642–1666), al-Kashani was so roundly attacked by those opposed to the prayer, on a variety of grounds, that he resigned his post and left the city. Although he privileged recourse to the traditions, compiling a multi-volume collection of the imams' traditions entitled *al-Wafi*, al-Kashani nevertheless ruled for the involvement of the *faqih* in the administration of *zakat* and *khums* 'by right of the *niyaba* (deputyship)'. His fellow opponent of *ijtihad*, Muhammad Tahir, upheld the obligation of the 'common people' to refer to the *fuqaha* whom he called 'the agents, bearers and narrators of the *hadiths* of *ahl al-bayt*'. This latter formula clearly equated the *fuqaha* with those mentioned in the tradition of Imam Jaʻfar, narrated via Umar b. Hanzala.

Muhammad Baqir al-Majlisi was appointed as Isfahan's Shaykh al-Islam in 1687. His Arabic-language *Bihar al-anwar* (Oceans of Lights) was the largest of the three great collections of the imams' traditions produced in these years. The *Bihar* includes many texts and much material of which few copies had been extant to that time. Al-Majlisi critically selected those materials and traditions that most effectively supported his own, larger, very contemporary project to focus on the imams and their revelation in order to dampen down the period's spiritual conflicts. With the same goal in mind, al-Majlisi also composed Persian-language works on matters of both belief and practice for lay believers. Many of these were in fact shortened forms of parts of the *Bihar*. Although he privileged the traditions, al-Majlisi was a firm advocate of the authority of the senior clerics during the imam's absence.

The increasing recourse to both earlier collections of the imams' traditions and essays by earlier generations of scholars over these years coincided with, and certainly encouraged, a marked upturn in the number of manuscript copies of these works produced from about 1640 onwards. Indicative figures suggest that from 1641 to 1688 over 200 copies of al-Tusi's *Tahdhib* were produced, compared with 60 over the previous century, and 6 from 1494 to 1543. More than 150 copies of *al-Kafi* appeared in the same 47-year period, compared to 52 over the previous 100 years and none from 1494 to 1543.[5] The effective 'rediscovery' of these earlier source materials and the appearance of a range of new essays and books, many in Persian – coupled with the expanding religious infrastructure – furthered the widespread establishment of Twelver Shi'ism as the dominant faith on the plateau. The faith endured as such through the fall of Isfahan to the Afghans in 1722, the scattering of some clerical elements to the Iraqi shrine cities and the Indian subcontinent, and the weakening of its status during the reign of Nadir Shah (r. 1736–1747). With pockets of believers also established in Lebanon, Iraq and India, the stage was set also for the complex, international religious dynamics that encouraged Akhbarism to find a hold in Iraq – and then fall, there and in Iran, to Usuli elements over the 18th and early 19th centuries.

Conclusion

While the roots of the present-day doctrines and practices of all Shi'i groups may be traced back through the centuries, the paths of each to what may be said to constitute the 'normative' today were continuously marked by internal debate and external challenges. The faithful of each community hold to a body of common doctrines and practices; both elite and non-elite believers also maintain varying views on a range of issues, with these being traceable to local cultural norms. There are therefore different, sometimes conflicting, understandings of what constitutes 'orthodoxy' both within those local communities, and between them and many others across the world of the Shi'a.

---

5   A. J. Newman, *Twelver Shi'ism: Unity and Diversity in the Life of Islam, 632 to 1722* (Edinburgh, 2013), Appendix II.

Not all Twelvers, for example, recognise *wilayat al-faqih* (the guardianship of the *faqih*) which is at the heart of Iran's Islamic Republican system of government. As well, not all believers agree with the precise manner in which different communities commemorate the death of Imam al-Husayn at Karbala.

The politics of the polities and, more recently, the nation-states in which believers have found themselves across the years have also had an impact on the localised developments in doctrine and practice. In the case of Iran, only in the 17th century were both the longevity of the Safawid polity and, concomitantly, the place of the faith in Iran, assured. More recently, such events as the Tobacco Protest of the late 19th century, the 1905 Iranian Constitutional Revolution, the fall and restoration of Muhammad Reza Shah Pahlavi (r. 1941–1979), the last shah of Iran, are inextricably bound up with the manner in which clerical authority in Iran has evolved and *wilayat al-faqih* came to be established.

The continued global presence of communities of the Shi'i faithful – most notably the Twelver, Ismaili and Zaydi, but also the Turkish and Syrian Alavi – further guarantees the presence of the aforementioned dynamics and believers' continuous engagement with issues of doctrine and practice. As in the past so in the present and the future, combinations of internal and external challenges and responses thereto, however contentious and controversial, guarantee longevity. A robust heritage of legal discourse shows every sign of remaining a vital part of Shi'ism.

Further Reading

Daftary, Farhad. *A History of Shi'i Islam*. London, 2013.

Gleave, Robert. *Scripturalist Islam: The History and Doctrines of the Akhbari Shi'i School*. Leiden, 2007.

Halm, Heinz. *Shi'ism*. 2nd ed. Edinburgh and New York, 2004.

Mallat, Chibli. *The Renewal of Islamic Law: Muhammad Baqer as-Sadr, Najaf and the Shi'i International*. Cambridge, 2003.

Modarresi Tabataba'i, Hossein. *An Introduction to Shi'i Law*. London, 1984.

Newman, Andrew. J. *The Formative Period of Twelver Shi'ism: Hadith as Discourse between Qum and Baghdad*. Richmond, 2000.

—— *Safavid Iran: Rebirth of a Persian Empire*. London, 2006.

—— *Twelver Shi'ism: Unity and Diversity in the Life of Islam, 632 to 1722*. Edinburgh, 2013.

Walbridge, Linda, ed. *The Most Learned of the Shia: The Institution of the Marja' Taqlid*. Oxford, 2001.

Yahia, Mohyddin. 'Introduction to Part IV: Shi'i Law', in Farhad Daftary and Gurdofarid Miskinzoda, ed., *The Study of Shi'i Islam*. London, 2014, pp. 253–270.

5

Intellectual Traditions

Paul E. Walker

Shi'i Islam revolves around a specific doctrine of the imamate: the notion that succession to the prophet belonged to Ali b. Abi Talib either by preference or absolute necessity. Upholding Ali's exclusive right to supreme leadership of the Muslim community might be a matter simply of faith or of inherited tradition; but it could also involve issues of intellectual principles, that is of rationally determined judgement. Can the succession of Ali be defended as an essential result, all others, including those accepted by non-Shi'i Muslims, failing the test of reason?

The Shi'i intellectual tradition insists that this is so, that it can argue forcefully not only for the imamate of Ali but that of his progeny as well. But is that all it comprises? Surely not, as we shall see. There are many additional features in Shi'i thought that separate it and set it apart, that give it a special character. But what exactly is an intellectual tradition and how do we define it? Within the broad spectrum of Islamic thought where does Shi'ism fit? What does it include or exclude? A good example here is the major difference between two schools of theology, the Mu'tazila and the Ash'ariyya, the former once supported by a considerable body of scholars but later falling into decline, the latter its chief competitor eventually gaining dominance and finally coming to define Sunni 'orthodoxy'. It is and was perfectly possible for a Shi'i to be also a Mu'tazili, the imamate being only one issue among many. Still a great proportion of Mu'tazilis were not Shi'is. By contrast no Shi'is, who often recognised and admitted some affinities with Mu'tazilis, subscribed to the key doctrines of the Ash'aris.

For our present purposes, which do not purport to be comprehensive on this score, intellectual tradition is best expressed as the undertaking of scholars working within a particular tradition. In the domain of scholarly pursuits, those to be examined involve issues and problems investigated by theoretical reasoning and the results obtained and then solved by applying the principles derived from that process. Even so, as with Islamic thinking generally, the topics of study comprise a vast set of fields ranging from fairly simple and readily accessible to the common believer to areas of subtle complexity and sophistication well out of the reach of any but a highly trained specialist.

The Making of the Shiʻi Intellectual Traditions

For the Shiʻa at large, there exist a wide array of topics that have been subject to scholarly treatment by its leading authorities: scripture and its interpretation, law and its application, the *hadith* of the imams, the imamate itself, prophecy, theology (*kalam*), philosophy and science (for example, physics and metaphysics) and many others. A given treatise by a Shiʻi author might discuss the following subjects: moral obligations and reason, man's best interest, the prophets, their miracles and the Quran, the imamate, the attributes of God, divine justice and features of natural philosophy, such as place, time, accidents, movement, the elements and mankind's position in the order of creation. Another might deal with the distinction between existence and essence and their relative importance, causality both temporal and ontological, God and His creating, motion and time, the divine attributes, God's speech and command, the nature of the afterlife, revelation and scripture, intellect and soul.

What Shiʻi authors had to say about each and how one might differ from another is an area not adequately investigated. There are, moreover, hundreds of writers and thousands of separate works to be considered. Much of this material, although reasonably well known in its own tradition (Imami material by Imami scholars, Zaydi by Zaydis and Ismaili by Ismailis), has not entered modern scholarship, which has been slow to pay attention to it except sporadically. More recently, however, the tide has turned. In the past two or three decades sound critical writing about the Shiʻi intellectual tradition has begun to appear in profusion, almost as a rising flood of information, far too much to be easily digested. However, thus far the separate Shiʻi traditions have remained separate. A proper history of Shiʻi intellectual endeavours should integrate what was in many ways always a single interconnected tradition.

Out of this large field of authors, topics and works, it is necessary here to focus on a selection, a few major figures and essential problems and sources of knowledge. One of the latter involves the role of Greek philosophy, its acceptance and adaption, in possible conflict with scripturally revealed doctrines. Another is how the Shiʻa, while affirming the absolute authority of the imam, have accorded special intellectual status to scholars and with them to a tradition of reasoned doctrines that depended on their efforts.

One answer points to the position of reason in the Shiʻi understanding of the roots and sources of religious truth. In contrast to the Sunnis, who do not accept reason as one of the *usul* (root-sources), the Shiʻa do. What is true or false, allowed or forbidden, upheld or rejected, can be determined by reason (*aql*). That distinction alone suggests why Shiʻism should be considered more rational than its opponents.

On the issue of supreme authority, few, if any, of the Shi'a would deny that the imam holds, theoretically, the highest rank. Were he accessible and could be consulted, his ruling must be accepted. However this condition is not and was not always possible. Each division of the Shi'a has a different position concerning the present imam and how his authority operates in practice. The Zaydis hold that the imam, who can be any descendant of Ali's sons, Hasan and Husayn, must also be the most knowledgeable member of this lineage. His knowledge is thus critical to his imamate; he will be the leading scholar among them. The Imamis (Twelver Shi'a) maintain the absolute authority of their imam, but admit that he is in hiding and thus not accessible for consultation. A community of religious scholars has for practical purposes taken his place. Among the Ismailis, there are two slightly different answers. One group upholds the imamate and authority of the living imam, who is in this case fully apparent (physically) and actively involved in governing his community. The other branch regards the chief *da'i* (*mutlaq*) as the highest authority on behalf of an absent imam who is himself not accessible.

If an intellectual tradition is defined by scholarship and the relative value of that scholarship depends on its authority, then when the Shi'a benefit from the active presence of an imam, the intellectual tradition they observe will be confined to the teachings of that imam. What role could others of lesser rank play? In the absence of the imam for whatever reason, another model of authority develops and the importance of individual scholars increases. What actually happened historically supports such a conclusion in part, but not always and not absolutely.

It is useful at this juncture to examine several cases, individual major figures, each with a solid claim to the highest regard, for clues to the development and propagation of the intellectual tradition that we are discussing. In this instance we look at two Ismailis, two Imamis and one who was both. They are Abu Ya'qub al-Sijistani and Hamid al-Din al-Kirmani, both Ismailis from respectively the 10th and early-11th centuries; al-Kirmani's nearly exact contemporary al-Shaykh al-Mufid, an Imami; Nasir al-Din al-Tusi from the 13th century, who was earlier an Ismaili and later an Imami; and finally Mulla Sadra, an Imami from the 17th century. It is, of course, fair to ask why these and not the many others. For one thing, the written work of these five is now reasonably available and thus accessible for study and investigation. Accordingly, modern scholarship about each of them is relatively abundant. Each, moreover, occupies a prominent place in the later manifestations of the intellectual tradition of which they were seminal figures.

Al-Sijistani was the leading voice of intellectual Ismailism during a period spanning the middle decades of the 10th century, from about 934 or earlier to 971 and perhaps a bit later. There were other important figures before him, from some of whom he drew doctrinal material and inspiration. His own writings display an attachment both to a previous set of Ismaili teachings and a newer, then fairly recently imported type of Neoplatonism, that is of philosophical ideals and concepts derived from the Greek legacy then entering the Islamic realm. Al-Sijistani combined them both and formed out of them a special synthesis, one part based on Neoplatonic philosophy and the other an Islamic (Ismaili) religious tradition.

Al-Kirmani flourished in the era of the Imam-caliph al-Hakim bi-Amr Allah (r. 996–1021). As an Ismaili authority of a fairly high rank, he supported the work of his predecessors, among them al-Sijistani. But he tried as well to reformulate the philosophical component of their teachings, replacing much of what they had proposed by a fresh interpretation. Principally the changes involve rejecting Neoplatonic concepts in favour of ideas taken from a form of Aristotelianism which closely parallels that advocated by the famous Muslim philosopher al-Farabi (ca. 872–950). These adjustments affected, in the main, doctrines of philosophy rather than those specifically of the Ismaili religious tradition. Although al-Kirmani was well regarded in his own time, al-Sijistani apparently retained his preeminence throughout the following century. Thereafter, most particularly in the Yemen where one later (Tayyibi) form of Ismailism survived, the situation was reversed, with al-Kirmani now on the top. The Tayyibi Ismailis up to the present regard al-Kirmani, along with al-Mu'ayyad fi'l-Din al-Shirazi (d. 1078), as the leaders in the intellectual tradition which they have inherited. Al-Sijistani is still studied, but his authority is less than theirs.

Abu Abd Allah Muhammad al-Nu'man, known as al-Shaykh al-Mufid (948–1032) became the leading theological spokesman of the Imami Shi'a and was already regarded as such by 987. In addition to standard Imami Shi'i positions, he adopted the doctrines of one school of Islamic theology, the Mu'tazila. Among the Imamis his influence was large and his students included nearly all of the subsequent generation of Imami scholars, among them al-Sharif al-Radi and his brother al-Sharif al-Murtada, and Abu Ja'far Muhammad al-Tusi.[1]

Nasir al-Din Muhammad al-Tusi belongs to a later period; his life spans three quarters of the 13th century from 1201 until his death in 1274. A prolific writer and expert in many fields, including the hard sciences of astronomy, biology, chemistry, physics and mathematics, he

---

[1]   Al-Sharif al-Radi (970–1015) and al-Murtada (967–1044) were consecutive official heads (*naqib*) of the Imami Shi'i community. Al-Radi is also famous as the compiler of the *Nahj al-balagha* (Peak of Eloquence). Abu Ja'far Muhammad al-Tusi is not to be confused with the much later al-Tusi, discussed below; he succeeded the brothers as head of the Shi'i community.

contributed to them as well as to philosophy. In religion he studied both Ismaili and Imami authorities, finally accepting early in his adult life a form of philosophical Ismailism. But, following the Mongol invasions of the 1250s, he switched his allegiance to the Imamis.

Muhammad b. Ibrahim al-Shirazi (1572–1640), known widely as Mulla Sadra, is the major intellectual figure of the Safawid era in Iran, but his fame has now spread elsewhere as well. Some consider him the most important Islamic philosopher after Ibn Sina. The complexity of his thought is formidable and many features of it are original to him. Thus, despite his Imami Shi'ism, he has attracted the attention of outsiders – most particularly those interested in what became of Islamic philosophy in later centuries, and how it compares either to the much earlier period or to European thought.

The Ismailis: al-Sijistani and al-Kirmani

Ismaili thought in its early formative period would be almost unintelligible without a background in philosophy, both Neoplatonism and Aristotelianism, each of which plays an essential part in the teachings of one of these major figures. It is not a matter of vague notions and superficial generalities, but of evidence that reveals the influence of specific works of Greek origin, and of a technical language in Arabic devised for the translation of them. The vocabulary employed by these Ismaili authors clearly indicates this one source of their ideas. Nevertheless, they deny vehemently that they are themselves philosophers – whom they generally regard, whether Greek or Islamic, as lacking a grasp of the ultimate truth. Some might have been brilliant and sections of what they wrote achieved a profound status; yet in the end, they failed to attain real validity and value.

But these Ismailis also insist on the absolute primacy of intellect, that is, reason in the created realm. For them the first created being is intellect. It is the sum and essence of all subsequent being; it governs and rules everything, the whole of the universe. As a corollary, revelation, which in some systems would thus be in conflict with intellect, is here not in opposition in any sense. Religious law and the scripture do not constitute a separate source, but rather they are each a manifestation of reason itself. In essence, the two – reason and revelation – are identical. Simply put, the very process of revelation produces an incarnation of universal intellect. A prophet converts timeless theoretical reality into a practical instrument for the benefit of human society on its path to eternal salvation.

Among the earliest Ismailis who had accepted this premise and thus started to express their Ismaili Shi'ism philosophically, two are especially important. They are al-Nasafi and al-Razi, both from the first decades of the 10th century, and both Neoplatonists who used the technical terms then fairly common with the philosophers such as the well-known al-Kindi. Many other Ismailis of the time knew and read the works of Muslim philosophers and such Greek importations as the so-called *Theology of Aristotle*, which was actually a paraphrase of the *Enneads* of Plotinus. By the time of al-Kirmani at the beginning of the next century, scientific and philosophical resources had expanded considerably, and his writings show that he had mastered all or most of them. By then a classical library in Arabic would have included nearly all of Aristotle plus various works of many other Greek authors.

Al-Sijistani from the middle of the 10th century thus drew upon a rich background, both of classical texts and of his predecessors among the Ismailis, some of whom had already incorporated in their teachings many ideas taken from Greek sources. Their purpose, however, was to explain Ismaili religious concepts, not to promote philosophy, certainly not as an alternative. Al-Sijistani continued this trend. His books and treatises are fairly numerous. In them he discusses, side by side, issues of critical importance for both Ismailism and for philosophy, sometimes overlapping the two, at others keeping them separate.

In general, his doctrines range systematically over a descending and ascending scheme, from the simple and universal to the complex and particular, from the One to the many, and back again. The study of creation, for him, means to reveal the structure of the universe beginning with the perpetually stable higher realm, and coming down progressively into the sphere of constant flux in the lower material world. Human souls are entangled in this lower realm but their salvation and eventual eternity lies in the upper world. Creation moves downwards from the foremost created being, the intellect, which is the first existent and is nearest to God Himself. Next, after intellect, comes soul, the universal form of soul not the individual. Then, going on downwards, is nature, which is in part simply a lower form of soul, its descending aspect. Following them the process changes from the sublime and spiritual to the mundane and corporeal. Nature at this reduced level generates the physical world, the earthly habitat of minerals, plants, animals – and above all of the highest species of animal, mankind.

For al-Sijistani the upward turn and the reverse is of major concern. As standard Ismaili doctrine, the return upwards is a historical process leading to the collective salvation of the human being. To lead the way there exists a second hierarchy parallel to intellect, soul and nature. It provides law and truth, and it prompts humans to seek a path away from the physical and sensate into the sublime spiritual world, from the realm of generation and corruption to the eternal world of intellect, wherein truth is never mixed with or masked by falsehood and deception. From his statements about this process and its details, we learn of several doctrines that now seem to be especially his.

His ideal of the One shows a particular concern to preserve its absolutely unqualified transcendence. Nothing and no concept can tie God to His creation. He is not the first in any sense because being first implies a second or third, thereby connecting the two. He is not the outer limit of things. Al-Sijistani insists that God is not a substance, not intellect; He is not a being or a cause. Attributions of this kind are falsely applied in His case, although they are often cited in Islamic works of theology or philosophy. Al-Sijistani devoted many chapters of his major books to refute such misleading concepts. It is and was common to claim that God is a thing not like any other thing. But that is wrong, al-Sijistani says. It would appear to maintain God's detachment but does not in actuality. The proper procedure is to systematically deny of God all such qualifications. He is not in a place, not in a time, not describable – but then continue by denying each of these denials. God is not a thing and He is not *not* a thing; not in a place and not *not* in a place, and so on. A simple set of negatives produces an intellectual satisfaction that is, he maintains, deceptive and lacking in rigour. The second finally achieves a clear separation between God and His creation.

To explain creation, which is here creation from nothing, *ex nihilo*, al-Sijistani like many of his predecessors, including the Ismailis al-Nasafi and al-Razi, depends on a special kind of creation denoted by the Arabic verb *abda'a*, which means in this instance to bring something into being from nothing. All other forms of creation involve fashioning a new thing out of a pre-existing matter. He is careful to call these other types of creation by a different name. What is created by the process of origination (*abda'a*) is first of all intellect. In moving from intellect to the next stage which is, for him, soul, a different verb is used; soul gushes (*inbajasa*) or proceeds (*inba'atha*) out of intellect.

A special characteristic of al-Sijistani's thought, a doctrine he shares with several others, inserts between God and intellect a command. God creates by fiat; He wills the universe into being. This command is the divine logos (*kalima*) but it is not an existent. Once issued it becomes the thing it brings into being, that is, intellect. There cannot be a second command. The cosmos has come into being; it will not revert to chaos.

The objective of God's command is intellect and the latter is the sum and principle of all being, the form of all things, both those manifest and those hidden, the wellspring of all spiritual and physical light. Thus some aspects of it enter all subsequent being. Soul comes out of it, less in rank and by contrast imperfect. To achieve perfection the soul begins to acquire what it can of the perfection of its predecessor. This process moves sequentially and thus temporally. Soul is in motion and it thereby creates time itself. But soul is not always focused on the higher world of intellect and, in moments of heedlessness, it turns towards the world it itself has made, namely nature and physical reality. There it becomes enthralled with sensate delight; it is forgetful of its source, having become disoriented. Only by proper reorientation, turning back upwards towards intellect, can it attain salvation.

Key items in this system indicate its Neoplatonic origin. One is the universality of intellect. It does not separate or break up into individual intellects, even at the cosmic level. Likewise soul is a single soul, a universal. Our souls are parts of this same universal soul.

What then is prophecy? Clearly the prophets are not simply philosophers. In fact for al-Sijistani, the law-giving prophets belong to the same genealogical lineage and they all share an extraordinary faculty not available to other humans. They have perfect access to the timeless truth of intellect and thus function in the physical world as its deputies. They convert universal reason into language in order to convey its benefits to other humans. As a result they formulate laws and compose scriptures, bringing about in the process a regime that governs the community they were sent to rescue. The final such messenger was Muhammad; his law was and is the most perfect of all those that came before him. But, since he has departed, there must be someone to preserve and defend his legacy in the meanwhile. Such a person will also understand better than anyone else how intellect became law and how the law indicates the intellectual reality on which it is based. This one individual unerringly traces the physical symbols, the language, in the law and scripture back to what is really real, and can thereby explain what the words used in it actually mean. He is the imam.

Turning now to al-Kirmani, we see almost immediately that many of the features in the thought of al-Sijistani have been abandoned. The changes represent a move from concepts that are decidedly Neoplatonist towards the Aristotelian leanings of al-Farabi and Ibn Sina. The single universal intellect becomes a descending series of intellects, each corresponding to one of the heavenly spheres. The world soul disappears. The individual human soul does not exist in any form prior to the body; it comes into being along with the body it inhabits. These are a few examples of the adjustments al-Kirmani hoped would find acceptance. Had they been adopted, the Ismaili intellectual tradition of his time and later would have been much closer to that suggested by al-Farabi and Ibn Sina.

Nevertheless, what al-Kirmani proposed, although sharing features with al-Farabi, is also markedly different in many ways. For him God is not the First Cause or the necessary being (*wajib al-wujud*) as the philosophers would have it. The initial element of a causal series is, despite its primacy, still a part of that series. The chain of intellects commences with an intellect, not with God. He is above and apart from it. Here al-Kirmani acknowledges a doctrine somewhat similar to al-Sijistani's double negation. God is utterly unknown and unknowable. Intellect might want to understand Him but simply cannot. God can no more be grasped by the intellect than the sun can be seen by the naked human eye. Even trying to do so produces harm. But how, then, do we understand references to Him in religious materials? Al-Kirmani's answer is that what we speak about is actually intellect at its highest and ultimate first level. It is not God, but as close to Him as humans can come. It suggests God but is not Him.

Creation begins with the unique act denoted by the verb *abda'a*, that of origination. It produces first intellect which is, thereafter, the absolute first of the cosmos: first being, first cause, first mover. It thinks, is thought, and is what is thought, all at once. It is the mover of all motions, the actuality that brings all potentiality into actuality.

From first intellect a second intellect appears. The first unintentionally radiates its joy at being itself. That blush generates an image which becomes a separate intellect as a reflection of the first. This process is called procession or emanation (*inba'atha*). As the second, this being clearly has rank and position; it is not alone or unique. But it retains some intellectual qualities. It is actual and not potential; it encompasses and preserves its own essence. In contrast to the first, it must conceive what it came out of as well as contemplate itself, thereby engendering a double aspect. It has a dual nature.

From these two aspects of the second intellect there issue a further procession of intellects and with them a parallel series of material entities. The former are the additional intellects of the heavenly spheres and their material forms, the planets. At a final stage, the last of these intellects creates our physical realm and its corporeal beings. Al-Kirmani assigns the governance and regulation of this world to the intelligences of the heavenly spheres. Each of these secondary intellects observes the veneration of God through perfect unchanging circular motion like, he notes, pilgrims circumambulating the Ka'ba. They also have a providential interest in our world, though in practice it is the closest of them, the tenth intellect, that is most directly involved. This is what the philosophers call the Active Intellect.

In direct contrast to the doctrine of al-Sijistani (and of the Neoplatonist), al-Kirmani taught that soul commences with the body. In the beginning it is formless and devoid of knowledge; nevertheless, it is the first perfection of the natural body. For it, intellect is a kind of soul and as a substance it has the possibility of surviving its body. Here, in this world, it depends on the senses and physical existence. It possesses instincts about its physical condition, but gradually acquires more than them, a form of knowledge that leads to its second perfection. Thereby it endures and continues beyond the death and dissolution of the body. Ultimately, based on its acquisition of true intellect, it will reach an eternal state.

The kind of knowledge necessary for this final development comes from the eternal realm. It is brought down from there by teachers, a special class of humans who have access to the Active Intellect. They are rare and unique, the great prophets and founders of religions, and at the end the messiah of the future. These men were the intellects of their time, the earthly image of the first intellect. At this present moment, the perfection of intellect in the physical world is the single living imam; he is the ultimate teacher, the master. Only he knows unerringly what is true because he, like the prophet, can see into the divine world as fully as any human can.

The Imamis: al-Mufid, al-Tusi and Mulla Sadra

A history of the Imami intellectual tradition has yet to be written, though the material for it has now grown into a formidably large collection of individuals and their works spanning many centuries and continuing into the present. However, for several reasons, al-Shaykh al-Mufid is a good figure to start with. And he provides an instructive point of comparison with his Ismaili contemporary al-Kirmani, as we shall see.

Imami scholarship prior to al-Mufid, notably that of his own teacher, Ibn Babuya al-Qummi, largely focused on collecting, sorting and preserving the traditions reported from the imams of the line they recognise. Al-Mufid then turned in a different direction, moving towards a form of Mu'tazili theology (*kalam*). For him, a theologian (*mutakallim*) – here counting himself among them – was one who employed reason and disputation to find the truth and to repel falsehood through argumentation and proof. As with the Mu'tazila in general, he thus added to the sources of religious knowledge reason itself, not alone, but together with revealed scripture. Thereafter, except in regard to the doctrine of the imamate, Imami theology took up the positions and concerns of the Mu'tazila. But that meant that it now belonged to an intellectual tradition more complex and sophisticated than that of the Imamis in the previous century; theology had become an accepted discipline.

Al-Mufid was himself acclaimed for his sharp mind and skill in debate. His house in the Shi'i district of Baghdad and the nearby mosque became centres of discussion attracting followers and members of opposing factions, from 987 to his death in 1032. Against the factions, which included some of the most famous theologians of his time, he wrote tracts and treatises, in addition to debating with them personally. Imamis elsewhere accepted his authority and the record shows evidence of his written responses to widely scattered communities of supporters. Unfortunately most of his writings, which may have numbered 200 in all, are known only by title. Many were refutations of all sorts of opponents. In the subsequent generation of Imami scholars, few, if any, had not at some time been his students; the list of them is lengthy and its members distinguished.

The principal concerns of al-Mufid, however, are theologically speaking fairly traditional. The issues that he is most apt to deal with fit and match well with those of Sunni theologians, such as the famous al-Ash'ari. His answers tend to be Mu'tazili, but the problems addressed are similar. Two examples may suffice to explain. On the question of the status of a grave sinner in this life – whether such a person may even so be accepted as a believer – he argued against the Mu'tazili position, which argues for a middle point between believer and unbeliever in this life, and condemnation in the next. For al-Mufid, the Prophet and the Imams might intercede to restore any member of their following. With regard to the place of reason, he rejected a major Mu'tazili doctrine that the truths of religion must be uncovered by reason, insisting instead that transmitted revelation is absolutely necessary for reason to acquire this knowledge. His Imami successors would go further and adopt outright the Mu'tazili position, but he did not.

In his discussion of these issues we can see the focus of his thought, what problems bothered him, and how he responded. The difference between him and the Ismaili thinkers cited earlier is striking, and the contrast is profound. No one would consider al-Mufid a philosopher. The matters he takes up belong to a different tradition, one that is first of all based in the historical development of religious concerns in the domain of traditional Islamic theology. Al-Sijistani and al-Kirmani have less concern for such questions; they are not of paramount importance for them and their thought is accordingly not rooted or confined to Islamic doctrine pure and simple, but to a scientific exploration of the cosmos and mankind's role in it. They were in this way far more philosophically inclined than al-Mufid, or for that matter any of the Imami theologians of his century and earlier.

That is, in part, why our next figure is so fascinating and his achievements so important. Nasir al-Din al-Tusi was for much of his life and career an Ismaili and therefore, as such, he almost certainly inherited and then absorbed the intellectual concerns of both al-Sijistani and al-Kirmani, along with other leading authorities in the Ismaili *da'wa*. An important additional example might be Nasir-i Khusraw. Yet because al-Tusi eventually converted to a form of Imami Shi'ism, he contributed to its intellectual tradition as well, in fact bringing the two together perhaps for the first time, and creating in the process a new synthesis. After him, Imami scholars tended to follow his lead. One result was that philosophy, possibly with some Ismaili influences, became an essential component of post-Tusi Imami thought.

Al-Tusi was born most likely into an Imami family. His father was also a scholar and his son Nasir al-Din acquired from him a wide-ranging knowledge of the sciences, philosophy and the doctrines of various Islamic groups, including the Ismailis. This openness to disparate fields and intellectual variety allowed him to move freely through the works of his most significant predecessors, chief among them Ibn Sina, but a long list of others as well, some of whom he studied with in person. By the time he was 32, he had completed his training and found a patron in the Ismaili governor of Quhistan, Nasir al-Din Muhtashim, for whom he composed his famous work on ethics, the *Akhlaq-i Nasiri*, named after this patron. Somewhere in the process, influenced by the Ismaili imam, he declared himself to be a follower. A spiritual biography he wrote in about 1246, the *Sayr wa suluk*, says as much. By this time he had arrived at Alamut where he was to remain on and off for about 20 years.

A critical step along this path was his realisation that intellect alone could not answer the most fundamental metaphysical questions. Such an inquiry would have intellect explaining itself, its own origin, which he doubted it could do. Reasoning, as promoted by the Aristotelian philosophers, properly begins with a premise known to be universally true, and proceeds through the syllogism to a sound conclusion. But the universal validity of the assumed premise is open to question. On what authority do we accept it? Ultimately there needs to be a source of unquestionable authority. Possibly the answer for al-Tusi, at least near the beginning of his career, lay in the imamate and specifically in the Ismaili imam.

We must assume that the Ismaili fortresses he visited and lived in for so long a period provided him with access to libraries rich in the classics of older Ismaili thought. Although the evidence for them as sources of his thought is not precise, it is reasonably clear in the books he wrote (or supervised), such as the *Rawda-yi taslim* (Paradise of Submission), while directly affiliated with the *da'wa*. In this work we find, for example, a doctrine of the divine command not dissimilar to that for which al-Sijistani was noted and for which he was criticised by al-Kirmani.

Faced with the onslaught of the Mongols, al-Tusi was commissioned to negotiate with them in 1256. The outcome included surrender and destruction, especially of the Ismaili movement as it had existed until then. However, al-Tusi survived and entered the service of new masters. As he did, he reverted to the Imamism of his origins. Some of his writing during this later period indicates his new affiliation clearly. The Mongols also built for him an astronomical observatory near Tabriz, which quickly became a major centre of scholarship of many kinds with its own substantial library, attracting important scholars who came there to work with al-Tusi and take advantage of its collections.

At the end of his life, he moved to Baghdad where he died in 1274. By then he had composed a vast number of works with as many as 165 separate titles. Significantly, many of them survive and that is most likely due to his growing fame even while he was alive. The range of subjects that he wrote about is equally impressive. A list would include astronomy, astrology, geomancy, mathematics, physics, mineralogy, medicine, jurisprudence, philosophy including logic, mysticism and theology. In most of these fields he made original contributions, some of extraordinary importance. By comparison his intellectual predecessors, especially those cited here, rarely if ever worked directly in more than a few of these fields. The Ismaili figures, while undeniably learned in the hard sciences (astronomy, biology, mineralogy, mathematics), as we can easily see from the detailed references to scientific facts in their writings, did not attempt their own investigations of these areas. From other sources and materials we know, however, that the Fatimid imam-caliphs did promote this kind of science. The famous astronomer Ibn Yunus (d. 1009) was sponsored by al-Hakim bi-Amr Allah (r. 996–1021). There are many other such cases. But none of those involved were themselves Ismailis; none were members of the *da'wa*. With the case of al-Tusi, we therefore witness a dramatic change since he was deeply committed to both the hard sciences and to theology and doctrinal expression.

In both phases of his work, the Ismaili and the Imami, one of his enduring contributions was the incorporation of philosophy. In the former case, he adapted it to support a particular view of the cosmological background to the imamate, especially in the period of *qiyama* (resurrection); in the Imami instance, he reformulated Shi'i theology to stress the importance of philosophical demonstration over religious dialectics. Several of his major treatises were written to defend Ibn Sina, one a commentary on the latter's *Isharat*, another to refute an Ismaili Neoplatonic text that had assailed him. Rescuing Ibn Sina from his detractors and rebuilding regard for him proved to be an enduring legacy for al-Tusi, as well for the great philosopher himself. In part, al-Tusi's explanations of his predecessor's work can often be clearer than the original. In addition, al-Tusi's major Imami theological work, the *Tajrid al-kalam* (Abstract of Theology) brought the terminology of metaphysics into that subject where it would remain. This one work of al-Tusi thereafter influenced nearly all Imami writings in this area, leading to the eventual fusion of theology and philosophy in the work of Mulla Sadra.

Muhammad Sadra al-Din al-Shirazi was the son of a prominent court official and thus of a privileged background. He acquired a taste for philosophy fairly early, and eventually realised that he required a teacher in order to attain greater depth in this subject than he could acquire himself. He had the means to find the best, and moved from Shiraz to the Safawid capital Qazwin in 1591, studying there with Baha al-Din al-Amili and Mir Damad, two highly important scholars at the royal court. There is much more to Mulla Sadra's training and the others he studied with, but here it simply needs be noted that he had access to the finest minds of the time.

Through them and the written legacy of major predecessors, he was in contact with a whole tradition of learning and debate. Mulla Sadra would have become familiar with many of these predecessors, but most especially with Ibn Sina and al-Suhrawardi, two individuals who influenced his thought directly. Another influential figure would have been Ibn al-Arabi (1165–1240). The concept of the unity of existence (*wahdat al-wujud*), famously attributed to Ibn al-Arabi, was criticised by those who upheld the primacy of essence as the primary reality of all. For these thinkers, existence is merely derivative, a mental phenomenon. This latter idea was the position of al-Suhrawardi and Mir Damad. Initially Mulla Sadra followed them. Eventually, however, the primacy of existence dawned on him and from then on he was on his own.

Lacking a suitable patron and no longer finding like-minded colleagues in Shiraz he went into a kind of retreat, isolating himself in the village of Kahak outside Qumm, in order to meditate. It was there that he began writing his great summation of philosophy and theology, the *Transcendent Wisdom of the Four Journeys of the Intellect* (known in Arabic commonly as *al-Asfar al-arba'a*). The four journeys explore first the subjects of ontology, existence, essence and movement; second, substance and accident; third, God's being and attributes; and fourth, humanity and its destiny. The confluence of philosophy and theology is clearly apparent. This period of solitude lasted about five years and it brought Mulla Sadra new insights and the ultimate value of intuitive experience. He came to understand that truths must be experienced in order to produce certainty. Such knowledge is not new, but the degree of certainty attached to it is. Therefore the nature of existence and its uniqueness must be experienced through a non-rationally based process. Once existence is conceptualised, it becomes essence and in so doing real existence is falsified. That which is directly experienced is existence, but that which is understood by the mind is an essence.

Al-Suhrawardi was well known for his theory of light; that it is the only reality and has greater and less intensities, a foundational idea of Illuminationism. Existence was for him a mere logical notion. Mulla Sadra made al-Suhrawardi's light existence instead – including the idea that it is the only reality, and most significantly, that it can be more or less intense. Existence, he held, is in perpetual motion climbing higher. It has priority and posteriority, perfection and imperfection, strength and weakness. Accordingly, it is systematically ambiguous. This movement ends with the Perfect Man who is a member of the divine realm, united with and among the attributes of God. Each stage in the process includes all of those lower, though the higher is more and more simple. The more something has of existence, the less it has of essence. The latter is only in the mind; it is not actually real. God has no essence at all. He is absolute existence. Essences are the bearers of contingency, mere modes of existence at a lower stage. Existence is radically particular; the mind thinks only generalities. Existence is never static but perpetually in motion, a motion of substance, from the more general and indeterminate to the concrete and determinant or integrated. God is all existence, yet nothing relative or contingent can be attributed to Him.

This brief account does not render the ideas of Mulla Sadra full justice by any means. He was a complex thinker, working at the outer limits of the Islamic intellectual tradition broadly speaking, and at the leading edge of Shi'i thought more specifically. But however brief it may be, it is enough to suggest the critically important nature of the whole picture, were we to go into it at the length that it deserves. And Sadra's legacy has grown accordingly in the modern era.

Conclusion

Of all the varied aspects of the Shi'i intellectual tradition we might have considered, the main focus here is the role of philosophy – its incorporation and use to express doctrines that cover not merely the fine points of law and religious practice, but of the whole universe, of its creation and mankind's place in it. In many ways, that represents the high point of the tradition itself. Still, these other aspects, such as legal doctrine, should not be ignored, though in the present case space does not permit including them.

Once focused on the introduction of philosophy and science, our view of the history of Shi'i thought must inevitably note the essential role played by the Ismailis of the 10th and 11th centuries. Al-Sijistani was not the first to employ philosophy to explain Ismaili Shi'ism, but he stands for us now as the most important figure in part because his major works survive. Although only recently finally published in sound critical editions, there is no reason now not to recognise his achievements and to acknowledge that he occupied a prime position at the very beginning of a trend running from him to Mulla Sadra – even though as yet we do not fully understand or perceive all the connecting links.

We have seen, however, how little of philosophy there is in the work of the Imami al-Mufid, in contrast to his contemporary al-Kirmani on the Ismaili side. That observation highlights the importance of al-Tusi. Surely we are permitted to claim that he functioned as a transition point between the older Ismaili figures and a new phase of Imami thought that was now fully conversant with philosophical ideas and concepts. This assertion is not to downplay the huge importance of Ibn Sina, but seeks to add an element not yet completely understood or recognised. In short, if we assume that al-Sijistani and al-Kirmani were sources for al-Tusi – that he had read both – what further traces of their work can we discern in the later Imami tradition?

Any answer is complicated by a situation of secrecy and extreme reticence about public disclosure among the agents of the Ismaili *da'wa*, who wrote for each other but not for non-Ismailis. Most were active in regions of the Islamic world where the dominant authorities were extremely hostile to them and their ideas. Moreover, the veil of secrecy applies to the facts of their lives about which we know, at this point, little or nothing. Thus it is necessary to question whether and when what they said reached an audience that could have included Imami Shi'is or even Sunnis. About this problem there are a few clues. One is the anti-Ismaili tracts composed by al-Ghazali (1058–1111). Clearly he had access to Ismaili writings, as did some other non-Ismailis, significantly including Ibn Taymiyya (d. 1328) who says he had read *al-Maqalid* (The Keys), a major book by al-Sijistani. Thus when al-Ghazali credits the Ismailis with a formidable system of thought based in philosophy, and Ibn Taymiyya comments that al-Sijistani was the best of them, those judgements support our view of his importance – and with him, of the critical role the Ismailis may have played in adding philosophy to the Shi'i intellectual tradition. There it took root and became in the long run the completely naturalised component that we find in the work of Mulla Sadra, where philosophy and theology appear intertwined, one with the other.

Further Reading

Daftary, Farhad, ed. *Intellectual Traditions in Islam*. London, 2000.

Leaman, Oliver. *Islamic Philosophy: An Introduction*. 2nd ed., Cambridge, 2009.

McDermott, Martin J. *The Theology of al-Shaikh al-Mufid (d. 413/1022)*. Beirut, 1986.

Rahman, Fazlur. *The Philosophy of Mulla Sadra*. Albany, NY, 1975.

Rizvi, Sajjad H. *Mulla Sadra Shirazi: His Life and Works and the Sources for Safavid Philosophy*. Oxford, 2007.

—— *Mulla Sadra and Metaphysics*. London, 2009.

al-Tusi, Nasir al-Din. *Contemplation and Action: The Spiritual Autobiography of a Muslim Scholar*, ed. and tr. S. J. Badakhchani. London, 1998.

—— *Paradise of Submission: A Medieval Treatise on Ismaili Thought*, ed. and tr. S. J. Badakhchani, with an introduction by H. Landolt and commentary by Ch. Jambet. London, 2005.

Walker, Paul E. *Early Philosophical Shiism: The Ismaili Neoplatonism of Abu Ya'qub al-Sijistani.* Cambridge, 1993.

—— *The Wellsprings of Wisdom*: A study of Abu Ya'qub al-Sijistani's *Kitab al-yanabi'.* Salt Lake City, 1994.

—— *Abu Ya'qub al-Sijistani: Intellectual Missionary.* London, 1996.

—— *Hamid al-Din al-Kirmani: Ismaili Thought in the Age of al-Hakim.* London, 1999.

6

Governance and Pluralism under the Fatimids (909–996 CE)

Shainool Jiwa

The medieval Mediterranean littoral was a region inhabited by peoples of diverse ethnic backgrounds and religious persuasions. This was evident in 10th-century Egypt, the mainstay of the Fatimid domains, a land in which lived Arabs, Turks, Greeks, Armenians, Berbers and Sudanese – among whom were Sunni and Shiʿi Muslims, Coptic, Melkite and Nestorian Christians, as well as Rabbanite and Qaraite Jews. It was in this milieu that the Fatimids established the first Shiʿi empire across the southern shores of the Mediterranean, from the Atlantic Ocean to the Red Sea.

Over the course of their two and a half centuries of rule, from 909 to 1171, the Fatimids, a Shiʿi Ismaili dynasty, developed a model of governance recognised both in medieval and modern times for its inclusive nature; particularly for the participation of Christians and Jews in the state administration. Doctrinally, their model was underpinned by a universalist notion of authority of the divinely designated imam-caliph. Pragmatically, the model evolved with their experience of governing diverse communities across a vast terrain. This led to a relationship between the state and its diverse subjects, which fluctuated with time and circumstance.

While participation of non-Muslims in the administration of Muslim polities was common in the formative period of Muslim rule, Fatimid governance has been presented in medieval Muslim chronicles and in modern scholarship as being exceptional in this regard. Varied arguments have been postulated as to why, ranging from inherent pluralism in the Fatimid approach to governance to pragmatic necessity, with the Fatimids as a Shiʿi minority seeking support from other minority groups.

This chapter examines the theoretical constructs that underpinned Fatimid governance and reviews the extent to which Fatimid policy was the result of the interplay between doctrinal commitments and their lived experience, tempered by local conditions and communal

dynamics. It focuses on the conceptual formulations of Fatimid governance that took shape in the reign of the fourth Fatimid Imam-caliph,
al-Mu'izz li-Din Allah (r. 953–975), and which came to be regarded as
the blueprint for Fatimid governance in Egypt.

In this chapter, the term religious pluralism refers to the accommo-
datory approaches which the Fatimids developed in their conceptual
framework for the governance of non-Ismaili subjects over the formative period of their empire, which spanned their 60-year reign in North
Africa and the first two decades of their rule in Egypt. In reviewing these
developments through a close reading of primary texts, the relationship
between doctrine and history is examined to elicit how the Fatimid
doctrinal formulations of governance evolved in tandem with their lived
experience, a dialectic that was enabled by the scope of authority with
which the Fatimid imam-caliph was invested, as the supreme authoritative source of law and doctrine.

Universalist Rule: The Fatimid Framework

Inherent to the monotheistic tradition, with its belief in a universal
God, are aspirations for the creation of a universal polity engendered for the realisation of salvation.[1] This notion was manifested in
the relationship between Christianity and the Roman Empire after
the conversion of the Emperor Constantine, and Islam subsequently
inherited the same predisposition to universalist rule.[2] The connection between religion and state was firmly established during the time
of the Prophet Muhammad and subsequently framed Islamic models
of leadership such as the imamate and the caliphate. In both Shi'i and
Sunni Islam, the continued saliency of the principle of universalism
was regarded as the culmination rather than a rupture of the historical
process.[3]

The same ideal of a universal order characterised the religio-
political vision of the Fatimids. Proclaiming his caliphate in Ifriqiya
(present-day Tunisia and eastern Algeria) in 909, the founder of the
dynasty, Abd Allah al-Mahdi, pronounced his descent from the *ahl
al-bayt*, the household of the Prophet Muhammad, and claimed to

---

[1]   This section of the article has been abridged from S. Jiwa, *The Founder of
Cairo: The Fatimid Imam-caliph al-Mu'izz and His Era* (London, 2013), where the
related arguments have been discussed extensively.
[2]   Garth Fowden is among the notable authors who have examined the relationship
between monotheism and universal sovereignty in his *Empire to Commonwealth:
Consequences of Monotheism in Late Antiquity* (Princeton, NJ, 1993).
[3]   Sumaiya Hamdani, *Between Revolution and State: The Path to Fatimid
Statehood* (London, 2006), pp. xvii–xviii.

be the only legitimate successor to the Prophet's mantle of temporal and religious leadership over the Muslim *umma*. The Fatimid investiture was rooted in the Imami Shi'i belief in the continuity of divine guidance inherited through a designated sequence of prophets and imams. They held that authority after Prophet Muhammad was only legitimately held by Ali b. Abi Talib, Muhammad's cousin and son-in-law, and thereafter upheld in an ordained line of imams from his descendants. The imams were considered to be the bearers of divine light and knowledge, as inherited from the Prophet and were the sole authoritative exponents of Scriptural interpretation, law and creed. As such, the manifestation of an imam in each age was indispensable, and allegiance to the Imam as 'God's Representative on Earth' was incumbent upon the believers.

The Fatimid claim to universal authority was asserted in direct opposition to that of the reigning Abbasid caliphs and was notably distinct, with the Shi'i model of the imamate harkening back to the notion of the Imam being authoritative in law and doctrine. In their early years the Abbasids had sought to realise a similar model. In the 10th century, they exerted strenuous efforts to stem the rising prestige of the proto-Sunni religious scholars, the *ulama*, with the caliph al-Ma'mun's so-called *mihna* (or 'trial'), the inquisition of Ahmad b. Hanbal being a case in point; but they were swimming against the consensual Sunni tide. The *mihna* had been instituted by al-Ma'mun (r. 813–833) to ensure he was recognised as the supreme authority on law and doctrine. Religious scholars were put through 'trials' to enforce their compliance with al-Ma'mun's position. Resistance by scholars such as Ahmad b. Hanbal (780–855) led to the eventual refutation of the caliph's stance. Consequently, by the time the Fatimids rose to power in the 10th century, a general consensus was being reached in the proto-Sunni schools of thought that it was not the caliph but the *ulama*, considered unrivalled bearers of the Prophetic 'tradition', who were the ultimate determiners of religious doctrine and practice. Though the theoretical necessity of the caliph as God's representative on Earth and embodying religious authority remained an abiding principle in Sunni Islam, his authority was increasingly symbolic.

In Imami Shi'i thought, the distinction between the functions of the imam and caliph received elucidation in the writings of Imams Muhammad al-Baqir (d. 733) and Ja'far al-Sadiq (d. 765). The imam was regarded as a spiritual teacher and guide who may or may not wield temporal power; the caliph was a worldly ruler, who claimed to govern with divine sanction. The Fatimids as 'imam-caliphs' were synthesising these roles – consistent with the paradigm of the Prophet as a religious and political leader in Medina, a synthesis which was inherited by the four caliphs who followed Muhammad. This paradigm was not sustained thereafter, and a de facto separation of roles had emerged as the norm by the early 9th century under the rule of the Abbasids.[4]

The Fatimid model of the caliphate was thus a novel phenomenon in the Muslim world of the 10th century, with the assertion that their imam-caliphs had divinely-mandated authority over doctrine and belief, as well as their legal and theological interpretations. Although the Zaydi Shiʿi model of the imamate emphasised superior knowledge as a qualification of the righteous imam, the Imami Shiʿi notion of the imam as the possessor of Divine Support (*taʾyid*) and inheritor of esoteric knowledge rendered his authority unrivalled. The distinction of the Fatimid model of governance stemmed from how the Fatimid imam-caliph, as ruler of a vast empire, exercised this authority. As authoritative exponents of doctrine, every Fatimid imam was able to reform and reformulate, to adapt and to alter, and thus to negotiate the relationship between the ruler and the ruled, as he deemed appropriate. The notion of the living imam as the ultimate arbiter of human affairs meant that the Fatimid sovereigns had the potential to be authoritarian, with unfettered power at their disposal. A study of the structures of their administration reveals that by and large, they maintained an inclusive approach to governance, but one which nonetheless gave rise to its own challenges.

The claim to universal authority remained the *raison d'être* of Fatimid rule, and conceptual articulations of the Fatimid imamate became an essential aspect of the Fatimid *daʿwa* literature, which proliferated in the 10th and 11th centuries in tandem with the expansion of the Fatimid Empire.

The growing availability over the past few decades of an increasing number of Fatimid texts has led to instructive insights on the vital issue of righteous rule and just governance. These texts allow for a close reading of Fatimid approaches to governance, as well as an understanding of their distinctiveness and the vicissitudes they underwent. Authors such as Hamdani, Brett, Halm, Walker, Lev, Madelung and Daftary have increasingly relied on these texts to enlarge on various aspects of this theme. Yet the systematic study of the evolution of the Fatimid model of governance remains to be done. In this chapter, while a range of Fatimid sources have been reviewed to develop a nuanced understanding of the developments in Fatimid governance, two documents in particular – the *ahd* of Ali as cited in al-Qadi al-Nuʿman's (d. 974) *Daʿaim al-Islam*,[5] and the *Aman* document as preserved both in the *Ittiʿaz al-hunafa* of

---

[4] Ira M. Lapidus, *A History of Islamic Societies* (2nd ed., Cambridge, 2002), pp. 99–102.

[5] Al-Qadi al-Nuʿman, *Daʿaim al-Islam*, ed. Asaf A. A. Fyzee (Cairo, 1951–1960), vol. 1, pp. 350–365, English trans. A. A. A. Fyzee, revised by Ismail K. Poonawala, *The Pillars of Islam* (New Delhi and Oxford, 2002–2004), vol. 1, pp. 436–456.

Taqi al-Din al-Maqrizi (1364–1442),[6] and the *Uyun al-akhbar* of Idris Imad al-Din (1392–1468),[7] have been closely examined for their value in tracing the shaping of Fatimid governance.

Towards a Fatimid Model of Governance

The universalist nature of the Fatimid model of authority led to two significant challenges following their assumption of political power. The first was the messianic and exclusivist demands of the segments of the Fatimid *da'wa* (religio-political mission) that brought them to power. The second was the expectations of inclusion required by the multi-ethnic and religiously diverse populace over whom the Fatimids came to rule in North Africa.

The messianic challenge came from within the movement that had led to the establishment of the Fatimid state. The Ismaili *da'wa*, which traced the Shi'i imamate in the line of Isma'il b. Ja'far al-Sadiq, aimed at replacing the Abbasids by promising an era of just rule under the sole legitimate Ismaili imam. In the 10th century, it gained particular momentum across many different regions of the Muslim world. The founding of the Fatimid state in North Africa was realised by the Kutama Berbers, amongst whom there had been previously some presence of Shi'ism and who, after 902, began in increasing numbers to adhere to the Ismaili *da'wa* under the leadership of the pioneering *da'i*, Abu Abd Allah al-Shi'i. Over the following years, the Kutama rallied around the *da'i*, forming an exclusivist community of believers. Based at Ikjan, a new urban centre which they characterised as their *dar al-hijra* (place of refuge), the Kutama under the *da'i* Abu Abd Allah expanded their rule in preparation of the inception of the empire of the Mahdi. Bringing the previous Abbasid-affiliated regime in the region, of the Aghlabids, to an end in 909, Abd Allah al-Mahdi was publicly proclaimed as the first Fatimid imam-caliph in 910.

This proclamation was the *da'wa*'s crowning glory. The successful proclamation gave vent to the messianic expectations of the mission, of the imam being the Mahdi, the saviour who would usher in an awaited utopia. An inherent expectation of this vision was the establishment of a polity in which belief in the imamate of al-Mahdi bi'llah was the

---

[6]   Taqi al-Din al-Maqrizi, *Itti'az al-hunafa bi-akhbar al-a'imma al-Fatimiyyin al-khulafa*, vol. 1, ed. Jamal al-Dīn al-Shayyal (Cairo, 1967); English translation of the section on the reign of al-Mu'izz by Shainool Jiwa as *Towards a Shi'i Mediterranean Empire: Fatimid Egypt and the Founding of Cairo* (London, 2009).

[7]   Idris Imad al-Din, *Uyun al-akhbar*, vol. 6, ed. al-Yalawi; English translation of the section on the reign of al-Mu'izz by Shainool Jiwa as *The Founder of Cairo: The Fatimid Imam-Caliph al-Mu'izz and His Era* (London, 2013).

exclusive qualification for social standing and power. However, the early Fatimid model of governance inevitably dashed some of these exclusivist aspirations, resulting in particular challenges for the nascent Fatimid state.

The second issue that pressed upon Fatimid governance was the demographic reality of the region. At the inception of Fatimid rule in North Africa, the key ethnic groups were the mainly urban Arabs and the native Berbers. The majority were Muslims, with Sunni Malikism especially dominant amongst the Arabs, their *ulama* unrivalled in influence, followed by a notable community of Hanafis and a small but distinct grouping of Shi'a. While many of the Berbers had embraced either Sunni or Shi'i Islam, a significant number were Kharijis, especially amongst the rural inhabitants of the region. Christian and Jewish communities were also present. Fractiousness between ethnic and religious communities was a recurrent feature in this period. The Berbers themselves divided along old tribal divisions, notably the rival Sanhaja and Zanata confederations, while Maliki Arabs vied with the Hanafis for authority at the Aghlabid court.

The demographic and communal context of North Africa presented the first Fatimid rulers with their second set of challenges. How were the Ismaili imam-caliphs to govern over this majority non-Ismaili population? What was to be the status of Sunni Muslims in a Shi'i Ismaili state? How were their legal systems and public rituals supposed to function? These were among the issues that were of paramount concern to the non-Ismaili subjects of the Fatimid state. They were, therefore, of salient importance to the Fatimids.

Al-Mahdi and al-Qa'im: The Early Fatimid Experience

The primary preoccupation of the first two imam-caliphs, al-Mahdi (r. 909–934) and al-Qa'im (r. 934–946) was defending the nascent Fatimid polity and establishing the parameters of Fatimid governance in ways that responded to the challenges noted earlier.

As Sumaiya Hamdani's erudite study of the early Fatimid texts on the transformation from their *da'wa* to the state demonstrates, among the first constituencies which al-Mahdi had to address was the coterie of *da'i*s who had brought the Fatimids to power, and who were ruling on his behalf prior to his arrival in North Africa.[8]

Their expectation was that the establishment of the Fatimid state would be followed by a fulfilment of the messianic expectations held

---

8   Hamdani, *Between Revolution and State*, pp. 26–29.

by a number of individuals within the *da'wa*. Of paramount importance to the Fatimid Imam-caliph al-Mahdi instead was the establishment of a functional administration for the nascent state. Consequently, tempering messianic and eschatological concerns regarding his reign was of immediate concern. The choice of his own regnal title, *al-Mahdi bi'llah* (the Rightly-Guided through God), which qualified the idea of his messianic status, and the appointment of his son Abu'l-Qasim al-Qa'im bi-Amr Allah as his successor in 912, thus signifying that there was to be a continuation of the Fatimid imamate, were important early measures that he took in this regard.

However, it was the model for Fatimid governance that was adopted that first emerged as the clearest indicator of the move from an exclusivist messianic community, as previously manifest in the *dar al-hijra*, to a more inclusive empire. Contrary to the custom of previously ruling *da'i*s, of maintaining exclusive control over their territories, al-Mahdi appointed administrators from a variety of religious and ethnic backgrounds, including those who had served in the previous Sunni Aghlabid administration. Among these were Ibn al-Qadim, a senior Aghlabid official who was given supervision of the *diwan al-kharaj*, the ministry responsible for taxation and finance, as well as the *barid* (postal service), and Ibn al-Qamudi who was retained for his expertise in supervising the official mint.

Al-Mahdi's approach led to the disaffection of some of the senior *da'i*s, including Abu Abd Allah al-Shi'i, who saw their messianic expectations thwarted. Divested of power and forced to the periphery of affairs, they clamoured for a restitution of what they considered to be their rightful position. They conspired to remove al-Mahdi, leading to their own executions in 911. A period of inter-*da'wa* warfare followed, where some members of the Kutama proclaimed a Berber youth as a rival *mahdi* in 912. Yet, significant elements of the *da'wa* remained loyal to al-Mahdi. This major rupture within the *da'wa* was strikingly similar to the Abbasid experience with their *da'wa* a century and a half earlier.[9] Yet the Fatimids did not follow the Abbasid precedent of dismantling the *da'wa* network, and subsequently it became an integral part of the Fatimid state apparatus. Over time, there developed a symbiotic relationship between the two, such that the *da'wa* became a state-sponsored network for the teaching of Ismaili doctrine and promoting allegiance to the Fatimid imam.

---

[9]   The initial Abbasid *da'wa* was infused with religious and messianic elements revolving around the claim that political authority should revert to the family of the Prophet. It was hastily dismembered however, once the newly installed Abbasid caliphs wished to cast themselves in a proto-Sunni mould, and therefore to rid themselves of their Shi'i, messianic past.

From the onset of Fatimid rule in North Africa, the Sunni Maliki *ulama* who dominated the region virulently opposed the Fatimid regime, an opposition that was catalysed by their hostility to Shi'i movements as well as from the undermining of their own power. Previously, the Maliki *ulama* had dominated the intellectual and religious scene in Qayrawan, functioning as the stewards of doctrine and piety and often exercising a significant degree of influence over the regional rulers. The establishment of the Fatimid state made it impossible for them to continue in this role. The Shi'i imam, the Fatimid caliph, had replaced them as the source of religious authority and legal instruction, thus depriving them of their traditional function in society as well as their means of livelihood.[10]

While the early Fatimid model signalled a generally inclusive attitude towards administration, in matters related to public ritual, law and religious affairs, they resolutely promoted an exclusively Shi'i stance. Not only were Sunnis unable to occupy any religious office, but the promotion of their *madhhab*s was circumscribed.

In 909, the first Ismaili judge (*qadi al-qudat*) was appointed over the staunchly Sunni, Maliki-dominated, city of Qayrawan. The *qadi* al-Marwarrudhi immediately banned the teaching of both the Maliki and Hanafi traditions. Though he was removed from office in 915, the precedent that the office of chief justice in Qayrawan and in other Sunni cities was to be held by a Shi'i official was established. A number of major judicial and administrative figures were appointed from the local Shi'i community, whose numbers now swelled with an influx of Hanafi converts.[11] The early Fatimid model of governance during which Shi'ism was the only publicly sanctioned religious tradition lasted 37 years, spanning the reigns of the first two imam-caliphs.

Opposition to Fatimid rule was most potently expressed however in 943 when the Khariji Berbers mounted a wide-scale anti-Fatimid rebellion led by Abu Yazid al-Nukkari (d. 947), supported in the main by the Zanata Berbers who felt they had been dispossessed following the Fatimid arrival. Forming an alliance with the Maliki *ulama* of Qayrawan, the rebellion threatened the very survival of Fatimid rule in North Africa.[12] Such was the severity of the insurrection that the death of the second Fatimid Imam-caliph al-Qa'im was kept secret until his

---

[10]   Hamdani, *Between Revolution and State*, p. 26.

[11]   Ibid., pp. 26–27.

[12]   The Berber Abu Yazid became a leading proponent of the Nukkar, a schism in the Khariji Ibadi movement, earning him the epithet al-Nukkari. His opposition to the Fatimids culminated in a major revolt in 943, which was only curbed by his defeat and subsequent death in 947. See Halm, *The Empire of the Mahdi*, pp. 329, 393, and S. M. Stern, 'Abu Yazid Makhlad b. Kaydad al-Nukkari', *EI2*.

successor, al-Mansur bi'llah (r. 946–953), had successfully quelled the rebellion.

Al-Mansur: The Broadening of the Fatimid Base

Al-Mansur's reign, rising from the embers of the Khariji revolt, marks the first major milestone in the evolution in the Fatimid model of governance. Following his successful restoration of Fatimid rule over the region, al-Mansur had the option to curb the Maliki *ulama* in Qayrawan and to revert to the earlier policy of appointing a Fatimid official over the city. However, in a change which Madelung notes was a 'momentous development in Islamic government',[13] the Fatimid imam-caliph explicitly recognised the Sunni *madhhab*s as a 'legitimate religious and legal community'. Al-Mansur's gesture of reconciliation with the Malikis was the first time that a Muslim legal school different from that of the ruling dynasty was given official recognition, and indicates that there was a notable broadening of the Fatimid approach to governance.

The shift was underlined by al-Mansur's appointment of a Maliki administrator over Qayrawan instead of an Ismaili or another Shi'i one. This was replicated across other Fatimid regions where Sunni *qadi*s were appointed to towns which had a Sunni majority, while retaining Ismaili *qadi*s in the Fatimid cities of al-Mahdiyya and al-Mansuriyya. Hence, two judicial systems with their own legal codes were given official sanction and support. In all likelihood, it is this development towards more inclusive governance which saw al-Mansur being held in particular regard by the Sunnis of Ifriqiya. As noted by Sumaiya Hamdani, this signalled a shift in the official Fatimid policy towards striking a balance between the propagation of the doctrines of Ismaili Shi'ism and ensuring that some form of acceptance of the Fatimid state by its non-Ismaili subjects could be generated.

However, this conciliatory arrangement presented a new set of challenges that would recur in subsequent phases of Fatimid rule, primarily in the form of disputes as to which code of law took precedence in matters related to public affairs. A case in point was the determination of the public calendar of events. The Ismaili approach of citing the new moon was based on astronomical calculations, whilst the Malikis required the visual sighting of the new moon as a necessary prerequisite for confirmation. This had a bearing on the celebration of communal

---

[13] Wilferd Madelung, 'A Treatise on the Imamate of the Fatimid Caliph al-Mansur bi-Allah', in C. F. Robinson, ed., *Texts, Documents and Artefacts: Islamic Studies in Honour of D.S. Richards* (Leiden, 2003), pp. 69–77.

Muslim festivals. Thus, when in 953 the Maliki judge of Barqa declared the celebration of the Eid was to be held on a different day to the official Fatimid date, this threatened schism in the performance of public ritual, and so he was arrested by the regional governor and eventually executed for refusing to comply with state policy.

An instructive manifestation of the broadening of the previously exclusive relationship between the imam and his believers, to one where the imam was the head of a state who provides oversight to all his people regardless of denomination, much like the shepherd providing care and protection to all his flock (*ra'iyya*), became evident in the reign of al-Qa'im, the predecessor to al-Mansur. The use of the term *ra'iyya* was by then widespread in Muslim political literature when referring to the relationship between the ruler and his subjects. In a sermon (*khutba*) to the people of Alexandria during the first Fatimid expedition to Egypt (913–915), recounted by the Yemeni Ismaili author Idris Imad al-Din, the second Fatimid Imam-caliph al-Qa'im proclaimed, 'The imam does not have the option to reduce the rights of his flock, nor is the flock to decrease the rights of their imam.'[14]

Under al-Mansur, this broadening scope of the conception of the imam's 'duty of care' is evident. In 946, al-Mansur announced a series of tax-remission measures in a sermon to the people of Qayrawan following the depredations of Khariji insurrections. The injunction expressly offered measures designed to alleviate the exactions on all his subjects – Muslim as well as non-Muslim.[15]

Universal Dhimma: Articulating Governance under al-Mu'izz li-Din Allah

It was during the reign of al-Mansur's son and successor, al-Mu'izz li-Din Allah, that the conceptual framing of an inclusive, universal imamate was systemically fostered. Al-Mu'izz's 22-year reign (953–975) witnessed the Fatimid conquest of Egypt in 969. The major expansion of the empire, into Egypt and then Palestine and Syria, brought forth a substantial series of new challenges.

The messianic undercurrent ever-present in the Ismaili *da'wa* from the time of al-Mahdi, was a central doctrinal issue with which al-Mu'izz had to contend. Early Ismaili doctrine in the pre-Fatimid period had postulated the nascent vision of the Mahdi as a single messianic

---

14   Paul E. Walker, *Orations of the Fatimid Caliphs: Festival Sermons of the Ismaili Imams. An Edition of the Arabic Texts and English Translation of Fatimid khutbas* (London, 2009), English text, p. 90, Arabic, p. 4.

15   Walker, *Orations*, p. 100.

saviour.[16] Under al-Muʿizz, the notion of the singular Mahdi was amplified, through the works of al-Qadi al-Nuʿman, to extend the function of a
Mahdi across a successive cycle of imams, each of whom would have his
designated share in realising the fulfilment of the messianic vision.[17] Yet,
while the messianic and eschatological expectations were thus extended
across time and space, and therefore receded to the horizon, the imam's
duty and responsibility to exercise inclusive care and protection, that is
his *dhimma*, was given immediacy.

Iman and Islam

Notions of governance under al-Muʿizz li-Din Allah received a systematic formulation in the writings of al-Qadi al-Nuʿman who was the
preeminent Fatimid jurist and scholar of his age.[18] The large corpus of
his scholarship, covering a range of disciplines including historiography,
adab, and *ta'wil* (esoteric interpretation) works, became major markers
in the formulation of Fatimid doctrine. Being a trusted companion and
disciple of al-Muʿizz, al-Nuʿman's writings had the seal of approval of
the imam himself. Al-Nuʿman was also the architect of the Fatimid legal
code. His magnum opus, the *Daʿaʾim al-Islam* (The Pillars of Islam),
was composed in the first decade of al-Muʿizz's reign and subsequently
became the preeminent legal text of the Fatimid state.[19] Of particular
interest in this chapter is that, alongside its stipulations regarding law,
the *Daʿaʾim* also articulated salient principles of Fatimid governance as
they had developed by the reign of al-Muʿizz.

The *Daʿaʾim* begins with arguably its most original contribution, the
Fatimid Ismaili theory of the imamate.[20] It singles out *walaya*, allegiance
and obedience to the imam as the premier condition of faith (*iman*),
and the first of the seven 'Pillars of Islam'. While resolutely upholding
the universal authority of the Fatimid imam and remaining engaged in
polemic with the major proponents and tenets of other Sunni and Shiʿi
*madhhab*s, the *Daʿaʾim* notably allows for the co-existence of variant
schools of thought in the Fatimid polity. Adopting the schema of the Shiʿi

---

[16] For an exposition of the role of the *mahdi* and messianic currents in Ismaili
history, see Farhad Daftary, 'Hidden Imams and Mahdis in Ismaili History', in B.
Craig, ed., *Ismaili and Fatimid Studies in Honor of Paul E. Walker* (Chicago, 2010),
pp. 1–22.
[17] Ibid., pp. 8–9, particularly note 12, which cites a number of primary and
secondary sources.
[18] Entering in the service of the Fatimids during the reign of al-Mahdi,
al-Nuʿman's lifetime of service culminated in his heading the judiciary as well as
the *daʿwa* during the reigns of al-Mansur and al-Muʿizz.
[19] Ca. 958–960.
[20] Al-Nuʿman, *Daʿaʾim*, English trans., vol. 1, p. xxxi.

Imam Ja'far al-Sadiq (d. 765), al-Nu'man emphasises the recognition of
the Fatimid imam as a prerequisite of *iman*, denoting its possessor as a
mu'min ('faithful', or believer). Nevertheless, he distinguishes between
iman (faith) and *islam* (submission), with the former encompassing the
latter, but the latter not including the former.[21] Thus, according to the
Da'a'im, one could be a Muslim without being a *mu'min*, and therefore
could follow the common Islamic laws. Consequently, when distinguishing between a *mu'min* and a Muslim, or between the *khassa* (elite)
and the *amma* (commoners), the former are privileged but the latter are
not condemned.[22] Rather, the *mu'min*s represent those who have access
to the esoteric (*batin*) understanding of reality, while the latter are those
who remain on the exoteric (*zahir*) plane. In a milieu where proponents
of many other *madhhab*s were engaged in placing their adversaries in
binary categories of belief and unbelief, the *Da'a'im* presented a hierarchical gradation. Thus it paves the way for the co-existence of *madhhab*s, as would be manifested in the premier political document of the
Fatimid age.

The Ahd: Principles of Good Governance

Among the exceptional features of the *Da'a'im* which scholars have
noted, besides the articulation of *islam* and *iman* as mentioned above,
is the inclusion of the document on governance known as the '*ahd* of
Ali' in the *Da'a'im*'s chapter on *jihad*. While the exact provenance of
the *ahd* has been a matter of scholarly debate, nonetheless its inclusion
in the *Da'a'im* is significant. As Wadad al-Qadi, who drew attention to
debates about the provenance of this text, notes, 'The *ahd* represents the
first political constitution of the Fatimid state after its final establishment as a *dawla*. ... With the '*ahd*'s incorporation in the *Da'a'im*, the
Da'a'im came to represent not only the paramount divine constitution
of the Fatimid state but also the civil constitution of the state.'[23] The
inclusion of the *ahd* in the *Da'a'im* thus made it part of al-Mu'izz's code
of practice, and a representation of the Fatimid mode of governance as
developed by his reign.

The *ahd*, as presented in the *Da'a'im*, provides a detailed exposition of good governance. It delineates specific guidelines to governors
and other administrators for governing the subjects of the imam with

---

[21] Represented in the writings of Imam Ja'far al-Sadiq by the image of two concentric circles, of *iman* and *islam*, one within the other; Hamdani, *Between*, p. 67.
[22] Ibid., p. 68.
[23] Wadad al-Qadi, 'An Early Fatimid Political Document', *Studia Islamica*, 48
(1978), p. 104.

justice.[24] While it notes briefly the responsibilities of subjects towards their rulers, its main focus is on enunciating the governors' responsibilities towards the population, to ensure their care and protection.

The *ahd* outlines a vision of an ideal government, prescribing particular requirements for the maintenance of an ideal socio-political order. Its understanding of the political order is one of a complex polity in which the governing officials and the subject population, who are compartmentalised into classes according to their function in society, exist in a cycle of co-dependency, each reliant on the proper functioning of the other.

A salient distinction of this *ahd* is that its principal focus is on the 'the satisfaction of the common people'. Accordingly, a governor is advised, 'Let the most cherished of affairs to you be that which is between the two extremes and the most comprehensive of them in relation to the obedience to God and the satisfaction of the common people.'

Throughout the text of the *ahd*, the subject population of the imam's realms, variously called the people, the subjects (*ra'iyya*) or the commonalty (*al-amma*), are conceived as the source of strength and resilience of the state. The *ahd* asserts that the totality of the affairs of the state, the ability to express power and even its ability to fight enemies all stem from the *amma*. Concurrently, their 'discontent' can be a cause of instability. Their protection and amelioration is therefore necessary to ensure good governance, and the provision of justice for them is vital as, 'it is upon that alone that the welfare of the servants [of God] and countries depends'.[25]

Significantly, the *ahd* is almost non-denominational in its tone, making it noticeably different from its recension in the *Nahj al-balagha*.[26] Its conception of a stable political order is based on ensuring peace as well as protection from harm for all segments of the population. Its prescription on the selection of governors and administrators, therefore, is based principally on merit and competence, so as to protect the people from 'nepotism, tyranny, arrogance, cruelty and other human excesses'. The *ahd* describes bad government as that which unleashes tyranny, arrogance, excessive punishment, cruelty, lust for wealth and possessions, and which causes hardship for the wealthy. It makes particular reference to the ills of favouritism by those in government, namely the undue preferences shown to others and to themselves by administrators and officials.[27]

---

24 Ibid., p. 73.
25 Al-Nu'man, *Da'a'im*, text, vol. 1, p. 355; trans., vol. 1, p. 441.
26 Al-Qadi, 'Early Fatimid Political Document', pp. 81–82.
27 Al-Nu'man, *Da'a'im*, text, vol. 1, p. 345; trans., vol. 1, p. 438.

The *ahd* thus provides a tangible marker for the evolution of Fatimid governance. The broader, more inclusive approach to governance as represented in the *Da'a'im* shows a significant gradation of the development of the Fatimid model from its beginnings as an dominant Ismaili administration concerned with establishing Ismaili legal systems and practices. The Fatimid model as espoused in the reign of al-Mu'izz received a further articulation in the stipulations of the *Aman* document, the Guarantee of Safety which the Fatimid general Jawhar al-Siqilli issued, on the instructions of al-Mu'izz, to the Egyptian population upon the Fatimid entry into Egypt in 969.

The Fatimid Guarantee of Safety

The *Aman* document was publically read out to the people of Egypt on the eve of the Fatimid conquest. It set out a blueprint for Fatimid governance. Its stipulations represent a practical manifestation of the principles of Fatimid governance, namely, an administration that sought social stability, justice and prosperity fostered by the universalist authority of the Fatimid imam-caliph. It reflected the developing conceptual underpinnings that emerged from 60 years of experience at the head of a state in North Africa. It subsequently became the standard by which the Fatimids reigned in Egypt for the next two centuries.

The import of the *Aman* document continued to reverberate in Egyptian historiography as well as in Ismaili writings over the subsequent centuries, such that its full recension survives in the extant writings of two 15th-century scholars, those of the erudite Mamluk historian Taqi al-Din al-Maqrizi as well as of the chief *da'i* of the Tayyibi Ismaili community in Yemen, Idris Imad al-Din.[28]

The Fatimids as the Sole Legitimate Universal Authority

The text of the *Aman* presents the Fatimid imam-caliph as the sole universal legitimate authority over the Muslim *umma*, to whom obedience is mandatory. It refers to al-Mu'izz both as the *amir al-mu'minin* (Commander of the Faithful), the most-commonly used title for the caliph, and as the *wali Allah* (the friend of God), implicitly referring to the Shi'i conception of the imamate. Subsequently, the *Aman* presents the relationship of the Fatimid imam and his

---

[28] The full *Aman* document has been translated and analysed in my earlier work, 'Inclusive Governance: A Fatimid Illustration', in A. B. Sajoo, ed., *A Companion to the Muslim World* (London, 2009), pp. 157–177.

subjects as a covenantal one, whereby the subject population, irrespective of denomination and background, are considered to be under
the *dhimma*, the canopy of the imam-caliph. The *Aman* thus iterates
al-Mu'izz's duty to redress the malaise afflicting the eastern Muslim
world, through his restoration of order in Egypt, offering protection
to the Muslims of Syria against Byzantine advances, and the establishment of the hajj, considered to be among the responsibilities of the
Muslim ruler.[29] The *Aman* then proceeds to offer the imam's *dhimma*
to those who are now directly under his care, proclaiming: 'I guarantee you God's complete and universal safety, eternal and continuous, inclusive and perfect, renewed and confirmed through the days
and recurring through the years.'

In their acceptance of the *Aman* all the Egyptians, regardless of their
religious persuasion, are considered to have entered into a bond with
the Fatimid imam which has divine sanction. Thus it is referred to as
an *ahd* (oath) of God, His *mithaq* (pact) and *dhimma* (guarantee of
protection).[30] The *dhimma* issued in the name of the Fatimid imam is
positioned as being also the *dhimma* offered by the Prophets and the
imams before him.[31]

As Michael Brett has pointed out, the Fatimids, drawing upon Shi'i
Imami notions of authority, were able to expand the narrower legalistic notions of *dhimma* of their time, which referred to the rights and
obligations of the 'people of the book' (*ahl al-kitab*), by reinvigorating
earlier notions of *dhimma* as expressed in the Prophet Muhammad's
own precedent in Medina, where Muslims, Jews and others, formed
part of the nascent *umma*, and were jointly responsible for its safety
and security.[32]

---

[29] The decades preceding 969 had seen a general breakdown of central authority
in the lands of Syria, Arabia and Iraq, initiated by the decline of Abbasid authority.
In Egypt and Syria in particular, the fragmentation of state authority following the
death of the regional ruler, Kafur, led to severe factional fighting and anarchy.
[30] By the 10th century, the issuance of an *Aman* was a distinct legal mechanism
across the Muslim world. It denoted a contractual relationship, usually between
two warring parties, whereby safety and security was guaranteed upon mutually
agreed terms. Its standard function was to guarantee the life and property of the
inhabitants, upon the takeover of a city.
[31] The *Aman* states: 'I promise to fulfil what I have pledged to you, in the name of
God's sacred covenant and protection, and by the covenant of His Prophets and
Messengers, and by the covenant of the Imams, our masters, the Commanders
of the Faithful, may God sanctify their souls, and by the covenant of our lord
and master, the Commander of the Faithful, al-Mu'izz li-Din Allāh, may God's
blessing be upon him.'
[32] Brett, *Rise of the Fatimids*, pp. 299–303.

Through this framework, the *Aman* sought to present a unifying vision of Islam, in which various Muslim traditions, Sunni and Shi'a, were accorded their own place for belief and practice. It thus marks a major milestone in the development of the inclusive Fatimid model. It notes:

> Islam consists of one *sunna* and a *shari'a* followed [by all] … You shall continue in your *madhhab*. You shall be permitted to perform your obligations according to religious scholarship, and to gather for it in your congregational and other mosques, and to remain steadfast in the beliefs of the worthy ancestors from the Companions of the Prophet, may God be pleased with them, and those who succeeded them, the jurists of the cities who have pronounced judgments according to their *madhhab* and *fatwa*s.

The *Aman* proceeds to demarcate how the ideals of the Fatimid model of governance are to be realised. It delineates four areas of responsibility which the Fatimid governance had to address: (a) provision of security and protection for all its subjects; (b) ensuring economic stability; (c) upholding justice; and (d) patronage of religious practice.

The imam's responsibility for the protection of the people and the provision of security form a central concern of the *Aman*. The text vouchsafes i) security of life and possessions, ii) the protection of borders from foreign invasion, iii) protection from crime, poverty and want, including the provision to supervise living conditions.

Thereafter, it focuses on the realisation of economic prosperity as an aspect of the imam's purview of protection. The *Aman* promises the restoration of trade through the safeguarding of trade-routes that had been previously cut off. It also promises monetary reform and the renewal of coinage, the debasement of which had plagued the country previously. It notes that all these measures were to be taken to enable the people 'to earn a living'.

Reflecting the importance of the notion of justice, the *Aman* offers the promise of equity and the eradication of injustice and transgression, with particular case for those who have been oppressed. More specifically, it stipulates the annulment of illegal and unjust taxes.

Finally, as regards the upholding the religious practices of Muslims from various *madhhab*s, the *Aman* promised the maintenance and upkeep of their mosques, their observance of the Ramadan rituals, the collection of the *zakat*, the performance of pilgrimage, and the undertaking of *jihad* as required.

Expressions of the Dhimma

While the *Aman* document enunciated these ideals of governance, it is in their pragmatic application in the Fatimid administration in Egypt that the proverbial rubber met the road. Al-Muʿizz li-Din Allah died in 975, just over two years after his arrival in Egypt. The application of the principles of governance therefore took place in the reign of his successor, al-Aziz (r. 975–996). These were realised through the creation of a broadly inclusive administration, a judicial system which accommodated the Sunni legal systems and the upholding of the various schools' practises of ritual worship which extended to the sponsorship and protection of non-Muslim places. Nonetheless, their approach also met with significant challenges. These included issues of ritual performance that contravened Fatimid Shiʿi practice, the issue of a plurality of legal systems in the public sphere, and critically, challenges arising from inter-confessional boundaries, expectations and notions of privilege.

Broadening Administration

The arrival of the Fatimids in 969 raised the possibility of an overhaul of the previous administration Instead, the Fatimid general Jawhar confirmed the continuity in office of the senior administrators from the previous Ikhshidid regime. Accordingly, Jaʿfar b. al-Furat was reconfirmed as the chief minister of the state.[33] Importantly, North African bureaucrats were appointed in joint positions with their Egyptian counterparts. This allowed for a gradual yet effective transition of expertise from one administration to the other.

Abu al-Faraj Yaʿqub b. Killis (d. 991), the first Fatimid vizier, was among the most illustrious administrators of his age. Having previously converted to Islam from Judaism, Yaʿqub's exceptional acumen led to his rapid promotion through the Fatimid state bureaucracy to become the first Fatimid vizier in Egypt. It was during his tenure that leading figures from both the Christian and Jewish communities achieved unrivalled prominence in the Fatimid judiciary.[34]

The Legal System

The integration of Sunni judges in the Fatimid judiciary illustrates the negotiation between the upholding of their own universalist claim, and

---

[33] Al-Maqrizi, *Towards a Mediterranean Empire*, p. 86.
[34] Isa b. Nasturus and Menashe b. Ibrahim respectively. The subsequent ascent of Fahd b. Ibrahim, the Christian fiscal administrator, during the final years of al-Aziz's reign further testified to the trend.

maintaining the legal validity of other Muslim schools of law. Upon his accession over Egypt, al-Mu'izz retained the Maliki *qadi* Abu Tahir as his Chief Justice, a role which the latter had occupied in the previous Ikhshidid administration. Reminiscent of the policy of co-existence followed by al-Mansur, al-Mu'izz also appointed a son of al-Qadi al-Nu'man, Ali b. al-Nu'man, alongside the Sunni *qadi*, an arrangement that continued under al-Aziz, until paralysis led the Sunni *qadi* to present his resignation in 976. Of the 16 years Abu Tahir served as chief *qadi* of Egypt, seven were thus in the service of the Fatimid caliphate.[35] Jurists from different Sunni and Shi'i *madhhab*s being appointed to the judiciary was fairly commonplace in subsequent Fatimid reigns.[36]

Ritual and Worship

During al-Aziz's reign, Muslim and non-Muslim communities were by and large permitted the performance of their religious rituals and obligations. The Fatimid sponsorship of mosques and congregational spaces was retained not only for the construction of new Fatimid mosques such as al-Azhar and al-Anwar, but was also extended to Sunni religious spaces. The latitude afforded to the Christian and Jewish communities in the maintenance of their places of worship and the performance of their religious rituals became one of the notable features of al-Aziz's reign, as recorded by Severus Ibn al-Muqaffa (d. 987), the Coptic bishop of al-Ashmunayn, who was among the most well-regarded theologians and writers of the Coptic Church in the early medieval period. It was the safeguarding of the Coptic spaces of worship by al-Mu'izz and al-Aziz that led Ibn al-Muqaffa to remark that there was 'great peace for the churches' in the reigns of these two sovereigns.

---

[35] Qadi Abu Tahir was born into a family of *qadi*s, and he himself had previously held positions as the *qadi* of Baghdad, Wasit and Damascus, and was one of the noted figures who set out from Fustat to negotiate the *Aman* with the Fatimid general, Jawhar. See al-Maqrizi, *Kitab al-Muqaffa*, ed. M. al-Yalawi (Beirut, 1991), vol. 5, pp. 189–190.

[36] The sources record that on his appointment as the Chief Justice, Ali b. al-Nu'man, nominated two deputies: his brother, Muhammad b. al-Nu'man and a Sunni Shafi'i jurist, Hasan ibn Khalil. Muhammad b. al-Nu'man in turn appointed a Hanafi jurist, Ibn Abi'l-Awwam, as the *qadi* of Fustat. The appointment of Ithna'ashari Shi'i jurists to the Fatimid judiciary is also recorded. In 991 Qadi Abd al-Aziz, the son of Qadi Muhammad b. al-Nu'man appointed a body of *ashraf* to pronounce judgments in the Mosque of Amr based on the *madhhab* of the *ahl al-bayt*. The following year, an Ithna'ashari Shi'i was commissioned with a similar responsibility. These references demonstrate that the Fatimid judiciary drew upon scholars from a variety of Shi'i as well as Sunni *madhhab*s.

The functioning of Christian religious life was further realised in the state protection of the performance of their public festivals. Al-Maqrizi notes in his *Khitat* that numerous Christian festivals were celebrated during the Fatimid era, including the Coptic New Year (Nawruz), the Nativity (*al-Milad*), the Epiphany (*al-Ghitas*), and Maundy Thursday amongst others. In a number of instances during the reigns of al-Aziz and his successors, the sources mention the Fatimid sovereigns' participation in the celebrations.

Challenges and Legacies

The Fatimid model of governance was not without its challenges, many of which came to the fore in the subsequent phases of their reign. These included issues relating to the prevailing custom in matters such as the sighting of the new moon, where there were significant variances between Sunni and Ismaili practice. Amongst the most critical challenges however were those concerned with managing the expectations of different religious communities. Muslim expectations of privilege vis-à-vis Christians and Jews were at times met by incidents of self-promotion and nepotism by the latter when in positions of power in the Fatimid administration. The sources note the reaction of certain segments of the Muslim population against the ascent of both Christians and Jews in the administration of al-Aziz. Elsewhere, cases are reported in al-Mu'izz and al-Aziz's time when some hard-line Sunni clerics protested vociferously against the rebuilding of churches in Fustat. The work was nonetheless allowed to progress, under the protection of Fatimid troops. On the other hand, al-Aziz is similarly recorded to have taken action against Christian bureaucrats who were leading figures in the administration when accounts of self-promotion at Muslim expense were brought to his attention. Among the distinctive social groups with which the first Fatimid sovereigns in Egypt were able to forge alliances were the *ashraf*, the lineal descendants of the Prophet, whose privileged status was well established by the 10th century. Their shared lineage afforded a common bond which enabled the *ashraf* to benefit from the Fatimid presence in Egypt, as much as it enabled the Fatimids to establish their rule in the region.

During the reigns of the later Fatimid imam-caliphs, it was the contest between power brokers from different ethnic groups at the Fatimid court that led to factional struggles and even outbreaks of violence from time to time. The divergent personalities and approaches of the Fatimid sovereigns and their overshadowing by the viziers from the time of Badr al-Jamali (d. 1094) onwards had a significant impact on the nature of Fatimid governance. Nonetheless, the Fatimid model of governance as articulated in the formative period of Fatimid rule, continued to remain an ideal point to which each successive Fatimid imam-caliph aimed to aspire, as well as the bedrock upon which they aimed to build the edifice of their reign during two centuries of Fatimid rule in Egypt – a unique Ismaili Shi'i legacy in Egypt.

Further Reading

Brett, Michael. *The Rise of the Fatimids: The World of the Mediterranean and the Middle East in the Fourth Century of the Hijra, Tenth Century CE*. Leiden, 2001.

Daftary, Farhad. *The Isma'ilis: Their History and Doctrines*. 2nd ed., Cambridge, 2007.

Fowden, Garth. *Empire to Commonwealth: Consequences of Monotheism in Late Antiquity*. Princeton, NJ, 1993.

Halm, Heinz. *The Empire of the Mahdi*, tr. M. Bonner. Leiden, 1996.

Hamdani, Sumaiya. *Between Revolution and State: The Path to Fatimid Statehood*. London, 2006.

Idris Imad al-Din. *Uyun al-akhbar wa funun al-athar*, vol. 5 and part of vol. 6, ed. Muhammad al-Yalawi. Beirut, 1985; English translation of the reign of al-Mu'izz by Shainool Jiwa as *The Founder of Cairo: The Fatimid Imam-caliph al-Mu'izz and His Era*. London, 2013.

Jiwa, Shainool. 'Inclusive Governance: A Fatimid Illustration', in Amyn B. Sajoo, ed., *A Companion to the Muslim World*. London, 2009, pp. 157–177.

Madelung, Wilferd. 'A Treatise on the Imamate of the Fatimid Caliph al-Mansur bi-Allah', in C. F. Robinson, ed., *Texts, Documents and Artefacts: Islamic Studies in Honour of D. S. Richards*. Leiden, 2003, pp. 69–77.

al-Maqrizi, Taqi al-Din. *Itti'az al-hunafa bi-akhbar al-a'imma al-Fatimiyyin al-khulafa*, vol. 1, ed., Jamal al-Din al-Shayyal. Cairo, 1967; English translation of the reign of al-Mu'izz by Shainool Jiwa as *Towards a Shi'i Mediterranean Empire: Fatimid Egypt and the Founding of Cairo*. London, 2009.

al-Nu'man, al-Qadi Abu Hanifa. *Da'a'im al-Islam*, ed. Asaf A. A. Fyzee. Cairo, 1951–1960. English trans. A. A. A. Fyzee, revised by Ismail K. Poonawala, as *The Pillars of Islam*. New Delhi, 2002–2004.

—— *Iftitah al-da'wa*, tr. Hamid Haji as *Founding the Fatimid State: The Rise of an Early Islamic Empire*. London, 2006.

al-Qadi, Wadad, 'An Early Fatimid Political Document', *Studia Islamica*, 48 (1978), pp. 71–108.

Walker, Paul E., ed. and trans. *Orations of the Fatimid Caliphs: Festival Sermons of the Ismaili Imams*. London, 2009.

7

Moral Authority in the Safawid State

Rula J. Abisaab

Leading Shi'i *ulama* in Ottoman Syria – most notably in Jabal Amil and Balabak al-Hirmil in modern-day Lebanon – engaged in fateful discourses beginning in the mid-14th century, building especially on the *ijtihadi* (interpretive) rationalism of the scholars of Hilla in Iraq as part of an innovative approach to law.[1] The intellectual developments at the Amili *madrasa*s reached their peak in the first half of the 16th century. Two outstanding Amili jurists or *mujtahid*s, Ali b. Abd al-Ali al-Karaki (ca. 1465–1534), known as al-Muhaqqiq al-Thani and Zayn al-Din al-Juba'i known as al-Shahid al-Thani (1506–1558), dominated the centres of Shi'i legal learning. They were to elicit enthusiasm as well as open resistance among a generation of scholars, with major ethical implications.

The two jurists and their students preserved an organic link to the Hilli tradition, and continued to adapt elements of the Shafi'i school to resolve methodological and conceptual problems within their juristic tradition. They turned to the verification of the four *hadith* collections,[2] the rationalisation of legal sources and the organisation of substantive law and its principles.[3] Al-Karaki was recognised for his commentaries on the legal works of al-Muhaqqiq al-Hilli (1205–1277), al-Allama al-Hilli (1250–1325), and Muhammad b. Makki al-Amili known as al-Shahid al-Awwal (1333–1384).[4] His thinking ranged over an enormous number of substantive rulings (*furu*), as reflected in his collections of legal inquiries (*masa'il*) and injunctions (*fatawa*, sing. *fatwa*). Al-Shahid al-Thani too, and his son Hasan Sahib al-Ma'alim, applied

---

[1] In this chapter, the term Shi'a refers to the Imami Twelver Shi'a unless indicated otherwise.

[2] These collections are *al-Kafi*, *Man la yahduruhu al-faqih*, *Tahdhib al-ahkam* and *al-Istibsar*.

[3] A. Tabataba'i, *Riyad al-masa'il* (Qumm, 1992), vol. 1 pp. 77–82.

[4] R. J. Abisaab, 'Karaki', *Encyclopedia Iranica*, vol. 15, pp. 544–547. See also M. al-Hassun, *Muqtatafat min mawsu'at hayat al-Muhaqqiq al-Karaki wa atharihi* (Beirut, 2003), pp. 20–30, 60–62.

diverse aspects of al-Allama's *usuli* (rationalist) legal thought and his methods of *hadith* verification, which distinguished between sound, good, reliable and weak accounts. The Amilis shaped the discipline of *dirayat al-hadith* (scrutiny of *hadith* reports and their verification) and developed its link to the juristic tradition.[5] *Kalam* and logic were useful in providing the Hilli and Amili jurists with forms of syllogistic and theological reasoning necessary for expanding the extra-textual sources of the law.[6] Even though al-Shahid al-Thani did not set foot in Iran, his writings travelled widely from one circle of legal learning to another in Iraq and Iran, and especially among al-Karaki's students. Meanwhile, the *usuli* juristic system became the prevalent and most authoritative basis for deriving the law under the Safawid monarchs in the 16th century. Through this system, the law was derived on the basis of the Quran, the *hadith*s, the consensus of the jurists and the rationalist principles of *ijtihad*. As it grew and gained support, the *usuli* system was attacked by a diverse group of scholars who saw it as an unwarranted shift in the ethical foundations of the Shi'i tradition. Among these critics were the *akhbari*s who rejected various aspects of *ijtihad* and *hadith* categorisation, as well as the high value given to extra-textual sources in deriving the law. They feared that the spiritual authority of the imams would be undermined through *hadith* scrutiny, and they challenged decisively the legal authority of the *mujtahid*s and the ethical basis for their emulation by the believer.

The Safawid shahs' espousal of Shi'ism in Iran during the early 16th century gave several Amili *mujtahid*s the opportunity to work within the rubric of a pre-modern state, which added another layer of ethical tension to the issue of the jurist's association with temporal rulers. These *mujtahid*s started applying formally the legal obligations and prohibitions defined by the Ja'fari school of law, hence the appearance of the first works devoted to legal principles (*al-qawa'id al-fiqhiyya*). Such works reflected a practical need to make available to the jurist and judge the range of legal cases and diverse rulings on them as well as addressing new ones.[7] The state's patronage of the *mujtahid*s starting with al-Karaki, allowed them in turn to play visible socio-political roles in Iranian society. With respect to al-Karaki, his association with the

---

[5]   Al-Shahid al-Thani, Zayn al-Din al-Amili, *al-Diraya* (Tehran, 1984), pp. 4–8; Hasan Sahib al-Ma'alim, *Muntaqa al-jum'an*, ed. A. Akbar al-Ghaffari (Qumm, 1362 Sh./1983); Baha al-Din al-Amili, *al-Wajiza fi al-diraya*, ed. M. al-Gharbawi, nos. 32 and 33, Year 8 (Qumm, 1992), pp. 387–439.

[6]   Al-Shahid al-Thani, Zayn al-Din al-Amili, *Rasa'il al-Shahid al-Thani*, vol. 2, ed. R. al-Mukhtari (Qumm, 2001), pp. 762–767.

[7]   See al-Shahid al-Awwal, *al-Qawa'id wa'l-fawa'id*, ed. Abd al-Hadi al-Hakim (Qumm, n.d.), vol. 1, pp. 4, 6, 92, 173; vol. 2, pp. 65–66, 133, 389.

shahs, his ruling on Friday prayer (*salat al-jum'a*), and his acceptance of Shah Tahmasp's gifts raised a host of ethical and moral considerations.[8] A number of *ulama* and *mutakallimun* (rationalist theologians) challenged his legal authority.

This chapter sheds light first on the authorisation of the *usuliyya* or what I term *ijtihadi* rationalism in 16th-century Iran, particularly through the writings of al-Shahid al-Thani and al-Karaki. As religious guides, these jurists were eager to implement the *shari'a*'s legal-ethical principles in a Shi'i society. Yet the methods, which they used to derive the law, and the new connections that emerged between legal authority and Safawid state patronage, had critical ethical consequences. I will discuss al-Karaki's enthusiasm for service to the Safawids as a means of spreading and systematising Shi'i law, as well as attaining personal power and economic stability. I will then turn to al-Shahid al-Thani and his approach to Safawid rule, and the state of legal scholarship in Iran.

Secondly, the chapter will engage with the lively controversy over the status of the Friday prayer, on which al-Karaki, and al-Shahid al-Thani had much to say.[9] I will discuss the overall implications of the *mujtahids*' diverse rulings, and the laity's increasing confusion. I will argue that the issuing of contradictory rulings on the Friday prayer, while being an integral feature of *ijtihadi* rationalism, led to an ethical impasse because the Friday prayer was tied to a central tenet in *usul al-din* (foundations of religion), namely the Imamate and the imam's authority. Doubts were raised among believers, be they scholars or laypersons, about the moral status of the prayer during the absence (in occultation) of the imam. It was no longer clear whether observing the Friday prayer was categorically permissible (*ja'iz*), or permissible under certain conditions, or obligatory for each and every believer (*wajib ayni*), or optional (*wajib takhyiri*) under certain conditions, or simply prohibited (*muharram*). The wide range of rulings also raised misgivings about the action (*amal*) to be taken by the believer in response to this knowledge. The divergence in the *mujtahids*' rulings on some legal questions displaced at times the ontological relation of these rulings (*ahkam*) to actions. In other words, it created confusion among believers as to whether the rulings correspond

---

[8]   On these rulings, see R. J. Abisaab, 'Karaki', *Encyclopedia Iranica*, vol. 15, pp. 544–547.

[9]   In exploring questions of Islamic ethics and moral philosophy related to this paper, I have consulted especially A. K. Reinhart, 'Islamic Law as Islamic Ethics', *Journal of Religious Ethics*, 11 (1986), pp. 186–203; W. Hallaq, 'Can the Shariah Be Restored?', in Y. Haddad and B. Stowasser, ed., *Islamic Law and the Challenge of Modernity* (Lanham, 2004); F. S. Carney, 'Some Aspects of Islamic Ethics', *Journal of Religion*, 63 (1983), pp. 149–174; and M. A. Amir-Moezzi, *The Divine Guide in Early Shi'ism: The Sources of Esotericism in Islam* (Albany, NY, 1994).

to good and evil in the real world, and whether they can reveal the actual moral knowledge intended by God.[10] Clearly, in situations where the ethical boundaries of the law become vague and the consequences of the legal act (observing the Friday prayer) are great, believers take precaution as the best action, in this case, preferring not to observe the Friday prayer. The tenets of Imamism, and the moral commitment to the Imamate as a locus of spiritual and temporal authority, seemed to have transcended the ethical guidelines offered by the *mujtahids* through these rulings.

Promoting *ijtihadi* Rationalism: al-Muhaqqiq al-Karaki and al-Shahid al-Thani

It is widely recognised that the migration of Arab scholars from Syria's Jabal Amil in Syria to Safawid Iran during the 16th and 17th centuries was momentous, and that a group of them came to shape Iran's legal, doctrinal and juridical history.[11] The teaching of the legal sciences was sophisticated and deep-rooted in Jabal Amil (and by extension, Balabak al-Hirmil), a region which comprises about three square miles, that is, approximately, a section of the district of Isfahan. It is during the Safawid period and through the agency of the Amilis that diverse branches of Perso-Arab intellectual inquiry brought forth new ideas and practices.

Shah Tahmasp's reign started in 1524, when he was only 10 years old, supported by the Qizilbash leader, Div Sultan Rumlu, his vicegerent and the actual decision-maker.[12] As various Qizilbash factions competed fiercely for ascendancy at the court in Tabriz, Div Sultan was eliminated. It was not until 1533 that Tahmasp reaffirmed his sovereignty over Iran against various military threats. Sufi perceptions and heterodox beliefs continued to feature in the religious experience of Tahmasp, but *shari'a*-based piety and reverence for the Prophet and the Twelve Imams became prominent.[13] Kishvar Rizvi notes that in the years 1537–1541, 'entirely new structures were erected' in the vicinity of the Ardabil shrine of Shaykh Safi which,

[10] See Reinhart, '*Islamic Law as Islamic Ethics*', pp. 193–194.

[11] See, for example, S. A. Arjomand, *The Shadow of God and the Hidden Imam* (Chicago, 1984); and R. J. Abisaab, 'Shi'ite 'Ulama of Jabal 'Amel', *Encyclopedia Iranica*, vol. 14, pp. 305–309; and her 'The '*Ulama* of Jabal 'Amil in Safavid Iran, 1501–1736: Marginality, Migration and Social Change', *Iranian Studies*, 27 (1994), pp. 103–122.

[12] C. P. Mitchell, 'Tahmasp I', *Encyclopaedia Iranica*.

[13] Tahmasb Safawi, *Tadhkira-yi Shah Tahmasb*, ed. A. Safari (Tehran, 1984), pp. 23, 33, 36–37.

would alter not only the spatial, but conceptual, boundaries of the shrine – away from a Sufism-centered institution focused on the cult of Shaykh Safi towards a dynastic edifice centered on the person of the Shah. The altered focus did not, however, undermine the customary practices of the Safawid order in which the Shah continued to play a central role.[14]

The impetus to implement standardised Shi'a belief and orthopraxy – carried out within the rubric of *ijtihadi* rationalism – was not only crucial to Safawid legitimacy but also the basis for legal organisation and social discipline in late medieval Islamic society. Rudi Matthee also draws attention to the need to control the 'unruly tribal element' and achieve 'unity through loyalty, leading to a growing emphasis on the Safawid State as a Shi'i polity – in contradistinction to the Sunni states surrounding it'.[15] Further, Shah Tahmasp's personal piety, especially his concern with ritual ablution, contributed to his reliance on clerics for guidance and remedy.

The reign of Shah Tahmasp, the longest of any Safawid monarch, witnessed the young state's increasing commitment to the observation of the *shari'a* on the basis of the Ja'fari school of law.[16] The Qizilbash's heterodox beliefs did not prevent them from supporting a number of Amili *ulama*, forging at times a practical alliance with them against crypto-Sunni Iranian notables. The military *amir*s were instrumental to the ascendancy of al-Karaki at the Safawid court and the promotion of his grandson, Husayn al-Mujtahid.[17] Around 1510 when al-Karaki was still in Najaf, he was given official recognition by Tahmasp's father, Shah Isma'il (r. 1501–1524), who offered him land grants and revenues (*kharaj*) as a hereditary endowment.[18]

---

[14]   Kishvar Rizvi, *The Safavid Dynastic Shrine: Architecture, Religion and Power in Early Modern Iran* (London, 2010), p. 79.

[15]   Rudi Matthee, *Persia in Crisis: Safavid Decline and the Fall of Isfahan* (London, 2012), pp. 175–176.

[16]   On religious syncretism, orthopraxy and the Amili *ulama* in Safawid Iran, see Arjomand, *The Shadow of God*, pp. 109–121, 132–144; his 'Two Decrees of Shah Tahmasp Concerning Statecraft and the Authority of Shaykh 'Ali al-Karaki', in his *Authority and Political Culture in Shi'ism* (Albany, NY, 1988), pp. 250–262; B. Scarcia Amoretti, 'Religion in the Timurid and Safavid Periods', in *The Cambridge History of Iran*, vol. 6: *The Timurid and Safavid Periods*, ed. Peter Jackson and L. Lockhart (Cambridge, 1986), pp. 640–646.

[17]   R. J. Abisaab, 'New Ropes for Royal Tents: Shaykh-i Baha'i and the Imperial Order of Shah 'Abbas (996–1038/1587–1629)', *Studies on Persianate Societies*, 1 (2003), pp. 29–56.

[18]   Ali b. Abd al-Ali al-Karaki, *Rasa'il al-Muhaqqiq al-Karaki*, ed. M. al-Hassun (Qumm, 1988), vol. 1, p. 237; H. M. Tabataba'i, *Kharaj in Islamic Law* (London, 1983), pp. 47, 54, 56–58.

Even though al-Shahid al-Thani's legal concepts and methodology were circulating in Shi'i *madrasa*s across the region, it was al-Karaki who was the most immediate and prominent manifestation of the Amili's *ijtihadi* rationalism in Najaf and Iran. Al-Karaki established new rulings and issued injunctions in various categories of Shi'i law.[19] He wrote commentaries on al-Allama's *Irshad al-adhhan, Mukhtalaf al-Shi'a* and *Tahrir al-ahkam*. Al-Karaki's *Jami al-maqasid* became the most useful and lucid commentary on al-Allama's *Qawa'id al-ahkam* at the time. Al-Karaki's commentary on *al-Alfiyya* of al-Shahid al-Awwal and his own treatise on worship and ablution, known as *al-Risala al-Ja'fariyya*, circulated widely among Iranian students and scholars. The circulation of these writings and others involving more elaborate legal discussions helped spread *usuli* approaches to *hadith* and methods of legal argumentation. Based on a collection of legal rulings provided by al-Karaki to Safawid governors and rulers, Ni'matullah al-Jaza'iri, an *akhbari* scholar, argued that al-Karaki played a crucial role in implementing the religious obligations and prohibitions, fixing prayer times as well as 'punishing criminals and the lawbreakers in Iran', in other words, creating through the *shari'a*, the basis for social discipline and order.[20] Another traditionist scholar, Yusuf al-Bahrani, noted that Tahmasp considered al-Karaki more qualified to decide clerical appointments than himself, and that through the Safawids, al-Karaki came to 'acquire' deputyship of the imam. Tahmasp pronounced that 'whomsoever [al-Karaki] dismisses from a post cannot be rehired and whomsoever he hires cannot be removed'.[21]

Al-Karaki's and al-Shahid al-Thani's methods and ideas took on a life of their own, having been adapted by numerous Iranian students and scholars. By looking at one group of students from Astarabad who studied with al-Karaki, we can perceive the spread of their legal scholarship and the promotion of Hilli-Amili *ijtihadi* rationalism.[22] These students studied works such as *Shara'i al-Islam* by al-Muhaqqiq al-Hilli

---

[19]　Muhammad Baqir al-Khwansari, *Rawdat al-jannat fi ahwal al-ulama wa'l-sadat* (Beirut, 1991), vol. 4, pp. 346–360; M. Afandi Isfahani, *Riyad al-ulama wa hiyad al-fudala*, ed. S. Ahmad al-Husayni (Qumm, 1981), vol. 3, pp. 441–460; Muhsin al-Amin, *A'yan al-Shi'a*, ed. H. al-Amin (Beirut, 1986), vol. 8, p. 208. Several students wrote commentaries on al-Karaki's *al-Risala al-Ja'fariyya* including his legal agent in Yazd, Yahya Sharaf al-Din b. Husayn b. al-Ishra al-Bahrani al-Yazdi. See A. Buzurg Tehrani, *Tabaqat alam al-Shi'a: Ihya al-dathir min al-qarn al-ashir* (Tehran, 1952), pp. 45, 205, 274.

[20]　Tabataba'i, *Riyad al-masa'il*, vol. 1, p. 90.

[21]　Ibid., pp. 90–91.

[22]　A few Astarabadi scholars also studied with Shaykh Ibrahim al-Qatifi, al-Shahid al-Thani and Husayn b. Abd al-Samad. See Tehrani, *Ihya al-dathir*, pp. 145–146, 205.

as well as *Qawaʿid* and *Tahdhib al-ahkam* by al-Allama, presumably through the commentaries of al-Karaki. Others studied and commented on al-Karaki's treatises dealing with worship and doctrinal questions. Sayyid Sharaf al-Din Ali al-Husayni Astarabadi, for one, wrote a commentary on al-Karaki's treatise, *al-Jaʿfariyya* known as *al-Fawaʾid al-gharawiyya*. He and Muhammad b. Abi Talib Astarabadi each translated into Persian al-Karaki's anti-Sunni polemical work, *Nafahat al-lahut fi laʿn al-jibt waʾl-taghut*. Abu al-Maʿali b. Badr al-Din al-Hasan al-Husayni al-Gharawi Astarabadi translated *al-Jaʿfariyya* into Persian and seems to have composed a treatise on questions of law, theology and logic.[23] Abu al-Maʿali's *Kad al-yamin wa araq al-jabin* addressed six knotty legal questions relating to inheritance (*mirath*); it was read and copied by al-Shahid al-Thani. Mir Safi al-Din Muhammad b. Jamal al-Din Astarabadi produced a commentary on al-Allama's *Tahdhib al-wusul ila ilm al-usul* in jurisprudence.[24] Meanwhile, a number of scholars from Astarabad were keen on circulating major works of law, jurisprudence and *hadith* scrutiny (*diraya*) authored by the *mujtahid*s. Muhammad b. Abd al-Rahim b. Dawud Astarabadi, for instance, copied a volume of al-Karaki's marginalia on *Qawaʿid* in 1524 in Najaf, while Muhammad Ashraf and Muhammad Baqir, the sons of Zayn al-Abidin Astarabadi, copied several legal treatises in 1561 (during their residence in Astarabad), most of them belonging to al-Karaki and some belonging to al-Shahid al-Thani. In 1571–1572, while residing in Shiraz, Muhammad Ashraf Astarabadi copied the *Dirayat al-hadith* of al-Shahid al-Thani, a critical *usuli* work categorising and scrutinising Imami *hadith*. Muhammad Baqir further copied al-Karaki's *Salat al-jumʿa* and al-Shahid al-Thani's concise treatise, *Takhfif al-ibad fi bayan ahwal al-ijtihad*, a work arguing that *ijtihad* was a legal duty incumbent upon jurists in every age, and that the legal opinions of a dead *mujtahid* are invalid.[25] Al-Karaki had discussed the conditions of *ijtihad* in *Risala fiʾl-man an taqlid al-mayt* and *Risala fiʾl-usul*, which reflected the convergence of his and al-Shahid al-Thani's views on the impermissibility of emulating a dead jurist, and the necessity of turning to a living jurist for legal guidance. Curiously, Mir Fadlullah Astarabadi's treatise, *Taqlid al-mayt*, challenges the views

---

[23] Afandi, *Riyad al-ulama*, vol. 5, p. 466. See Tehrani, *Ihya al-dathir*, p. 249.

[24] Ibid., p. 205.

[25] Jamal al-Din b. Abd Allah Jurjani wrote a commentary on al-Allama's juristic work, *Tahdhib al-wusul ila ilm al-usul*. See Tehrani, *Ihya al-dathir*, p. 121. Abd al-Salam Astarabadi copied al-Allama's *Irshad al-adhhan* from a copy owned by his teacher Muhammad Dawud Astarabadi in 1558–1559. Taj al-Din Hasan Astarabadi Jurjani, a student of al-Karaki also copied *Irshad*. See Tehrani, *Ihya al-dathir*, pp. 48–49.

of al-Shahid al-Thani against the legal emulation of a deceased jurist.[26] The objection to such emulation became an *usuli* tenet at the time and appears to have played itself out in different ways among the *mujtahid*s.

Sealing *ijtihad*: An Oxymoron?

In 1532, Shah Tahmasp proclaimed al-Karaki the deputy (*na'ib*) of the Hidden Imam and depicted him as the 'seal of *mujtahids*' (*khatam al-mujtahidin*).[27] This proclamation was a novelty not only to the Iranian scholars and theologians, but also to the Amili *mujtahid*s themselves who shaped the tradition of *ijtihadi* rationalism. To be sure, asserting that a *mujtahid* is the ultimate and final legal authority let alone the 'deputy' (though in a limited manner) of the Hidden Imam violated the pluralistic nature of legal authority as envisaged by these jurists. Jurists who meet the conditions for practising *ifta* (deriving legal opinions) all have equal claims to legal authority, even if they cannot guarantee that each and every legal ruling will be correct. The *mujtahid*s had rejected the legal maxim prevalent among Sunni jurists that 'every *mujtahid* is correct' (*kull mujtahid musib*).[28] For the Shi'a, *mujtahid*s may issue erroneous rulings but since they are morally obligated to provide legal guidance to believers, they attain a reward merely by striving to derive the law. Al-Karaki and al-Shahid al-Thani were among first leading *mujtahid*s to reject the opinions of *al-mujtahid al-mayt* (dead jurist), a position, which became prevalent among the *usuli*s afterwards.[29] Al-Karaki insisted that there was a consensus (*ijma*) against the emulation of a dead *mujtahid*.[30] He proceeded to delineate three reasons for its impermissibility. First, with the passing of the *mujtahid* his pronouncements also become 'deceased', and can no longer carry legal weight. Second, since

---

[26]   Al-Shahid al-Thani wrote a treatise on the same question presumably responding to al-Husayn b. al-Hasan al-Amili, who sent this treatise in turn to Mir Fadlullah Astarabadi.

[27]   Abd al-Husayn Khatunabadi, *Waqa'i al-sinin wa'l-a'wam* (Tehran, 1352 Sh./1973), p. 360; Iskandar Beg Munshi, *Tarikh-i alam-ara-yi Abbasi*, ed. M. Isma'il Rizvani (Tehran, 1957), vol. 1, pp. 229–231; Khwansari, *Rawdat al-jannat*, vol. 7, pp. 168–169; and W. Madelung, 'al-Karaki', *EI2*, vol. 4, p. 610.

[28]   Abu Ishaq Ibrahim b. Ali b. Yusuf al-Shirazi, *al-Luma fi usul al-fiqh* (Beirut, 2003), p. 130; Abu Hamid al-Ghazali, *al-Mustasfa fi ilm al-usul* (Beirut, 1994), pp. 361–362. Most, but not all, Mu'tazilis and Ash'aris accepted the validity of the maxim that every *mujtahid* is correct with respect to questions of substantive law.

[29]   Al-Fadil al-Tuni, Abd Allah b. Muhammad al-Bushrawi al-Khurasani, *al-Wafiya fi usul al-fiqh*, ed. M. Husayn al-Ridawi al-Kashmiri (Qumm, 2013), pp. 301–304.

[30]   Rasul Ja'fariyan, *Kawushha-yi tazih dar bab-i ruzgar-i Safawi* (Qumm, 1383/1964–1965), pp. 40–41.

the indicants (*dala'il*) upon which the jurist relies to issue an opinion are probative (*zanni*), the authoritativeness (*hujjiyya*) of his opinion is temporary (*waqti*). The basis for this authoritativeness lies then in the *mind* of the *mujtahid*; when he dies, such authoritativeness departs with him. Finally, the believer is enjoined to emulate the most knowledge-able and pious (*awra*) jurist. This is not possible with respect to deceased jurists.[31]

On the matter of al-Karaki's status as 'seal of *mujtahid*s', the circle of *usuli* jurists at large could not accept this either literally or as binding in any way. Indeed, al-Karaki subscribed to a pluralistic juristic ethic where no one *mujtahid* is 'correct', even if there is one 'correct' legal opinion. *Mujtahid*s like him found the attempt of qualified jurists to derive the correct opinion ethical in and of itself, and thus accepted the multiple bases of legal authority within the circle of Twelver Shi'i jurists. To his opponents, however, al-Karaki appeared to be acting upon the titles bestowed on him by the shah, hence breaching the ideal ethical disentanglement from worldly positions and ambitions.

Another jurist from Jabal Amil, Husayn b. Abd al-Samad al-Juba'i al-Harithi al-Amili (1512–1576), who also joined the Safawid court, strongly challenged the shah's bestowal of the title on al-Karaki. He took it upon himself to change the ruling of al-Karaki on the Friday prayer, and to undermine the role of the ruler in ranking jurists. Ibn Abd al-Samad tried to convince Tahmasp I of the need to re-implement public obser-vance of the Friday prayer for the benefit of common believers. Aiming to restore virtue to the practice of *ijtihad*, he declared that 'no *mujtahid* has been saved from a critic or a person from a deficiency'.[32] The contin-uous renewal of legal rulings was necessary, he warned the shah, and argued that common believers must not emulate the opinions of a dead *mujtahid* – not even al-Karaki. In his bid to restore credibility to the *mujtahid*s, he expressed his disapproval of the way the Safawid state had come to restrict legal authority to a few. For a jurist like Ibn Abd al-Samad, 'sealing' *ijtihad* might well appear to be an oxymoron: closing up legal inference violated the ethical essence of *usuli* jurisprudence.

For a host of Iranian and Arab *ulama*, the extent of al-Karaki's authority was seen as a serious threat. His emulators from among the *mufti*s and judges were already forming the principal legislative and judicial system of the young Safawid state. The emergence of this Shi'i state created a critical shift in the moral status of certain legal acts, such

---

[31] Ja'fariyan, *Kawushha-yi*, p. 42.
[32] Husayn b. Abd al-Samad, 'Risala fi al-husur wa'l-bawari wa sahm al-imam', in A. Ha'iri, et al. ed., *Fihrist-i kitabkhana-yi majlis-i shuray-i milli*, Collection 1836 (Tehran, 1926–1978), pp. 217–221, folio 3a.

as the observation of the Friday prayer and the jurist's acceptance of gifts and land revenues from the temporal ruler. The scholar Ibrahim b. Sulayman al-Qatifi, for one, had refused the gifts of Shah Ismaʿil, insisting that it was prohibited to accept them from an illegitimate ruler during the imam's occultation. Al-Karaki debunked each of al-Qatifi's views, arguing that such acts were not only proper but also religiously beneficial.[33] Al-Karaki had accepted the land grants offered to him by the shah as a hereditary endowment, along with revenues from land tax.[34] He validated his position on the basis of earlier legal opinions given by major jurists such as Shaykh al-Taʾifa al-Tusi, al-Allama, Ibn Idris al-Hilli, and al-Shahid al-Awwal. For al-Qatifi, however, and many others, al-Karaki's actions ran counter to the prevalent opinion among Imami jurists. But al-Karaki noted that these grants were beneficial to Iraqi villagers, and that the land revenues could be used to improve the conditions of Shiʿi believers as well as strengthen Twelver Shiʿism. In the late 16th century, al-Muqaddas al-Ardabili supported al-Qatifi's views, finding the acceptance of *kharaj* revenues illicit. Equally important was his view that it was permissible to emulate the dead jurist, denouncing the *ijtihadi* rationalist methods upon which the support for the prohibition (*hurma*) of this emulation was based. Al-Muqaddas had no compunction about investing his own independent reasoning in deriving the law, while 'ignoring the opinions and views of previous scholars'.[35] But unlike the Amili *mujtahid*s, he rejected association with the Safawid rulers despite an invitation from Shah Abbas; serving temporal rulers was for him unethical. In contrast, several Amili *mujtahid*s who followed al-Karaki's lead found the benefits of associating with temporal rulers an occasion for discarding moral precaution. The coming section will shed light on al-Shahid al-Thani's approach to the Safawids.

Al-Shahid al-Thani and the Safawid State: 'Does anyone reject dignity but a donkey?'

Iranian and Arab *ulama* extolled al-Shahid al-Thani's juridical knowledge and authoritative *ijtihad* before the mid-16th century.[36] His distin-

---

[33] Al-Karaki's treatise on *kharaj*, 'Qatiʿat al-lajaj fi tahqiq hill al-kharaj', was composed in 1510 in Najaf before he entered the service of the Safawids.

[34] Al-Karaki, *Rasaʾil al-muhaqqiq al-Karaki*, vol. 1, pp. 237, 238, 244–245. On the question of *kharaj*, see Tabatabaʾi, *Kharaj*, pp. 47, 54, 56–58.

[35] Hossein Modarressi, *Introduction to Shiʿi Law*, p. 51. Al-Muqaddas wrote two treatises, the first doubting the legality of accepting *kharaj* revenue from temporal rulers, and the second declaring it absolutely prohibited.

[36] See Rida al-Mukhtari's introduction to al-Shahid al-Thani, Zayn al-Din al-Amili, *Munyat al-murid fi adab al-mufid waʾl-mustafid* (Qumm, 1989),

guished career and the circumstances of his death were also discussed in major Safawid chronicles such as Qadi Ahmad Ghaffari's *Tarikh-i jahan-ara*, Shirazi's *Takmilat al-akhbar*, Rumlu's *Ahsan al-tawarikh*, Qummi's *Khulasat al-tawarikh* and Munshi's *Alam-ara-yi Abbasi*.[37] They stressed his martyrdom at the hands of the Ottomans, though the precise details surrounding his execution are contested and unclear. The matter of al-Shahid al-Thani's approach to the Safawid state was until recently open to speculation. It can now be answered with confidence, both on the basis of his final stance on the Friday prayer, and an epistle addressed to him by his devoted student Husayn b. Abd al-Samad.[38] My assessment in this respect brings a corrective to assertions about al-Shahid al-Thani's negative appraisal of the Safawids and about Amili scholarly migration to Iran at this time. Even though Ibn Abd al-Samad's epistle was given the title *al-Rihla*, depicting events of his journey to Iran, it does not provide the kind of geographical knowledge and ethnographic detail known to the medieval genre of *rihla* literature. His work seems to belong to the genre of epistolary literature, where an actual or fictitious friend or confidant is addressed in highlighting by selective incidents and encounters during one's journey. In this epistle, themes appear that interweave scriptural, legal, historical and literary materials, giving us valuable insights into the author's state of mind about what he hoped to achieve by writing it. One can corroborate some of his statements by reference to historical and biographical sources. We do know, for instance, from these sources that Ibn Abd al-Samad left Jabal Amil to escape economic hardship, as well as Ottoman discrimination and religious repression.

The epistle sheds new light on al-Shahid al-Thani's view of migration to Iran and the association of fellow Amili jurists with the Safawids.

pp. 9–88; D. J. Stewart, 'The Ottoman Execution of Zayn al-Din al-'Amili', *Die Welt des Islams*, 48 (2008), pp. 289–347; R. J. Abisaab, 'The Shi'a "*ulama*", the *madrasa*s, and Educational Reform in the Late Ottoman Period', *Ottoman Studies*, 36 (2010), pp. 155–183.

[37] Al-Shahid al-Thani, Zayn al-Din al-Amili, *Munyat al-murid*, pp.13–17; Qadi Ahmad b. Muhammad Ghaffari, *Tarikh-i jahan-ara* (Tehran, 1962), p. 304; Hasan-i Rumlu, *Ahsan al-tawarikh*, vol. 1, ed. C. N. Seddon (Baroda, 1931), p. 406; A. Beg Shirazi, *Takmilat al-akhbar: Tarikh-i Safaviyya az aghaz ta 978 hijri qamari*, ed. Abd al-Husayn Nava'i (Tehran, 1990), pp. 112–113; Qadi Ahmad b. Sharaf al-Din al-Husayni al-Qummi, *Khulasat al-tawarikh* (Tehran, 1980), vol. 1, p. 398f.; and Iskandar Beg Munshi, *Tarikh-i alam-ara-yi Abbasi*, vol. 1, pp. 246–247.

[38] Al-Shahid al-Thani, Zayn al-Din al-Amili, 'Salat al-Jum'a', *Rasa'il al-Shahid al-Thani*, vol. 1, ed. R. al-Mukhtari and G. al-Qaysari (Qumm, 1421/2001), pp. 173–249; Y. Tabaja, 'Risalat al-Shaykh Husayn b. Abd al-Samad al-Amili, walid al-baha'i ila ustadhihi al-Shahid al-Thani', *al-Minhaj*, 8 (2003), pp. 152–195.

In the introduction to the epistle, Ibn Abd al-Samad explains that his shaykh (al-Shahid al-Thani):

> urged me to write to him about what occurs during my journey and charged me with detailing what transpires during my sojourn, out of his kindness for he has prepared me for such an endeavour, and expressed concern for me in accordance with his current and past tendency. In compliance with his wishes and kind benevolence, I pursued his generous command, as was my habit, present and past.[39]

Al-Shahid al-Thani had urged Ibn Abd al-Samad to write about his journey to Iran, having 'prepared' him intellectually and socially to embark on this journey. Clearly, al-Shahid al-Thani was eager to learn from Ibn Abd al-Samad about his encounters and what he experienced before and after arriving in Iran.

Persistent themes in Ibn Abd al-Samad's epistle are his professional frustration, the social restrictions he faced in Jabal Amil, as well as fear of 'enemies'. These features can be easily corroborated in the biographical and historical sources. In one place, he notes that he could not bear the harm caused by 'the state of the enemies', that is the Ottomans, and doubted the prudence of staying away from the just state (*dawlat al-adl*), that is, the Safawid state. He went to great length to show that worldly gains were not the motive for his journey to Iran, but rather his longing to practice his faith publicly. He writes that the 'necessity of migration from the territory of injustice – where it is impossible to express [Shiʿi] rituals of faith – is strong and receives approval ... *for what harm is worse than preventing the spread of knowledge through those qualified to do so*' (emphasis is mine).[40] 'Knowledge' here relates to expertise about the foundations of his faith, Shiʿism, and the legal obligations, which jurists like him are prevented from spreading in Ottoman Syria. Devin Stewart claims that Ibn Abd al-Samad meant by the above statement that the pursuit of knowledge by Shiʿi scholars was blocked, that 'circumstances in Ottoman territories deny Shiʿa scholars adequate access to learning.'[41] But this runs counter to the well-known fact that the Amili scholars cultivated a very sophisticated level of learning in Ottoman Syria. Stewart's conclusion appears to be based on a misreading of the original Arabic. Ibn Abd al-Samad argued that Ottoman rule had caused a grave harm

---

[39]   Tabaja, 'Risalat al-Shaykh Husayn', p. 157.

[40]   Ibid., p. 162.

[41]   D. J. Stewart, 'An Episode in the ʿAmili Migration to Safavid Iran: Husayn ibn ʿAbd al-Samad al-ʿAmili's Travel Account', *Iranian Studies*, 39 (2006), pp. 481–508, at pp. 501–502.

to Shi'i scholars who were prevented from spreading their knowledge about God's law to the believers, and so benefitting them. It is important to stress that Ibn Abd al-Samad does not appear to be polemical here, and presents this view largely as undisputed. To this point, I will add other critical pieces of evidence that confirm al-Shahid al-Thani's support for migration to Iran and association with the Safawids.

Immediately after laying out these aforementioned reasons for leaving Ottoman territories to live in Iran, Ibn Abd al-Samad adds that his shaykh does not need advise from him about what course of action he must take with respect to the question of migration. He goes on to note that al-Shahid al-Thani was experiencing similar if not worse professional and personal hardships in Ottoman Syria, yet he is

> much too knowledgeable to be warned about [the dangers of] an axe or persuaded to observe a *sunna* (exemplary prophetic or Imami act) ... but these [words of mine] give vent to a heavy heart and offer an answer to an inevitable question or one [earlier] mentioned.[42]

The inevitable question may have something to do with the safety of his shaykh, who ends up being killed at the hands of the Ottomans. In other words, his shaykh appears to show no hesitancy about the soundness of migration, yet he has not decided to migrate. Both of these elements are present in this and other parts of the epistle. Al-Shahid al-Thani did not need convincing about the dangers of staying in Jabal Amil, and the benefits of implementing the *sunna* in Safawid Iran. As such, whatever reasons al-Shahid al-Thani had for remaining in Jabal Amil, they had to be personal and social, not political.

This position becomes indisputable when Ibn Abd al-Samad reiterates that his decision to migrate to Iran was motivated by 'recovery of dignity' and 'safety', boldly declaring: 'Does anyone reject dignity but a donkey?'[43] Such a declaration would be utterly insulting to al-Shahid al-Thani if the latter had expressed even a slight reservation about migration to Iran, or had questioned Ibn Abd al-Samad's association with the Safawid monarchs. This one statement in the epistle shows that so much ink has been wasted over extrapolations about the definite objections of al-Shahid al-Thani to Safawid Shi'ism, or his preference for associating with the Ottomans over the Safawids. Ibn Abd al-Samad clearly stated in the epistle that he would be honoured by his service to the Safawid state. Based on this assessment, Stewart's claim that Ibn Abd al-Samad

---

[42] Tabaja, 'Risalat al-Shaykh Husayn', p. 162.
[43] Ibid., p. 163.

wrote this epistle to apologise to al-Shahid al-Thani for seeking 'safety and fortune in Iran' can be put to rest.[44]

The same is true of the view that aversion to the heterodox Shi'ism of the Safawids was the main deterrent for prominent Amili jurists (such as al-Shahid al-Thani) from migrating to Iran, or entering into the Safawids' service.[45] Historically, there has been some flexibility in the relationship between the jurist and the temporal ruler, as long as the ultimate moral position is upheld, namely, only the Imam's rule can be considered legitimate. We have several examples of Shi'i jurists from Buyid Baghdad who associated with Zaydi rulers and Abbasid caliphs, as well as other Sunni rulers.[46] We also have the cases of Nasir al-Din Tusi (1201–1274) and others who served the Mongol Ilkhanid rulers known for their shamanistic pagan beliefs mixed with Christian and Buddhist practices.[47] Despite the difference in context between one case and the other, the prevalent motive for such an association with temporal rulers is pragmatic. It aims to provide public benefit for Shi'i believers or/and alleviate repressive measures against them, as well as advance the *ulama*'s social and professional interests. The purported connection between the Amilis' decision to migrate to Persia and the type of Shi'ism (heterodox) professed by the Safawids overlooks other factors, as well as the ethical obligation which the *mujtahid*s perceived to implement God's law. Their heterodox views notwithstanding, the Safawids' implementation of Imami legalism as the basis of social order and moral authority in society was deemed sufficient by these Amili *mujtahid*s to justify their service.

---

[44] Stewart, 'An Episode in the 'Amili Migration', p. 506. In a succeeding article, Stewart offers an opposite view of al-Shahid al-Thani's stance: 'Polemics and Patronage in Safavid Iran: The Debate on Friday Prayer during the Reign of Shah Tahmasb', *Bulletin of the School of Oriental and African Studies*, 72 (2009), pp. 427–429.

[45] A. Newman, 'The Myth of the Clerical Migration to Safawid Iran: Arab Shiite Opposition to Ali al-Karaki and Safawid Shi'ism', *Die Welt des Islams*, 33 (1993), pp. 66–112.

[46] To cite just two major instances: Ibn al-Junayd associated with Buyid and Ghaznavid rulers, and al-Shaykh al-Tusi associated with the Abbasid caliph al-Qa'im (r. 1031–1075).

[47] J. Pfeiffer, *Twelver Shi'ism in Mongol Iran* (Istanbul, 1999). On the association of Shi'i *ulama* with Hulegu Khan, see G. Lane, *Early Mongol Rule in Thirteenth-Century Iran: A Persian Renaissance* (New York, 2003), pp. 32–35, 250.

Al-Shahid al-Thani and the Iranian Mutakallimun (Theologians)

Ibn Abd al-Samad and al-Shahid al-Thani shared important views about Iran's leading scholars, showing that they tied ethics to legal guidance rather than to theological (*kalam*) scholarship. This is developed further in Ibn Abd al-Samad's epistle. On the one hand, he dramatises the ills of the 'Persians' and of the 'Arabs': 'intermingling with the Persians after the Arabs I thought would offer me two joint virtues. Rather, I gained the worse from both ethnic groups!' Persia, on the other hand, appears to be flawless except for a group of inept clerics practising jurisprudence (*qada*) and issuing legal opinions (*ifta*), thus committing errors and causing dissension. Ibn Abd al-Samad found many clerics in Iran unfit to administer the *shari'a* due to their impiety, greed and lack of expertise. The only devices they carried to the court, he wrote, were 'a pen and an inkpot'.[48]

This critique resonated with al-Shahid al-Thani. He paid homage to Shaykh Ali al-Karaki whom he counted among the few leading *mujtahid*s of his age.[49] Al-Shahid al-Thani denounced scholars who opposed al-Karaki or failed to recognise the authoritative knowledge that was the basis for his legal rulings. Meanwhile, al-Shahid al-Thani found fault with the prevalence of the rational disciplines in Iran, especially *kalam* and logic (*mantiq*), and their growth at the expense of the legal-religious disciplines. He remarked on the subsidiary knowledge which these scholars had of the legal-religious disciplines, especially *hadith*. It was not merely futile to pursue these rational fields of study, but also disruptive for achieving a moral life defined by the *shari'a*. If these scholars, al-Shahid al-Thani added, were to spend but part of their lives cultivating the learning of the *shari'a*, they would embrace the ethical foundations of knowledge, because this type of knowledge is made obligatory by God.[50] Quite simply, the rational disciplines were inconsequential for the fulfilment of the believer's moral obligations towards God. Even though al-Shahid al-Thani was a *mujtahid* who utilised syllogistic reasoning to derive the law, he argued that logic, presumably as an independent field of study, is not fully reliable and its examination has limited benefits for the legal scholar.[51] Curiously, he also seemed displeased with the sense

---

[48]   Tabaja, 'Risalat al-Shaykh Husayn', pp. 178, 181.

[49]   Al-Shahid al-Thani, Zayn al-Din al-Amili 'Taqlid al-mayt', *Rasa'il al-Shahid al-Thani*, vol. 1, ed. Rida al-Mukhtari and Abbas al-Muhammadi, p. 37.

[50]   Ibid., p. 55.

[51]   Al-Shahid al-Thani, Zayn al-Din al-Amili, 'al-Iqtisad wa'l-irshad ila tariq al-ijtihad fi ma'rifat al-mabda wa'l-ma'ad wa ahkam af'al al-i'bad', *Rasa'il al-Shahid al-Thani*, vol. 2, ed. Rida al-Mukhtari, pp. 762–767.

of superiority, which the *mutakallimun* (theologians) felt towards legal scholars, and so appeared unsettled about the scholarly authority they were claiming in Safawid society. The clashes between the *mutakallimun* of Shiraz, and some of their students, and al-Karaki were well known, but here we see the ethical dimensions of these clashes and the claims of both groups to scholarly authority.

Evidently, al-Shahid al-Thani questioned the piety and ethical commitment of the theologians, noting that they had revived the 'religion of Aristotle and his like from among the philosophers', pulling themselves away from God. A number of these *mutakallimun* and their students found a host of al-Karaki's rulings, taken with his deputyship, unacceptable. Even though a number of these *mutakallimun* were linked to the Safawid court and accepted various appointments and grants from the monarchs, their views on the Friday prayer came close to the traditional pietistic skepticism about the symbols of temporal rule. Kamal-al-Din Husayn Ilahi Ardabili (1465–1543), a student of the prominent *mutakallim*, Jalal-al-Din Dawani (1426–1502), issued an injunction that the performance of the Friday prayer was unlawful during the occultation (*ghayba*) of the imam.[52] He considered its performance a violation of the ethical guidelines of the Imamate; like most of the *ulama* in Najaf and Iran at the time, he considered precaution the only moral act possible during *ghayba*. On occasion, the challenge to the authority of *mujtahid*s like al-Karaki was based not on ethico-legal considerations but on competing mathematical calculations, such as on the proper direction of the *qibla*.

The Controversy over the Friday Prayer

Historically, Shi'i jurists like Shaykh al-Ta'ifa and al-Allama have advanced slightly different positions on the Friday prayer. The variation can be seen at times across the range of their comprehensive and abridged legal manuals and discussions. For instance, Shaykh al-Ta'ifa in one of his works emphasised the obligatory status of the Friday prayer, arguing that believers are '*madhunun fihi muraghghabun fihi*' (given permission and encouraged to hold it) – but in another considers its observance merely tolerable during *ghayba*.[53] These differences may not always be substantive, and at times they are dictated by the genre

---

[52] R. Pourjavady, *Philosophy in Early Safavid Iran: Najm al-Din Mahmud al-Nayrizi and His Writings* (Leiden, 2011), p. 43.

[53] Al-Shahid al-Thani, Zayn al-Din al-Amili, 'Risala salat al-jum'a', *Rasa'il al-Shahid al-Thani*, vol. 1, pp. 221–223, 222–225 (first stance); p. 195 (second stance).

of writing. In other cases, differences may mark an actual shift in the jurists' ruling on the question over time.

In the treatise on the Friday prayer which he completed in 1515, al-Karaki argued that the Imami *ulama* had agreed that the Imami jurist who possesses all the qualifications for deriving the law is the deputy of the Hidden Imam in all legal matters where the deputyship applies, except perhaps in imposing penalties for the most egregious crimes (*hudud*) or of death (*qatl*).[54] He stressed the imam's direct role in holding the Friday prayer, or appointing a general deputy (*na'ib amm*) to carry it out.[55] He concluded that if the presence of such a deputy is required during the imams' era then it is even more essential during the *ghayba*. The congregational prayer, in his view, must be held by a designated *mujtahid*, qualified to act as the deputy of the Hidden Imam, in a general (*amma*) capacity. In this respect, he emphasised the comprehensive rather than partial (*mutajazzi*) knowledge of the deputy. Only in the presence of such a deputy who possesses 12 innate abilities and acquired fields of knowledge, is it possible then for the Shi'a to perform the Friday prayer. Even though al-Karaki insisted on the propriety of the Friday prayer, he went to great length to show that it is not absolutely obligatory; in the absence of the imam, its observation was optional (*wajib takhyiri*).

Al-Shahid al-Thani completed a treatise on the Friday prayer in 1554, a few years before his execution by the Ottomans. Like al-Karaki, he looked favourably on the Safawid state's espousal of Imamism and stressed the religious benefit of associating with it.[56] His views about the Friday prayer and its conditions, however, contradicted al-Karaki's rulings. He argued that al-Karaki's support for its optionality during *ghayba* cannot be supported by the textual sources – and sought to have it regarded as obligatory (*al-wujub al-ayni*). This stance, like that of his student Ibn Abd al-Samad, was rare among the *mujtahid*s, most of whom supported its optionality.[57] Al-Shahid al-Thani prayed for forgiveness of the jurist who failed to make the Friday prayer obligatory, and who erred by supporting its optionality. In *ijtihadi* rationalism, such an 'error' did not make al-Karaki's ruling unethical – and the jurist earned

---

[54] Al-Muhaqqiq al-Karaki, 'Risala salat al-jum'a', in *Rasa'il al-Muhaqqiq al-Karaki*, vol. 1, pp. 142–145. Al-Karaki presents the general guidelines about Friday prayer in *Jami al-maqasid fi sharh al-qawa'id* (Beirut, 1991), vol. 2, pp. 374–380.

[55] Al-Karaki, 'Risala salat al-jum'a', pp. 144–146, 158–160.

[56] Al-Shahid al-Thani, Zayn al-Din al-Amili, 'Risala salat al-jum'a', *Rasa'il al-Shahid al-Thani*, vol.1, pp. 173–249.

[57] Interestingly, Fadil al-Hindi, a leading *mujtahid* of the late Safawid period, supported the absolute prohibition on holding the Friday prayer, also a rare position for *mujtahid*s to take.

his due moral reward for striving to bring the benefit of God's law to society. But the differences among prominent *mujtahid*s on this question contributed to the confusion about the status of Friday prayer, and to criticisms of the exercise of *ijtihad*.[58] Al-Shahid al-Thani expressed his forceful support for the Safawids whose rule enabled the removal of the barriers to observing an 'exalted obligation' which could now be held 'in many lands of faith especially during this time'.[59]

He also addressed the matter of juristic deputyship, insisting that any pious prayer leader could convene the Friday prayer. There was no need to secure the presence of a leading jurist who carried all the qualifications of a *mufti* or *mujtahid*, or one exclusively designated by the imam to hold the Friday prayer. The Imami *ahadith* (reports), he concluded, supported the view that convening the Friday prayer was not conditional upon the presence of the Just Ruler, the awaited imam. Through his ruling on the Friday prayer, we get a clear statement from al-Shahid al-Thani stressing the Islamic basis of Safawid rule.

* * *

Disagreement over the status of the Friday prayer intensified after al-Shahid al-Thani's time, with fresh implications for ethics and legal authority in the shadow of the Safawid state. This disagreement occurred between scholars who were not even associated with the Safawid court or seeking posts and grants from the rulers. The differences were largely informed by the new political reality of Iran's Shi'i state and the need to re-establish the moral status of particular legal acts. Some of these acts, which were in abeyance or unsystematically observed under Sunni rulers, such as the Friday prayer, had to be discussed anew. The reality of the Shi'i state also brought a shift in the jurists' social-political status, because it transformed the informal power of a few individual jurists into formally recognised clerical authority. As the legal authority of the *mujtahid*s changed under the protection of the Shi'i state, so did its ethical consequences. Meanwhile, jurists such as Ibn Abd al-Samad affirmed that *ijtihadi* rationalism in fact prevents the abuse of legal power, for no scholar can hold an exclusive or ultimate legal-religious authority – and error is part of the pluralistic ethic of jurisprudence.

---

[58]   Husayn b. Abd al-Samad, *al-Iqd al-Husayni (al-Tahmasbi)*, ed. S. J. Modarressi Yazdi (Yazd, n.d.), pp. 3–6, 31–33; Mulla Muhsin-i Fayd Kashani, *Dah risala*, ed. R. Ja'fariyan (Isfahan, 1992), p. 281; Husayn b. Shihab al-Din al-Karaki, *Hidayat al-abrar ila tariq al-a'imma al-athar*, ed. R. Jamal al-Din (Baghdad, 1977), pp. 3–4.
[59]   Al-Shahid al-Thani, Zayn al-Din al-Amili, 'Risala salat al-jum'a', p. 189.

Further Reading

Abisaab, Rula Jurdi. *Converting Persia: Religion and Power in the Safawid Empire*. London, 2004.

Arjomand, Said Amir. *The Shadow of God and the Hidden Imam*. Chicago, 1984.

Chehabi, H., ed. *Distant Relations: Iran and Lebanon in the Last 500 Years*. Oxford, 2006.

Eickelman, Dale F. 'Islam and Ethical Pluralism', in Sohail H. Hashmi, ed., *Islamic Political Ethics: Civil Society, Pluralism, and Conflict*. Princeton, NJ, 2002, pp. 115–134.

Hallaq, Wael B. *Authority, Continuity and Change in Islamic Law*. Cambridge, 2001.

—— *Shari'a: Theory, Practice, Transformation*. Cambridge, 2009.

Hourani, George F. *Reason and Tradition in Islamic Ethics*. Cambridge, 1985.

Johansen, Baber. *Contingency in a Sacred Law: Legal and Ethical Norms in the Muslim Fiqh*. Leiden, 1999.

Modarressi, Hossein. *Crisis and Consolidation in the Formative Period of Shi'ite Islam*. Princeton, NJ, 1993.

Reinhart, A. Kevin. *Before Revelation: the Boundaries of Muslim Moral Thought*. Albany, NY, 1995.

8

Devotional Practices

Ali S. Asani

Shiʻi devotional life is generally associated with reverence for Ali, the first Shiʻi Imam, subsequent imams, and other members of the Prophet's family (*ahl al-bayt*).[1] Veneration of these figures is, to be sure, an important marker of Shiʻi piety, but it is not – historically or currently – unique to the Shiʻa. Indeed, even a cursory glance at Islamic devotional practices reveals numerous examples of such reverence among many other Muslim communities. Ali in particular holds an important role in almost all interpretations of Islam; in most Sufi conceptualisations, for example, he is regarded as an important spiritual teacher from whom nearly all *tariqa*s, or Sufi orders, trace their spiritual descent. Sunni Muslims maintain that he was among the first to accept Muhammad's teachings and among the closest of his disciples, as attested by his marriage to his daughter, Fatima. They also celebrate his wisdom and courage, and he is their fourth caliph. A shrine dedicated to him in Mazar-i Sharif in Afghanistan is visited by Sunni as well as Shiʻi Muslims. Reverence for the Prophet's family among non-Shiʻi groups is not restricted to Ali, however. A mosque in Cairo, which houses a shrine containing the head of Ali's martyred son, Husayn, is visited by millions of Sunni Muslims annually. Such examples illustrate that it is more accurate to conceive of reverence for Ali and the *ahl al-bayt* not as a binary – in which 'Shiʻi' is equated with veneration of the Prophet's family – but rather as a continuum, in which these figures play a variety of roles across the devotional practices of Muslims generally.

It is the theological and cosmological frameworks through which the Shiʻi imams, and the *ahl al-bayt*, are conceived that distinguishes Shiʻi practices from those of other Muslim groups. According to the Shiʻa, Ali was not only Muhammad's legitimate temporal successor, but also his spiritual heir. God endowed him and the subsequent imams in his lineage with the knowledge to interpret the deeper esoteric aspects of the

---

[1] The author gratefully acknowledges the assistance of Andrew Halladay in researching his chapter in this volume.

revelation, thereby charging them with the task of leading the community along the path of righteousness. Hence, for the Shi'a, faith in God and the Prophet is incomplete without faith in Ali and the imams – a belief that is reflected in the third statement of the Shi'i *shahada* (testimony of faith), which affirms that Ali, and by extension all subsequent imams, are near to God: 'Ali, the Master of the Believers, is the friend (*wali*) of God.' Key to the shaping of Shi'i devotional practices, whether expressed in rituals or in pietistic literature, is the notion of *walaya*; in its most basic sense, the word evokes a sense of stewardship – that the imam should guard, protect and guide his community. Importantly, it also implies a nearness to God, before whom the imam can act as an intermediary for his community. More figuratively, but no less importantly, *walaya* demands admiration and love. Just as children love their parents – their social guardians – so too do the Shi'a show love towards their spiritual protectors, their imams. This feature of Shi'i thought, as we shall see shortly, provides an important lens through which to understand Shi'i devotional practices.

Over time, Shi'i understandings of their imams acquired a cosmological significance in which the imamate came to be interpreted as a primordial institution of divine guidance parallel to that of prophethood. Each prophet preceding Muhammad was associated with an imam, whose identity was not known publicly, but who interpreted and safeguarded prophetic revelation. Just as the prophets were linked through the light of prophethood, so too were the imams linked by the light of the imamate. In Shi'i belief, Muhammad, as the last prophet, made this primordial institution known to the world. During his last pilgrimage in 632, at the oasis of Ghadir Khumm, he declared: 'He whose master I am, Ali is his master.' For the Shi'a, this historic declaration is so central to the history of the imamate that Shi'i communities commemorate its anniversary in various ways on 18 Dhu'l-Hijja, the 12th month of the Islamic calendar. Among the Dawoodi Bohra Ismailis, for instance, the festival of Ghadir Khumm provides the occasion for the faithful to renew their oath of allegiance to the imam just as those who were present at the historic event at Ghadir Khumm offered their allegiance to Ali. On the anniversary of the event, Bohras fast and attend special midday prayers, after which they may listen to a sermon and devotional poetry.

We must be careful, however, not to map the above articulation of the imamate onto the succession crisis that followed Muhammad's death. These ideas crystallised only about three centuries later, and derived in part from the Shi'i imams themselves, who increasingly pointed to the Quran not only to justify their political legitimacy, but to underscore their role in the salvation of humankind. These doctrinal developments were deeply enmeshed in historical circumstances. While some imams were regarded as scholars or spiritual authorities by the wider Muslim community, for the most part their political fortunes, together with those of their followers, were highly unfavourable; most of the early imams were murdered or put under some form of surveillance, and attacks on their supporters were common and relentless. A theological framework developed, particularly among the Twelver Shi'a, to articulate the legitimacy of the imams in the light of their persecution and political defeat, and to expound a cosmic order that valorised the redemptive nature of their suffering.

The emergence of distinctly Shi'i devotional practices must be, therefore, understood in the context of these interconnected doctrinal and historical developments. As the tenor of Shi'i devotional practices shifted, not only did they emphasise love and devotion to the imams, but also their martyrdom, suffering and role in salvation. Shi'i ritual practices also came to require specific spaces, other than the mosque, where they could be performed, leading to the appearance of the *Husayniyya* or *Imambara* among the Twelver Shi'a and the *jamatkhana* among the Ismaili Shi'a.

Political and social circumstances, therefore, fostered a gradual divergence of devotional practices among early Muslim communities, ultimately manifesting the divisions we now know as Shi'i and Sunni. A similar awareness of historical, political, cultural and social factors helps us explain the diverse devotional practices in the Shi'i community itself. To illustrate, let us now turn to an event that has played a significant role in defining Shi'i devotional practice, and which is regarded as emblematic of the suffering of the imams, and of the righteous more generally: the martyrdom of Imam Husayn and his followers at Karbala on 10 Muharram 680.

Remembering Karbala

The event itself is addressed elsewhere in this volume from other perspectives. My aim, therefore, is not to retell this well-known story, but rather to explore the ways in which socio-political and historic circumstances have shaped the Shi'i devotional practices surrounding it. If we return to the idea that reverence for the *ahl al-bayt* is a continuum, we can see that the mourning for Husayn's martyrdom is not exclusive to the Shi'a. For them, however, the event represents not merely a usurpation of political power, but a cosmic struggle between good and evil as well as being the ultimate symbol of the suffering which the righteousness must endure. The extent of the tragedy of Husayn's martyrdom can only be understood if we recall that, from a Shi'i view, the imam not only represents political and spiritual authority, but is an object of supreme love and admiration. This dimension has coloured the ways in which Shi'i devotional rituals have been conceptualised and practised. The most ubiquitous expression of these rituals occurs during the month of Muharram, particularly the first ten days, when special gatherings or *majalis* (sing. *majlis*) are held in *Husayniyya*s or *Imambara*s to commemorate the martyrdom of Imam Husayn. These *majalis* often contain several elements such as the recitation of the *durud*, or blessings on the Prophet Muhammad and his family; the *soz*, a type of lament poetry sung in melodic tune; the *salaam*, a lyrical elegy containing references to the Karbala tragedy with reflections on the nature of human life and existence; the *marsiya*, or elegy, and the *zikr*, a type of sermon recited by a professionally-trained *zakir* (preacher) during which the virtues and merits of the Prophet's family, together with the hardships they experienced, are recounted with refined oratorical skills. In addition to these *majalis*, some form of which appears in most Shi'i communities, there are other practices which are unique to certain regions, including the *taziya* play in Iran, its indigenised forms in South Asia and Trinidad, and other Muharram commemorations in India (especially *matam*). The importance of Muharram, we shall see, extends also to the realm of devotional literature where it finds expression in such genres as the Persian *rawzeh khani*, the Urdu *marsiya*, and the Sindhi *Shah jo risalo*, particularly the section called *Sur Kedaro*. I will now briefly turn to each of these examples, both ritualistic and literary, in turn.

Among the most well known of the Shi'i devotional practices concerning Karbala is the Iranian form of theatre called the *taziya*, the literal meaning of which is 'mourning'. This tradition was especially widespread in Iran during the late Qajar period; due principally to political factors, its popularity declined somewhat during the 20th century.[2] Yet even in its diminished form, the *taziya* is central to the Muharram experience in Iran, and enjoys an especially exalted place in rural communities. In practice, *taziya* in Iran refers to several rituals, though the best known is a re-enactment of Husayn's martyrdom during Muharram. Many scholars have equated it with the 'passion play,' though an analysis of the tradition reveals few parallels with Western traditions. It is, rather, strongly enmeshed in Persian cultural and political traditions, especially pre-Islamic traditions of theatre and visual representation. Especially notable in this regard was a pre-Islamic theatrical practice which depicted the death of Siyawush, a legendary Persian hero. I do not mean to suggest that Husayn merely replaced Siyawush in this tradition – indeed, substantial evidence cautions against this – but rather that it

---

[2] Kamran Scot Aghaie. *The Martyrs of Karbala: Shi'i Symbols and Rituals in Modern Iran* (Seattle, WA, 2004), p. 12.

was natural that Shi'i communities in Iran would represent Karbala in a way that was continuous with pre-existing cultural practices.

Today, *taziya* productions in Iran can vary from lavish performances with professional actors to comparatively modest ones by local amateurs. Audience participation is central to the performance; actors may vary their lines or even entire scenes so as to elicit the strongest possible emotional response from the audience. To guide viewers in their inter-pretation of the characters and events, the colours of actors' costumes symbolise the allegiance of their characters: those in green represent the force of good – that is, the family of the Prophet – while those in red are associated with the malevolent forces of Yazid and the Umayyads. Iranian *taziya* performances permit a flexibility almost unknown in modern Western theatre. Even before the performance, the audience may play an active role in preparing costumes or the set, donating – according to one's means – household objects or funds. Doing so ensures the audience's investment in the performance and its aims: to remember the suffering of their beloved Husayn, the archetype of the suffering of the righteous more generally. Pursuant to these aims, the performance does not purport to be a historical rendering of Karbala, but rather to reflect its cosmological significance. Anachronistic figures, such as Mary or Alexander the Great, may appear on the stage together. Lines may be added or improvised that have little basis in recorded sources. Though such versatility may appear bewildering to those unaccustomed to the genre, through the lens of the *taziya* they are both natural and appropriate. Karbala, after all, was not merely a historical event, but a cosmological battle of good against evil; in this way, the blending of the performance and the audience, together with the addition of characters and lines, are permissible – even inevitable – in the endeavour to depict a battle not only in its earthly, but its cosmological, terms. In this way, a good *taziya* performance aims to transport its audience back to the fields of Karbala, so that the distant historical event feels intimately real and present. In this regard, Peter Brooks, a noted Western theatre director and producer, comments on the transformative power of the *taziya*:

I saw in a remote Iranian village one of the strangest things I have seen in theatre: a group of four hundred villagers, the entire population of the place, sitting under a tree and passing from roars of laughter to outright sobbing – although they knew perfectly well the end of the story – as they saw Husayn in danger of being killed, and then fooling his enemies, and then being martyred. And when he was martyred, the theatre became a truth – there was no difference between past and present. An event that was told as happening in history 1300 years ago actually became a reality in that moment.[3]

In a South Asian context, the tradition of the *taziya* – though introduced to the region through contacts with Persian culture – came to refer not to performances, but instead to miniature mausoleums constructed for the body of the martyred Husayn which mourners carry through the streets. In addition, mourners may hold *alam*s, or standards, associated with the Prophet's family. Frequently, the procession includes an elaborately decorated riderless horse which represents the steed of the beheaded Imam Husayn. Like the *taziya* performances in Iran, the *taziya* mausoleums in South Asia are closely associated with Muharram rituals. They are often carried silently (*chup taziya*) during processions, after which they are buried or, in many cases, immersed in water. Although some *taziya*s are constructed for long-term use, in general – and especially today – they are designed to be disposable. Their composition has ranged from bamboo and paper, which is common among the general population, to ivory and glass, such as those designed for the Nawabs of Lucknow whose legendary processions included an elephant trained to trumpet '*Ya Husayn, Ya Husayn*'. Like the *taziya* plays in Iran, *taziya* mausoleums in South Asia are enmeshed in local historical and social circumstances. From a devotional perspective, the tradition enables Shi'i communities to symbolically complete a pilgrimage to distant Karbala. It is also reminiscent of certain Hindu rituals, revealing that as the tradition moved to the Subcontinent it assimilated local practices. A particularly striking parallel, for instance, is the Ganesha Chaturthi festival, in which icons of Ganesh are immersed in water. Whether or not the *taziya* processions in India drew inspiration from these practices, such resemblances – together with their emphasis on the universal theme of suffering – have extended the appeal of the *taziya* well beyond the Shi'i, or even Muslim, communities.

Just as the *taziya* came from Iran to South Asia, where its expression was adapted to its Indic milieu, the tradition travelled from the subcontinent as well, again acquiring a distinctly indigenous garb in its new locales. In the early 19th century, for example, Shi'i sepoys (soldiers in the employ of the British Raj) introduced the tradition to west Sumatra, where it still thrives. Following the example of the *taziya* rituals of South Asia, the *tabuik*s of Southeast Asia – as the bamboo tombs of Husayn came to be called – are lowered into the water. Here, however,

---

[3]   As quoted in Peter J. Chelkowski, 'Iran: Mourning Becomes Revolution', *Asia*, 3 (1980), p. 36.

the immolation is typically accompanied by local music and dramatic performances, including reenactments of the battle of Karbala.

The South Asian form of the Muharram ritual was also exported elsewhere in Southeast Asia in a process that was, as in Sumatra, often enmeshed in colonial structures. A particularly noteworthy case is that of Penang; various factors, including British expulsion of Indian Shi'i convicts from India, together with the Shi'i sepoys who oversaw them, brought the Muharram ritual to the island. Although a significant Shi'i population did not remain in Penang, the Muharram ritual has endured. The Boria theatrical tradition, today considered an integral part of Penang culture, is ultimately derived from the Muharram rituals that Shi'i Indian groups brought to the island.

A few decades later, beginning around 1845, British economic interests exported the *taziya* tradition further still – indeed, out of Asia altogether. As Indians came to the Caribbean in mass numbers, typically as indentured labour, the ritual came with them. Far from home, the Shi'i community in Trinidad used the *taziya* to cement social bonds and remember their homeland. The practice also acquired important political consequences, of which the British were grudgingly aware, in that the tragedy of Karbala had a striking relevance in the hardships of colonial rule. Most importantly, the appeal of the Hosay – as the commemoration of 'Husayn' is called in Trinidad – came to transcend the Indian Shi'i community from which it derived; indeed, the Hosay has become symbolic of an ecumenical national culture irrespective of ethnic and religious affiliation. The particulars of this tradition are discussed elsewhere in this volume.[4]

The *taziya*, of course, is not the only tradition associated with Muharram. Among the most notable, and contentious, of the Muharram practices is *matam*, which – especially in its South Asian context – refers to acts during Muharram that demonstrate mourning for Husayn. This is often manifested as the ritual beating of the chest (*sineh-zani*), usually in time to the recitation of poetry that recounts the events of Karbala (*nauha*). In some cases, however, *matam* becomes an expression of self-violence (*zanjeer-zani*); instead of hands, the use of chains, knives and other objects amplify the suffering of those who undergo *matam*. Controversy surrounds many aspects of these practices; its adverse physical effects – leading to serious health risks or even death – have drawn protests from many, including prominent voices within the Shi'i community. From a religious perspective, too, the spilling of blood leaves one ritually unclean, and therefore unable to partake in communal prayer, an important part of the Muharram ritual. However, bewildering

---

4   See Chapter 15 ('Diasporas').

as these aspects of *matam* may seem at first, if we peer beyond the controversy we can glean something of their significance. At one level, pain during *matam* serves to bridge the gap between the suffering of the community and the trials of Husayn, who endured the ultimate agony at Karbala. The physical infliction of wounds also demonstrates a readiness to have suffered with him,[5] and more abstractly but no less vitally, to participate even now in the cosmic battle against evil which the event symbolises. Perhaps above all, the intensity of the *matam* allows those who participate in it to push beyond seeing Husayn as a mere political, or even spiritual, leader. Rather, self-violence demonstrates an eagerness to partake of the ultimate sacrifice for their beloved, Imam Husayn.

Rituals are not the only means by which Shi'i communities commemorate Muharram. Various literary genres, too, constitute an integral part of the Muharram experience for most Shi'a. As we have seen above, many rituals are themselves imbued with literary dimensions – such as the *taziya* – and it is sometimes difficult to disentangle the two. Indeed, the *taziya* itself can be said to have emerged from one of the most enduring literary traditions surrounding Muharram in Iran: the *rawzeh khani*. The tradition came to prominence during the early 16th century, when Husayn Vaez Kashifi's poem *Rawzat al-shuhada* (The Garden of the Martyrs), became well known.[6] This work synthesised many of the existing Karbala narratives while incorporating some original material. What is distinctive about this influential composition is the manner in which Kashifi blended into it the popular genre of the *ghazal*, or love lyric, into his narrative, thereby substantially increasing the popularity of the text. During Muharram, specially trained reciters performed sections of the work, or sometimes the work in its entirety. The tradition eventually became known as the *rawzeh khani*. Though many of its elements were later incorporated into the *taziya*, the *rawzeh khani* should still be regarded as a distinct tradition, especially because it is often performed separately. True to the tradition from which Kashifi's text emerged, the *rawzeh khani* is seldom a verbatim recitation of the *Rawzat al-shuhada*. Embellishments, modifications and substitutions are very much an accepted part of the genre. Sometimes the *Rawzat al-shuhada* is not included at all. Like the *taziya* with which it is associated, the *rawzeh khani* aims to produce an emotional response in its audience by figuratively transporting them back to the plains of Karbala through a dramatic recalling of the tragedy. Indeed, the sure

---

[5] For more on these points, see Syed Akbar Hyder, *Reliving Karbala: Martyrdom in South Asian Memory* (Oxford, 2006), p. 52.

[6] Aghaie, *Martyrs*, pp. 12–13.

sign of a gifted reciter is the ability to move the audience to tears. The best reciters carefully choose their words and skilfully vary the tone of their voice to generate emotions, often by evoking filial and parental love. Not surprisingly, members of the audience will often burst into unrestrained sobbing, slap their foreheads and beat their chests as they lament. Apart from demonstrating piety, tears carry soteriological significance in that crying for Husayn and his companions is said to secure one a place in heaven.

A closely related literary form is the Urdu *marsiya*. In its broadest sense, *marsiya* implies an elegy for the dead, usually – though not always – for persons of religious or spiritual importance. Much more commonly, however, the word refers to an epic genre of poetry that laments Husayn's martyrdom at Karbala. Like other associated traditions, the *marsiya* is typically recited during the first ten days of Muharram – often at places deemed to have spiritual significance, such as the tombs of spiritual, and certain political, leaders. Though unmistakably Persian in its origin, the Urdu *marsiya* – like the *taziya* on the subcontinent – demonstrates a marked independence from its source tradition. Its symbols and imagery are imbued with a distinctly subcontinental imagery, and it achieved a centrality in the Muharram traditions of South Asia that it had not known in Iran.

The *marsiya* has been – and remains – an important dimension of Muharram practices for many Shi'i communities throughout the subcontinent. The height of the genre's popularity not to say its quality, however, is generally associated with Lucknow during the 19th century. Having the largest concentration of Shi'i communities in South Asia and a rich tradition of poetry recitation, Lucknow was thus a natural space in which the tradition could mature and expand. An individual poem before this period had typically been limited to around 40 stanzas. But in Lucknow it was extended to permit potentially hundreds of stanzas to be included in a single poem, thereby providing ample opportunity for the unfolding of details and vignettes about the events of Karbala. Many of the *marsiya* poets who achieved fame during this period, such as Mir Babar Ali Anis (1803–1874) and Mirza Salamat Ali Dabir (1803–1875), made indelible contributions to the Urdu literary canon.

Many of these Muharram genres, as we have seen, are shared across large sections of the Muslim world, in each case adapting to, and drawing from, the local conditions. Some genres, however, are not merely indigenised forms of earlier Arabo-Persian literary traditions, but are instead of a wholly local provenance. Perhaps the most well-known example is the *Sur Kedaro* from Shah Abdul Latif's classic Sindhi composition, *Shah jo Risalo*. To be sure, this work – like the *rawzeh khani* and the *marsiya* – is often recited or sung, but its literary form and function are wholly embedded in the traditions of Sindh from which it emerged.

Shah Abdul Latif Bhittai (1689–1752) is often regarded as the greatest of all Sindhi poets; his pre-eminent role in Sindhi literature, together with his strong emphasis on Sufi themes – especially love and music – have led some scholars to compare him favourably to the Persian poet Rumi. His poetry includes many mystical themes, and has been assembled into the collection *Shah jo Risalo*. This text has a central place in the literary consciousness not only of Muslim Sindhis, but has enjoyed enduring popularity among Hindu Sindhis as well. The allure of the text, in part, is due to its strong reliance on Sindhi folk traditions; stock figures and stories from Sindhi folklore – including pre-Islamic figures – occupy a central place in the text, thereby giving it a distinctly local flavour while ensuring its appeal across religious divides. In this way, the works of Shah Abdul Latif have emerged as an important symbol of Sindhi identity, irrespective of national, religious, or class boundaries.

Given the widespread appeal of Shah Abdul Latif, it is hardly surprising that his poetry has come to be associated with Sindhi Muharram rituals. *Sur Kedaro* – one of the chapters of the *Shah jo Risalo* – holds an especially important place in the Muharram rituals of Sindh. The first part of this section recounts the martyrdom of Husayn at Karbala, and later sections praise the heroism of the subsequent imams in the face of evil. Though they may not meet political triumph on earth, Shah Abdul Latif says, the imams – together with those who support them – are sure to reap their reward in heaven. Many sections of the *Risalo*, when recited, have been associated with the inducing of strong emotional reactions from its audiences. We might say that this is particularly so with the *Sur Kedaro*, which calls upon its listeners to join in the greater fight against evil. The events of Karbala, to be sure, embody this fight, but that battle continues, and the onus is on everyone to join with the leaders of the righteous – the imams.

Visualising Piety

Literary narratives, as we have seen, are often enmeshed in larger rituals associated with Muharram. In many cases – as with the *taziya* – these rituals have strong visual elements. Another example of the fusion of the literary and visual dimensions is in the ritual of *pardeh-dari*, in which story tellers (*pardeh-dar*) travel from village to village carrying large canvasses (*pardeh*) depicting scenes from the battle of Karbala. As *pardeh-dar*s sing the *taziya*, they point to scenes and characters on the canvas as they appear in the narration. Frequently, the canvas will also include scenes of the hereafter in which the enemies of Husayn are punished while his supporters enjoy heavenly rewards.

That visualisation is an important element of Shi'i ritual aesthetics is substantiated by the widespread depictions of Shi'i holy persons on objects ranging from large posters, wall-hangings and banners, to small stickers and medallions to be worn around the neck or kept in pockets or wallets. While historical personalities are depicted in paintings, contemporary figures of authority are often portrayed through mass-produced photographs. While these objects can be found in Shi'i homes or spaces of worship, they also feature prominently in public spaces in predominantly Shi'i communities. As Ingvild Flaskerud argues in her study, these depictions are central to 'the recollection of Divine will, saintly power, dissemination of religious knowledge, transformation of emotions … and the understanding of ethical values and spiritual experiences.'[7] The *panj tan-i pak* (the 'Five Holy Persons' – Muhammad, Ali, Fatima, Hasan and Husayn), together with later Shi'i imams, are often depicted in an idealised form that, through their facial expressions, represents such virtues as bravery and kindness. Frequently, appropriate textual references will anchor these images to a specific religious personality. Thus, images of Ali may have the phrase '*La fata ila 'Ali, la sayf ila dhu'l-fiqar*' (There is no hero save Ali, no sword save Dhu'l-Fiqar) which is a popular reference to Ali's bravery and chivalry as well as his legendary two-pointed sword, Dhu'l-Fiqar (pronounced as 'Zulfiqar' in Persian, Urdu and many other languages). These images serve not as objects of worship but rather as visual symbols that direct the viewer to qualities that he or she should seek to embody. From a theological perspective, they act as tangible reminders of the deep metaphysical relationship between the imams and their devotees. In this regard, these representations may also serve a talismanic function as many people believe they have the power to ward off evil and convey *baraka*, or spiritual blessing.

The Imam as Intercessor

The doctrine of *walaya*, which is essential to the Shi'i conceptualisation of the imamate, is also central to Shi'i devotional practice. *Walaya* not only implies a closeness to God, as explored above, but has come to imply that the Shi'i imams – whether living or dead, absent or present – have the power to intervene before God on behalf of their community. Many, for example, have credited an imam (or the imams collectively) with healing illnesses and solving personal problems, among other miracles. As well, many amongst the Shi'a believe that the imams, being near to God, can intervene to secure their salvation. Such notions, as we shall see, have heavily influenced Shi'i devotional practices.

---

[7]　Ingvild Flaskerud, *Visualizing Belief and Piety in Iranian Shi'ism* (London and New York, 2010), p. 2.

Belief in intercession is such that it has affected not only formal rituals, but has been woven into the daily lives of many Shi'a. The phrases '*Ya Ali madad*' (O Ali, help!), '*Ya Ali adrikni, Ya Ali agisani*' (O Ali come to my help, O Ali come to my rescue), and '*Ya Ali mushkil gusha*' (O Ali, solver of difficulties), though commonly chanted during Muharram rituals and at Shi'i holy places – are often recited by the faithful at times of difficulty or before undertaking even simple tasks. The use of these phrases, predictably, varies across Shi'i communities, and attempts to fully describe their role and function surpasses the scope of the current study. Sometimes a phrase or its usage may become associated with a particular Shi'i group or region; '*Ya Ali madad*,' for instance, is often linked to its use as a greeting among members of the Nizari Ismaili community, though it is used by other Shi'i groups as well. In addition to such phrases, many Shi'a also recite the invocatory prayer '*Nadi Ali*' – 'Call Ali, who is the manifestor of miracles, you shall surely find him a helper in your difficulties, all worries and sorrows will soon disappear on account of your authority, O Ali, O Ali, O Ali.' Popularly believed to have been revealed by the archangel Gabriel to the Prophet Muhammad at a crucial moment at the battle of Khaybar so that he could secure victory with Ali's assistance, this prayer is said to be so powerful that it is often used for talismanic purposes. For example, a sick person may be given some water over which the *Nadi Ali* has been recited, or a mother may recite the prayer over her child as a means of protecting it from harm. The remarkably different contexts in which the Shi'a use this prayer and other invocations underscores their belief that Ali – and by extension all imams – are very much active in the world and responsive to the needs of their supplicants.

Another ritual that draws upon the intercessory powers of the imams and the *panj tan-i pak* are the *mujizat kahani*s (miracle stories) in South Asia, a tradition exclusive to women. Since it is especially common for women not to attend the Friday prayer in South Asia, a rich culture of household rituals has developed. Far from merely providing an alternative space for the Friday prayer, for many South Asian Shi'i women the home constitutes a social and religious space for a wide variety of customs. The *mujizat kahani*s are arguably the most prominent. Like many of the rituals we have encountered, *mujizat kahani*s must be understood within the cultural context in which they developed. Indeed, no similar custom has been identified in the *hadith*s or the Quran;[8] the practice, rather, is similar to the Hindu practice of fasting (*vrat*s) for the fulfilment of certain wishes. The observance of the *vrat* ritual is

---

[8]   Vernon James Schubel, *Religious Performance in Contemporary Islam: Shi'i Devotional Rituals in South Asia* (Columbia, SC, 1993), pp. 37–38.

associated with a whole treasure trove of stories. After reciting a particular story, the supplicant makes a request and often performs an associated devotional prayer, or *puja*. The *mujizat kahani*s, similarly, relate specific stories about a holy figure – usually Muhammad, Fatima, or an imam – and are recited after one has fasted so that a particular request may be answered. Sometimes the story is read as the request is made, but more commonly it is recited only once the wish has been fulfilled, after which follows the distribution of sweets. The nature of these supplications vary substantially, from appeals to cure serious illnesses to more mundane matters. Due to their ubiquity, *mujizat kahani*s have come to constitute a critical part of devotional life for many Shi'i women in the subcontinent. Like the tradition of the *vrats*, standardised versions of *mujizat kahani*s are widely available in bookshops, generally in highly readable Urdu or in other regional languages. Depending on the story and the request, stories may be read aloud among two, three, or more women. Incense is generally lit before the reading, and silence and serenity is expected from all participants.

Perhaps the best-known *mujizat kahani* is known as *Janab-i Sayyida ki Kahani*, among other titles. Though versions of the story vary substantially, each emphasises miracles associated with Fatima – both during her life and subsequently. Today, the best-known version is clearly an amalgamation of several tales, which reveals the organic way in which the story – together with the tradition itself – has developed.[9] The reader will note that the very tradition of the *mujizat kahani* is manifest within the stories themselves.

In the framing narrative of *Janab-i Sayyida ki Kahani*, a woman faints upon hearing that her son has fallen into a kiln and is presumed dead. While unconscious, a mysterious woman visits her, telling her that Fatima can intercede to save her son. If he survives, the woman says, then the mother must recite the story of Fatima. After she awakes and hears that her son is alive, the woman searches for a suitable person to recite Fatima's story. In her search, she meets the same mysterious woman from her vision. After telling the mother to distribute sweets, the woman reads several stories about Fatima.

In one such story, Fatima has been invited to a non-Muslim wedding. Concerned that her modest appearance will be inappropriate at the lavish wedding, Fatima prays to God that she will not embarrass herself. God responds by beautifying her clothes and endowing her with radiant features. The bride of the wedding, upon viewing the erstwhile simple Fatima, dies from shock. Horrified, Fatima prays to God to resurrect the woman. After Fatima performs ablutions and calls on her authority

---

9   This version relies heavily on Schubel, *Religious Performance*, pp. 39–47.

as the Prophet's daughter, the bride stands up, reciting the *shahada*.
Amazed at the spectacle, the entire wedding party converts to Islam.

In returning to the tale's framing story, the mysterious woman – now
understood to be Fatima – disappears, her work done. Though this is only
one version of this popular tale, this rendition reveals much about the
tradition of *mujizat kahani*s more generally. First, it demonstrates that
Fatima – and, by extension, her husband and descendants – are capable
of interceding before God on behalf of their supplicants. It reveals, too,
that even in death, Fatima is believed to be very much active in world
affairs, and appears – either figuratively or in a guise – in moments of
need. Most interesting, perhaps, is that this *mujizat kahani* is clearly
conscious of the larger *mujizat kahani* tradition. In this way, those who
recite this story are recalling examples of those who have done so before
them. The associated actions – including the prayer and the distribution
of sweets – are also included by way of instruction.

Another means by which the Shiʿa believe that they can secure the
blessing of Ali and other imams is visiting their tombs, where their
intercessory powers are said to be particularly strong. This tradition
of tomb veneration is shared with many other Muslim communities,
notably those who visit shrines of Sufi teachers, mystical poets and
prominent religious scholars to seek *baraka*, or spiritual blessings. For
the Shiʿa, the resting places of the imams and the *ahl al-bayt* – Najaf,
Karbala, Baghdad, Samarra (all in Iraq), Mashhad (Iran), Damascus
and Medina – have been sites of veneration and pilgrimage for centuries. At these shrines, pilgrims not only express their reverence but
humbly request the assistance of the imams in overcoming whatever
material and spiritual problems they may face. Frequently, they knot a
string or tie a cloth on the railing surrounding the tomb as a reminder
of their request, or even attach a written note addressed to the imam.
The power and sanctity of these major tomb shrines is often made
accessible to Shiʿi populations outside the Middle East through local
versions. For example, the north Indian city of Lucknow – once the
capital of a Shiʿi polity – has its own Najaf and Karbala shrines located
in predominantly Shiʿi neighbourhoods. Devotees believe these local
shrines, being spiritually connected to their counterparts in Iraq, have
substantial *baraka*. The belief in their power is such that pious devotees
strive to be buried near the sacred precincts so as to ensure their salvation. Not surprisingly, therefore, scores of graves surround these local
shrines. In southern India, not far from the city of Hyderabad – named
in honour of Ali (also known as 'Hyder,' or 'lion,' on account of his
valour), is the *Koh-i Mawla Ali*, which contains the sacred handprint
of Ali, and is considered one of the region's most renowned religious
shrines. Every year, during the *mawlid* celebrating the birth of Ali and
the *urs* commemorating the discovery of the relic, the shrine attracts

thousands of pilgrims of all faiths. Similar traditions exist throughout the wider Muslim world, notably in Central Asia.

At these South Asian shrines, it is customary for pilgrims to offer silver or metallic replicas of different parts of the body afflicted with illness, or physical objects such as cars and houses, in the hope that through the intercession of the imams that part of the body will be cured of its ill or the object acquired. They may, in return for the donation of a few coins, select a votive from a box which – in addition to replicas of body parts – includes silver balls representing stones or tumours and miniature replicas of passports, diplomas, houses, cars, motor scooters and even airplanes symbolising the yearning to travel. When their requests are fulfilled, the pilgrims return to the shrine to pray and may also make a monetary donation for food for the poor.

Political realities have often impeded access to Shi'i pilgrimage sites. Wahhabi groups, which fiercely oppose all intercessory interpretations of Islam – such as Shi'ism and Sufism – have not only prohibited the veneration of the tombs of the four early imams (Hasan, Ali Zayn al-Abidin, Muhammad al-Baqir and Jafar al-Sadiq) buried at the Baqi cemetery in Medina, but have systematically undertaken their destruction. The restrictions and regulations imposed by the regime of Saddam Husayn, together with the instability of the country more generally, long impeded pilgrimage to the shrines in Iraq. Relative stability in recent years, however, has reinvigorated pilgrimage there; the city of Najaf – the site of the shrine of Ali – has seen the construction of a new international airport as well as the proliferation of other amenities aimed at stimulating religious tourism among Shi'i communities all over the world. Although the politics of Iraq have been heavily influenced by sectarian tensions, in some cases these tombs – their Shi'i significance notwithstanding – are revered even by local Sunni communities. Many Sunnis in Samarra, for instance, hold the local al-Askari Mosque, which contains the tombs of the tenth and eleventh Imams of the Twelver Shi'a, as a venerable site and an object of local pride.

We have repeatedly seen that local contexts strongly shape local practices, and the case of pilgrimage is no exception. The Imam Reza shrine in Mashhad, for instance, is strongly enmeshed in Iranian Shi'i culture; situated near Iran's eastern border, the site has long acted as a Mecca of sorts for those unable to travel to the holy city in Arabia. Just as Muslims who complete the pilgrimage to Mecca acquire the title Hajji, those who visit Mashhad can use the title Mashhadi (or Mashti) in recognition of their piety. Similar to the many sites of religious learning that have developed around Mecca and Medina, Mashhad contains some of Iran's greatest religious institutions, libraries and museums – affirming its spiritual and cultural significance for Iranian Shi'i communities.

Tragically, the tombs of the Twelver Shi'i imams have long endured attacks and other acts of destruction. The 2006 and 2007 bombings of al-Askari Mosque, mentioned above, are recent examples, and an attack at the shrine of Imam Reza in 1994 is another. In both cases, the shrines have been rebuilt – and even expanded. From a theological perspective, many Shi'is view these attacks as yet further confirmation of the persecution that the imams and their communities must endure. Continuing to visit these shrines and financing their reconstruction and expansion is thus seen as an act of great piety.

Shi'i pilgrimage is not only limited to the shrines of the imams however. A particularly illustrative case is the Baqi cemetery close to the Prophet's tomb in Medina. The cemetery contains the graves of several early Islamic figures closely associated with Muhammad, including his son Ibrahim, daughter Fatima, several of his wives, and the early Shi'i imams. Although the site is of great historical significance to all Muslims, in 1925, after taking the city, the Wahhabis demolished many of these tombs and severely restricted the performance of any religious rituals there. In lieu of visiting the Baqi, for much of the 20th century many Shi'a have made pilgrimage to Bab al-Saghir, a cemetery in Damascus, close to the Umayyad Mosque, that contains the grave of Umm Kulthum, the daughter of Ali and Fatima, as well as Bilal, the close companion and preferred muezzin of Muhammad. It also contains cenotaphs that commemorate several figures beloved of the Shi'a but whose actual graves are in Baqi cemetery. Yet the spiritual significance of Bab al-Saghir does not derive wholly, or even principally, from its graves and cenotaphs, but rather from its associations with the early imams and the battle of Karbala. The Umayyad caliph Yazid I buried the heads of the martyrs of Karbala at Bab al-Saghir; though they were later removed, many believe that their former presence has had a lasting spiritual effect on the site. Ali b. Husayn (Zayn al-Abidin), Husayn's son and heir, was also imprisoned there; the places in which he performed *wudu* and his daily prayers, together with other areas associated with his imprisonment, are especially venerated. Shi'i groups from across the world have travelled to the site seeking the *baraka* with which it is associated. Such pilgrimages often include the ritual execration of the enemies of Husayn and his companions – especially Yazid. In addition to visiting the shrines of the imams, it is also customary for groups such as the Bohra Ismailis to visit the tombs of their *da'i*s, or religious leaders, in Yemen and India.

The Poetry of Love

In addition to pilgrimage, poetry of various genres has been a powerful medium through which the Shi'a express love and devotion (*walaya*) to their imams. Over the centuries, innumerable poems have been composed in classical languages such as Arabic, Persian and Urdu, utilising diverse literary forms, the most prominent being the *qasida*, a panegyric of Arabic origin. The *musadda*s, or six-verse stanza, has been a favourite form for the composition of long elegiac poems, particularly those that honour Imam Husayn. In South Asia, Shi'i artistes have also employed the *ghazal* and the *qawwali*, forms of poetry usually associated with Sufi groups. Forms of devotional poetry in languages and idioms specific to certain regions or communities have also developed. One such example is the *ginan*s, or 'hymns of wisdom', associated with the Nizari Ismailis of South Asia. The *ginan*s are attributed to one of several medieval preacher-poets, referred to as *pir*s or *sayyid*s, believed to have been sent to the subcontinent by Ismaili imams living in Iran to propagate Ismaili concepts and ideas. In the process they composed songs in local languages as a way of providing instruction on a variety of doctrinal, ethical and mystical topics. Although composed several centuries ago, *ginan*s are recited daily in *jamatkhana*s (houses of congregation) wherever Nizari Ismailis from the subcontinent have settled. In the *ginan*s, the *pir*s represented themselves as guides who knew the whereabouts of the long-awaited tenth *avatara* of the deity Vishnu – Ali, and by extension his successor imams in the Nizari Ismaili lineage. In this way, the *pir*s strove to portray the imams as the culmination of the Vaishnavite tradition, enabling them to present Ismaili Shi'i notions of the imam within an Indic framework. One of the major themes of the *ginan*s is the relationship between the disciples and the imam, who is the repository of knowledge and inheritor of a pre-eternal and cosmic light (*nur*), expressed beautifully through the following verses:

> Construct a boat from the name of Ali and fill it with Truth
> When the winds of love blow, the True Master will surely guide
> it to the shore of salvation.
> Apply the collyrium (*kajal*) of Love to your eyes, let the Beloved
> be the garland around your neck.[10]

In representing this relationship, the *ginan*s draw on local Indic literary traditions of love symbolism in which the disciple is represented as a *virahini*, the woman longing for her beloved. Best exemplified in Indic traditions by Radha and the *gopi*s (cowmaids) in their yearning for Krishna, in the *ginan*s the *virahini* becomes symbolic of the human soul who is experiencing *viraha* (longing) for the beloved, almost always

---

[10] Ali Asani, 'Satpanthi Ismaili Songs to Hazrat Ali and the Imams', in Barbara Metcalf, ed., *Islam in South Asia in Practice* (Princeton, NJ, 2009), p. 52.

identified as the imam. As a result, the *ginan*s often portray the believer as a *virahini* by employing the feminine voice, although their authors are predominantly male. Some *ginan*s mention a covenant (*kol*) of love between the bride-soul and the imam, a covenant that includes the promise of a marriage and marital bliss (*suhag*). This may be an allusion to the primordial covenant of *alast* – central to Islamic mysticism – that binds all of creation with God through love.

> How tired are my eyes from waiting expectantly:
> When will my Lord come?
> So that knowing him to be present before me, I may pay my respects
> Beloved, bowing humbly, I will greet you.
> Sweet Lord, I remember your name
> O Lord, I remember your name
> O Master, I remember your name.
>
> My Master, I have been in love with you since I was a child
> I am in love with the Lord of the Light
> How can the ignorant possibly understand this?
> Sweet Lord, I remember your name
> O Lord, I remember your name
> O Master, I remember your name.[11]

This survey has shown that a particular cosmological framework – the doctrine of *walaya* – is integral to, and distinctive of, the devotional practices of Shi'i communities throughout the world. *Walaya* implies not only the imam's authority and nearness to God – in addition to his intercessory powers – but calls upon humanity to demonstrate their love for him. But we have seen that doctrine alone cannot sufficiently explain the ways in which devotional practices are articulated and enacted throughout the world. The historical experience of persecution has strongly influenced the ethos of many Shi'i practices. By looking at doctrine and history together, therefore, we are better equipped to understand a wide variety of devotional practices – from the *matam* in South Asia to the *taziya* in Iran. And though *walaya* and historical experience are integral to Shi'i religious experience, we have seen that cultural contexts heavily inflect local practices, from the Hosay in Trinidad to the *virahini* in Sindh. The rich diversity of their expression has thus become a characteristic marker of Shi'i devotional life.

---

[11] Asani, 'Satpanthi Ismaili Songs', pp. 56–57.

Further Reading

Aghaie, Kamran Scot. *The Martyrs of Karbala: Shi'i Symbols and Rituals in Modern Iran*. Seattle, WA, 2004.

Asani, Ali S. *Ecstasy and Enlightenment: The Ismaili Devotional Literature of South Asia*. London, 2002.

Chelkowski, Peter J. *Ta'ziyeh, Ritual and Drama in Iran*. New York, 1979.

—— *Eternal Performance: Ta'ziyeh and Other Shi'ite Rituals*. London and New York, 2010.

Flaskerud, Ingvild. *Visualizing Belief and Piety in Iranian Shi'ism*. London and New York, 2010.

Hyder, Syed Akbar. *Reliving Karbala: Martyrdom in South Asian Memory*. Oxford, 2006.

Luft, Paul and Colin Turner, ed. *Shi'ism: Critical Concepts in Islamic Studies*. New York, 2008.

Padwick, Constance. *Muslim Devotion: A Study of Prayer-Manuals in Common Use*. London, 1961.

Pinault, David. *The Shi'ites: Ritual and Popular Piety in a Muslim Community*. New York, 1992.

Waugh, Earle. 'Everyday Tradition', in Amyn B. Sajoo, ed., *A Companion to Muslim Cultures*. London, 2012, pp. 21–35.

9

Shi'i Communities in History

Farhad Daftary

Islam is a major world religion, with some 1.3 billion adherents scattered in almost every region of the globe, especially in the Middle East, Asia and Africa. Currently, around 15 per cent of the Muslim population of the world belongs to various communities of Shi'i Islam, with the Sunni Muslims accounting for the remaining 85 per cent. The Shi'i Muslims themselves are comprised of a number of major communties, including the Ithna'asharis or Twelvers who account for the largest numbers, the Ismailis and the Zaydis.

In addition to their significant numbers, around 200 million, Shi'i Muslims have played a key role, proportionately much greater than their relative size, in contributing to the intellectual and artistic accomplishments of Islamic civilisation. Indeed, Shi'i scholars and literati of various communities and regions, including scientists, philosophers, theologians, jurists and poets, have made seminal contributions to Islamic thought and culture. There have also been a multitude of Shi'i dynasties, families or individuals who variously patronised scholars, poets and artists as well as numerous institutions of learning in Islam. Amongst such major Shi'i dynasties, particular mention should be made of the Buyids, the Fatimids, the Hamdanids and the Safawids, as well as a host of lesser dynasties of North Africa, the Middle East and South Asia. In sum, the Shi'i Muslims have contributed significantly over the entire course of Islamic history to the richness and diversity of Islamic traditions, enabling Islam to evolve not merely as a religion, but also as a major world civilisation.

The unified nascent Muslim community, or *umma*, of the Prophet Muhammad's time soon split into numerous rival factions and lesser groups, as Muslims disagreed on a range of fundamental issues after the death of the Prophet in 632. Modern scholarship has shown that at least during the first three centuries of their history, marking the formative period of Islam, Muslims lived in an intellectually dynamic and theologically fluid milieu characterised by a multiplicity of communities of interpretation and schools of thought with a diversity of views on a range of religio-political issues.

The early Muslims were confronted by many gaps in their religious knowledge and understanding of the Islamic revelation, which revolved around issues such as the attributes of God, the nature of authority and the definitions of true believers and sinners, amongst other theological concerns. It was during this formative period that different groups and schools of thought began to articulate their doctrinal positions and gradually acquired their distinctive religious identities and designations. In this effervescent atmosphere, Muslims engaged in lively discourses and disputations on a variety of religio-political issues, while ordinary Muslims as well as their scholars moved rather freely between different communities of interpretation. In terms of theological perspectives, which remained closely linked to political loyalties, pluralism in early Islam ranged from the stances of those Muslims, later designated as Sunnis, who endorsed the historical caliphate and the authority-power structure that had actually emerged in Muslim society to various religio-political communities, notably the Shi'a and the Khawarij, who aspired towards the establishment of new orders and leadership paradigms.

In this emerging partisan context, the medieval religious scholars (*ulama*) of the Sunni Muslims produced a picture of early Islam that is at great variance with the findings of modern scholarship on the subject. According to this Sunni narrative, endorsed unwittingly by the earlier generations of orientalists, Islam was from the beginning a monolithic phenomenon with a well-defined doctrinal basis from which different groups deviated over time. In other words, Sunni Islam was portrayed by its exponents as the 'true' interpretation of Islam, while all non-Sunni Muslim communities of interpretation, especially the Shi'a, who had supposedly 'deviated' from the right path, were accused of heresy (*ilhad*), innovation (*bid'a*) or even unbelief (*kufr*). The Shi'a, who elaborated their own paradigmatic model of 'true Islam', soon disagreed among themselves, however, regarding the identity of the legitimate spiritual leaders or imams of the community. As a result, the Shi'a were soon subdivided into a number of major communities as well as several minor groupings.

In such a milieu of theological pluralism and diversity of communal interpretations, abundantly recorded in the heresiographical tradition of the Muslims, obviously general consensus could not be attained on designating any one interpretation of Islam as the 'true Islam'. To make matters more complicated, different regimes lent their support to particular doctrinal positions that were legitimised in their state by their *ulama*, who in turn were accorded a privileged social status in society. It is important to bear in mind that many of the original and fundamental disagreements among Sunnis, Shi'is and other Muslims will in all likelihood never be satisfactorily explained and resolved, mainly because of a lack of reliable sources, especially from the earliest centuries of Islamic history. Needless to add that the later writings of the historians, theologians, heresiographers and other categories of Muslim authors display variegated 'sectarian' biases.

In spite of its relative significance, however, Shi'i Islam has received very little scholarly attention in the West. And when it has been discussed, whether in general or in terms of its subdivisions, it has normally been treated marginally, often as a 'heterodoxy', echoing the attitude of Sunni Muslims who have always accounted for the majority share of Muslim society. Scientific orientalism, based on the study of textual evidence, began in Europe in the 19th century. European scholars now started to produce their studies of Islam on the basis of manuscripts, which had been written mainly by Sunni authors and reflected their particular perspectives. Consequently, the orientalists, too, studied Islam according to the Sunni stances of their original sources; and, borrowing classifications from their own Christian contexts, they treated the Sunni interpretation of Islam as 'orthodoxy', in contrast to Shi'ism which was taken to represent 'heterodoxy', or at its extreme a 'heresy'. The Sunni-centric approach to the study of Islam has continued to hold prominence to various degrees in Western scholarship on the subject. At the same time, Shi'i studies have also remained extremely marginalised in Muslim countries outside Iran and Iraq with their vibrant religious seminaries and Shi'i theological traditions as well as massive collections of Shi'i manuscripts. Increased accessibility to Shi'i texts, during more recent times, promises to bring about drastic revisions in the approaches of Western scholars to Islamic studies.

Origins and Early History of Shi'i Islam

The origins of Islam's main divisions into Sunni and Shi'i may be broadly traced to the crisis of succession to the Prophet Muhammad, who died in 632 after a brief illness. The successor to Muhammad could not be another prophet or *nabi*, as it had already been made known through divine revelation that Muhammad was the 'seal of the prophets' (*khatam al-anbiya*). However, a successor was needed in order to ensure the continued unity of the nascent Islamic community. According to the Sunni view, the Prophet had left neither formal instruction nor a testament regarding his succession. Amidst much ensuing debate, this choice was resolved by a group of Muslim notables who elected Abu Bakr, a trusted Companion of the Prophet, as successor to the Messenger of God (*khalifat rasul Allah*), a title which was soon simplified to *khalifa* (whence the word 'caliph' in Western languages). By electing the first successor to the Prophet, these Muslims had now also founded the distinctive Islamic institution of the caliphate (*khilafa*).

Abu Bakr and his next two successors, Umar and Uthman, belonging to the influential Meccan tribe of Quraysh, were among the earliest converts to Islam and the Prophet's Companions. Only the fourth of the so-called 'rightly-guided caliphs', Ali b. Abi Talib (r. 656–661), who occupies a unique position in the annals of Shi'i Islam, belonged to the Prophet's own clan of Banu Hashim within the Quraysh. Ali was also very closely related to the Prophet, being his cousin and son-in-law, bound in matrimony to the Prophet's daughter, Fatima.

It is the fundamental belief of the Shi'a of all branches that the Prophet had designated Ali as his successor, a designation (*nass*) instituted through divine command and revealed by the Prophet at Ghadir Khumm shortly before his death. The Shi'a have also interpreted certain Quranic verses in support of Ali's designation. Ali himself was firmly convinced of the legitimacy of his own claim to Muhammad's succession, based on his close kinship and association with him, his intimate knowledge of Islam as well as the merits of his early deeds in the cause of Islam. Indeed, Ali made it plain in his speeches and letters that he considered the Prophet's family or the *ahl al-bayt* to be entitled to the leadership of the Muslims as long as there remained a single one of them who recited the Quran, knew the *sunna* and adhered to the religion of the truth.[1] And from early on, Ali did have a circle of supporters who believed he was better qualified than any other Companion to succeed the Prophet. This minority group expanded in time and in Ali's brief caliphate became generally designated as the *shi'at Ali*, or the 'party of Ali', and then simply as the Shi'a.

The Shi'a also held a particular conception of religious authority that set them apart from the other Muslims. They believed that Islam contained inner truths that could not be understood directly through human reason. Thus, they recognised the need for a religiously authoritative guide, or imam as the Shi'a have traditionally preferred to call their spiritual leader. In addition to being the guardian of the Islamic revelation and leader of the community, as perceived by the majority of the Muslims, the succession to the Prophet was seen by the Shi'a as having a key spiritual function connected with the elucidation and interpretation of the Islamic message. And for the Shi'a the Prophet's family, or the *ahl al-bayt*, provided the sole authoritative channel for elucidating fully the teachings of Islam. These ideas, which may not be attributed entirely to the earliest partisans of Ali, eventually found their full elaboration in the central Shi'i doctrine of the imamate.

---

[1] W. Madelung has produced an exhaustive analysis of the historiography on this subject in his *The Succession to Muhammad: A Study of the Early Caliphate* (Cambridge, 1997).

Pro-Ali sentiments and broad Shi'i tendencies persisted in Ali's life-time; and the early Shi'a survived Ali's murder in 661 and numerous subsequent tragic events. After Ali, his partisans in Kufa, to where Ali had transferred his capital to confront a challenge to his authority by Mu'awiya, the governor of Syria, recognised his eldest son al-Hasan as his successor to the caliphate. Under obscure circumstances, al-Hasan abdicated a few months later in favour of Mu'awiya, whose power had become unchallengeable. Mu'awiya was speedily recognised as the new caliph, and he was to found the first dynasty in Islam, the Umayyads, which stayed in power for nearly a century. Meanwhile, following his peace treaty with Mu'awiya, al-Hasan had retired to Medina and abstained from any political activity. However, the Shi'a continued to regard him as their imam after Ali.

After al-Hasan's death in 669, the Kufan Shi'a revived their aspira-tions for restoring the caliphate to the Prophet's family and invited al-Hasan's younger brother al-Husayn, their new imam, to rise against the Umayyads and restore the legitimate rule of the *ahl al-bayt*. Having decline to pledge allegiance to Mu'awiya's son Yazid, al-Husayn finally responded to these summons and set out from the Hijaz for Kufa. On 10 Muharram 61/10 October 680, al-Husayn and his small band of relatives and companions were ruthlessly massacred at Karbala, near Kufa, where they had been intercepted by an Umayyad army. The martyrdom of the Prophet's grandson, together with numerous other members of the *ahl al-bayt*, infused a new religious fervour in the Shi'a and contributed significantly to the consolidation of the Shi'i ethos and identity. It also led to the formation of radical trends among the Shi'a. The earlier Kufan Shi'a had remained relatively moderate in their stance on the historical caliphate. Henceforth, the passion motif and the call for repentence and martyrdom became integral aspects of Shi'i spirituality. Later, the Shi'a began to commemorate the martyrdom of Imam al-Husayn annually on 10 Muharram, known as *Ashura*, with special ceremonies and the so-called *taziya* performances.

During its first half-century, Shi'ism remained unified, and main-tained an almost exclusively Arab composition with a limited appeal to non-Arab Muslims, the so-called *mawali*. These features changed with the next important event in the early history of Shi'i Islam, the move-ment of al-Mukhtar b. Abi Ubayd al-Thaqafi, who launched his own Shi'i campaign with a general call to avenge al-Husayn's murder. Winning the support of the majority of the Kufan Shi'a, al-Mukhtar claimed to be acting on behalf of Ali's then only surviving son, Muhammad b. al-Hanafiyya, whose mother hailed from the Banu Hanifa; he was half-brother to al-Hasan and al-Husayn, Ali's sons by Fatima. Ibn al-Hanafiyya, who declined to assume the active leadership of the move-ment and remained in Medina (the traditional residence of the Alids), was proclaimed by al-Mukhtar as the imam and Mahdi, or the 'divinely-guided one', the messianic saviour imam and restorer of true Islam who would establish justice on earth and deliver the oppressed from tyranny.

The concept of the Mahdi was a very important doctrinal innovation, and proved particularly appealing to the *mawali*, the Aramean, Persian, Berber and other non-Arab converts to Islam who, under the Umayyads, were treated as second-class Muslims. As a large and underprivileged social class, and aspiring to the establishment of an order based on the egalitarian precepts of Islam, the *mawali* provided a major recruiting ground for any movement opposed to the exclusively Arab hegemony of the Umayyads. They became particularly drawn to al-Mukhtar's movement and Shi'ism, calling themselves the *shi'at al-mahdi*, or 'party of the Mahdi'. With the help of the *mawali*, al-Mukhtar readily won control of Kufa in an open revolt in 685. The Shi'a now avenged Imam al-Husayn, killing those responsible for the massacre at Karbala. However, al-Mukhtar's success was short-lived. In 687, he was defeated and killed together with thousands of his *mawali* supporters. But the movement founded by al-Mukhtar survived his demise.

The 60-odd years intervening between the revolt of al-Mukhtar and the Abbasid revolution mark the second phase in the early history of Shi'i Islam. During this period different Shi'i groups, consisting of both Arabs and *mawali*, came to coexist, each one having its own line of imams and propounding its own doctrines. Furthermore, the Shi'i imams now hailed not only from the major branches of the extended Alid family, namely the Hanafids (descendants of Muhammad b. al-Hanafiyya), the Husaynids (descendants of al-Husayn b. Ali) and, later, the Hasanids (descendants of al-Hasan b. Ali), but also from other branches of the Prophet's clan of Banu Hashim. This is because the Prophet's family or the *ahl al-bayt*, whose sanctity was supreme for the Shi'a, was then still defined broadly in its old Arabian tribal sense. It, therefore, covered the various branches of the Banu Hashim, including the Alids as well as the descendants of the Prophet's two paternal uncles, namely, the Talibids, descendants of Abu Talib through both of his sons Ali and Ja'far al-Tayyar (d. 629) and the Abbasids, descendants of al-Abbas (d. 653). In sum, the Fatimid and non-Fatimid Alids as well as many non-Alid Hashimids, all belonging to the Banu Hashim, apparently qualified as belonging to the *ahl al-bayt*. It was after the Abbasid revolution that the Shi'a came to define the *ahl al-bayt* more restrictively to include only the Fatimid Alids, covering both the Husaynids and the Hasanids.

In this fluid and often confusing setting, Shi'ism evolved in terms of two main branches or factions, the Kaysaniyya and the Imamiyya, each with its own internal divisions; and, later, another Alid movement led to the foundation of yet another major Shi'i community, the Zaydiyya. There were also those Shi'i *ghulat*, individual theorists with small groups of followers, who existed in the midst or on the fringes of the major Shiʻi communities. For information on these early Shiʻi groups and their subdivisions, we must rely mainly on the heresiographical literature of the Muslims produced by later generations of scholars with their own sectarian perspectives.

A radical branch, in terms of both doctrine and policy, evolved out of al-Mukhtar's movement and accounted for the majority of the Shiʻa until shortly after the Abbasid revolution. This branch, breaking away from the religiously moderate attitudes of the early Kufan Shiʻa, was generally designated as the Kaysaniyya by the heresiographers. The Kaysaniyya, comprising of a number of interrelated groups, and recognising various Hanafid Alids and other Hashimids as their imams, drew mainly on the support of the *mawali* in southern Iraq, Persia and elsewhere, though many Arabs were also among them. Heirs to a variety of pre-Islamic traditions, the *mawali* played a crucial role in transforming Shiʻism from an Arab party of limited size and doctrinal basis to a dynamic movement.

In the ideas expounded by the Kaysani Shiʻi groups we have the first Shiʻi statements of the eschatological doctrines of *ghayba*, the absence or occultation of an imam whose life has been miraculously prolonged and who is due to reappear as the Mahdi; and *rajʻa*, the return of a messianic personality from the dead, or from occultation, sometime before the Day of Resurrection (*qiyama*). The closely related concept of the Mahdi had now acquired a more specific eschatological meaning as the messianic deliverer in Islam, with the implication that no further imams would succeed the Mahdi during his occultation. On Ibn al-Hanafiyya's death in 700, the bulk of the Kaysaniyya recognised his son Abu Hashim as their next imam. And on Abu Hashim's death in 716, a majority of his Kaysani followers, known as the Hashimiyya, acknowledged the Abbasid Muhammad, a great-grandson of the Prophet's uncle al-Abbas, as their new imam. This party continued to be known as the Hashimiyya and later also as the Abbasiyya, and it served as the main instrument of the Abbasid movement, which succeeded in overthrowing the Umayyads.

Meanwhile, there had appeared another major branch or faction of Shiʻism, later designated as the Imamiyya, the common heritage of the Twelver and the Ismaili Shiʻis. The Imami Shiʻis, who like other Shiʻi Muslims of the Umayyad period were centred in Kufa, adopted a quiescent policy in the political field while doctrinally they subscribed to some of the radical views of the Kaysaniyya, such as the condemnation of the early caliphs before Ali. The Imamiyya traced the imamate through al-Husayn b. Ali's sole surviving son, Ali b. al-Husayn Zayn al-Abidin, the progenitor of the Husaynid line of the Alid imams. He retired to Medina and adopted a quiescent attitude towards the Umayyads, and later towards al-Mukhtar's movement. It was after Zayn al-Abidin's death around 714 that the Imamiyya began to gain some importance under his son and successor Muhammad b. Ali, known as al-Baqir, who engaged in active Shi'i teachings in the course of an imamate of some 20 years.

Imam Muhammad al-Baqir concentrated on teaching and expounding the rudiments of the ideas that were to become the legitimistic principles of the Imami branch of Shi'i Islam. Above all, he seems to have concerned himself with the religious rank and spiritual authority of the imams who possessed what was considered to be a divinely inspired knowledge (*ilm*). He taught that the world was in permanent need of such an imam. He is also credited with introducing the principle of *taqiyya*, the precautionary dissimulation of one's true religious belief and practice that was to protect the imam and his followers under adverse circumstances. This principle was later adopted by the Twelver and Ismaili Shi'is, while it did not find any particular prominence in Zaydi doctrine. Imam al-Baqir's legal and ritual teachings comprised many of the features that were later regarded as distinctive aspects of Imami Shi'i law.[2]

On Imam al-Baqir's death, around 732, the majority of his Imami Shi'i followers recognised his eldest son Ja'far, later called al-Sadiq (the Trustworthy), as their new imam, being designated as such by the *nass* of his father. The Imamiyya expanded significantly and became a major religious community during the long and eventful imamate of Ja'far al-Sadiq, the foremost scholar and teacher amongst the Husaynid Alids. In the earlier years of Imam al-Sadiq's long imamate, the movement of his uncle Zayd b. Ali Zayn al-Abidin, al-Baqir's half-brother, was launched in 740 with some success, leading to the formation of the Zaydiyya community of Shi'i Islam.

Meanwhile, the Abbasids had learned important lessons from all the abortive Kaysani Shi'i revolts against the Umayyads. Consequently, they paid particular attention to developing the organisation of their own movement. The Abbasid *da'wa* was cleverly preached in the name of *al-rida min al Muhammad*, an enigmatic phrase which spoke of an unidentified person belonging to the Prophet's family. This slogan aimed to maximise support from the Shi'is of different groups who commonly upheld the leadership of the *ahl al-bayt*.

However, the Abbasid victory in 750 proved a source of utter disillusionment for the Shi'a, who had all along expected an Alid, rather than an Abbasid, from the *ahl al-bayt* to succeed the Umayyads to the caliphate. The animosity between the Abbasids and the Alids was accentuated when, soon after their accession, the Abbasids began to persecute

---

[2]   See Arzina R. Lalani, *Early Shi'i Thought: The Teachings of Imam Muhammad al-Baqir* (London, 2000), especially pp. 84–95, 114–126.

many of their former Shi'i supporters and the Alids. Shi'i disappointment was further aggravated when the Abbasids renounced their own Shi'i past and became the spiritual spokesmen of Sunni Islam. With these developments, many of those remaining Kaysani Shi'is who had not been absorbed into the Abbasid movement now rallied to the side of Imam Ja'far al-Sadiq, who thus emerged as the main rallying point for Shi'is of diverse backgrounds, apart from the Zaydi Shi'is who followed their own imams.

Meanwhile, Imam al-Sadiq had gradually acquired a widespread reputation as a religious scholar. He was a reporter of *hadith*, and was later cited as such in the chain of authorities accepted by Sunni Muslims as well. He also taught *fiqh*, or jurisprudence, and has been credited with founding, after the work of his father, the Imami Shi'i school of religious law (*madhhab*), named Ja'fari after him. Imam al-Sadiq was accepted as a teaching authority not only by his Shi'i partisans but by a wider circle that included many of the piety-minded Muslims of Medina and Kufa, where the bulk of the Imamiyya had continued to be located. In time, a noteworthy group of scholars assembled around him, comprising some of the most eminent jurist-traditionists and theologians of the time, such as Hisham b. al-Hakam (d. 795), the foremost representative of Imami scholastic theology (*kalam*). Indeed, the Imami Shi'is now came to possess a distinctive body of ritual, as well as theological and legal doctrines.

As a result of the intellectual activities of Imam al-Sadiq and his circle of learned associates, the basic conception of the Imami Shi'i doctrine of the imamate was now elaborated. This doctrine, expressed in numerous *hadith*s reported mainly from Imam al-Sadiq, is preserved in the earliest corpus of Imami *hadith* compiled by al-Kulayni (d. 940).[3] This central Imami Shi'i doctrine, which was essentially retained by the later Ithna'asharis and Ismailis, was founded on a belief in the permanent need of mankind for a divinely-guided and infallible (*ma'sum*) imam who, after the Prophet Muhammad, would act as the authoritative teacher and guide of men in all their spiritual affairs. Although the imam, who can practise *taqiyya* when necessary, is entitled to temporal leadership as much as to religious authority, his mandate does not depend on his actual rule. The doctrine further taught that the Prophet himself had designated Ali b. Abi Talib as his legatee (*wasi*) and successor by an explicit designation (*nass*) under divine command. However, the majority of the Prophet's Companions had ignored this designation.

---

[3] See Abu Ja'far Muhammad b. Ya'qub al-Kulayni, *Kitab al-hujja*, the first book of his *al-Usul min al-kafi*, ed. A. A. al-Ghaffari (Tehran, 1388/1968), vol. 1, pp. 168–548.

After Ali, the imamate was to be transmitted by the rule of the *nass* from father to son through the descendants of Ali and Fatima; and after al-Husayn b. Ali, it would continue in the Husaynid line until the end of time. This Husaynid Alid imam, the sole legitimate imam at any time, is in possession of special knowledge (*ilm*), and has perfect understanding of all aspects and meanings of the Quran and the message of Islam. Indeed, the world could not exist for a moment without such an imam, who is the proof of God (*hujjat Allah*) on earth. The imam's existence is so essential that recognition of and obedience to him were made the absolute duty of every believer (*mu'min*).

Having established a solid doctrinal basis for Imami Shi'ism, Imam Ja'far al-Sadiq, the last of the early Shi'i imams recognised by both the Ithna'asharis and the Ismailis, and counted as the sixth for the former and the fifth for the latter, died in 765. The dispute over his succession caused historic divisions in the Imami Shi'i community, leading to the eventual formation of independent Ithna'ashari and Ismaili communities.

The Twelvers

On Imam Ja'far al-Sadiq's death in 765, his succession was simultaneously claimed by several of his sons. As a result, the Imami Shi'is now split into various groups, one of which eventually acquired the designation of the Ithna'ashari or Twelver, recognising a line of 12 imams, starting with Ali b. Abi Talib and ending with Muhammad b. al-Hasan who was acknowledged as the eschatological Mahdi.

The majority of Imam al-Sadiq's Imami partisans recognised his eldest surviving son Abd Allah al-Aftah as his successor to the imamate. And when Abd Allah died a few months later, many of his followers turned to his younger half-brother Musa al-Kazim, who already had an Imami following of his own. Musa al-Kazim, later counted as the seventh imam of the Twelvers, soon received the allegiance of the majority of the Imami Shi'a, including the most renowned scholars in al-Sadiq's entourage. Imam Musa al-Kazim strengthened and further developed the rudimentary organisation of his Imami group by appointing agents to supervise his followers in different localities. However, in line with the tradition established by his predecessors, he too refrained from all political activity. Nevertheless, he was not spared the persecutions of the Abbasids. He was arrested several times and banished to Iraq on the orders of the fifth Abbasid caliph, Harun al-Rashid (r. 786–809), who had retained the anti-Shi'i policies of his predecessors. Imam al-Kazim died in 799 in a Baghdad prison, perhaps due to poisoning, as the Twelvers claim in the case of almost all their imams.

On Musa al-Kazim's death his Imami Shi'a split into several sects. A significant group now acknowledged his son Ali al-Rida as their next imam, later counted as the eighth in the line of the Twelver imams. The contemporary Abbasid caliph, al-Ma'mun, attempted to achieve a reconciliation between the Abbasids and Alids by appointing Ali al-Rida as his heir apparent in 816. This attempt proved futile, however, as Ali died in 818 in Khurasan, where he had joined the entourage of al-Ma'mun. A new city near Tus, called Mashhad (the martyr's place), grew up around Ali al-Rida's tomb and became the most important Shi'i shrine in Persia. A group of Imam al-Rida's Shi'a traced their imamate for three more generations in his progeny down to their 11th imam, al-Hasan al-Askari, with minor schisms. These imams, too, were brought to Baghdad or Samarra (for a while the Abbasid capital), and watched closely by the agents of the Abbasid regime.

On Imam al-Hasan al-Askari's death in 874, his Imami Shi'a partisans experienced a serious crisis of succession, and subdivided into numerous splinter groups, of which only one (the Imamiyya proper) was to survive as the Twelver Shi'a.[4] This main body, later designated specifically as the Ithna'ashariyya, eventually held that a son named Muhammad had been born to al-Hasan al-Askari in 869 and that the child had been kept hidden out of fear of Abbasid persecution. They further held that Muhammad had succeeded his father to the imamate while remaining in concealment as before. Identified as the Mahdi and its equivalent *qa'im* (the 'riser'), Muhammad was expected to reappear in glory before the final Day of Judgement to rule the world in justice.

According to the Twelver Shi'i tradition, the occultation of Muhammad al-Mahdi fell into two periods. During his initial 'lesser occultation', covering 874–941, the hidden imam remained in regular contact with his community through four successive representatives, who acted as intermediaries between him and his followers. But in the 'greater occultation', initiated in 941 and still continuing, the hidden imam has chosen not to have any representative while living on earth and participating in worldly experience. The Mahdi enjoys a miraculously prolonged life, as explained in numerous Twelver theological treatises. Twelver Shi'i scholars have written extensively on the eschatological doctrine of the occultation (*ghayba*) of their twelfth, hidden Imam-Mahdi and the conditions that would need to prevail before his return (*raj'a*). By the first half of the 10th century, when the line of the 12 imams had been identified, those Imami Shi'is believing in that series of

---

4   See Abu Muhammad al-Hasan b. Musa al-Nawbakhti, *Kitab firaq al-Shi'a*, ed. H. Ritter (Istanbul, 1931), pp. 79–94; Sa'd b. Abd Allah al-Qummi, *Kitab al-maqalat wa'l-firaq*, ed. M. J. Mashkur (Tehran, 1963), pp. 102–116; and E. Kohlberg, 'From Imamiyya to Ithna-'Ashariyya', *Bulletin of the School of Oriental and African Studies*, 39 (1976), pp. 521–534; reprinted in his *Belief and Law in Imami Shi'ism* (Aldershot, 1991), article XIV.

imams became known as the Ithna'ashariyya or Twelvers, and as such they were distinguished from all earlier or contemporary Imami Shi'i groups.

In the first phase of their religious history, stretching from its origins to the occultation of the twelfth imam, the Imami (Ithna'ashari) Shi'a benefited from the direct spiritual guidance and teachings of their imams. It was in the second phase of their history, from around 874 until the Mongol invasions of the 13th century, that Twelver scholars (*ulama*) emerged as influential guardians and transmitters of the teachings of their imams, compiling collections of Imami *hadith* and formulating Imami law. This phase coincided with the rise of the Buyids, in Persia and Iraq, as overlords of the Abbasids. The Buyids were originally Zaydi Shi'is from Daylam, in northern Persia, but after establishing their own dynasty, they supported Mu'tazilism and Shi'ism without allegiance to any specific branch, though they may have been more inclined towards Twelver Shi'ism.

The earliest comprehensive collections of the sayings and teachings of the Twelver imams, which were first transmitted in Kufa and elsewhere, were compiled in Qumm, in Persia. By the 9th century, Qumm was already the chief centre of Imami Shi'i learning, whereas in Kufa the Shi'a were divided into many rival factions, including especially the Zaydis. It was thus in Qumm that the traditions of the Imami Shi'i imams were first collected systematically by al-Kulayni (d. 940), in his *Kitab al-kafi*, which came to be recognised as the first of the four canonical collections of Imami *hadith*. These works deal with Imami theology and jurisprudence. The traditionist school of Qumm, which rejected all forms of *kalam* theology based on extensive use of independent reasoning (*aql*) and instead relied on the traditions of the Prophet and the imams, reached its peak in the works of Ibn Babawayh (d. 991), also known as Shaykh al-Saduq.

In the course of the 10th century, the traditionist school of Qumm began to be overshadowed by the rise of a rival school – the school of Imami theology (*kalam*) in Baghdad, which adhered to the rationalist theology of the Mu'tazila and also produced the principles of Imami (Twelver) Shi'i jurisprudence (*usul al-fiqh*) based on a legal methodology opposed to unqualified adherence to *hadith*.[5] The school of Baghdad, thus, assigned a fundamental role to reason (*aql*) in theology and jurisprudence. The first leader of the 'rationalist' Imami school of Baghdad was Shaykh al-Mufid (d. 1022), who criticised Ibn Babawayh's emphasis

---

[5]　See W. Madelung, 'Imamism and Mu'tazilite Theology', in T. Fahd, ed., *Le Shi'isme Imâmite* (Paris, 1970), pp. 13–28; reprinted in his *Religious Schools and Sects in Medieval Islam* (London, 1985), article VII.

on *hadith* and rejection of reasoning. In contrast al-Mufid argued for the methodology of *kalam*, religious disputation or reasoned argumentation; a methodology developed by the Mu'tazili theological school in Baghdad.

Shaykh al-Mufid was succeeded as chief authority of the Baghdad school and head of the Imami Twelver community by his student Sharif al-Murtada Alam al-Huda (d. 1044), a descendant of Imam Musa al-Kazim and also head (*naqib*) of the Alid family. He went further than al-Mufid and insisted, like the Mu'tazila, that the basic truths of religion could be established by reason (*aql*) alone. Even the transmitted *hadith*s were to be subjected to the test of reason rather than being accepted uncritically. Sharif al-Murtada's younger brother Sharif al-Radi (d. 1015) is responsible for having compiled the *Nahj al-balagha* (The Way of Eloquence), an anthology of the letters and sermons of Ali b. Abi Talib, which is regarded as one of the most venerated books of the Twelvers. Other Shi'i communities also hold this book in high esteem. Muhammad b. al-Hasan al-Tusi (d. 1067), known as Shaykh al-Ta'ifa, was another prominent member of the Baghdad school, and he became the most authoritative early systematiser of Twelver law. He also partially rehabilitated the school of Qumm and its reliance on traditions. However, the school of Qumm itself disintegrated in the 11th century, and its traditionist focus remained dormant in Twelver Shi'i thought until it was restated vigorously by Muhammad Amin al-Astarabadi (d. 1624), the reviver of the so-called Akhbari school.

Meanwhile, Twelver Shi'i communities had appeared in many parts of the Iranian world, not only in Qumm and Rayy, but also in different towns of Khurasan and Transoxania, as well as in central Persia, including Kashan, Isfahan, Hamadan and Qazwin. Minority Twelver communities also existed in Khuzistan and in the coastal region of northern Persia. The tombs of sayyids and descendants of the imams were now widely scattered throughout Persia, demonstrating that Twelver Shi'ism was well established, mainly in terms of small minority communities, in much of the Iranian world before the Mongol invasions. Outside Persia, Shi'i Islam received a serious blow when the Sunni Saljuqs succeeded the Shi'i Buyids. But the situation of the Shi'a improved when the non-Sunni Mongols established their rule in southwestern Asia. By then, a number of local dynasties in Iraq and Syria adhered to Twelver Shi'ism and patronised the efforts of their *ulama*. With the collapse of the Qarmati state of Bahrayn in 1077, a number of Twelver communities also began to gain influence in eastern Arabia and other localities around the Persian Gulf. Foremost among these local Twelver dynasties were the Mazyadids who had their capital at Hilla on the banks of the Euphrates. Indeed, from the beginning of the 12th century Hilla was established as an important centre of Shiʻi activity, and it later superseded Qumm and Baghdad as the main centre of Twelver scholarship.

Meanwhile, Sharif al-Murtada's basic approach to *kalam*, holding that reason was the sole source of the fundamentals of religion, had become widely accepted in Twelver Shiʻi circles. The same approach was later basically adopted by Khwaja Nasir al-Din al-Tusi (d. 1274), then the chief exponent of Imami *kalam*, and his disciple Ibn al-Mutahhar al-Hilli (d. 1325), who represented the last school of original thought in Twelver theology. Subsequently, with a few exceptions, Twelver scholars mainly produced commentaries (*sharh*) on, or restatements of, the earlier teachings. Indeed, with the Mongol invasions and the work of Nasir al-Din al-Tusi a third phase was initiated in the intellectual history of Twelver Shiʻism, which lasted until the advent of the Safawid dynasty in 1501.

Nasir al-Din al-Tusi, who spent some three decades in the fortress communities of the Nizari Ismailis of Persia and temporarily converted from Twelver to Ismaili Shiʻism, was the first Imami scholar to have been at once a theologian and a philosopher, having been particularly influenced by the philosophy of Ibn Sina (d. 1037), known in Europe as Avicenna. In this third phase, the influence of al-Tusi in both theology and philosophy was a key factor, while close relations also developed between Twelver theology and the Sufism of Ibn al-Arabi (d. 1240). Al-Tusi's student Ibn al-Mutahhar al-Hilli had lasting influence on the development and theoretical foundations of Twelver jurisprudence. Having argued against the reliability of *hadith*, and following in the tradition of the Baghdad school, he then reorganised jurisprudence so as to make reason its central focus, as well as introducing new principles of legal methodology. Indeed, he provided a theoretical foundation for *ijtihad*, the principle of legal ruling by the jurist (*faqih*) through reasoning (*aql*). In his *Mabadi al-wusul*, Allama al-Hilli expounds the principle of *ijtihad*, which is exercised by *mujtahid*s who, he argues, are fallible unlike the infallible imams. A *mujtahid* can, therefore, revise his decision. *Ijtihad* also allowed for *ikhtilaf*, or differences of opinion, among *mujtahid*s. Allama al-Hilli's acceptance of *ijtihad* represents a crucial step towards the enhancement of the authority of the *ulama* in Twelver Shiʻism in the absence of a manifest imam. *Ijtihad* also gained importance within Zaydi Shiʻism, but it was rejected by the Ismailis. It should also be added here that a major difference between the later Twelver Shiʻi doctrine of *ijtihad* and the Sunni doctrine is that Twelver Shiʻis do not allow for the *ijtihad* of the jurists who are no longer alive or of their books.

Meanwhile, Shiʻi tendencies had been spreading in Persia and Central Asia since the 13th century, creating a more favourable milieu in many predominantly Sunni regions for the activities of the Shiʻa (both Twelvers and Ismailis) as well as a number of movements with

Shi'i inclinations. In this connection, particular reference should be made to the Hurufi movement, whose doctrines were later adopted by the Bektashi dervishes of Anatolia, and the Nuqtawis who split off from the Hurufis. There were also the Twelver-related Musha'sha who ruled from Khuzistan, and under whose persecutionary policies Hilla lost its prominence as a centre of Twelver learning to Jabal Amil in Lebanon. These movements normally entertained chiliastic or Mahdist aspirations for the deliverance of the oppressed and underprivileged groups. Instead of propagating any particular form of Shi'ism, however, a new syncretic type of popular Shi'ism was now arising in post-Mongol Central Asia, Persia and Anatolia, which found its culmination in early Safawid Shi'ism. Marshall Hodgson designated this as 'tariqah Shi'ism', as it was transmitted mainly through a number of Sufi orders (tariqas) then being formed.[6] These Sufi orders remained outwardly Sunni, while being particularly devoted to Ali and the *ahl al-bayt*. Ali was in fact included in the chains (silsilas) of the spiritual masters of these Sunni Sufis. In this atmosphere of religious eclecticism, Alid loyalism became more widespread, and Shi'i elements began to be superficially imposed on Sunni Islam. It was under such circumstances that close relations developed between Twelver Shi'ism and Sufism, and also between Nizari Ismailism and Sufism, in Persia.

A fourth phase may be identified in the historical development of Twelver Shi'ism, from the establishment of Safawid rule in 1501 to around 1800. Post-Mongol Persia was politically fragmented, while Shi'i sentiments and Alid loyalism had continued to spread, especially through the Sufi orders. One of the Sufi orders that played a leading role in spreading Shi'ism in predominantly Sunni Persia was the Safawiyya *tariqa*, founded by Shaykh Safi al-Din (d. 1334), a Sunni Muslim. The Safawid order spread rapidly in Adharbayjan, eastern Anatolia and other regions, acquiring influence over several Turcoman tribes. Subsequently, the order was transformed into a militant revolutionary movement. A later Safawid master, Shaykh Haydar (d. 1488), was responsible for instructing his Sufi soldier followers to adopt the scarlet headgear of 12 gores commemorating the 12 imams, for which they became designated as the Qizilbash, a Turkish term meaning redhead.

The eclectic Shi'ism of the Qizilbash Turcomans became more clearly manifested when the youthful master of the Safawiyya, Isma'il, presented himself to his Qizilbash followers as the representative of the hidden imam, or even the awaited Mahdi himself, also claiming divinity. With the help of his Qizilbash followers, Isma'il seized Adharbayjan from the Aq Qoyunlu dynasty and entered their capital, Tabriz, in 1501. He now

---

6   Marshall G. S. Hodgson, *The Venture of Islam* (Chicago, 1974), vol. 2, pp. 493ff.

proclaimed himself *shah* (king), and at the same time declared Twelver Shi'ism the official religion of his newly-founded Safawid state.

The Safawids, as noted, originally adhered to an eclectic and extremist type of Shi'ism which was gradually disciplined and brought into conformity with the 'mainstream' of Twelver Shi'ism. However, in order to enhance their legitimacy, Shah Isma'il (r. 1501–1524) and his immediate successors claimed variously to represent the hidden Mahdi, in addition to constructing an Alid genealogy for their dynasty, tracing their ancestry to Imam Musa al-Kazim. Shi'i Islam was imposed over the subjects of Safawid Persia rather gradually. As Persia did not have an established class of Twelver religious scholars, however, the Safawids were obliged for quite some time to invite theologians and jurists from the Arab centres of Twelver scholarship, notably Najaf, Bahrayn and Jabal Amil in southern Lebanon, to instruct their subjects. Foremost among these Arab Twelver *ulama*, mention should be made of Shaykh Ali al-Karaki al-Amili (d. 1534), known as the Muhaqqiq al-Thani, who adhered to the Hilla school of Imami *kalam* theology with its recognition of *ijtihad* for the qualified scholars, combined with *taqlid*, or authorisation of the majority who emulated the *mujtahids*. Shaykh al-Karaki also ruled emphatically against the permissibility of following a dead *mujtahid*, as practised in Sunni Islam.

The Safawids encouraged the training of a class of Twelver legal scholars, who could consider themselves empowered by the hidden imam, and transferred some of his functions to themselves. The training of the Twelver scholars was facilitated through the establishment of a number of religious colleges. By the time of Shah Abbas I (r. 1587–1629), the greatest scion of the dynasty who established the Safawid capital at Isfahan, Twelver Shi'i rituals and practices, such as regular visitations (*ziyara*) to the shrines of the imams and their relatives at the *atabat* – Najaf, Karbala and other shrine cities in Iraq – as well as in Mashhad and Qumm in Persia, had gained wide currency.

The Safawid period witnessed a renaissance of the Islamic sciences and Shi'i scholarship. Foremost among the intellectual achievements of the period were the original contributions of a number of Twelver scholars belonging to the so-called 'school of Isfahan'.[7] These scholars integrated a variety of philosophical, theological and gnostic traditions within a Shi'i perspective into a metaphysical synthesis known

---

[7]   See H. Corbin, *Islamic Philosophy*, tr. L. Sherrard (London, 1993), pp. 338–348; and S. H. Nasr, *Islamic Philosophy from its Origins to the Present* (Albany, NY, 2006), pp. 209–233. For selected works in translation of several key members of this school, see S. Hossein Nasr and M. Aminrazavi, ed., *An Anthology of Philosophy in Persia*, vol. 5: *From the School of Shiraz to the Twentieth Century* (London, 2015), pp. 119–368.

as *al-hikma al-ilahiyya*, divine wisdom or theosophy. The founder of this school was Muhammad Baqir Astarabadi (d. 1630), better known as Mir Damad, a Twelver theologian and philosopher who was also the *shaykh al-Islam*, or chief religious authority, of Isfahan. However, the most important representative of the 'school of Isfahan' in theosophical Shiʻism was Mir Damad's principal student, Sadr al-Din Muhammad Shirazi (d. 1640), better known as Mulla Sadra. He produced his own synthesis of four major schools of Islamic thought, namely *kalam* theology, Avicennan peripatetic philosophy, the illuminationist philosophy of Shihab al-Din Yahya al-Suhrawardi (d. 1191) and gnostic-mystical traditions (*irfan*), particularly the Sufism of Ibn al-Arabi.

The Twelver *ulama*, especially the jurists (*fuqaha*) amongst them, played an increasingly prominent religio-political role in the affairs of the Safawid state. This trend reached its climax under the last Safawids, with Muhammad Baqir al-Majlisi (d. 1699), who held the highest clerical offices and consolidated the influence of the Twelver hierocracy. The author of an encyclopedic Imami *hadith* collection, the *Bihar al-anwar* (Seas of Lights), al-Majlisi, like many other jurists, was opposed to philosophers and Sufis. The Twelver *ulama* also disagreed among themselves on certain theological and juristic issues, and now became particularly divided into two opposing camps, generally designated as Usuli and Akhbari, reflecting their stances on the role of reason versus traditions (*hadith* or *akhbar*) in religious matters. From early on, opposing traditionist and rationalist trends had existed within Twelver Shiʻism, as expressed by the schools of Qumm and Baghdad. As noted, the traditionist Akhbari school of Qumm lost its early prominence to the rationalist Usuli school of Baghdad that adopted Muʻtazili *kalam* principles. However, by the early 17th century, Mulla Muhammad Amin al-Astarabadi (d. 1624) had articulated the Akhbari position afresh, and effectively became the founder of the revived Akhbari school. He sought to re-establish Shiʻi jurisprudence on the basis of traditions (*akhbar*) rather than the rationalist principles (*usul*) of jurisprudence used in *ijtihad*. Indeed, al-Astarabadi attacked the very idea of *ijtihad* and branded the Usuli *mujtahids* as enemies of religion. Al-Astarabadi recognised the *akhbar* of the imams as the most important source of law, required also for correct understanding of the Quran and the Prophetic traditions, because the imams were the divinely appointed and infallible interpreters of these sources.

The Akhbari school flourished for almost two centuries in Persia and the shrine cities of Iraq. In the second half of the 18th century, when Twelver Shiʻism was already widespread in Persia, the Usuli doctrine found a new champion in Muhammad Baqir al-Bihbahani (d. 1793), who defended *ijtihad* and successfully led the fight against the Akhbaris in Persia and Iraq. Thereafter, the Akhbaris rapidly lost their position to the Usulis, who now emerged as the prevailing school of jurisprudence in Twelver Shi'ism. The re-establishment of the Usuli school led to an unprecedented enhancement in the authority of the Twelver *ulama* under the Qajar monarchs of Persia and in modern times. Meanwhile, Twelver Shi'ism had also spread in southern Lebanon and certain regions of the Indian subcontinent.

It was during the fifth and final phase of Twelver history, stretching from around 1800 to present times, that Twelver Shi'i jurisprudence acquired its current form, advocating the Usuli doctrines of *ijtihad* and *taqlid*. The victory of the Usuli *ulama* was accompanied by the development of the religious scholars into a hierarchical class of *mujtahids* in Qajar Persia during the 19th century. A group of qualified Twelver scholars selected on the basis of their knowledge of the principles of jurisprudence (*usul al-fiqh*) were now widely permitted to practise *ijtihad*, reaching binding decisions. At the same time, ordinary Twelver Shi'i were to follow such a qualified *mujtahid* designated as *marja-i taqlid* (Arabic, *marja al-taqlid*), the 'source of emulation' or the 'supreme exemplar'. The triumph of the Usuli school thus divided the Twelver Shi'i community into *muqallids*, persons obliged to practise *taqlid*, and *mujtahids*, those qualified to practise *ijtihad*. In principle every *mujtahid* could be a *marja-i taqlid*, but in practice only one or very few at any time have been recognised as such. By the final decades of the Qajar period (1779–1925), the Twelver clergy had evolved into an important social class in Persia with much influence and active participation in the country's public affairs.

Reza Shah, founder of the Pahlavi dynasty of Persia (1925–1979), as part of his modernisation policies systematically curtailed the privileged position of the Twelver *ulama* in Persian society. In particular, he excluded them from the country's judiciary and educational systems, fields previously under the control of the clergy. Under Reza Shah's son and successor, Mohammad Reza Shah Pahlavi (1941–1979), the clergy gradually regained, at least partially, some of their traditional privileges in Persia, more commonly designated as Iran in the West since 1936.

By the 1960s, a strand of clerical opposition to the regime in Iran had become solidified under the leadership of Ayatullah Sayyid Ruhullah Khumayni (d. 1989), who articulated the doctrine of *vilayat-i faqih* (Arabic, *wilayat al-faqih*), or 'guardianship of the jurist', holding that the Twelver *ulama/fuqaha* were effectively heirs to the political authority of the 12 imams. He argued that the right to rule devolves from the imams to the jurists, during the occultation of the twelfth imam, because they are best qualified to comprehend the divine revelation of the *shari'a*; and this right would devolve to a single jurist (*faqih*) if he succeeded in establishing a government. It was on such a doctrinal basis that Ayatullah Khumayni organised and led a revolutionary movement establishing the Islamic Republic of Iran in 1979.

The historical evolution in the authority/power paradigm of the Twelver *ulama* from the first articulation to the principle of *ijtihad* had thus reached its extreme and ultimate conclusion in the establishment of a theocratic Islamic state with its leader (*rahbar*) as the *vali-yi faqih* (the 'guardian jurist'), conceived as the full representative of the hidden Mahdi of the Twelver Shi'a. In such a state, the Twelver *ulama* in general, and the *vali-yi faqih* in particular, would enjoy a unique constitutional position of religious authority with unlimited political power.

The Ismailis

Representing the second most important Shi'i community, the Ismailis have had their own complex history. The history of the Ismailis as an independent Shi'i community may be traced to the dispute over the succession to Imam Ja'far al-Sadiq, who died in 765. As related in the majority of the available sources, Imam al-Sadiq had originally designated his second son, Isma'il, the eponym of the Isma'iliyya, as his successor to the imamate by the rule of *nass*. According to the Ismaili religious tradition, Isma'il survived his father and succeeded him in due course. However, most non-Ismaili sources relate that Isma'il predeceased his father. At any rate, Isma'il was not present in Medina or Kufa at the time of Imam al-Sadiq's death, when three of his brothers simultaneously claimed the succession. As noted above, this confusing succession dispute split the Imami Shi'a into several groups, two of which may be identified with the earliest Ismailis.

One group denied the death of Isma'il in his father's lifetime, maintaining that he was the true imam after al-Sadiq. Designated as *al-Isma'iliyya al-khalisa*, or the 'Pure Ismailis', these Imami Shi'is now awaited Isma'il's return as the Mahdi. A second group of the earliest Ismailis, known as the Mubarakiyya, affirmed Isma'il's death during the lifetime of his father, and now recognised his son Muhammad as their imam after al-Sadiq.[8] Before long, Muhammad b. Isma'il, the seventh imam of the Ismailis, went into hiding, marking the initiation of the *dawr al-satr*, or period of concealment, in early Ismaili history, which lasted until the emergence of the Ismaili imams as Fatimid caliphs in 909.

It is certain that for almost a century after Muhammad b. Isma'il, who died around 795, a group of Ismaili leaders worked secretly for the creation of a unified revolutionary movement against the Abbasids. These leaders did not openly claim the imamate for three generations. Abd

---

[8]   Al-Nawbakhti, *Firaq*, pp. 57–62; and al-Qummi, *Kitab al-maqalat*, pp. 80–81, 83.

Allah, the first of these leaders, had in fact organised his campaign around the central doctrine followed by the bulk of the earliest Ismailis, who had eventually acknowledged Muhammad b. Isma'il as the awaited Mahdi. As explained later by the Ismaili imams, this was a *taqiyya* tactic adopted to safeguard the early leaders of the movement, who were Alid imams descended from Ja'far al-Sadiq, against Abbasid persecution. At any rate, Abd Allah eventually found refuge in Salamiyya, in central Syria, disguising himself as a merchant. Henceforth, Salamiyya served as the secret, central headquarters of the early Ismaili movement. The Ismailis now referred to their movement as *al-da'wa al-hadiya* (the rightly guiding mission) or simply as the *da'wa*.

The sustained efforts of Abd Allah and his successors began to bear fruit in the early 870s, when numerous Ismailis *da'is* appeared in southern Iraq and other regions. In 874, Hamdan Qarmat was converted to Ismailism in the Sawad of Kufa. Hamdan and his chief assistant Abdan organised the *da'wa* in southern Iraq and adjacent regions, where the Ismailis became generally known as the Qaramita, after their first local leader. The *da'wa* in Yemen was initiated in 881 by Ibn Hawshab Mansur al-Yaman (d. 914). By 893, the *da'i* Abu Abd Allah al-Shi'i (d. 911) was already active among the Kutama Berbers of North Africa. Meanwhile, Abu Sa'id al-Jannabi had been active as a *da'i* in eastern Arabia, then known as Bahrayn. It was also in the 870s that the Ismaili *da'wa* was initiated in the Jibal, the west-central and northwestern parts of Persia, where the *da'is* adopted a new conversion policy, targeting the elite and the ruling classes. The same policy was later adopted successfully, at least temporarily, by the *da'is* of Khurasan and Central Asia.[9]

By the early 890s, a unified and expanding Ismaili movement had replaced the earlier Kufan-based splinter groups. This movement was centrally directed from Salamiyya by leaders who made every effort to conceal their true identity. The leaders of the early Ismaili *da'wa* were, however, in contact with the *da'is* of different regions, propagating a revolutionary religio-political message in the name of the hidden Imam-Mahdi Muhammad b. Isma'il, whose advent was then anticipated. Centred on the expectation of the imminent emergence of the Mahdi, who would establish the rule of justice in the world, the Ismaili *da'wa* of the 9th century had a great deal of messianic appeal for under-privileged groups of diverse social backgrounds. The early Ismaili *da'wa* also achieved particular success among those Imami Shi'is of Iraq and

---

[9]   Samuel M. Stern, 'The Earliest Isma'ili Missionaries in North-West Persia and in Khurasan and Transoxania', *Bulletin of the School of Oriental and African Studies*, 23 (1960), pp. 56–90; reprinted in his *Studies in Early Isma'ilism* (Jerusalem and Leiden, 1983), pp. 189–233.

elsewhere who had hitherto acknowledged Musa al-Kazim and certain of his descendants as their imams. It was particularly in the confusing circumstances following the death of al-Hasan al-Askari in 874, later counted as the 11th imam of the Twelvers, that large numbers of these Imamis responded to the summons of the Ismaili *da'wa*. Indeed, most of the early Ismaili *da'is* hailed from such Imami Shi'i backgrounds.

In 899, soon after Abd Allah al-Mahdi, the future Fatimid caliph, had succeeded to the central leadership of the *da'wa* in Salamiyya, Ismailism was rent by a major schism.[10] Abd Allah had now felt secure enough to claim the imamate openly for himself and his predecessors, the same individuals who had organised and led the early Ismaili *da'wa*. Later, he explained that, as a form of *taqiyya*, the central leaders of the *da'wa* had adopted different pseudonyms, also assuming the rank of *hujja* (proof or full representative) of the absent Muhammad b. Isma'il. Abd Allah further explained that the earlier propagation of the return of Muhammad b. Isma'il as the Mahdi was itself another dissimulating measure, and that the Mahdi was, in fact, a collective code-name of every true imam in the progeny of Ja'far al-Sadiq.

Abd Allah al-Mahdi's reform split the then unified Ismaili *da'wa* and community into two rival branches. One faction remained loyal to the central leadership and acknowledged continuity in the Ismaili imamate, recognising Abd Allah al-Mahdi and his Alid ancestors as their imams, which in due course became the official Fatimid Ismaili doctrine. On the other hand, a dissident faction, originally led by Hamdan Qarmat (d. 933) and Abdan (d. 899), rejected the reform and maintained their belief in the Mahdism of Muhammad b. Isma'il. Henceforth, the term Qarmati came to be applied more specifically to the dissident Ismailis who did not acknowledge Abd Allah al-Mahdi and his predecessors as well as his successors in the Fatimid dynasty, as their imams. The dissident Qarmatis acquired their most important stronghold in Bahrayn, where a Qarmati state was founded in the same eventful year 899 by Abu Sa'id al-Jannabi (d. 913). Soon after these events, Abd Allah left Salamiyya and embarked on a historic journey which ended several years later in North Africa where he founded the Fatimid caliphate.

The early Ismailis elaborate the basic framework of a system of religious thought which was further developed or modified in the Fatimid period, while the Qarmatis followed a separate doctrinal course. Central to the Ismaili system of thought was a fundamental distinction between the exoteric (*zahir*) and the esoteric (*batin*) aspects of the sacred

---

[10] See F. Daftary, 'A Major Schism in the Early Isma'ili Movement', *Studia Islamica*, 77 (1993), pp. 123–139; reprinted in his *Ismailis in Medieval Muslim Societies* (London, 2005), pp. 45–61.

scriptures, including the Quran, as well as the religious commandments and prohibitions of the law. They further held that the *zahir*, the religious laws enunciated by the prophets, underwent periodical changes, while the *batin*, containing the spiritual truths (*haqa'iq*), remained immutable and eternal. These truths, representing the message common to Judaism, Christianity and Islam, were explained through *ta'wil*, or esoteric interpretation, which often relied on the mystical significance of letters and numbers.

The esoteric truths (*haqa'iq*) formed a gnostic system of thought for the Ismailis, representing a distinct worldview. The two main components of this system were a cyclical history of revelations or prophetic eras (*dawrs*) and a cosmological doctrine. The Ismaili cyclical conception, applied to Judaeo-Christian as well as several other pre-Islamic religions, was developed in terms of seven eras of different speaker-prophets (*natiqs*) recognised in the Quran. This view was also combined with the Ismaili doctrine of the imamate which had been essentially inherited from the earlier Imamiyya.

The Fatimid Phase in Ismaili History

The Fatimid phase represents the 'golden age' of Ismaili Shi'ism, when the Ismailis possessed a state of their own and Ismaili scholarship and literature attained their summit.[11] The foundation of the Fatimid caliphate in 909 in Ifriqiya, covering modern-day Tunisia and eastern Algeria in North Africa, marked the crowning success of the early Ismailis. The religio-political *da'wa* of the Isma'iliyya had finally led to the establishment of a state or *dawla* headed by the Ismaili Imam Abd Allah al-Mahdi (r. 909–934). The new dynasty came to be known as Fatimid (Fatimiyya), derived from the name of the Prophet's daughter Fatima, to whom al-Mahdi and his successors traced back their Husaynid Alid ancestry.

In line with their universal claims, the Fatimid caliph-imams did not abandon their *da'wa* activities on assuming power, as they aimed to extend their rule over the entire Muslim *umma*. However, they concerned themselves with the propagation of the Ismaili *da'wa* mainly after transferring the seat of the Fatimid state in 973 to Egypt, where Cairo was founded in 969 as their new capital city. The religio-political messages of the *da'wa* were disseminated by networks of *da'i*s within the Fatimid dominions as well as in other regions, referred to as the *jaza'ir*. Indeed, it was in non-Fatimid regions, especially Yemen, Persia and

---

[11]   The historiography of this phase is fully discussed in Paul E. Walker, *Exploring an Islamic Empire: Fatimid History and its Sources* (London, 2002).

Central Asia, that the Fatimid Ismaili *da'wa* achieved its lasting success. The Ismailis comprised a minority within Fatimid Egypt where the bulk of the subjects remained Sunni with a significant community of Coptic Christians.

However, the Fatimid *da'wa* was particularly concerned with educating the Ismaili converts in esoteric doctrines, known as *hikma* or wisdom. As a result, a variety of lectures, known as the *majalis al-hikma*, or 'sessions of wisdom', were organised for the Ismaili initiates. Many of these *majalis* delivered by the chief *da'i* (*da'i al-du'at*), were in due course collected and committed to writing, such as the *Ta'wil al-da'a'im* of al-Qadi al-Nu'man (d. 974) and the *Majalis* of al-Mu'ayyad fi'l-Din al-Shirazi (d. 1078). Another of the main institutions of learning founded by the Fatimids was the Dar al-Ilm, the House of Knowledge. This institution, founded in Cairo in 1005, taught a variety of religious and non-religious subjects and it was also equipped with an extensive library. Many *da'is* received at least part of their education at the Dar al-Ilm. The Ismaili *da'wa* also paid special attention to the selection and training of the *da'is*, who became scholars in theology and other subjects.[12]

It was during the Fatimid phase that the Ismaili *da'is*, who were at the same time the learned scholars of their community, produced what were to be regarded as the classical texts of Ismaili literature, dealing with a multitude of exoteric and esoteric subjects as well as *ta'wil*, which became the hallmark of Ismaili thought.[13] In the course of the 10th century, the *da'is* of the Iranian lands set about harmonising Ismaili Shi'i *kalam* theology with Neoplatonism and other philosophical traditions into complex metaphysical systems of thought. This led to the development of a unique intellectual tradition of 'philosophical theology' within Ismaili Shi'ism. The major early proponents of this tradition were the *da'is* Muhammad b. Ahmad al-Nasafi (d. 943), Abu Hatim al-Razi (d. 934), Abu Ya'qub al-Sijistani (d. after 971) and Hamid al-Din al-Kirmani (d. after 1020).[14] These Iranian *da'is* wrote for the elite and the educated strata of society, aiming to attract them intellectually. This may explain why they expressed their theology, always revolving

---

[12] For more details, see Ahmad b. Ibrahim al-Nisaburi, *al-Risala al-mujaza al-kafiya fi adab al-du'at*, ed. and tr. V. Klemm and P. E. Walker as *A Code of Conduct: A Treatise on the Etiquette of the Fatimid Mission* (London, 2011); H. Halm, *The Fatimids and their Traditions of Learning* (London, 1997), pp. 23–29, 41–45, 71–78; and P. E. Walker, 'Fatimid Institutions of Learning', *Journal of the American Research Center in Egypt*, 34 (1997), pp. 179–200; reprinted in his *Fatimid History and Ismaili Doctrine* (Aldershot, 2008), article I.
[13] See I. K. Poonawala, *Biobibliography of Isma'ili Literature* (Malibu, CA, 1977), pp. 31–132.
[14] Paul E. Walker, *Early Philosophical Shiism: The Ismaili Neoplatonism of Abu Ya'qub al-Sijistani* (Cambridge, 1993), pp. 67–142.

around the central Imami Shiʿi doctrine of the imamate, in terms of the then most fashionable intellectual themes, yet without compromising the essence of their religious message. Nasir-i Khusraw (d. after 1070), who spread the *daʿwa* in Badakhshan (now divided between Tajikistan and Afghanistan), was the last eminent member of this 'Iranian school' of Ismailism.[15]

From early on, the Fatimids also concerned themselves with legal matters. The process of codifying Ismaili law had already started in Abd Allah al-Mahdi's reign when the precepts of Imami Shiʿi law were put into practice. However, at the time there still did not exist a distinctly Ismaili *madhhab* or school of jurisprudence. The promulgation of an Ismaili *madhhab* resulted mainly from the efforts of al-Qadi Abu Hanifa al-Nuʿman b. Muhammad (d. 974), the foremost Ismaili jurist, who was officially commissioned to prepare legal compendia. He codified Ismaili law by systematically collecting the firmly established *hadith*s transmitted from the *ahl al-bayt*, drawing on existing collections. Al-Qadi al-Nuʿman's efforts culminated in his *Daʿaʾim al-Islam* (The Pillars of Islam), which served as the official code of the Fatimid state. The authority of the infallible Alid imam and his teachings became a principal source of Ismaili law, after the Quran and the *sunna* of the Prophet.[16] In comparison with the Twelver and the Zaydi Shiʿi *madhhab*s, the legal literature of the Ismaili Shiʿis is extremely meagre.

The Fatimid caliph-imam al-Hakim's reign (996–1021) witnessed the opening phase of what was to become known as the Druze religion. A number of *daʿi*s who had come to Cairo from Persia and Central Asia, notably al-Akhram (d. 1018), Hamza and al-Darazi (d. 1019), began to propagate certain extremist ideas regarding al-Hakim and his imamate. Drawing on the traditions of the Shiʿi *ghulat* and the eschatological expectations of the early Ismailis, these *daʿi*s founded a new religious movement proclaiming the end of the era of Islam and the abrogation of its *shariʿa*. By 1017, the opening year of the Druze era, Hamza and al-Darazi also publicly declared al-Hakim's divinity. It was after al-Darazi that the adherents of this movement later became known as Daraziyya or Duruz; hence their general designation as Druzes. The Fatimid *daʿwa* organisation in Cairo launched a campaign against this movement; and, subsequently, the Druzes were persecuted in Fatimid

---

[15]   See, for instance, Nasir-i Khusraw, *Kitab jamiʿ al-hikmatayn*, ed. H. Corbin and M. Muʿin (Tehran and Paris, 1953); English trans., *Between Reason and Revelation: Twin Wisdoms Reconciled* by E. Ormsby (London, 2012).

[16]   Ismail K. Poonawala, 'The Evolution of al-Qadi al-Nuʿman's Theory of Ismaili Jurisprudence as Reflected in the Chronology of his Works on Jurisprudence', in F. Daftary and G. Miskinzoda, ed., *The Study of Shiʿi Islam: History, Theology and Law* (London, 2014), pp. 295–351.

Egypt. The Druze movement eventually found its greatest success in Syria.

Ismaili *da'wa* activities reached their peak, especially outside the Fatimid dominions, in the long reign of al-Mustansir (r. 1036–1094), even after the Sunni Saljuqs had replaced the Shi'i Buyids as overlords of the Abbasids in 1055. The *da'is* won many converts in Iraq, Persia, Central Asia and Yemen, where the Sulayhids ruled as the vassals of the Fatimids from 1047 until 1138. One of the most eminent *da'is* of al-Mustansir's time was Nasir-i Khusraw (d. after 1070), who spread the *da'wa* in Central Asia. Meanwhile, by the time local tribes had uprooted the Qarmati state of Bahrayn 1077, other Qarmati groups in Persia, Iraq and elsewhere had either disintegrated or switched their allegiance to the Ismaili *da'wa* of the Fatimids.

On al-Mustansir's death in 1094, the unified Ismaili *da'wa* and community split into two rival factions, as his heritage was claimed by two of his sons. The deceased caliph-imam's original heir-designate, Nizar (d. 1095), was deprived of his succession rights by the all-powerful Fatimid vizier al-Afdal, who installed Nizar's younger half-brother on the Fatimid throne with the title of al-Musta'li bi'llah (r. 1094–1101). The imamate of al-Musta'li was also recognised by the Ismaili communities of Egypt, Yemen and western India. On the other hand, the Ismailis of Persia, then led by Hasan-i Sabbah, supported the succession rights of Nizar and his descendants. The two factions were later designated as the Musta'liyya and the Nizariyya.

The Musta'lian Ismailis themselves split into Hafizi and Tayyibi branches on the assassination of al-Musta'li's son and successor al-Amir in 1130. Al-Amir's successor on the Fatimid throne, al-Hafiz (d. 1149), and the later Fatimid caliphs were acknowledged as imams by the *da'wa* headquarters in Cairo and the Musta'lian Ismailis of Egypt and Syria and by part of the community in Yemen. These Musta'lian Ismailis, known as the Hafiziyya, did not survive long after the downfall of the Fatimid dynasty in 1171. On the other hand, the Musta'lian community of Sulayhid Yemen recognised the imamate of al-Amir's infant son al-Tayyib and became known as the Tayyibiyya. Indeed, with the demise of the Fatimid dynasty, Musta'lian Ismailism survived only in its Tayyibi form.

The Tayyibi Ismailis

Tayyibi Ismailism found its permanent stronghold in Yemen, where it received the initial support of the Sulayhid dynasty. Queen Arwa (d. 1138), then effective ruler of Sulayhid Yemen, became the leader of the Tayyibi *da'wa* and severed her ties with Cairo and the Fatimid regime. Nothing is known of the fate of al-Tayyib, who was probably murdered on the orders of the Fatimid caliph, al-Hafiz. According to Tayyibi tradition, however, al-Amir had earlier placed his infant son in the custody of a group of trusted *da'is*; and, they in due course succeeded in hiding al-Tayyib, making it possible for the Tayyibi imamate to continue in his progeny. The Tayyibi Musta'lian Ismailis are of the opinion that their imamate has been handed down among al-Tayyib's descendants to the present time, with all these Tayyibi imams having remained in concealment.

The history of Tayyibi Ismailism in Yemen is a history of the activities of the various *da'is* who led the *da'wa* in the absence of their imams, and their relation with the Zaydis and other local dynasties of medieval Yemen. The Tayyibi *da'wa* received its initial support from the Sulayhid queen al-Sayyida Arwa, who had been looking after the affairs of the Ismaili *da'wa* in Yemen for some time, with the help of the *da'i* Lamak b. Malik al-Hammadi (d. ca. 1098) and then of his son Yahya (d. 1126). It was soon after 1132 that the Sulayhid queen broke off relations with the Fatimid regime and declared al-Dhu'ayb b. Musa al-Wadi'i (d. 1151) as *al-da'i al-mutlaq*, or *da'i* with absolute authority, to lead the Tayyibi *da'wa* on behalf of the hidden imam, al-Tayyib. This marked the foundation of the independent Tayyibi *da'wa*. Al-Dhu'ayb's successors have retained the title of *da'i mutlaq* to the present day. Idris Imad al-Din (d. 1468), the 19th *da'i mutlaq* of the Tayyibis, was also a major Ismaili historian; his works include the *Uyun al-akhbar*, a comprehensive seven-volume history of Ismailism from its beginnings until the opening phase of Tayyibi Ismailism.

The Tayyibis have preserved a good portion of the Ismaili literature of the Fatimid period. And in the doctrinal domain they have maintained many of the Fatimid traditions. They also retained the established interest of the Ismailis in cyclical sacred history and cosmology, which served as the basis for their gnostic, esoteric *haqa'iq* system of religious thought with its distinctive eschatological and salvational themes. The Tayyibis have continued to use al-Qadi al-Nu'man's *Da'a'im al-Islam*, regarding it as their most authoritative legal compendium.

Meanwhile, the Yemeni *da'is* had maintained close relations with the Tayyibi community of western India, where the Ismaili converts of mostly Hindu descent had become known as Bohras. The head of the Indian Tayyibi *da'wa* was regularly appointed by the *da'i mutlaq* residing in Yemen. With the establishment of Mughal rule in India in 1572, the Bohras began to enjoy a certain degree of religious freedom; and they were no longer severely persecuted or forced to convert to Sunni Islam.

On the death of the 26th *da'i mutlaq*, Da'ud b. Ajabshah in 1589, a heated dispute over his succession led to the permanent Da'udi-Sulaymani schism in the Tayyibi *da'wa* and community, reflecting Indian-Yemeni rivalries. By then, the Tayyib Bohras in India, who outnumbered their Yemeni co-religionists, desired to attain their independence from Yemen. Henceforth the Indian Bohra Tayyibis, known as Daʾudis, and the Yemeni Tayyibis, known as Sulaymanis, followed different lines of *daʻi*s, starting with their 27th *daʻi*. The Daʾudi *daʻi*s continued to reside in India, while the headquarters of the Sulaymani *daʻwa* remained in Yemen. The Sulaymanis represent a minority within the Tayyibi community. Subsequently, the Daʾudi Bohras themselves were further subdivided because of periodic challenges to the authority of their *daʻi mutlaq*. For all branches, the *daʻi*s are designated, like the imams, by the *nass* of their predecessor. Since the 1920s, Bombay (Mumbai) has served as the administrative headquarters of the Daʾudi *daʻi*. The Sulaymani Tayyibis of Yemen have not experienced succession disputes and schisms; and since the middle of the 17th century, their leadership has remained hereditary in the same Makrami family. The traditional seat of the Sulaymani *daʻi*s was located in Badr, Najran, in northwestern Yemen, annexed to Saudi Arabia in 1934.

The Nizari Ismailis

The Nizari Ismailis have had their own complex history and distinctive doctrinal development. From early on, the Nizari Ismailis, who had broken away in 1094 from the Fatimid regime, were preoccupied with their revolutionary campaign and their survival in an extremely hostile environment. Accordingly, they produced military commanders rather than highly trained *daʻi*s addressing a host of intellectual issues, as did the Ismailis of the Fatimid period or the Tayyibis of Yemen. Furthermore, adopting Persian as the religious language of the community, the early Nizaris (those outside Syria) did not have ready access to the Ismaili literature of earlier times which had been written in Arabic. The early Nizari Ismailis of the Alamut period (1094–1256) did, nevertheless, maintain a sophisticated intellectual outlook and a literary tradition, propounding their teachings in response to changing circumstances.

By the time of the Nizari-Mustaʻli schism of 1094, Hasan-i Sabbah (d. 1124), who preached the Ismaili *daʻwa* within the Saljuq dominions in Persia, had already emerged as the leader of the Persian Ismailis. Originally a Twelver Shiʻi, Hasan had operated as a *daʻi* in Persia after his conversion. His seizure of the fortress of Alamut in 1090, in northern Persia, had in fact signalled the foundation of what would become the Nizari Ismaili state of Persia; it also marked the initiation of the open revolt of the Persian Ismailis against the oppressive rule of the Sunni Saljuqs. This revolt, cleverly organised and led by Hasan from Alamut, was also an expression of Persian 'national' sentiments, as the alien rule of the Saljuq Turks was greatly detested by Persians of different social classes. In the dispute over the succession to al-Mustansir, as noted,

Hasan-i Sabbah supported Nizar's cause and severed his relations with the Fatimid regime. By this decision, Hasan had now also founded the independent Nizari Ismaili *da'wa* on behalf of the Nizari imams, who after Nizar remained inaccessible for several decades. Nizar himself was captured by the Fatimid forces after the failure of his revolt and then executed in Cairo in 1095.

Soon Hasan-i Sabbah acquired a network of fortresses in several regions of Persia, which served as bases for operations against the Saljuqs. And later, by the opening decade of the 12th century, he extended his activities to Syria by sending *da'is* there. However, Hasan did not succeed in uprooting the Saljuqs; and, the Saljuqs, despite their much superior military power, failed to dislodge the Nizaris from their mountain strongholds. By the final years of Hasan-i Sabbah, Ismaili-Saljuq relations had entered a phase of stalemate, which lasted even under the Saljuqs' successors in Persia.[17]

Hasan-i Sabbah was also a learned theologian and is credited with restating in a more rigorous form the old Shi'i doctrine of *ta'lim*, or authoritative teaching by the 'imam of the time'. He expounded this doctrine in a Persian treatise entitled *al-Fusul al-arba'a* (The Four Chapters), which was preserved fragmentarily in Persian and in Arabic by al-Shahrastani (d. 1153).[18] Emphasising the autonomous teaching authority of each imam in his own time, the doctrine of *ta'lim* became the central doctrine of the Nizaris who, henceforth, were often designated as the Ta'limiyya. The intellectual challenge posed to the Sunnis by the doctrine of *ta'lim*, which also refuted the legitimacy of the Abbasid caliph as the spiritual spokesman of all Muslims, brought a reaction from the Sunni establishment. Many Sunni scholars, led by Abu Hamid Muhammad al-Ghazali (d. 1111), sought to refute this Ismaili doctrine.

Meanwhile, the Nizaris had been eagerly expecting the emergence of their imam, who had remained inaccessible since Nizar's demise in 1095. The fourth lord of Alamut, Hasan II (r. 1162–1166), to whom the Nizaris refer with the expression *ala dhikrihi'l-salam* (on his mention be peace), declared the *qiyama* or Resurrection in 1164, initiating a new phase

---

[17] See Carole Hillenbrand, 'The Power Struggle between the Saljuqs and the Isma'ilis of Alamut, 487–518/1094–1124: The Saljuq Perspective', in F. Daftary, ed., *Mediaeval Isma'ili History and Thought* (Cambridge, 1996), pp. 205–220; and F. Daftary, 'Ismaili-Seljuq Relations: Conflict and Stalemate', in E. Herzig and S. Stewart, ed., *The Age of the Seljuqs* (London, 2015), pp. 41–57.

[18] Abu'l-Fath Muhammad b. Abd al-Karim al-Shahrastani, *Kitab al-milal wa'l-nihal*, ed. A. M. Wakil (Cairo, 1968), vol. 1, pp. 195–198; and S. J. Badakhchani, 'Shahrastani's Account of Hasan-i Sabbah's Doctrine of Ta'lim', in M. A. Amir-Moezzi, ed., *Islam: Identité et altérité. Hommage à Guy Monnot* (Turnhout, 2013), pp. 27–55.

in the religious history of the Nizari community. Relying extensively on Ismaili *ta'wil* and earlier traditions, however, Hasan II interpreted the *qiyama*, the long-awaited Last Day, symbolically and spiritually. Accordingly, the *qiyama* meant merely the manifestation of unveiled truth (*haqiqa*) in the person of the Nizari imam; and it represented a spiritual resurrection only for those who acknowledged the rightful imam of the time and were thus capable of understanding the truth, or the esoteric essence of Islam. The imam proclaiming the *qiyama* would be the *qa'im al-qiyama* or the 'lord of resurrection', a rank higher than that of an ordinary imam. In due course, Hasan II himself was recognised as the imam and *qa'im*. Henceforth, the Nizaris acknowledged the lords of Alamut as their imams, descendants of Nizar b. al-Mustansir.

In the reign of Ala al-Din Muhammad (r. 1221–1255), the penultimate lord of Alamut, the Nizari leadership made a sustained effort to explain the different doctrinal declarations and religious policies of the lords of Alamut within the terms of a coherent theological framework. It is mainly in the Ismaili works written or supervised by the eminent Shi'i philosopher and theologian Nasir al-Din al-Tusi (d. 1274), who spent some three decades during this time in Nizari fortress communities and converted to Ismailism, that we have an exposition of the Nizari thought of the Alamut period.[19]

The surrender of the fortress of Alamut to the all-conquering Mongol hordes led by Hülegü himself, in 1256, sealed the fate of the Nizari state. Rukn al-Din Khurshah, the Nizari imam and the last of the lords of Alamut, was murdered in Mongolia in 1257, where he had gone to see the Great Khan. The Mongols now massacred large numbers of Nizaris, also destroying their fortresses in Persia. In Syria, where the Nizaris attained the peak of their power and fame under their most eminent *da'i*, Rashid al-Din Sinan (d. 1193), the sectarians attracted the attention of the Crusaders, who made them famous as the Assassins. The Syrian Nizaris were spared the Mongol debacle. However, by 1273 all the castles of the Syrian Nizaris had fallen into Mamluk hands. The Syrian Nizaris were permitted to remain in their traditional abodes as loyal subjects of the Mamluks and Ottomans.

In the Post-Alamut phase of their history, the Nizari Ismaili communities, scattered from Syria to Persia, Central Asia and South Asia, elaborating a diversity of religious and literary traditions in different languages. They also resorted to widespread *taqiyya* practices under Sunni, Twelver Shi'i, Sufi and Hindu guises, in addition to guarding

---

[19] See especially Nasir al-Din al-Tusi, *Rawda-yi taslim*, ed. and tr. S. Jalal Badakhchani as *Paradise of Submission: A Medieval Treatise on Ismaili Thought* (London, 2005).

secretly their limited literature. For several early centuries of this period, when the Nizaris of various regions were effectively deprived of any systematic form of central leadership, their communities developed independently under the local leadership of their own *da'i*s, now also designated as *pir*s, *shaykh*s and *khalifa*s, who established their own hereditary dynasties.

Meanwhile, a group of Nizari dignitaries had managed to hide Rukn al-Din Khurshah's son, Shams al-Din Muhammad (d. ca. 1310), who in due course succeeded to the imamate. An obscure dispute over his succession split the line of the Nizari imams and their followers into the Qasim-Shahi and Muhammad-Shahi (or Mu'mini) branches. The Muhammad-Shahi imams transferred their seat to India in the 16th century, and by the end of the 18th century this line had become discontinued. Nizari Ismailism has survived mainly through its Qasim-Shahi faction, represented in modern times by their imams known as the Aga Khans.

In the early Post-Alamut centuries, the Persian Nizaris disguised themselves especially as Sufis, without establishing formal affiliations with any of the Sufi orders then spreading across Persia and Central Asia. By the middle of the 15th century, Ismaili-Sufi relations had become well established throughout the Iranian lands. Indeed, a type of coalescence had emerged between these two independent esoteric traditions in Islam that shared common doctrinal grounds. This explains why the Persian-speaking Nizaris have regarded some of the greatest mystic poets of Persia, such as Farid al-Din Attar and Jalal al-Din Rumi, as their co-religionists. Soon, the dissimulating Persian Nizaris adopted more visible aspects of the Sufi orders. Thus, the imams appeared to outsiders as Sufi *pir*s or masters, while their followers adopted the typically Sufi appellation of *murid* or disciple.

By the middle of the 15th century, the Nizari imams of the Qasim-Shahi line had emerged in the village of Anjudan, near Qumm, in Central Persia, initiating the so-called Anjudan revival in Nizari *da'wa* and literary activities. Imam Mustansir bi'llah (d. 1480), who carried the Sufi name of Shah Qalandar, is the first of the Nizari imams of his line to be definitely settled in Anjudan. The imams now successfully began to reorganise their *da'wa* activities and reassert their authority over various Nizari communities, especially in Central Asia and India. The imams gradually replaced the local hereditary leaders with their own loyal *da'i*s. The Anjudan period in Nizari history, lasting until the end of the 17th century, also witnessed a revival in the literary activities of the Nizaris. Many authors, notably Abu Ishaq Quhistani (d. after 1498), now began to produce doctrinal works. The post-Alamut Nizaris essentially retained the teachings of the Alamut period, especially as elaborated after the declaration of the *qiyama*. With the advent of the

Safawids, who proclaimed Twelver Shi'ism as their state religion in 1501, the Persian Nizaris also successfully adopted Twelver Shi'ism as another form of disguise.

The Nizari *da'wa* of the Anjudan period achieved particular success in the Indian subcontinent, where the Hindu converts originally belonging to the Lohana caste became generally known as Khojas. The Nizari Khojas developed an indigenous religious tradition known as Satpanth or 'true path' (to salvation), as well as a devotional literature, the *ginans*. Composed in a number of Indic languages, the hymn-like *ginans* were transmitted orally for several centuries before they were recorded, mainly in the special Khojki script developed in Sind within the Khoja community. The authorship of the great majority of the *ginans* is traditionally attributed to a few early *da'is*, such as Shams al-Din and Sadr al-Din, more commonly referred to in India as *pirs*.[20]

By the middle of the 18th century, the Qasim-Shahi Nizari imams had transferred their seat to the province of Kirman, closer to the pilgrimage route of the Khojas who then regularly travelled to Persia to see their imam and deliver their religious dues. The Khojas were by then acquiring increasing significance in the Nizari Ismaili community, in terms of both their numbers and financial contributions to the treasury of the *da'wa*. In Kirman, the imams also became involved in political activities. The 44th Imam, Abu'l-Hasan Ali, was appointed around 1756 to the governorship of Kirman by Karim Khan Zand, founder of the Zand dynasty of Persia. The Nizaris and their imams now had also developed close relations with several leading Ni'mat Allahi Sufis and supported the revival of the order's activities in Kirman.

The modern period in the history of the Nizari Ismailis commenced with Hasan Ali Shah (1804–1881), who succeeded to the imamate of the Nizaris in 1817 as their 46th imam. He was given the honorific title of Agha Khan (Aga Khan), meaning lord and master, by Fath Ali Shah (r. 1797–1834), the second Qajar monarch of Persia, who also appointed the youthful imam to the governorship of Qumm. Later, Hasan Ali Shah, Aga Khan I, was appointed to the governorship of Kirman by Fath Ali Shah's grandson and successor, Muhammad Shah Qajar (r. 1834–1848). Subsequently, after some prolonged confrontations between the Nizari imam and the Qajar establishment, Aga Khan I left Persia permanently in 1841. He eventually settled in Bombay in 1848. In India, Aga Khan I devoted much of his time and resources to defining the distinctive religious identity of his Khoja following, who had dissimulated for centuries under various guises. In 1866, matters were eventually brought

---

[20] See Ali Asani, *Ecstasy and Enlightenment: The Ismaili Devotional Literature of South Asia* (London, 2002).

before the Bombay High Court, which legally established the status of the Nizari Khojas as a community of 'Shi'a Imami Ismailis'.

Aga Khan I's grandson, Sultan Muhammad Shah, Aga Khan III (1877–1957), led the Nizaris as their 48th Imam for 72 years. Aga Khan III, too, made systematic efforts to set the identity of his followers apart from that of other religious communities, particularly the Twelver Shi'is, who for long periods had provided dissimulating covers for the Nizari Ismailis of Persia and elsewhere. The Nizari identity was defined and explained in numerous constitutions that the imam promulgated for his followers, especially in India, Pakistan and East Africa. Furthermore, he increasingly concerned himself with reform and modernisation policies that would benefit not only his own followers but other Muslims as well. Aga Khan III worked vigorously to reorganise the Nizari Ismailis into a modern Shi'i Muslim community with high standards of education, health and social well-being for both men and women, also developing a network of councils for administering the affairs of his community.

On his death in 1957, Aga Khan III was succeeded by his grandson Prince Karim, Aga Khan IV, known to his followers as Mawlana Hazar Imam Shah Karim al-Husayni. The present Harvard-educated Imam of the Nizari Ismailis, the 49th in the series, has substantially expanded the modernisation policies of his predecessor, also developing a multitude of new programmes and institutions of his own for the benefit of his community. At the same time, Aga Khan IV has concerned himself with a variety of social, economic and cultural issues and initiatives which are of wider interest to Muslims and the developing countries. Indeed, he has created a complex institutional network, generally referred to as the Aga Khan Development Network (AKDN), for implementing numerous projects in a wide variety of domains.[21] In the field of higher education, his major initiatives include The Institute of Ismaili Studies, the Aga Khan University, the University of Central Asia and the Global Center for Pluralism.

As an impressive Muslim leader, Aga Khan IV has also devoted much of his resources to promoting a better understanding of Islam, not merely as a religion with a multiplicity of expressions and interpretations but also as a major world civilisation with its plurality of social, intellectual and cultural traditions. In pursuit of these aims, he has founded an apex institution known as the Aga Khan Trust for Culture (AKTC).

---

[21] For details, see M. Ruthven, 'The Aga Khan Development Network and Institutions', in F. Daftary, ed., *A Modern History of the Ismailis* (London, 2011), pp. 189–220; and F. Daftary and Z. Hirji, *The Ismailis: An Illustrated History* (London, 2008), pp. 176–245.

The AKTC's mandate now covers a host of initiatives, projects and institutions, including the Aga Khan Award for Architecture, and the Aga Khan Museum, established in Toronto in 2014. The Nizari Ismailis have emerged as progressive Shi'i Muslim minorities in more than 25 countries of the world. And in every country of Asia, the Middle East, Africa, Europe and North America where they live as religious minority communities and loyal citizens of their adopted states, they generally enjoy exemplary standards of living while retaining their distinctive religious identity as well as devotion to their 'imam of the time'.

The Zaydis

The Zaydis represent another major Shi'i community. The general influence and geographic distribution of the Zaydiyya branch of Shi'i Islam, named after their fourth imam, Zayd b. Ali Zayn al-Abidin (d. 740), have been relatively more restricted compared with those of the Twelvers and the Ismailis.[22] In fact, after some initial success in Iraq, the Zaydi Shi'i imamate remained confined mainly to the Caspian region in northern Persia, and then, more importantly, to Yemen, where Zaydis have continued to live up to the present. The Zaydis have produced an impressive volume of literature over the centuries, which remains largely unpublished.[23]

The Zaydi branch of Shi'i Islam developed out of Zayd's abortive revolt. While Muhammad al-Baqir was acknowledged by the majority of the Imami Shi'a as their imam, his half-brother Zayd too acquired a reputation for his religious learning and he transmitted *hadith* from his father, amongst others. Subsequently, the Kufan Shi'a, who had never lost hope of uprooting the Umayyads, contacted Zayd and promised him extensive support if he rose against the Umayyads. However, when the battle was finally joined in 740, as had happened in the past, only a fraction of the number expected actually responded to Zayd's call to arms. In the event, the revolt was brutally suppressed in Kufa and Zayd was killed, his end reminiscent of the fate of his grandfather, Imam al-Husayn.

A Zaydi movement developed out of Zayd's revolt, and eventually crystallised as the Zaydi branch of Shi'i Islam. The movement was initially led by Zayd's eldest son Yahya, who fled from Kufa to Khurasan and concentrated his activities in that eastern region remote from the

---

[22] This section draws extensively on the work of Professor Wilferd Madelung, including especially his *Der Imam al-Qasim ibn Ibrahim und die Glaubenslehre der Zaiditen* (Berlin, 1965), a major study of early Zaydi history and thought.
[23] See S. Schmidtke, 'The History of Zaydi Studies: An Introduction', *Arabica*, 59 (2012), pp. 185–199.

centre of Umayyad administration. Yahya found some support amongst the local Shiʿa who had been exiled to Khurasan by successive governors of Iraq. Counted as one of the Zaydi imams, whose list has never been completely fixed, Yahya was eventually tracked down by the Umayyads and killed in battle in 743. Subsequently, the early Zaydis were led by another of Zayd's sons, Isa (d. 783), and others recognised as their imams. In early Abbasid times, groups of Zaydis participated in a number of abortive Alid, mainly Hasanid, revolts in the Hijaz, Iraq and elsewhere. By the middle of the 9th century, however, the Zaydis had shifted their rebellious activities to the mountainous region of Daylam in northern Persia, and to Yemen, remote from the centres of Abbasid power. Soon, the Zaydis actually succeeded in establishing two territorial states in these regions.

Zaydi Shiʿism was initially formed during the 8th century by the merger of two currents in Kufa, designated in heresiographical literature as the Batriyya and the Jarudiyya, also referred to as the 'weak' and the 'strong' traditions. The two groups disagreed especially with regard to the legitimacy of the rule (or imamate) of the caliphs preceding Ali, and the significance of the special knowledge attributed by the Shiʿa to the *ahl al-bayt*. Representing the moderate faction of the early Zaydiyya, the Batriyya upheld the caliphates of Abu Bakr and Umar. They argued that though Ali was the most excellent (*al-afdal*) of Muslims to succeed the Prophet, nevertheless the caliphates of his first two predecessors who were less excellent (*al-mafdul*) were valid, because Ali himself had pledged allegiance to them. In the case of the third caliph, Uthman (r. 644–656), the matter was more complicated. The Batri Zaydis either abstained from judgement or repudiated him for the last six years of his caliphate. The Batriyya, by contrast to Jarudiyya, did not ascribe any particular religious knowledge to the *ahl al-bayt*, or to the Alids, and accepted the knowledge (*hadith*) transmitted in the Muslim community generally. They also allowed the use of individual reasoning (*ijtihad* or *ra'y*) in religious matters in order to establish legal precepts. Furthermore, the Batriyya were indeed closely affiliated to the Kufan traditionist school, and with the latter's absorption into Sunni Islam in the 9th century, the Batri Zaydi tradition also disappeared. Thereafter, the more radical views of Jarudiyya on the imamate prevailed in Zaydi Shiʿism.

The Jarudiyya adopted some of the more radical doctrines of the Imami Shiʿis. Thus, they rejected the legitimacy of the caliphate of the caliphs before Ali. They held that the Prophet himself had designated Ali as his legatee (*wasi*) and implicitly as his successor, and that the majority of the Companions had gone astray for not supporting Ali's legitimate imamate. Consequently, the Jarudi Zaydis rejected the *hadith*s transmitted by these Companions and the Sunni traditionists as sources of the law, accepting only those handed down by the Fatimid (Hasanid and Husaynid) Alids. The Jarudiyya also ascribed superior knowledge in religious matters to the *ahl al-bayt*. However, in contrast to the Imami Shi'is, they did not confine legal teaching authority to their imams only, but accepted in principle the teaching of any member of the *ahl al-bayt* qualified by his religious learning.

By the 10th century, Zaydi doctrine, influenced by Jarudi and Mu'tazili elements, had been largely formulated. The Zaydis were less radical than the Imami Shi'is in their condemnation of the early caliphs and the Muslim community at large. Initially the Zaydis did not confine the legitimate imams to descendants of Ali, and accepted other Talibids, descendants of Ali's father Abu Talib, as suitable for their imamate. By then, however, the majority of the Zaydis considered only the Fatimid Alids, descendants of al-Hasan and al-Husayn, as legitimate candidates for their imamate. They also held that the first three imams, Ali, al-Hasan and al-Husayn, had been imams by designation (*nass*) of the Prophet himself. However, the designation had been unclear and obscure, *khafi* or *ghayr jali*, so that its intended meaning could be understood only through investigation.

After al-Husayn, the imamate could be claimed by any qualified descendant of al-Hasan and al-Husayn who was prepared to launch an uprising (*khuruj*) against the illegitimate rulers and issue a formal summons (*da'wa*) for gaining the allegiance of the people. Religious knowledge, ability to render independent ruling (*ijtihad*) and piety were emphasised as the qualifications of the imam, in addition to his Alid ancestry. Whilst the Zaydis did not generally consider their imams as divinely protected from error and sin (*ma'sum*), they later attributed such immunity to the first three imams. There were periods without any Zaydi imam; and, in practice, at times there was more than one. Due to high requirements in terms of religious learning, the Zaydis often backed Alid pretenders and rulers as summoners (*da'is*) or as imams with restricted status (*muhtasibun* or *muqtasida*) rather than as fully authoritative imams, known as *sabiqun* (sing. *sabiq*).

Thus, the Zaydis elaborated a doctrine of the imamate that clearly distinguished them from Imami Shi'ism and its two subsequent branches, the Twelvers and the Ismailis. In line with the points mentioned above, the Zaydis did not recognise a hereditary line of imams, nor did they attach any significance to the principle of the *nass*, central to the Imami doctrine. Initially, as noted, the Zaydis were prepared to accept any member of the *ahl al-bayt* as an imam, but later their imams were restricted to Fatimid Alids. According to Zaydi doctrine, if an imam wished to be recognised he would have to assert his claims publicly in a rising (*khuruj*) and sword in hand if necessary, in addition to having the required religious knowledge (*ilm*) and other qualifications. Many

Zaydi imams were, therefore, learned scholars and authors. Indeed, the Zaydis were not prepared to acknowledge quiescent claimants to the imamate. This explains why they did not recognise Zayd's father, Ali Zayn al-Abidin, or Zayd's brother, Muhammad al-Baqir, as imams. For the same reasons, in contrast to the Twelvers and the Ismailis, the Zaydis excluded the imamate of minors. They also rejected the eschatological idea of a concealed Mahdi and his return (*raj'a*) in the future. As a result, messianic tendencies remained rather weak in Zaydi Shi'ism. Their emphasis on activism also made the observance of *taqiyya* generally alien to Zaydi teachings. The Zaydis did, however, develop a doctrine of *hijra*, the obligation to emigrate from lands under the domination of unjust, non-Zaydi, rulers.

In theology, the Kufan Zaydiyya, like the early Imamiyya, were predestinarian and strongly opposed to the Qadariyya and the Mu'tazila. However, they later developed, similarly to the Imamis, closer relations with the Mu'tazili rationalist school of *kalam* theology. By the 10th century, the Zaydis had adopted practically all of the principal Mu'tazili tenets, including the unconditional punishment of the unrepentant sinner – a tenet rejected by the Twelvers and the Ismailis, for whom the imam plays a key role as intercessor for his followers. In religious law, the Zaydis initially relied on the teachings of Zayd himself and other early Alid authorities, such as Ja'far al-Sadiq. They also relied on the claimed consensus of the *ahl al-bayt*. By the end of the 9th century, however, four Zaydi legal schools (*madhhab*s) had emerged on the basis of the teachings of four different Zaydi authorities, including Imam al-Qasim b. Ibrahim al-Rassi (d. 860) founder of the school that later prevailed in Yemen as well as among a faction of the Caspian Zaydis.

Zaydi Shi'ism and Alid rule became closely intertwined in the mountainous provinces of Tabaristan, Gilan and Daylaman, in the Caspian region of northern Persia. Zaydi doctrines were first effectively disseminated in northern Persia by some of the local followers of the Hasanid Alid Zaydi Imam al-Qasim al-Rassi, who lived and taught on the Jabal al-Rass near Medina. As a result, al-Rassi's theological and legal teachings, which were only partially in agreement with Mu'tazili tenets, were spread in western Tabaristan (today's Mazandaran) in the Caspian region, known in medieval times as Daylam. In 864, the Hasanid Alid al-Hasan b. Zayd led the local Daylamis in a revolt against the region's Tahirid governor, who ruled on behalf of the Abbasids, and established the first Zaydi Alid state in Tabaristan with its capital at Amul. On his death in 884, al-Hasan b. Zayd was succeeded by his brother Muhammad; these two Alid brothers, who adopted the regnal title of al-Da'i ila'l-Haqq were not generally recognised as full imams, as there were some doubts regarding the justice of their rule. The first period of Zaydi Alid rule in Tabaristan came to an end in 900, at least temporarily, when Muhammad b. Zayd was defeated and killed in battle by the Samanids, who restored Daylam to their Sunni rule.

In 914, Zaydi Alid rule was re-established in Tabaristan by the Husaynid al-Hasan b. Ali al-Utrush (d. 917), known as al-Nasir li'l-Haqq. He had earlier converted many Daylamis and Gilis, and was generally recognised as an imam. In fact, al-Nasir became the founder of the school of Zaydi Shi'ism distinctive to the western Caspian region, in distinction from the older school of Qasimiyya prevalent in Daylam and later in Yemen. A learned scholar with numerous works on theology and law, al-Nasir's legal and ritual teaching, reflecting his own *ijtihad*, differed somewhat from the doctrine of Imam al-Qasim al-Rassi, which had been adopted earlier by the Zaydis of the Caspian region.

Henceforth, the Caspian Zaydis became divided into two rival schools (*madhhab*s) and communities, designated after their founders as Nasiriyya, concentrated in eastern Gilan and most of Daylaman (or Rudbar), and Qasimiyya, located mainly in western Tabaristan and Ruyan. There was much antagonism between the two Caspian Zaydi communities, who often supported different imams, *da'i*s or *amir*s. Matters were further complicated by ethnic differences and the close ties existing between the Caspian Qasimiyya and the Zaydis of Yemen. Prolonged Zaydi sectarian hostilities finally ceased in the Caspian region when around the middle of the 10th century Muhammad al-Mahdi li-Din Allah (d. 970), an imam of the Qasimiyya ruling from Gilan, declared both doctrinal schools as equally valid, because they were based on the *ijtihad* of legitimate imams. This ruling became generally accepted by the Caspian Zaydis who, nevertheless, remained divided in terms of their adherence to the two schools.

In the meantime, after the collapse of the second Zaydi Alid state of Tabaristan in 928 under Samanid attack, other Alid rulers had appeared in the Caspian provinces. In 932, Hawsam, and later Lahijan, in Gilan, became the seats of the Zaydi Alid dynasty of the Tha'irids, who reigned as *amir*s without claiming the Zaydi imamate, as well as other Alid rulers supporting the Nasiriyya school. At the same time, a number of Alids recognised as Zaydi imams by the Qasimiyya were active in Daylaman, with their seat at Langa. However, in the course of the 12th century, the Caspian Zaydis lost much of their prominence to the Nizari Ismailis, who had then successfully established themselves in Daylaman with their seat at Alamut. Subsequently, the Zaydis, now restricted mainly to eastern Gilan, were further weakened by incessant factional fighting and Alid rivalries. However, minor Zaydi Alid dynasties and Zaydi communities survived in the Caspian region until the 16th century, when Persian Zaydis converted to Twelver Shi'ism under Safawid rule over Persia. Henceforth, Zaydi Shi'ism was confined to Yemen.

In Yemen, Zaydi rule and an imamate were founded in 897 by the Hasanid Alid Yahya b. al-Husayn, grandson of Imam al-Qasim al-Rassi, who had the honorific title of al-Hadi ilaʼl-Haqq. With the help of some local tribes he established himself at Saʻda, in northern Yemen, which remained the stronghold of Zaydi Shiʻism, *daʻwa* activities and scholarship in Yemen. Soon, the Yemeni Zaydis came into conflict with the Ismailis, and Zaydi-Ismaili adversarial relations persisted throughout the centuries in Yemen. Imam al-Hadi expanded the Zaydi community in Yemen, also receiving support from groups of Caspian Zaydis who migrated to Yemen from 898.

Imam al-Hadiʼs theological doctrine was generally very close to the views of the contemporary Muʻtazili school of Baghdad. Concerning the imamate, he adopted the radical Shiʻi stance of the earlier Jarudi Zaydis, condemning the early caliphs before Ali. In religious law, al-Hadiʼs teachings were essentially based on the doctrine of his grandfather, Imam al-Rassi. Imam al-Hadiʼs legal doctrine was further elaborated by his sons, Muhammad al-Murtada (d. 922) and Ahmad al-Nasir li-Din Allah (d. 934), who were consecutively recognised as imams. Imam al-Hadiʼs legal teachings, collected and further developed later, provided the foundation of the Hadawiyya legal school, named after him, which became the only authoritative *madhhab* for the Zaydis of Yemen, and was adopted also in parts of the Caspian Zaydi community.

Having firmly established the Zaydi imamate in Yemen, which was to continue until 1962, Imam al-Hadi died in 911. His descendants, after his two sons, quarrelled incessantly among themselves and failed to be acknowledged as imams amongst the Yemeni Zaydis. The Zaydi imamate of the Rassid line was restored in Yemen in 999 by al-Mansur biʼllah al-Qasim al-ʻIyani (d. 1003), a descendant of Imam al-Rassi. Al-Mansurʼs son and successor al-Husayn, also recognised as an imam, made the unusual Zaydi claim of being the promised Shiʻi Mahdi, adopting the title of al-Mahdi li-Din Allah. He was killed in battle in 1013, but his remaining Zaydi followers denied his death and awaited his return, as traditionally expected from the Mahdi. These schismatic Zaydis, known as the Husayniyya, survived until the 15th century; they were led by the relatives of al-Husayn, who did not claim the imamate since the Mahdi could not be succeeded by any further imam. These Rassid Alids, who ruled merely as *amir*s awaiting the return of al-Husayn al-Mahdi, had numerous confrontations with the Ismaili Sulayhids who ruled over parts of Yemen as vassals of the Fatimids.

A second splinter Zaydi sect, known as the Mutarrifiyya, appeared in northern Yemen in the course of the 11th century. Named after its founder, Mutarrif b. Shihab (d. 1067), the Mutarrifiyya represented a pietist and ascetic, rather than a revolutionary, Zaydi movement. Mutarrif recognised the Zaydi teachings of the earlier imams and authorities, but rejected those of the contemporary Zaydi imams as well as the doctrines of the Caspian Zaydiyya. Furthermore, the Mutarrifis interpreted the acceptable Zaydi teachings in an arbitrary manner and developed a theology that deviated significantly from the Mu'tazili theology incorporated widely into Zaydi Shi'ism. The Mutarrifiyya founded numerous *hijras* or 'abodes of emigration', where they engaged in worship and ascetic practices. The Mutarrifi Zaydis, too, disappeared by the 15th century.

Meanwhile, the Zaydi imamate and fortunes were once again restored in Yemen by al-Mutawakkil Ahmad b. Sulayman (r. 1138–1171), who favoured the unity of the Zaydi communities and, therefore, recognised the equal legitimacy of the Yemeni and Caspian imams and their teachings. As a result, certain Yemeni imams were now acknowledged by the Caspian Zaydis; and numerous Zaydi texts of Caspian provenance were brought to Yemen. A key role was played in these unifying developments by Shams al-Din Ja'far b. Abi Yahya (d. 1178), a Zaydi jurist and scholar who originally adhered to Ismaili Shi'ism. He founded a Zaydi school that held that the Zaydi imams of the Caspian provinces were equal in their authority to those in Yemen.

The Zaydi imamate prevailed in Yemen even after the occupation of southern Arabia by the Sunni Ayyubids in 1174, though the power of the Zaydi imams was now considerably curtailed. Under these changed circumstances, the Yemeni Zaydis were at times obliged to cultivate better relations with the Sunni Muslims through modifying some of their own doctrines. For instance, Imam al-Mu'ayyad bi'llah Yahya b. Hamza (r. 1329–1349) praised the early caliphs as the Companions of the Prophet and deserving respect equal to that accorded to Ali. In later centuries, especially as the Zaydi imams extended their rule to the predominantly Sunni lowlands of Yemen, the Zaydis attempted in a more sustained fashion to achieve a certain doctrinal rapport with their Sunni subjects. In particular, they favoured the 'neo-Sunni school' that emerged in Yemen out of the teachings of Sayyid Muhammad b. Ibrahim al-Wazir (d. 1436), and, later, Muhammad b. Ali al-Shawkani (d. 1834). This 'neo-Sunni school' was primarily influenced by Sunni traditionalism, the Hanbali Sunni school of jurisprudence and the teachings of Ibn Taymiyya (d. 1328). On the other hand, the Yemeni Zaydis maintained their perennial hostility towards the Sufis, even though an ascetic Zaydi school of Sufism had been founded in Yemen in the 14th century.[24] The Yemeni Zaydis also

---

[24] See W. Madelung, 'Zaydi Attitudes to Sufism', in F. de Jong and B. Radtke, eds, *Islamic Mysticism Contested: Thirteen Centuries of Controversies and Polemics* (Leiden, 1999), pp. 124–144; reprinted in his *Studies in Medieval Shi'ism* (Farnham, 2012), article VI.

had prolonged conflicts with the Yemeni Ismailis, and wrote polemical treatises refuting their doctrines.

The final phase of the Zaydi imamate in Yemen commenced with al-Mansur biʾllah al-Qasim b. Muhammad (r. 1597–1620), founder of the Qasimi dynasty of Zaydi imams who ruled over much of Yemen until modern times. He branded the Sufis, like the Ismailis, as the Batiniyya and qualified to be considered as 'heretics'. The Zaydi persecution of the Sufis in Yemen continued until the abolition of the Zaydi imamate in the 20th century. Meanwhile, after the first Ottoman occupation of Yemen ended in 1636, Sanʿa served as the capital of an independent Zaydi state and imamate for more than two centuries until 1872, when Yemen once again became an Ottoman province. During this period, marked by rivalries over the succession in the Qasimi Zaydi dynasty as well as incessant tribal conflicts, the Zaydi imamate itself was transformed into a form of dynastic rule. The Zaydi rulers and imams now succeeded one another normally on a dynastic basis, without possessing the required religious knowledge and other qualifications expected of the imams according to Zaydi tradition. The imams, thus, effectively became kings or sultans, lacking the charisma and spiritual qualities enjoyed by the earlier Zaydi imams.

In its final stage lasting until 1962, the Zaydi rule and imamate were handed down amongst the members of the Hamid al-Din family of the Qasimis, starting with al-Mansur Muhammad b. Yahya Hamid al-Din (r. 1890–1904). Al-Mansur was succeeded by his son al-Mutawakkil Yahya, who pursued a policy of complete isolation; and on his assassination in 1948, he was succeeded by his son al-Nasir Ahmad who ruled until his own death in 1962. Ahmad's son, Muhammad al-Badr, ruled for only one week before he was deposed by a group of army officers who declared a republic in Yemen.

The Zaydi imamate has not been claimed since Muhammad al-Badr's death in 1996 in exile in England, which is a permissible state of affairs according to Zaydi doctrine. Thus, the Zaydi Shiʿis currently remain without an imam of any status, while the very nature of Zaydi Shiʿism has undergone a fundamental transformation, largely characterised by Sunnification. The modern Yemeni state has in fact pursued an anti-Zaydi policy in the guise of Islamic reform. The official ideology in Yemen has favoured the neo-Sunni school while marginalising the Zaydi *ulama* who have effectively lost their influential position in the state.

Further Reading

Amir-Moezzi, Mohammad Ali. *The Spirituality of Shi'i Islam: Beliefs and Practices*, tr. H. Karmali. London, 2011.

Crone, Patricia. *Medieval Islamic Political Thought*. Edinburgh, 2004.

Daftary, Farhad. *The Isma'ilis: Their History and Doctrines*. 2nd ed., Cambridge, 2007.

—— *A History of Shi'i Islam*. London, 2013.

Daftary, Farhad and Gurdofarid Miskinzoda, ed. *The Study of Shi'i Islam: History, Theology and Law*. London, 2014.

Haider, Najam. *Shi'i Islam: An Introduction*. Cambridge, 2014.

Halm, Heinz. *Shi'ism*, tr. J. Watson and M. Hill. 2nd ed., Edinburgh, 2004.

Kohlberg, Etan, ed. *Shi'ism*. Aldershot, 2003.

Madelung, Wilferd. *Studies in Medieval Shi'ism*, ed. S. Schmidtke. Farnham, 2012.

—— 'Zaydiyya', *EI2*, vol. 11, pp. 477–481.

Modarressi, Hossein. *Crisis and Consolidation in the Formative Period of Shi'ite Islam*. Princeton, NJ, 1993.

Momen, Moojan. *An Introduction to Shi'i Islam: The History and Doctrines of Twelver Shi'ism*. New Haven, CT, 1985.

Newman, Andrew J. *Twelver Shi'ism: Unity and Diversity in the Life of Islam, 632 to 1722*. Edinburgh, 2013.

Qutbuddin, Tahera. 'The Da'udi Bohra Tayyibis: Ideology, Literature, Learning and Social Practice', in F. Daftary, ed., *A Modern History of the Ismailis*. London, 2011, pp. 331–354.

Sobhani, Ja'far. *Doctrines of Shi'i Islam: A Compendium of Imami Beliefs and Practices*, tr. and ed. R. Shah-Kazemi. London, 2001.

10

Remembering Fatima and Zaynab: Gender in Perspective

Zayn Kassam and Bridget Blomfield

In the Muslim sacred universe, the central configuration connecting divine guidance to the realm of creation rests in the figure of the Prophet Muhammad, through whom the Quran was revealed. Ali, the cousin and son-in-law of Muhammad, is considered to be the true spiritual and temporal legatee of the Prophet in his twin roles as receiver of divine guidance and leader of the nascent community of Muslims. For the Shi'a, Muhammad's daughter and Ali's wife, Fatima, takes on special significance in her role connecting the prophetic lineage of Muhammad with the lineage of the imams. This chapter considers Fatima, her daughter Zaynab, women associated with the events at Karbala, and Fatima's descendant Nafisa, as exemplars for the faithful in ways that shape and are shaped by the sacred universe. A section on women holding key political positions during the time of the Fatimids illustrates the engagement of Shi'i women in public life. The chapter ends with the manner in which Fatima and Zaynab are remembered today, and continue to embody models of courage, perseverance and resistance and agency for Shi'i women in particular.

Fatima

Fatima is the cherished daughter of the Prophet Muhammad, born to the Prophet and his first wife Khadija in 605, though she is also considered in Shi'i sources to have been born later. Known for her piety, endurance and industriousness, she was consoled at the death of her mother by her father, who said that the angel Jibril (Gabriel) had informed him that God had built a palace for her in Paradise. Tradition relates that her father turned down several offers of marriage for her but accepted Ali's, whom she is thought to have married in 622 or 623, a marriage that began in straitened circumstances until the general lot of Muslims improved after the battle of Khaybar in 629. The marriage ended ten years later with her death. The *tasbih* (repetition of names or phrases as an act of glorification and supplication) of Fatima dates from the early period of her marriage, when, according to tradition, in a state of exhaustion, Fatima asked her father for a servant girl to help her. Her father asked if instead she would like something of greater value than the entire world, upon which he taught her to recite *Allahu akbar* 34 times, *al-hamdu li'llah* 33 times, and *subhan Allah* 33 times. Although not directly mentioned in the Quran, exegetes have connected verses such as 33:33 to her, in which '*ahl al-bayt*' is understood by Shi'i exegetes to refer to Muhammad, Ali, Fatima, Hasan and Husayn, the latter two being the sons of Ali and Fatima. Relations between A'isha, the Prophet's youngest wife, and Fatima may have been strained, according to a *hadith* report that 'A'isha disapproved of what Fatima used to say' (Bukhari, 7:63:245). After her father's death, Fatima was drawn into the dispute over succession in two ways. First, according to Shi'i tradition, the pregnant Fatima suffered injuries and broken ribs at the hands of Umar when he came to the household to exact Ali's loyalty to Abu Bakr, designated by influential members of the community as the first caliph after Muhammad. The result was Fatima's miscarriage of her unborn son Muhsin and, a few months later, her death during the month of Ramadan. Second, the confiscation of the Prophet's properties led Fatima to appeal to Abu Bakr for her share, comprising the estate of Fadak, which she claimed to have been gifted to her by her father, and her share from the battle of Khaybar. She was denied both by the new caliph on the grounds that the Prophet had said that 'prophets do not leave behind an inheritance', and his wealth should be used as *sadaqa* for charitable purposes. It is said that she asked for news of her impending death to be withheld until after she had been buried so as prevent the possibility of Abu Bakr officiating at her funeral. She was survived by her husband Ali, their two sons, Hasan and Husayn, and their two daughters, Zaynab and Umm Kulthum.

Sahih al-Bukhari, widely regarded as one of the most trusted *hadith* collections by Sunni Muslims, narrates a tradition from the Prophet's youngest and favourite wife A'isha, according to which Fatima is lauded as holding the position of mistress of all the women on earth and in Paradise (4:56:819). In addition, Fatima holds a tremendously important place in the historical development of Shi'ism. She is the 'mother of the imamate' by giving birth to the first living male heirs of the Prophet Muhammad. As such, in addition to the intrinsic qualities that make her a model for the faithful, especially Shi'i women, Fatima has over the centuries developed a spiritual significance that is central to the Shi'i worldview. Adored by her father, according to Shi'i tradition, Fatima's birth was surrounded by light. She is referred to as Fatima al-Zahra, 'the radiant, luminous, most shining one' and is considered pure and spotless, a heavenly intercessor. The 12th-century Shi'i scholar Ibn Shahrashub connects Fatima's radiance to *walaya*: 'God created Paradise from the light of His countenance; He took this light, and threw it; with a third of it He struck Muhammad, with another third Fatima, and with the remaining third Ali and the People of the House.'[1] The renowned and influential Shi'i scholar al-Majlisi (d. 1699), in explaining why Fatima is titled al-Zahra, recounts a *hadith* in which the light normally attributed to the sun's rays at daybreak, during the day, and evening are seen to be emanating from Fatima – a light that endures until the birth of Husayn, after which it proceeds through each of the subsequent imams. Identifying this light as the *nur Muhammadiyya*, the light of the Prophet, it is inherited by his descendants through Fatima. Indeed, she represents the confluence of two lights (*majma al-nurayn*), bringing the *tanzil* ('that which descends', that is, revelation) of Muhammad (exoteric knowledge) together with the *ta'wil* ('that which is taken back to its source', that is, its interpretation) of Ali (esoteric knowledge). Anointed as the Pure One, Fatima is born pure and dies pure, and does not menstruate. Thus she was honoured with the title *batul* (virgin). She is considered the womb of the world, the mother of all things. 'God created Fatima from the light, first a spirit without a body, then he touched us with His right hand and His light shone in us.'[2] The Prophet Muhammad related that Fatima is 'a pure and blessed child; and that the Almighty God will indeed create my lineage through her, and will choose from my lineage a number of *a'imma* [imams] appointing them as His *khulafa* [caliphs] on His earth after the completion of His revelation.'[3] He added: 'Fatima is a part of me; what hurts her hurts me, and what pleases her pleases me. Verily God becomes angry when Fatima is angry and is pleased when she is pleased.'[4]

As a redemptrix, it is believed that, 'on the day of Resurrection, Fatima will stand at the gate of Hell, and on the forehead of every man will be written '*mu'min*' [believer] or '*kafir*' [unbeliever].'[5] Yet if the sinner has loved Fatima and wept on behalf of her suffering and the suffering of her family, 'lover' will be stamped between his eyes and she will intercede on his behalf so that he is not sent to burn in hell. The shedding of tears in

[1]   Cited in Karen Ruffle, *Gender, Sainthood, and Everyday Practice in South Asian Shi'ism* (Chapel Hill, NC, 2011), p. 82.
[2]   Jawahir al-Amili, as quoted by Mahmoud Ayoub, *Redemptive Suffering in Islam: A Study of the Devotional Aspects of Ashura in Twelver Shi'ism* (The Hague, 1978), p. 56.
[3]   Mostafa Hosayni, *Sayyedat Nesa al-Alamen: Chief of the Women of the World* (UK, 2003), p. 28.
[4]   Ibn Babawayh, *Ma'ani al-akhbar*, ed. Ali Akbar al-Ghaffari (Tehran, 1959), p. 303.
[5]   Ali Shariati, *Shariati on Shariati and the Muslim Woman*, tr. Laleh Bakhtiar (Chicago, 1996), p. 214.

honour of Fatima and her family, the *ahl al-bayt* (People of the House) is critically important in Shi'i soteriology. The eminent 11th-century theologian, al-Shaykh al-Mufid, reports that Fatima stands at the gates of Paradise on the Day of Judgment, and will be compensated for her own suffering by being granted the power to save all those who pray to her. She carries the *jami'a*, a scroll that is 70 yards long. Upon this scroll is written everything that humanity needs to know until the end of time.

As the wife of Imam Ali she becomes the mother of the imamate. Many of the imams were martyred, making her the mistress of the House of Sorrows. Her sons Hasan and Husayn were martyred defending Islam. For the Shi'a, she maintains a status similar to the Virgin Mary for many Christians, a mother whose son, Jesus, was also martyred. Both Mary and Fatima are considered role models for women who have suffered and been oppressed, and who have experienced injustice.

Fatima represents the perfect woman as an earthly, human creature but also as an instrument of divine means for attaining spiritual wholeness. Her piety is depicted in stories narrated in *hadith*s, in the writings of Shi'i scholars, and in modern-day narratives both oral and written detailing her as generous, given to simplicity, and modest. One such story describes her gift to a poor woman. Not knowing that Fatima was soon to be married, the woman told Fatima that she had no dress to wear to her own wedding. Fatima took her wedding dress and gave it to the poor woman. God, so impressed by this selfless action, gifted Fatima with heavenly garments. 'He showed them a Being, adorned with a myriad of glittering lights of various colours, who sat on a throne, a crown on her head, rings in her ears, a drawn sword by her side.'[6] Fatima was given the gift of 'heavenly clothes' from the angel Jibril and on the day of her wedding, 70,000 angels accompanied her. This heavenly clothing can be interpreted as a mantle that concealed and enveloped her mystical powers. Her robes of light shield and protect anyone that turns towards her in need. Such imagery suggests that if one remains faithful, pious, and charitable there are heavenly rewards after death.

As a holy woman, Fatima transforms suffering through her faith and her ability to surrender to the will of God. She is the mistress of heaven and earth and is a mediator between this world and the next. Her significance not only derives from her connections to her illustrious family, but from her own merits, as expressed by the late Iranian intellectual, Ali Shariati:

---

[6] Louis Massignon, 'Die Ursprunge und die Bedeutung des Gnostizismus im Islam', *Eranos Jahrbuch*, 5 (1937), pp. 64–65.

I wanted to say, Fatimeh is the daughter of noble Khadijeh.
I saw, this is not Fatimeh.
I wanted to say, Fatimeh is the daughter of Muhammad.
I saw, this is not Fatimeh.
I wanted to say, Fatimeh is the wife of Ali.
I saw, this is not Fatimeh.
I wanted to say, Fatimeh is the mother of Hasan and Husayn.
I saw, this is not Fatimeh.
I wanted to say, Fatimeh is the mother of Zaynab.
Still, I saw that this is not Fatimeh.
No, she is all of these but all of these are not Fatimeh.
Fatimeh is Fatimeh.[7]

After the 1979 Iranian revolution, cemeteries in Iran were renamed *bihisht*, the Persian word for paradise, with the largest cemetery in Tehran being called Behesht-e Zahra, the Paradise of Zahra, Zahra the Mother of Martyrs, thus symbolically portraying the notion that 'the holy female figure, after which the cemetery is named, will be viewed as the mother of those who are no longer with us.' Fatima is the heavenly figure that in her earthly life embodies piety, patience and perseverance. Her daughter Zaynab, also beloved by the Shi'a, became a focal point of resistance to oppression as she became an outspoken granddaughter of the Prophet Muhammad in demanding justice for her martyred family. After the death of her mother, Zaynab continued the female legacy of the Prophet Muhammad's family and the message of justice in Islam.

Zaynab

Zaynab bint Ali, the third child of Ali and Fatima, is thought to have been born in 626. Referred to as Sayyida Zaynab, she exemplifies the essence of bravery and courage due to her role in the aftermath of Karbala, to which place she had accompanied her brother Husayn. Following his decapitation and the loss of many of his companions (traditionally numbered at 72), including her two sons Aun and Muhammad, Zaynab along with other captives was marched to Damascus, Yazid I's capital. It was there, at Yazid's palace that Zaynab offered the first *majlis* of lamentation mourning the deaths of her brother Husayn and their kinsmen, continued today in the rites observed during the first ten days of the month of Muharram. Women especially relate to her because she embodied the empowered woman, angered sister and outraged mother when she delivered her

---

[7]   Ali Shariati, 'Fatimeh is Fatimeh', quoted from Laleh Bakhtiar, tr., *Shariati on Shariati and the Muslim Woman* (Chicago, 1996), p. 216.

famous monologue at the court of Yazid. Reminding Yazid that he was the descendant of his father and grandparents who had been set free by her grandfather at the surrender of Mecca, she called him to task for pulling out 'the roots of piety and virtue' and for shedding the blood of the sons of the Prophet 'under the clouds of oppression and justice'.[8] Her radical assumption of authority won her the admiration of her people and even more deeply the loyalty and love of women. Her courage was enormous, to such a degree that in some communities she is simply referred to as al-Sayyida (descendant of the Prophet) without the use of a first name. Her second courageous act concerns the order given by the governor of Kufa sentencing Ali Zayn al-Abidin, the sole surviving son of Husayn, to death. Throwing herself over him, she declared to the governor that to kill Ali, he would first have to kill her. Thus, as protector of fatherless children, Zaynab is compared to 'the shining moon and the heroine of all time' as she is seen as being 'above man'.

> Don't call her a woman, she is above man, she is more faithful than a man
> Don't call her a woman, there is no one more courageous than Zaynab
> Don't call her a woman, there is no one more knowledgeable than Zaynab
> In her bravery and wisdom so similar to Haydar Safdar (Ali)
> Who is the one with pious knowledge, the protector of women's interest?[9]

Considered the source of wisdom for women, she is called Zinat, the Jewel of Paradise, the light of God. Zaynab embodies the perfect balance of the masculine and feminine attributes that many saints reflect. Eshtehardi describes her qualities as such:

> Her personality was like Khadija's, her modesty and chastity like her mother Fatima's, and the sweetness of her speech was like her father Ali's, her revolutionary dream and patience was like her brother Hasan's, her courage and strength of heart was like her brother Husayn's.[10]

---

8   Abu'l-Fazl Ahmad b. Abi Tahir, *Balaghatun Nisa*, available online at: http://www.al-islam.org/probe-history-ashura-dr-ibrahim-ayati/chapter-32-sermon-lady-zaynab-court-yazid.
9   F. Shirazi, 'The Daughters of Karbala: Images of Women in Popular Shi'i Culture in Iran', in Kamran Scot Aghaie, ed., *The Women of Karbala* (Austin, TX, 2005), pp. 109–110.
10   Mohammad Mohammadi Eshtehardi, *Hazrat-e Zaynab, payam resan-e*

She is a constant reminder that the human spirit will fight against and triumph over oppression and is seen as a heroine by Shi'i Muslim women, not as a victim. She died in 682, six months after being released by Yazid. Her tomb in Cairo at the Sayyida Zaynab Mosque is considered to be her final resting place, although a similar claim is made for the mosque of the same name in Damascus.

The Women of Karbala

The events of Karbala and its aftermath are, 'refracted through a woman's universe because the women survived the battle',[11] and offer an occasion for a memorial signifying the centrality of Fatima and Zaynab to the Shi'i sacred narrative. Already mentioned are Fatima's roles as the progenitrix of the imams and her redemptive role as their grieving mother beginning with the slaughter of her son Husayn and followed by the sufferings experienced by subsequent imams and members of her family, the *ahl al-bayt*. Fatima is commemorated each Muharram (also known as 'the month of Zaynab') in the *zaban-i hal* (biographical sketches) recited at *nawha* (lamentations) and *taziya*, the theatrical performances similar to a passion play that recollect, re-enact and recount the lives of the Prophet, Fatima and the 12 imams, also known as the 'Fourteen Infallibles' of the Ithna'ashari Shi'a. The *taziya* serves to revitalise and reinforce Shi'i identity and the commitment to working for justice, revolutionary if need be, as evidenced during the 1979 Iranian Revolution, against oppression. Zaynab stands out for her role in naming and defying Yazid I's oppression of her kinsmen and community, for initiating the mourning rites for her brother Husayn, and for shielding her nephew Ali Zayn al-Abidin and saving him from death, thereby playing a critical role in the continuation of the imamate. Thus, Zaynab, too, becomes an intercessor for those who grieve for the holy family.

In addition, there were other women associated with Karbala who played lesser but significant roles, and several studies of lamentation rites and the *taziya*s mention dozens of female characters who take part in the story of Karbala. The women most often mentioned are female relatives or women connected in some way to the holy family, for example, apart from Fatima and Zaynab, mother and sister, respectively, of Imam Husayn, Khadija, his grandmother; his sister Umm Kulthum; his wife, Umm Layla, or Shahrbanu, mother of Husayn's slain infant Ali Asghar; his four

---

shahidan-e Karbala (Tehran, 1997), p. 9, cited in Kamran Scot Aghaie, ed., *The Martyrs of Karbala* (Seattle, WA, 2004), p. 126.
[11] Ruffle, *Gender, Sainthood, and Everyday Practice*, p. 99.

daughters, Kulthum, Sakina, who begs her uncle Abbas to fetch water for the thirsty camp, whose access to the river has been cut off by Yazid's army, Fatima (her cousin Qasim's bride, also known as Fatima Kubra, who lost her husband on their wedding day), and little Ruqayya, forced to walk barefoot in captivity to Damascus, where she died; Umm Salama, the Prophet's wife who helped bring up Hasan and Husayn; a Christian convert; and Qasim's mother. Often included is a woman named Tuwih, who sheltered Husayn's messenger and exemplifies loyalty to the imam. These women are portrayed as exemplars, as loyal, moral, courageous and pious individuals who endured suffering due to oppression. They mourn the martyrdom of their menfolk, who were sacrificed for the sake of justice, and suffer humiliation in captivity after burying their dead. Some of them, such as the fighter Wahb's wife Haniya, attempt to dash into the battlefield and are called back by Imam Husayn; their sacrifice thus consists of giving up their loved ones in battle, as did Wahb's mother in sending him into battle. Umm Kulthum, Zaynab's sister, and Sakina, Husayn's four-year-old daughter, join Zaynab in calling oppressive men and betrayers of Husayn's cause, such as the Kufans, to task, regardless of their station. In contemporary rituals, supplicants offer prayers at the reconstructed bridal chamber of Qasim and Fatima to seek help for resolution in matters pertaining to marriage, while at the grave of Ruqayya, help is sought for matters pertaining to children.[12]

Kamran Scot Aghaie argues that Shiʿi symbols and rituals such as the *taziya* affect women on many levels: personally for psychological, emotional, spiritual and soteriological effects; for articulating gender ideals and the passing on of gender-specific identities; for establishing and preserving social bonds, identities and status; and finally, for reinforcing social norms for women while providing opportunities for independence, influence and public social participation for some women. The symbolism of Karbala, he notes, communicates several messages concerning women:

> First, the greatest and most worthy social status for women derives from piety, along with devotion to Islam and the family of the Prophet. Second, women had the ability, and the authority to preserve, transmit, and articulate the values of Shiʿism. Third, the precedent was established for women to encourage or even demand that the men in their family conform to religious ideals of behavior. And finally, women

---

[12] Ingvild Flaskerud, "'Oh, My Heart Is Sad. It Is Moharram, the Month of Zaynab.' The Role of Aesthetics and Women's Mourning Ceremonies in Shiraz", in Aghaie, ed., *The Women of Karbala*, p. 88.

were given the right, or even the responsibility, to challenge male authority when a man acted in an impious manner, even if he was the ruling caliph.[13]

Fatima's legacy in Egypt: Sayyida Nafisa

Fatima had another distinguished female descendant, Sayyida Nafisa, the great-granddaughter of her son Hasan. Born in Mecca in 762, she moved to Medina as a young child with her father, Hasan al-Anwar, son of Zayd al-Ablaj, son of Hasan, son of Fatima and Ali. There she became renowned for her renunciation (*zuhd*) and piety (*taqwa*), her knowledge of the Quran, the *hadith* and the law, her frequent visits to Muhammad's grave, and her pilgrimages to Mecca. It is said that she also studied with the great jurist, Malik b. Anas. She was married to Ishaq al-Mutamin, son of the Imam Jafar al-Sadiq, the great-grandson of Husayn and to avoid the persecution then faced by the *ahl al-bayt*, emigrated with him from the Hijaz to Egypt, where there is a mosque bearing her name. Her husband returned to Medina when appointed governor there by the Abbasids, and did not return to Egypt until she died in 824. She bore him two children, a son, al-Qasim, and a daughter, Umm Kulthum.

The titles attached to her name, Nafisa, meaning precious, attest to her spiritual and temporal knowledge, her steadfastness in piety and prayer, and the love and esteem with which she was held: *al-tahira* (the Lady of Purity), *al-ilmi wa'l-ma'rifa* (the Lady of Knowledge and Gnosis), *al-abida* (the Lady of Divine Servanthood), *al-darayn* (the Lady of Two Realms, that is, this world and the next), *sahiba al-karamat* (the Mistress of Miracles), *sayyida ahl al-fatwa* (Distinguished Lady among those pronouncing legal rulings), *umm al-awajiz* (the Mother of the Elderly), and *al-Misriyyin* (the Lady of the Egyptians). These titles indicate what has come down about her through history and hagiography. She was learned, and counted luminaries such as the jurist al-Shafi'i and the mystic Dhu al-Nun al-Misri among her interlocutors and students. Her piety was of such renown that people came from near and far to seek her blessings: hagiographies recount her decision to leave Egypt due to the throngs that came to seek the blessings of the *ahl al-bayt*, leaving little time for prayer and the discomfiture of imposing on the hospitality of the governor of Egypt, who had hosted the family in Cairo. The intervention of the governor, his gift of a larger residence, and the pleas of the people for her not to leave Egypt convinced her to stay. Numerous accounts are given of the miracles she performed for those who sought

---

[13] Kamran Scot Aghaie, 'The Gender Dynamics of Moharram Symbols and Rituals in the Latter Years of Qajar Rule', in *The Women of Karbala*, pp. 54–55.

her aid directly or through prayer, such as curing a blind girl, intervening when the Nile did not rise one year as expected, preventing a ship from sinking, helping a woman who spent her life spinning wool to support her family, freeing a prisoner through her intercession, and seeing people through their difficulties. A pilgrimage to Mecca occasioned the vivid appearance of the spirit of Ibrahim (Abraham), who remained her guide till the end of her days.

Fatimid Women

The legacy of Fatima continues with the Fatimids, an Ismaili Shiʻi dynasty that ruled from 909 to 1171 – and as Delia Cortese and Simonetta Calderini observe, 'the only Islamic dynasty to be named after a woman'.[14] At its height, the Fatimid empire stretched from the Atlantic coast in North Africa to the Red Sea, and included within its jurisdiction Palestine, Syria, Lebanon, Jordan, Sicily, the Red Sea coast of Africa, Yemen, Tihama and the Hijaz. In Cairo, ca. 970, al-Azhar was established as a place of learning by the Fatimids, considered one of the first universities in the world, and paying homage in its name to Fatima, who was titled al-Zahra (the Radiant or Resplendent), hence the name al-Azhar. Al-Qadi al-Nuʻman (d. 974), the foremost jurist of the Fatimids, held that Fatima's *khutba* or speech about the dispute over Fadak – the estate she inherited from her father – was to be understood symbolically: Fadak stood for the Prophet's bequest to her in her role as progenitrix of the imams subsequent to Ali. The issue of injustice with regard to a woman's inheritance, as in the case of Fatima, led al-Nuʻman to specify that if a woman was the sole survivor of a deceased person, then she should inherit the full amount, regardless of her gender. Such a view is echoed in more widespread Shiʻi inheritance practices as well. 'Shiʻi inheritance law ... gives more rights than does Sunni law to certain female relations, especially daughters, and to relations on the female as well as the male side', observes Nikkie Keddie. 'This may be in part because the imams' descent from the Prophet passed through the female line...'.[15] Fatima's name or titles are found on Fatimid coins and talismans; her birthday was commemorated as a holiday; and the recitation of her *tasbih* was thought to garner blessings the weight of a thousand good deeds.

---

[14] Delia Cortese and Simonetta Calderini, *Women and the Fatimids in the World of Islam* (Edinburgh, 2006), p. 232.

[15] Nikkie R. Keddie, *Women in the Middle East: Past and Present* (Princeton, NJ, 2007), p. 28.

Two other major female figures are associated with the Fatimids – Sitt al-Mulk, and Queen Arwa, titled al-Sayyida al-Hurra, of the Ismaili Sulayhid dynasty in Yemen. The first counts Fatima as her direct forebear, being the daughter of her descendant al-Aziz, the fifth Fatimid imam-caliph, while the second was a staunch supporter of the Fatimid cause. Sitt al-Mulk, the daughter of al-Aziz, was born in 970 in Mansuriyya. Endowed with natural political gifts, Sitt al-Mulk is said to have lived in an exquisitely appointed palace, employed close to 4,000 slave-girls, had an army division called al-Atufiyya, trained by her employee Atuf, as part of her entourage, and patronised the building of several *hamam*s (bathhouses) and with her mother, the construction of the Jami al-Qarafa, the second mosque to be built by the Fatimids after al-Azhar. At her father's death in 996, she sought to block the designated heir, her half-brother al-Mansur, to be known as al-Hakim bi-Amr Allah, from acceding to the imamate by staging what historical sources have termed a palace coup d'état, which was successfully thwarted by al-Hakim's guardian, the eunuch Barjawan. Historians have seen in this episode evidence of a broader struggle between the *maghariba*, those army factions from North Africa who had supported the dynasty from its rise, and the *mashariqa*, the soldiers from the eastern Islamic heartlands who had increasingly been imported by al-Aziz to manage the affairs of the caliphal administration. Barjawan rapidly consolidated his power, leading Sitt al-Mulk to withdraw from political interference while lavishing her younger half-brother with gifts. However, the assassination of Barjawan by al-Saqalibi, her ally in the attempted palace coup, facilitated her rise to power.

Al-Hakim not only conferred land and titles upon her but made her his key advisor on all matters relating to state. One example was his deft handling of grievances stemming from tax burdens in Syria upon her advice. However, al-Hakim's handling of several other crises over the next decade – including an anti-Fatimid revolt in North Africa, judicial and monetary problems in Egypt, the Jarrahid revolt in Palestine, and the movement in the *da'wa* proclaiming the divinity of al-Hakim – led to a rift between himself and Sitt al-Mulk. The historian al-Maqrizi asserts that al-Hakim's attempts to rein in the intrigues of the womenfolk of the palace resulted in either the banishment or drowning of a large number of the women. The historian Ibn Taghribirdi reports that Sitt al-Mulk offered refuge to al-Hakim's wife Amina and their son Ali at this time. In addition, several key functionaries close to Sitt al-Mulk were punished or killed, causing the princess once again to withdraw from public life. In 1021, al-Hakim disappeared, leaving a trail of torn and bloodied clothes, causing medieval historians to speculate that Sitt al-Mulk was likely to have been behind the attack and disappearance. Cortese and Calderini note that:

Ever since, the shadow of suspicion has been hanging over her and, alas, it is to her reputation as a possible fratricidal murderer that ultimately she owes her fame. Several reasons have been adduced for her supposed action; fear for her personal safety; the increasingly bizarre behaviour of her brother, especially against women; his elimination of several of her closest collaborators; and her disapproval of her brother's succession plans.[16]

However, the Fatimid courtier al-Quda'i noted half a century later that Sitt al-Mulk exposed the Berber chief, Ibn Dawwas, as the person responsible for the murder and had him killed by the deceased imam-caliph's men. It remains unclear whether or not al-Hakim's policies and measures were attempts to wrest power away from a politically ambitious Sitt al-Mulk, or perhaps responses to wider economic and political conditions in the Mediterranean.

Following al-Hakim's disappearance and likely death, Sitt al-Mulk, like her forebear Zaynab, is once again seen as responsible for ensuring that the direct line of the progeny of Fatima succeeded to the imamate, which would otherwise have passed to a grandson of al-Mahdi, still a Fatimid but not of the direct hereditary line. As de facto ruler of the Fatimid state between the death of al-Hakim and the proclamation of the next imam-caliph in 1021, she reportedly ordered a series of killings aimed at protecting the young al-Zahir, while also taking action to persecute the *da'is* responsible for proclaiming al-Hakim's divinity. She lifted restrictions placed by the deceased caliph on women, Christians, Jews, music and wine, allowing non-Muslims to restore their houses of worship, reclaimed land grants that had been disbursed, reinstated taxes abolished by al-Hakim, and restored the financial affairs of the state to order,[17] while also working to re-establish diplomatic relations and negotiations with the Byzantine emperor in connection with the expansionist policies of Byzantium in the eastern Mediterranean. In 1021, the 17-year-old Ali, son of al-Hakim, was proclaimed imam-caliph under the title al-Zahir li-I'zaz Din Allah. Sitt al-Mulk died, ostensibly of diarrhoea, in 1023.

Turning now to the medieval Yemeni queen, Arwa, she bore witness in her will to 'Fatima, the "radiant and pure", as the fifth among the elected *ashab*, or People of the House'.[18] Born around 1048 in Haraz, Arwa was raised by the queen-consort Asma at the palace of the founder of the Sulayhid dynasty, the Fatimid *da'i* and sultan, Ali b. Muhammad

---

[16] Cortese and Calderini, *Women and the Fatimids*, p. 123.

[17] Yaacov Lev, *State and Society in Fatimid Egypt* (Leiden, 1991), pp. 36–37.

[18] Cortese and Calderini, *Women and the Fatimids*, p. 135.

al-Sulayhi. The Sulayhids ruled Yemen for the better part of a century, and Ali, the son of a well-respected Shafi'i judge from the Banu Hamdan tribe, espoused the Fatimid cause and ruled as their vassal, establishing San'a as his capital and having the *khutba* pronounced in the name of the Fatimid Ismaili imam-caliphs throughout his dominions. Viewed by the Fatimids as a strategically important outpost for their *da'wa* activities, especially for those in India, Yemen was also important for military, political and commercial reasons to the Fatimids. In 1067, Ali and Asma were taken captive by the Najahids of Zabid; Ali was killed while Asma was eventually rescued by her son Ahmad al-Mukarram (d. 1084), whom she assisted in dealing with the affairs of state until her own death in 1074.

Under Asma's tutelage, the young Arwa was educated in letters, the Quran, history, poetry, and was noted for her beauty, piety and intelligence. She was married to Ahmad al-Mukarram in either 1065 or 1069, upon which she received the revenue of Aden as a dowry from her father-in-law, Ali. Her husband's war injuries sustained in 1074–1075 made him a paraplegic shortly after the death of his mother Asma. While al-Mukarram remained nominally the ruler of the Sulayhid state, Arwa effectively took charge, moving the capital from San'a to Dhu Jibla, and having her name read in the *khutba* after that of the Fatimid Imam-caliph al-Mustansir as a sign of her authority. Her son, Ali Abd al-Mustansir, confirmed as ruler by the Fatimid state after the death of her husband, died some six years after his father. Arwa remained the effective queen of the Sulayhid territories, increasingly beset by tribal fighting, till her death in 1138, leaving behind no living heirs and hence marking the end of the Sulayhid dynasty. Buried in the Friday Mosque at Dhu Jibla, where a shrine to her exists to this day, she is remembered fondly by Yemenis as Bilqis al-Sughra, the 'little' Queen of Sheba.

The Fatimid Imam-caliph al-Mustansir's death in Cairo in 1094 led to a crisis over the succession, with some Ismailis confirming the succession of his son Nizar, and others opting to support the claims of his son al-Musta'li. Sayyida Hurra threw her support and allegiance behind the latter, and a dispute over the succession to al-Musta'li's son al-Amir led to a conflict between the supporters of his son al-Tayyib and those of his cousin al-Hafiz. Queen Arwa upheld the succession of al-Tayyib, and is consequently to be credited for the success of the Tayyibi Ismaili *da'wa*, which continues to have followers in Yemen, the Indian subcontinent and other parts of the world. Her role in preserving Fatimid Ismaili manuscripts and her 'devotion to Ismailism and the cause of al-Tayyib found its final expression in her will in which she bequeathed her renowned collection of jewellery to Imam al-Tayyib'.[19] In Tayyibi

---

[19]   Farhad Daftary, 'Sayyida Hurra: The Isma'ili Sulayhid Queen of Yemen', in

sources, she is acknowledged as a *hujja*, the highest rank in any region's *da'wa* hierarchy, thus combining the political role of head of state (*malika*) with the spiritually authoritative role of the head of the *da'wa* (*hujja*) in Yemen. Daftary, in contrast to Cortese and Calderini, writes that the Fatimid Imam-caliph al-Mustansir appointed her the *hujja* of Yemen shortly after her husband's death – the first time such a post had ever been given to a woman. Cortese and Calderini note only that a *sijill* (letter) from Imam al-Mustansir confirms her as the authority to whom all Yemeni *da'i*s should report, but that the term *hujja* is not used except in Tayyibi sources. Regardless, her significant role in the affairs of the Fatimid *da'wa* in Yemen and the Indian subcontinent cannot be contested, nor her role in the establishment of the independent Tayyibi *da'wa*, which survived the fall of both the Sulayhids and the Fatimids, with the Fatimid legacy continuing in the Nizari Ismaili *da'wa*.

Fatima and Zaynab Today

The contemporary legacy of Fatima and Zaynab is especially visible in connection with the 1979 Iranian Revolution. As noted earlier in this chapter, the Iranian revolutionary ideologue Ali Shariati conceptualised Fatima as a person in her own right, rather than as instrumentally important in relation to her father, the Prophet Muhammad, her husband Ali, the first imam, and her sons Hasan and Husayn. For Shariati, Fatima stands as a paradigm of courage, patience and steadfastness, as well as faith and piety. As such, he called upon Iranian women to mobilise against injustice in their own right, not for the sake of their menfolk. Yet he provides very little actual information about her apart from her connections to the male figures of note in her life. Indeed, Shariati's stance ends up being largely instrumentalist in mobilising religious women to the cause of the revolution. In a similar vein, he draws upon Zaynab to assert:

> When Zaynab saw that the revolution had begun, she left her family, her husband and her children, and joined the revolution. It was not for the sake of her brother Husayn, who was the leader of this revolution, that she joined it. She did so because of her own responsibility and commitment to her society, her religion and her God. When she saw that a struggle and revolution had begun against an oppressive system, she joined the revolution and was beside her brother Husayn at all stages of

---

Gavin R. G. Hambly, ed., *Women in the Medieval Islamic World* (New York, 1998), p. 127.

those difficult days. Even after the martyrdom of Husayn and his companions, she carried the flag of the continuation of Karbala's revolution. She performed her mission thoroughly, perfectly and fairly. She performed her mission with strength and courage. She expressed with words the truth that Husayn expressed with blood. She shouted out against tyranny in any land. She distributed the seeds of revolution in any land that she entered, either free or as a captive. It is no accident that Muslims, wherever they are, show a great and deep sympathy towards the Prophet's family and love them.

Yes! All of these miracles belonged to a woman! Thus when a woman, a conscious and responsible, committed woman sees such heroics from a woman who belonged to Fatima's family, she understands where she must look, how she must be. She realises that a woman of any age and any century can emulate this model.[20]

For the Iranians supporting greater roles for women in the public sphere after the revolution, Zaynab has become a torchbearer for her speech and for speaking out in the face of injustice – at the same time that her memory was mobilised in the infamous vigilante group Dokhtaran-i Zaynab to enforce sartorial conventions for women.

For contemporary Shi'i communities, in the re-enactments of Karbala conducted annually wherever Ithna'ashari Shi'a gather to observe Muharram rites (including in South Asia and the Western diaspora), the incorporation of Fatima and Zaynab in the ritual presents a powerful model for emulation by women in every aspect of their lives. In addition to these two key figures, there is the example of the 11-year-old Fatima Kubra, daughter of Husayn, who was married to the 13-year-old Qasim, son of Hasan, on the day that he lost his life at Karbala. His exploits on the battlefield and her tragedy are remembered in the *mehndi* (henna) gatherings, *marsiya*s (elegies), and moving speeches delivered by *zakir*s (orators) on the seventh day of the mourning assemblies of Muharram. In her work on South Asian Karbala traditions observed in Hyderabad, India, Karen Ruffle notes that Fatima Kubra symbolises the importance of fulfilling one's duty despite any hardships encountered, for men and women alike in their roles as members of a family as well as a community. Rendered a bride and widow on the same day, her story invokes both joy and sorrow; this is typically linked, in the South Asian cultural context, to states of auspiciousness and inauspiciousness in the *azadar*s (mourners),

---

[20] Ali Shariati, available online at: http://www.shariati.com/english/woman/woman3.html.

calling upon both their sympathy and grief. Interestingly, widowhood is perceived as a form of protection for the young Fatima, for it prevents Yazid from forcibly marrying her off, as he could had she been a virgin of marriageable age. Her action in becoming a bride only to be made a widow is seen as the willing sacrifice she makes to send her husband into battle to preserve the faith; and she consents to her subsequent widowhood to preserve her family. In the Indic context, with its significations of the inauspiciousness of the widow, the hardship that Fatima Kubra undergoes is subverted by her sacrifice to save the holy family from despoliation – and also by the modelling of the ideals of wifehood and widowhood to mourners. At the same time, as regards her aunt Zaynab, as Lara Deeb observes in relation to Lebanese Ashura rituals:

> The incorporation of women into Ashura as active participants in the *masirat* [lamentation processions], and the reformulation of Zaynab as the ideal role model for women ... have occurred in part self-consciously and represent an active engagement with discourses and arguments about Islam, gender, and modernness that extend beyond Shi'ism and Lebanon. ... women are utilising the example of Sayyedeh Zaynab as an outspoken, strong, and compassionate activist to push the boundaries of what is acceptable and expected for pious Lebanese Shi'a women.[21]

Conclusion

In her study of contemporary Shi'i women's *azadari* or mourning rituals in southern California, Bridget Blomfield finds that women participants draw great solace and comfort, as well as models for handling the profound stresses brought upon by migration, often from war-torn contexts, to North America. In addition, personal suffering triggered by ill-health, unemployment, loss of loved ones and grief and the traumas resulting from dislocation, connect to and put a perspective on the suffering experienced by Fatima and Zaynab; this allows women to empathise with the women of the *ahl al-bayt* while also drawing moral support from their piety and their courage.

The town of Sayyida Zaynab (south of Damascus), originally founded as a refugee camp for Palestinians in 1949, was subsequently settled by the Iraqi Shi'a fleeing the conflict in Iraq, as well as Twelver Shi'a students from India, Pakistan and Afghanistan attending nearby

---

[21] Lara Z. Deeb, 'From Mourning to Activism: Sayyedeh Zaynab, Lebanese Shi'i Women, and the Transformation of Ashura', in Aghaie, ed., *The Women of Karbala*, pp. 359–360.

seminaries. It was also much frequented by Shi'i tourists from Iran and the Persian Gulf states. The town became an alternative centre of pilgrimage and learning when the sites of Karbala and Najaf were inaccessible due to regional and international conflict. Indeed, in her examination of Zaynab's sainthood in Syria, Edith Szanto sees the town as living in a 'state of exception': the state imposed laws and regulations (such as withholding the right to vote, buy property, or in some case, to hold employment) to allow it to better control a population that was not strictly Syrian but resident within its sovereign borders. Szanto finds that women undermine this state of exception to connect with the *ahl al-bayt* and to make spiritual and material progress. Typically, they draw upon the intercession (*shafa'a*) of Sayyida Zaynab through vows and ritual feasts such as the *sufra* offered in her name, to ask for healing (*shifa*) and aid for problems concerning health, family life, work, or other difficulties. Interviews with women show that Shi'i women exhibit agency in their lives as they strive to attain 'a good life' through serving Sayyida Zaynab, calling upon her to heal and intercede, drawing strength from her to educate their children and others on how to live a good life.

The challenges that Shi'i women face must necessarily be understood in their specific historical, political, legal and social settings. For example, in Iran, Shi'i women found that divorce laws left them in poverty as often their bridal endowments (*mahr*) were rendered worthless due to inflation or the death of their husband in war. Iranian women activists took recourse to the women's press to raise this, and to amend Iranian Islamic law to identify strategies to tackle inequalities associated with current marital regulations. Consequently, Ayatollah Khomeini had the law amended in 1982 to require that marriage contracts must accord a wife half the husband's wealth upon divorce. Regardless of the issue to be addressed, the figures considered in this chapter provide, as Vincent Cornell notes, the double subjectivity of sainthood, authority and guidance in the sense of *wilaya* on the one hand, and of love and closeness in the sense of *walaya* on the other.[22] The upshot for the Shi'i woman is that such figures provide exemplary guidance as she endures her afflictions, and a spiritualised connection with sacred and linear history in addressing them, while also opening up spaces for women to embrace leadership roles in arenas ranging from the spiritual to the political.

---

[22]   Vincent J. Cornell, *Realm of the Saint: Power and Authority in Moroccan Sufism* (Austin, TX, 1981).

Further Reading

Ayoub, Mahmoud. *Redemptive Suffering in Islam: A Study of the Devotional Aspects of Ashura in Twelver Shi'ism*. The Hague, 1978.

Beck, Lois and Guity Neshat, ed. *Women in Iran from 1800 to the Islamic Republic*. Urbana, IL, 2004.

Bierman, Irene A. *Writing Signs: The Fatimid Public Text*. Berkeley, CA, 1998.

Blomfield, Bridget, 'The Heart of Lament: Pakistani-American Muslim Women's Azadari Rituals', in Peter Chelkowski, ed., *Eternal Performance: Taziyah and Other Shi'ite Rituals*. Chicago, 2010.

—— 'The Image of Fatimah', in J. A. Morrow, ed., *Islamic Images and Ideas, Essays on Sacred Symbolism*. Jefferson, NC, 2014.

Corbin, Henry. *Spiritual Body and Celestial Earth: From Mazdean Iran to Shi'ite Iran*, tr. Nancy Pearson. Princeton, NJ, 1977.

Deeb, Lara. *An Enchanted Modern: Gender and Public Piety in Shi'i Lebanon*. Princeton, NJ, 2006.

Hyder, Syed Akbar. *Reliving Karbala: Martyrdom in South Asian Memory*. New York and Oxford, 2006.

Kassam, Zayn R., ed. *Women and Islam*. Santa Barbara, CA, 2010.

Mir-Hosseini, Ziba. *Islam and Gender*. Princeton, NJ, 1999.

Najmabadi, Afsaneh. *Women with Mustaches and Men without Beards: Gender and Sexual Anxieties of Iranian Modernity*. Berkeley, CA, 2005.

Schubel, Vernon. *Religious Performance in Contemporary Islam: Shi'i Devotional Rituals in South Asia*. Columbia, SC, 1993.

Shariati, Ali. *Shariati on Shariati and the Muslim Woman*, tr. Laleh Bakhtiar. Chicago, 1996.

Thurkill, Mary F. *Chosen among Women: Mary and Fatima in Medieval Christianity and Shi'ite Islam*. Notre Dame, IN, 2007.

11

Art and Architecture

Jonathan M. Bloom

Over the centuries Shi'i Muslims have made or appreciated many works of art and architecture – what we today call 'Islamic' art. This is not to say that an artist, artisan, patron or viewer in the medieval world who professed Zaydi, Ismaili or Imami beliefs, *thought* that he or she was producing or enjoying specifically 'Shi'i' art. Indeed, it is unlikely that Muslims at large thought that they were engaged in a specifically 'Islamic' art, since this is entirely a modern idea. It is therefore more rewarding to look within the wider context of the visual arts of the Islamic lands for forms and content that relate specifically to the Shi'ism of their makers, patrons and viewers.

Now this is not an easy task. While the Shi'a at various times and places certainly placed special meanings in particular forms and motifs, there are few instances where these meanings were deemed so obviously sectarian that Sunnis found them objectionable, thus imperative to destroy or deface a particular work of art or architecture. Perhaps the most obvious example is al-Azhar, the mosque in Cairo that is today the centre of Sunni 'orthodoxy'. It was actually built by the Shi'i Fatimids in the 10th century, and many of its original parts survive to this day.

In the absence of 'exclusively' Shi'i forms or motifs in the greater realm of Islamic art, identification with Shi'ism rests primarily on the *content* of the words inscribed on buildings and objects, and these words – often taken from the Quran – can be interpreted in different ways. For example, although the Shi'a consider certain Quranic verses such as 33.33 ('People of the House') to refer specifically to the Prophet's family and the Shi'i imams, all Muslims everywhere revere the entire text of the Quran. Sunnis may interpret these particular verses very differently to refer to the Prophet's tribe or clan, but would never think of removing Quranic verses from an inscription. Thus, many inscriptions on the exteriors of Fatimid mosques in Cairo were probably intended to have specifically Shi'i content, but they have remained visible on the wall despite centuries of subsequent Sunni rule.

Even such practices as the veneration of the family of the Prophet Muhammad, which appear to be specific to the Shi'a, may not indicate Shi'i patronage. For example, the purported tomb of the Prophet's son-in-law Ali at Mazar-i Sharif in Afghanistan as well as the tomb of the eighth Twelver Imam Reza at Mashhad in Iran have historically been the foci of generalised devotion to the Prophet's family by Shi'i and Sunni alike, a phenomenon that Robert McChesney has termed *ahl al-baytism*.[1]

Although the Shi'a were present in virtually all Muslim societies throughout history, and Shi'i individuals undoubtedly were involved in the production of specific works of art, they have played significant roles in artistic production mainly during the periods when their political control and circumstances allowed for the production of art. There was no real opportunity for a Shi'i art before the emergence of various Shi'i dynasties – notably the Fatimids in North Africa and Egypt and the Buyids in Iran and Iraq – during the 10th century, an era that has sometimes been called the 'Shi'i century' because it seemed as if Shi'ism was on the ascendant in many regions simultaneously.

The regions and historical periods in which circumstances might provide quite strong evidence of Shi'i art are Yemen under the Zaydi Imams (r. 897–1962) and the Ismaili Sulayhids (1047–1138); North Africa, Egypt and Syria under the Fatimids (r. 909–1171); Iran first under the Buyids (934–1055) and later under the Safawids (r. 1501–1732) and their Zand (r. 1751–94) and Qajar (1779–1925) successors, and finally the Deccan under the Bahmani (r. 1347–1527), Nizamshahi (r. 1490–1636) and Qutbshahi (r. 1490–1687) sultans. For various reasons, the historical record is incomplete. Although these periods had the *potential* for artistic production, in actuality this production may not have survived or yet been identified; moreover, the Shi'a are also known to have produced art under nominally Sunni rule.

This chapter focuses on representative examples from these historical periods. In contemporary countries with large Shi'i populations such as Iran, Iraq, Syria and Lebanon, artists and architects continue to produce works of art with Shi'i content, but exploration of their art must lie outside the scope of the present discussion. In recent years there has been much discussion about whether the catch-all term 'Islamic art' should be replaced by more narrowly focused regional, chronological or dynastic categories. In a similar vein, one may question to what extent the Shi'ism of artists and patrons might be reflected in art and architecture, in contrast to more general regional, chronological and dynastic tendencies in the arts of the Islamic lands.

---

[1]   Robert McChesney, *Waqf in Central Asia: Four Hundred Years in the History of a Muslim Shrine, 1480–1889* (Princeton, NJ, 1991).

Architecture: Traditional Types

We know very little about the earliest structures erected over sites of particular importance to the Shi'a, such as Najaf and Karbala, where Ali b. Abi Talib and al-Husayn b. Ali respectively were buried. They appear to have been given some sort of monumental expression in relatively early times, despite *hadiths* recounting the Prophet's disapproval of putting any structure over a grave. According to Ibn Hawqal, in the early 10th century the Hamdanid ruler of Mosul built a large *qubba* (dome) over Ali's grave and adorned it with precious carpets and curtains;[2] in 979–980, the Buyid ruler Adud al-Dawla built a mausoleum there where he and his two sons were themselves eventually buried.[3] Husayn's grave at Karbala began to attract pilgrims from a very early date; in 850–851 the Abbasid caliph al-Mutawakkil destroyed the tomb and had the ground levelled and sown. Although the caliph prohibited pilgrims from visiting the site, when Ibn Hawqal visited Husayn's tomb in 977 it was covered by a large domed *mashhad* (martyrium) with doors on either side.[4] Although these particular structures commemorated figures of special importance to the Shi'a, there is no evidence that there was anything specifically Shi'i in their form, for in this period domes were increasingly used to cover the graves of important political and religious figures, whether Sunni or Shi'i, and the connection between Shi'ism and the growing practice of venerating the dead may have been overstated.[5]

The proclamation of the Fatimid imamate in early 10th-century North Africa provided the first real opportunity for an overtly Shi'i architecture and art, but the early Fatimid rulers did not build tombs, and their surviving mosques show that they were perfectly content to adapt local North African forms of architecture, with some modifications, suggesting that there was little, if any, Shi'ism in their architecture. The first Fatimid mosque at Mahdiyya on the Tunisian coast, for example, seems to have been largely a smaller-scale copy of the nearby mosque of Qayrawan, a hotbed of Maliki resistance to Fatimid rule. Although the Fatimid builders emulated the Qayrawan mosque in most respects, they replaced its massive tower opposite the *mihrab* with an

---

[2]   Abu'l-Qasim Ibn Hawqal, *Kitab surat al-ard*, ed. J. H. Kramers (Leiden, 1967), p. 163.
[3]   E. Honigmann and C. E. Bosworth, 'al-Nadjaf', *EI2*, vol. 7, pp. 859–861.
[4]   Ibn Hawqal, *Kitab surat al-ard*, p. 166.
[5]   Oleg Grabar, 'The Earliest Islamic Commemorative Structures', *Ars Orientalis*, 6 (1966), pp. 7–46; Christopher S. Taylor, 'Reevaluating the Shi'i Role in the Development of Monumental Funerary Architecture: The Case of Egypt', *Muqarnas*, 9 (1992), pp. 1–10.

Figure 11.1 Portal of the Congregational Mosque in Mahdiyya.

Figure 11.2 Interior of al-Azhar Mosque, Cairo.

imposing projecting portal, presumably because the Shi'a at this period disapproved of building minarets.

In this instance, they relied on a *hadith* of Ali saying that the call to prayer should not be given from any place higher than the roof of a mosque. The presence of the projecting portal, which is a new feature in Islamic architecture, might also have led contemporary viewers – particularly those familiar with Shi'i *hadith* – to recall the saying of the Prophet, 'I am the city of knowledge, and Ali is its gate.' This interpretation might have been strengthened if such a saying had been inscribed on the portal, but curiously no Fatimid inscriptions survive from this mosque, although there are spaces for them on the portal and inscriptions were to become a hallmark of later Fatimid architecture.[6]

It is equally difficult to identify any specifically Shi'i content in Fatimid architecture after the fourth Imam-caliph al-Mu'izz (r. 953–975) decided to move the dynastic seat from North Africa to Egypt. Al-Azhar (begun 970), the first Fatimid mosque in Egypt, may have been planned in North Africa but it fits squarely in the Egyptian traditions of construction, as does the Mosque of al-Hakim, built several decades later.

The Mosque of al-Hakim did have a projecting portal and al-Azhar may have had one as well, suggesting that the portal was an element of continuing importance in Fatimid architecture. In addition to the by-now-standard dome in front of the *mihrab* found in many mosques, the Mosque of al-Hakim has two additional domes in the rear corners of the prayer-hall, and it is possible that al-Azhar had them as well. Architectural historians tend to agree that builders use domes to mark places of particular importance, but the exact meanings of these domes remains undiscovered. Similarly, North African builders of the Fatimid period gave several of their mosques an additional dome at the courtyard end of the aisle leading to the *mihrab*. Such domes were added in the 10th century to the mosques of Tunis and Qayrawan, for example, and in the 12th century the Fatimid caliph al-Hafiz ordered one added to the courtyard of al-Azhar in Cairo. While these additional domes may have been built for particular Shi'i purposes, their survival (despite centuries of subsequent Sunni use of the buildings) argues against such a restrictive interpretation.

Unusually, the Mosque of al-Hakim was given a pair of towers – one cylindrical, the other a tapering octagonal prism – at the ends of the main façade. Like the portal, they were decorated with Quranic and foundation inscriptions stating that they were added to the mosque in 1002–1003, more than a decade after work on the project had begun. A

---

[6]   Jonathan M. Bloom, *Arts of the City Victorious: Islamic Art and Architecture in Fatimid North Africa and Egypt* (London, 2007), pp. 23–30.

decade later, in 1010–1011, the patron ordered the towers hidden behind huge stone bastions. It is obvious that these towers had some specific meaning at the time, but it is difficult if not impossible to determine what that meaning was, since no other Fatimid mosque – before or after – had anything like them.

Like the Mosque of al-Hakim, other Fatimid mosques in Cairo were richly decorated with inscriptions that invoked blessings on the ruling imam-caliph and quoted Quranic verses that may have underscored Fatimid ideology. In most cases these inscriptions have survived untouched over the centuries, suggesting that few people actually took the time to read them and understand what their patrons might have been trying to express. Although many Fatimid mosques are extant, the absence of contemporary *mihrabs* in the major Fatimid mosques to survive in central Cairo (e.g., the Mosques of al-Azhar, al-Hakim, al-Aqmar and al-Salih Talaʾi) compared to their survival in remote shrines (e.g., the Mashhad al-Juyushi, Ikhwat Yusuf and Sayyida Ruqayya) *may* indicate that these missing *mihrabs* once contained Shiʿi content that later generations of Sunnis found objectionable and removed, although it is hazardous to argue from negative evidence. In addition, many of these smaller Fatimid shrines have three *mihrabs* – a larger central one flanked by smaller ones on either side – but a theological explanation for this feature has not yet been found, just as the exact meaning of the *mihrab* has never been adequately explained.[7]

At the mosque of Qayrawan, a large marble slab to the left of the *mihrab* is thought to have been brought as a trophy from the long-destroyed Fatimid mosque of Sabra-Mansuriyya outside Qayrawan.[8] In the upper right spandrel of its arched design it has a circular motif containing four words written radially that share the letter *mim*: *al-hamd liʾl-hamid al-mabdi al-amid*, 'Praise to the Praised, the Creator, the Resurrector.'[9] The unusual phrase is not specifically Quranic, and seems to have been chosen for its epigraphic potential to make a radial design sharing the common letter *mim*. Logic demands that a corresponding radial inscription, presumably containing Shiʿi praises on the Prophet's family, perhaps with the common letter *ayn*, once decorated

[7]   K. A. C. Creswell, *The Muslim Architecture of Egypt* (Oxford, 1952–1959), vol. 1, *passim*. Alexandre Papadopoulo, ed. *Le Miḥrāb dans l'architecture et la religion musulmanes: Actes du colloque international tenu à Paris en Mai 1980* (Leiden, 1988).

[8]   Jonathan M. Bloom, 'Erasure and Memory: Aghlabid and Fatimid Inscriptions in North Africa', in Antony Eastmond, ed., *Viewing Inscriptions in the Late Antique and Medieval Worlds* (Cambridge, 2015).

[9]   Bernard Roy and Paule Poinssot, *Inscriptions arabes de Kairouan* (Paris, 1950), p. 16.

Figure 11.3 Mihrab area in the Great Mosque of Qayrawan.

the upper left corner of the plaque; but it may have been abraded away to remove all traces of what later Sunni worshippers might have found objectionable.

One of the most characteristic architectural features of the two centuries of Fatimid rule in Egypt is the proliferation of small shrines over the graves of notable individuals in the cemeteries of Cairo and Aswan. Some of these structures are simple domed cubes built of brick, but others were more elaborate structures with domed chambers flanked by subsidiary rooms and courtyards. It has often been suggested that the proliferation of tombs in Egypt at this time was a phenomenon linked to the particularly Shi'i veneration of the descendants of the Prophet, but Egyptians had begun to build tombs already in the 9th century long before the arrival of the Fatimids, and patrons erected them in such other regions as Iran and Central Asia. The veneration of the descendants of the Prophet was not linked to Shi'is alone.[10]

Just as later Sunnis seem to have been able to accept (or ignore) possibly Shi'i forms and inscriptions in Fatimid Egyptian architecture, the Shi'a were able to do the same. For example, despite the Alid *hadith* about the place of the call to prayer (which some considered to be of questionable reliability), most Shi'is eventually accepted minarets as a universal symbol of Islam and an appropriate part of mosque design, whether or not they were actually used for the call to prayer. The general acceptance of the minaret, which was initially introduced as a sign of (Sunni) Islam, illustrates a broader trend in the general history of Islamic art: in the absence of a clergy charged with maintaining specific interpretations for particular forms, specific meanings tended to revert to the most widely-held opinion.[11]

The Buyid rulers of Iran and Iraq (r. 934–1055) were nominally Shi'i, first Zaydi and then Imami, but little of their artistic production has survived, and of that, much is of doubtful authenticity, for many forged 'Buyid' objects were produced in the 20th century. The Buyid ruler Adud al-Dawla is known to have restored several Shi'i shrines in Iraq and Iran, but some wooden panels purportedly from a cenotaph he ordered for Ali's tomb at Kufa with inscriptions praising the family of the Prophet use incorrect titulature and may be 20th-century forgeries, much like the 'Buyid' textiles – some with Shi'i inscriptions – that appeared on the art market in the 20th century.[12]

---

[10] Grabar, 'Earliest Islamic Commemorative Structures'; Taylor, 'Reevaluating the Shi'i Role'.

[11] See Jonathan M. Bloom, *The Minaret* (Edinburgh, 2013).

[12] Sheila S. Blair, *The Monumental Inscriptions from Early Islamic Iran and Transoxiana*, Supplements to *Muqarnas* (Leiden, 1992), pp. 41–46; Jonathan M. Bloom, 'Fact and Fantasy in Buyid Art', *Oriente Moderno*, 22 (2004), pp. 387–400.

From the 11th century in Iran the construction of small shrines dedicated to descendants of the Prophet and the imams provides evidence for the growth of popular forms of Shi'ism. Shi'i scholars recognised that pilgrimage to these structures, which are known by a variety of names, such as *imamzada* (descendant of an imam), *astana* (threshold), *marqad* (resting place, mausoleum), *buqa* (revered site), *rawza* (garden/tomb), *gunbad* (dome), *mashhad* (place of martyrdom), *maqam* (site/abode), *qadamgah* (stepping place) and *turbat* (dust, grave), was a valid form of devotion.[13] While few, if any, of these structures have survived unmodified from this early date, the octagonal pavilion at Natanz, which is now incorporated into the congregational mosque there, may give some idea of the type, although there is no evidence that it was built to commemorate an imam.[14]

The Ghaznavids (r. 962–1186) were the Buyids' great rivals in the east, but the fluidity of Sunni-Shi'i patronage at this time can be seen when the staunchly Sunni Mahmud of Ghazna (997–1031) rebuilt the sanctuary of Imam Reza at Mashhad after his father, Sabuktagin, had destroyed it. Suri, Mahmud's governor of Khurasan, is also recorded as having added a minaret to the shrine.[15] Under the equally Sunni Saljuq dynasty (1037–1194), patronage was equally flexible, especially in regions where there were significant Shi'i populations. In Aleppo, for example, the Shi'i *qadi* Abu'l-Hasan Muhammad b. al-Khashshab erected a beautiful stone minaret (recently destroyed in Syria's civil war) in 1090–1094 during the reign of the Saljuq sultan Malikshah. An inscription on the third storey accords praises on Muhammad and Ali; the inscription on the fourth storey quotes Quran 5:55, a text with particular resonance for the Shi'a, about your 'friends' (*awliya*) being God and his Messenger, for the Shi'i profession of faith states not only that Muhammad is God's messenger but adds that Ali is His friend.[16] The structure paradoxically therefore reflects the strong Shi'i tendencies of the population of Aleppo and its environs, where the *muezzin*s continued to use the Shi'i call to prayer despite the advent of Saljuq rule. It was only about 50 years after the construction of the minaret that Nur al-Din, the Ayyubid ruler,

---

[13] H. Algar and P. Varjavand, 'Emamzada', *Encyclopaedia Iranica*, vol. 8, pp. 395–412.

[14] Sheila S. Blair, 'The Octagonal Pavilion at Natanz: A Reexamination of Early Islamic Architecture in Iran', *Muqarnas*, 1 (1983), pp. 69–94.

[15] James W. Allan, *The Art and Architecture of Twelver Shi'ism: Iraq, Iran, and the Indian Sub-Continent* (London, 2012), p. 18.

[16] Ernst Herzfeld, *Inscriptions et monuments d'Alep. Matériaux Pour un Corpus Inscriptionum Arabicarum, Deuxième Partie: Syrie du Nord* (Cairo, 1954–1955), vol. 1, pp. 152–153.

Figure 11.4 Mihrab in the Winter Prayer Hall of the Congregational
Mosque, Isfahan.

was forced to prohibit use of the Shiʻi formula, although Shiʻi shrines continued to receive patronage from Sunnis and the Shiʻa alike.[17]

The Saljuqs were succeeded in the 13th century by the Ilkhanid (Mongol) rulers of Iran and Iraq (r. 1256–1353). Ghazan (r. 1295–1304), converted to Islam in 1295 and took the name Mahmud; his brother and successor Öljeitü (Uljaytu; r. 1304–1316) who had been baptised a Nestorian Christian, converted to Islam and later in his life vacillated between Sunni and Shiʻi Islam. One of the most magnificent examples of Ilkhanid art, a *mihrab* in the winter prayer hall of the Congregational Mosque of Isfahan signed by the master craftsman Haydar in July 1310, memorialises Oljaitu's Shiʻi beliefs.

Otherwise indistinguishable from contemporary Sunni works, the *mihrab* is inscribed with a historical text as well as Quranic verses, sayings of the Prophet's family, and pious invocations. The arch around the tympanum, for example, contains 4:59, admonishing believers to 'obey God, His prophet *and those charged with authority among you*.' The verse is the only one of 11 Quranic citations about obedience to God and His prophet that includes the phrase, which is usually understood to refer to those appointed to represent the Prophet's authority in his absence and hence of particular significance to the Imami Shiʻa.[18]

This particular Quranic verse on the Isfahan *mihrab* is explained by means of a *hadith* recorded by Jabir b. Zayd al-Jufi (d. ca. 720), who is said to have heard the *hadith* from Jabir b. Abd Allah, a Companion of the Prophet and transmitter of *hadith* held in high esteem by the Shiʻa. The *mihrab* inscription says that when Jabir heard about the revelation of the particular Quranic verse (4.59), he asked the Prophet, 'Who are those charged with authority to whom obedience is due?' Inscribed around the lower frames of the *mihrab* is the Prophet's answer, 'My successors' followed by the names of the Twelve imams. The large framing band around the *mihrab* contains sayings attributed to Muhammad and Ali about building mosques, and another inscription in interlaced kufic over the lower arch gives the profession of faith in the form typically used by the Shiʻa.

We have no idea whether the stucco-carver Haydar was a Sunni or Shiʻi. The same craftsman also designed the stucco decoration at the shrine complex at Natanz, Iran, which honoured Sunni members of the Kubrawiyya Sufi order who adhered to the Shafiʻi school of law but who also held members of the Prophet's family in special reverence. At

---

[17] Stephennie Mulder, *The Shrines of the Alids in Medieval Syria: Sunnis, Shiʻis and the Architecture of Coexistence* (Edinburgh, 2013), Ch. 2.

[18] Sheila S. Blair, 'Writing about Faith: Epigraphic Evidence for the Development of Twelver Shiʻism in Iran', in Fahmida Suleman, ed., *People of the Prophet's House* (London, 2015), p. 111.

Figure 11.5 Mosque of Gawhar Shad, Shrine of Imam Reza, Mashhad.

Natanz, the façade of the *khanaqah* (hospice) of the Sufi mystic Abd al-Samad bears the expression 'Ali is the friend of God'. Such inscriptions in all likelihood reflect a general veneration of the Prophet's family by contemporary Sufis.[19] The stucco carver Haydar, therefore, seems to have taken work wherever he could find it. The Isfahan *mihrab* was one part in an ultimately unsuccessful state-sponsored campaign to introduce Twelver Shi'ism to Iran, which also included the issuance of coins bearing the Shi'i profession of faith and blessings on the Twelve imams.[20] Contemporary accounts indicate that there was substantial resistance to the imposition of Shi'ism, and it would be another two centuries before Imami Shi'ism became the state religion of Iran.

Timur's son Shah Rukh (r. 1405–1447), his wife Gawhar Shad (d. 1457) and their Timurid successors – although Sunnis – were major patrons of the shrine of Imam Reza at Mashhad, which was extensively transformed and enlarged in this period. Of the additions, the most important is a large four-*iwan* mosque ordered by Gawhar Shad in 1416–1418, constructed by the noted architect Qawam al-Din Shirazi, and decorated with a spectacular tile inscription designed by Shah Rukh's son Baysunghur.[21] Although honouring a figure of the utmost importance to Iranian Shi'is, there is nothing particularly Shi'i in any of the architecture or its decoration.

Today the most outstanding features of the great Shi'i shrines at Mashhad and Qumm in Iran and Najaf, Karbala and Samarra in Iraq are their gilded domes, *iwans* and minarets, which appear to have been first added under the Safawids (r. 1501–1732), who made Shi'ism the official religion in their realm.

The earliest example of architectural gilding appears to have been at Mashhad, under Shah Tahmasp in the 1530s.[22] Although the Safawids established their capital first at Tabriz and then at Qazwin in northwestern Iran, they did not build new Friday mosques before Shah Abbas I erected one in his new capital at Isfahan. This seems to have been the result of uncertainty about their legality. In the first half of the 16th century, Shi'i scholars continually debated the issue,

---

[19] Sheila S. Blair, 'Persian Lustre Ware by Oliver Watson' (review), *Ars Orientalis*, 16 (1986), pp. 176–177.

[20] Sheila S. Blair, 'The Coins of the Later Ilkhanids: Mint Organization, Regionalization and Urbanism', *American Numismatic Society Museum Notes*, 27 (1982), pp. 211–230; and her 'The Coins of the Later Ilkhanids: A Typological Analysis', *Journal of the Economic and Social History of the Orient*, 26 (1983), pp. 295–317.

[21] Lisa Golombek and Donald Wilber, *The Timurid Architecture of Iran and Turan* (Princeton, NJ, 1988), pp. 328–331.

[22] Allan, *Twelver Shi'ism*, p. 29.

Figure 11.6 Golden dome of the Shrine of Fatima, Qumm.

focusing on the absence of the Mahdi. Some scholars asserted that the Friday prayer was not obligatory in the absence of the Mahdi, being permissible only if conducted by an eligible *mujtahid*, the most learned of Shiʻi religious scholars. Others, however, insisted that the Friday prayer was obligatory in all circumstances. It was only in the early 17th century that the Safawids finally decided that the Friday prayer was obligatory in all circumstances, and began to build Friday mosques, but again, there is nothing exclusively Shiʻi in their form or decoration apart from the choice of texts from the Quran and the *hadith*.[23] Alid *hadith* are found on the portal and inside the Masjid-i Shah (1612–1638) in Isfahan, for example.

Furnishings for mosques and shrines often carried inscriptions that made specific Shiʻi allusions. For example, ablution basins carved from blocks of stone and bearing Shiʻi inscriptions are found in the Masjid-i Shah, as well as in the earlier Masjid-i Jami and the Imamzada Ismaʻil there in Isfahan. They follow an earlier tradition exemplified by the great stone basin in Qandahar (1490), but the Safawid basins

---

[23] Ibid., pp. 51–52.

bear two particular types of Shi'i inscriptions: one in Arabic in *thuluth* script giving the names of the Fourteen Infallible Ones (Muhammad, Fatima and the Twelve imams), the second in Persian in *nasta'liq* mentioning Husayn. The Isfahan basin, for example, includes the words 'For the thirsty this basin was completed. It was donated for the king of the oppressed, Husayn b. Ali. May whoever drinks water curse Ibn Ziyad', a clear reference to the events surrounding Husayn's martyrdom at Karbala centuries earlier.[24] Shi'i messages also appear on the silver-plated doors of Safawid religious buildings, such as those on the Madrasa-yi Chahar Bagh (1706–1714) in Isfahan. These include the *hadith*, 'I am the city of knowledge, and Ali is its gate', already found in the Fatimid period, as well references to the ship of learning (*safina*), a reference reflecting the idea of the safe sailing of the ship of the Prophet's family.

Metal plaques with appropriately Shi'i inscriptions were used as fittings in mosques and shrines, where they might be set into the wooden valves of doors, but the most elaborate examples were incorporated into the metal grilles that enclose the cenotaphs over the graves of the imams and their descendants. A gilded openwork steel plaque containing the words 'and of his brother, the lion of God, named Ali' against a delicate scrolling background in the David Collection, Copenhagen, was part of a set inscribed with an Arabic poem in honour of the Fourteen Infallible Ones. The set was designed by the noted 17th-century Safawid calligrapher Muhammad Riza al-Imami, who signed inscriptions at many of the major shrines including Qumm and Mashhad. Several sets of similar plaques are known, including others inscribed with the same poem, indicating that such items were extremely popular.[25]

An attitude somewhat comparable to the Safawid questioning of the legality of congregational mosques developed among the Tayyibi Ismailis who flourished in Yemen after breaking with the Fatimid Ismailis of Egypt. The Tayyibis believed that the Friday sermon, which normally would be delivered from a *minbar* or pulpit to the right of the *mihrab*, could be pronounced only in the presence of a manifest imam; as a result Da'udi Tayyibi mosques are characterised by the absence of *minbar*s, although the Fatimids had commissioned and used them.[26] The Nizaris, the main Ismaili group who branched from Egyptian Ismailism in 1094, brought their faith first to Iran and then to India.

---

[24] Ibid., p. 57.
[25] Sheila S. Blair and Jonathan M. Bloom, *Cosmophilia: Islamic Art from the David Collection, Copenhagen*, with essays by Kjeld von Folsach, Nancy Netzer and Claude Cernuschi (Chestnut Hill, MA, 2006), p. 97.
[26] Farhad Daftary, *The Isma'ilis: Their History and Doctrines* (2nd ed., Cambridge, 2007), p. 29.

Figure 11.7 Openwork steel plaque, Iran, 17th century.

The tombstone of Satgur Nur (dated 1094), a missionary sent from Iran to India, is located at Nawsari near Surat.[27] In the early 14th century the missionary Shams al-Din focused his work in Sind and Multan, where he was eventually buried; his mausoleum at Multan (Shah Shams Tabriz) remains the focus of popular veneration, although in form it is indistinguishable from other mausoleums at Multan commemorating Sunni figures.

Architecture: New Types

Sadr al-Din, the individual who was instrumental in propagating the Nizari *daʿwa* in early 15th-century India, is credited with building the first Nizari *jamatkhana* (assembly and prayer hall) at Kotri in Sind, and the *jamatkhana* subsequently became the characteristic architectural feature of Nizari Ismaili communities in South Asia, although other Muslim communities, both Sunni and Shiʿi, used the same term to refer to buildings other than mosques where religious and social ceremonies were performed. No single form or style, however, was required for the *jamatkhana*, so the realisation of each depended on such local features as location, materials available, architectural practice and size of the community.

The introduction of the *jamatkhana* as a specifically architectural type for the Ismailis of South Asia was followed elsewhere in South and West Asia by the development of other types of buildings for use by the Shiʿa. In the Deccan under the Nizamshahi and Qutbshahi rulers, for example, the outstanding type of Shiʿi monument is the *ashur khana*, designed to accommodate the annual ceremonies commemorating the martyrdom of Imam Husayn, on *ashura*, the tenth day of Muharram. A distinctive feature of the Qutbshahi *ashur khana* is a central hall, open along its long side, with its roof supported by a row of columns or

---

27 Daftary, *Ismaʿilis*, p. 442.

piers and an arcade.[28] The most splendid example is the Badshahi Ashur Khana in Hyderabad, constructed in 1596 by Sultan Muhammad Quli Qutb Shah, with a main hall about 40 metres long, 30 wide and some 12 high. Open on one side to a courtyard, its flat roof is supported by stone pillars. In 1611, its walls were decorated with ornate polychrome mosaic tiles, the finest in India, with representations of the *alam*s (see below) kept in the building for use during ceremonies.

In Bengal and Lucknow a similar type of building, known as an *imambara*, combining the Arabic word *imam* and *barhi*, the Bengali word for mansion, is the focus of the Muharram processions and also the place where *alam*s are kept and displayed. The earliest recorded is the Husaini Dalan in Dacca, built in 1642; the second is an early 18th-century building in Hughli, also in Bengal. The largest and most famous is the Bara, or Great, Imambara, built by Asaf al-Dawla in 1784 in Lucknow. It consists of three interlocked forecourts, each with high and impressive gateways, and a central court containing not only the *imambara* but also a mosque. Like the Badshahi Ashur Khaneh in Hyderabad, the Great Imambara in Lucknow is an enormous structure, here covered by a vault 50 metres long and 15 metres wide flanked by two galleries half the width.[29]

Another type of specifically Shi'i building that survives from Lucknow under the Nawabs is the *karbala*, supposedly a copy of the holiest Shi'i shrine in Iraq commemorating the battlefield and burial place of Husayn. Although these structures are intended to be copies of the original shrines in Iraq, most of their features are more imaginative rather than exact. The finest is the Talkatora, probably built during the reign of Nawab Saadat Ali Khan (1798–1814).

In Zand and Qajar Iran, special buildings known as *tekiyeh*s began to be built for the performance of *taziya*, the Shi'i passion play.[30] They are first mentioned in Astarabad in 1786 and Shiraz in 1787. In the 19th century, the Royal Albert Hall so impressed Nasir al-Din Shah Qajar, when he visited London in 1873, that he built an equivalent auditorium next to the Gulistan Palace in Tehran to be used as a *tekiyeh*. The well-known depiction of it by the court artist Kamal al-Mulk shows that unlike its model, it was never roofed.[31] By the 1860s, *tekiyeh*s often outnumbered mosques and *madrasa*s in Iranian cities. They were built in a variety of ways, some resembling private houses but others, such as that of Amir Chaqmaq in Yazd, with a decidedly monumental character of superposed arches flanked by minarets. Still others resembled

[28] Allan, *Twelver Shi'ism*, p. 75.
[29] Ibid., pp. 76–77.
[30] Markus Ritter, *Moscheen und Madrasabauten in Iran 1785–1848, Architektur zwischen Rückgriff und Neuerung* (Leiden, 2006), pp. 434–436.
[31] Allan, *Twelver Shi'ism*, p. 58.

Figure 11.8 Tekiyeh of Amir Chaqmaq, Yazd.

*zur-khana*s, the traditional gymnasium having an octagonal arena surrounded by seating alcoves.[32]

Finally, the *saqqa-khana*, or public drinking fountain, took on a particular meaning in Shi'i Iran. Although public water fountains and water-dispensaries are typical of virtually all Islamic lands, in Iran the *saqqa-khana* reminded Shi'is of the struggle of Abu'l-Fazl Abbas to get water from the Euphrates at the battle of Karbala, in the course of which he lost both his hands. Some of these fountains may be a simple alcove in a wall, but larger ones are often decorated with popular religious paintings and guarded with protective latticework. Passers-by can touch the lattice and hang a padlock or a piece of cloth there. The form gave its name to an Iranian art movement of the 1960s, whose members introduced motifs derived from Iranian folklore and Shi'i folk art into their work.[33]

Portable Arts

Apart from items used in specifically Shi'i contexts, such as Muharram rituals, there are relatively few examples of exclusively Shi'i themes

---

[32] Ibid., p. 60.
[33] Ehsan Yarshater, 'Contemporary Persian Painting', in Richard Ettinghausen and Ehsan Yarshater, ed., *Highlights of Persian Art* (Boulder, CO, 1979), pp. 362–377.

in the general history of Islamic art, and many of the motifs that may appear specifically Shi'i can be also interpreted in other ways. For example, while the five-fingered hand can be seen as a specifically Shi'i symbol in Indian contexts, it has a long history in ancient civilisations and throughout the Islamic lands (particularly in North Africa) as a more general symbol against the evil eye known as the *khamsa* (five) or Hand of Fatima.[34] Likewise, the motif of a double-bladed sword is normally understood in Shi'i contexts to represent Dhu'l-Faqar, the famous double-edged or double-bladed sword that Muhammad gave to Ali, but its interpretation as a specifically Shi'i symbol is more problematic. Although it often appears in Indian contexts, it also appears on Ottoman flags and Maghribi banners, both staunchly Sunni environments. For example, a silk pilgrims' banner from 17th-century North Africa in the Harvard Art Museums is decorated with a large representation of Dhu'l-Faqar inscribed with verses from 48:1–4, but none of the extensive inscriptions on the banner mentions Ali; instead, the association seems to be military: Ali was famed among Sunni and Shi'i alike for his heroism and military exploits.[35]

Textiles were perhaps the most important industrial product of medieval Islamic societies and their production often reached extraordinary artistic heights, although their inherent fragility has meant that few have survived the vicissitudes of time. Medieval Islamic rulers regularly gave their courtiers textiles, known as *tiraz*, embroidered, woven or painted with inscriptions bearing their names and titles. A group of Yemeni *iqat* textiles, in which the cotton threads were dyed in patterns before weaving, with painted inscriptions in gold naming rulers and asking God's blessings on Muhammad are some of the earliest surviving examples of art known to have been produced under Shi'i rulers, but no specifically Shi'i content has been identified in either their style or technique.[36]

The Fatimid period is known for the extent and richness of its artistic production, whether textiles, metalwares, ceramics or carved objects of ivory, rock-crystal or wood. Nevertheless, it has been hard to find explicitly Shi'i content in it. Fatimid *tiraz* textiles contain blessings on the ruler and Quranic inscriptions, but these do not appear very different from contemporary *tiraz* produced for Sunni rulers. Coins, which bear Quranic inscriptions in an angular kufic script, are somewhat of an exception.

---

[34] J. T. P. de Bruijn, 'Khamsa', *EI2*, vol. 4, p. 1009.

[35] Anthony Welch, *Calligraphy in the Arts of the Muslim World* (Austin, TX, 1979), pp. 76–77.

[36] Sheila S. Blair, 'Legibility Versus Decoration in Islamic Epigraphy: The Case of Interlacing', in I. Lavin, ed., *World Art: Themes of Unity in Diversity. Acts of the XXVIth International Congress of the History of Art* (University Park and London, 1989), pp. 329–334.

Fatimid coins initially followed Aghlabid and Abbasid prototypes but increasingly developed a distinct format. The coins of al-Mu'izz introduced strongly Shi'i slogans (e.g., Ali is the Friend of God) accompanied by a new concentric design that made their quality (they were nearly pure gold) self-evident. Some scholars have proposed that the Shi'i Fatimids preferred angular 'kufic' scripts while their Sunni rivals preferred the new 'rounded' scripts, but such an interpretation does not withstand close examination.[37] Other scholars have expanded this dubious argument to claim that the Shi'i Fatimids also preferred organic and vegetal ornament over the new style of geometric ornament supposedly favoured by their Sunni rivals, but this hypothesis too does not take all the relevant evidence into account. The Fatimids used geometric designs as well as vegetal ones, without regard to confessional affiliation.[38]

A rare exception is the unusual design of the central panel on the *tabut* of Husayn – a large wooden box-shaped object standing over the spot where the purported head of Husayn, the Prophet's grandson – was interred in Cairo. The design of the *tabut*'s central panel is based on a seven-pointed star and is flanked by inscriptions and geometric panels which may have been intended to make an Ismaili reference. Fatimid theology accorded the number seven unusual prominence, though the arts of the Fatimids do not normally place unusual emphasis on the number seven.[39] The reference was subtle, so that later generations of Sunnis found nothing objectionable in its presence and the *tabut* survives to this day. As we shall see in the case of the later arts of Iran, forms and techniques do not normally convey sectarian messages in Islamic art, though words may.

Other examples are more problematic: a 10th-century earthenware bowl from northeastern Iran or Central Asia in the David Collection, Copenhagen may or may not be an example of Shi'i content. It is decorated on the interior with an inscription written in red and black slips, or liquid clay, 'He who believes in recompense [from God] is generous with gifts,' a proverb attributed not only to the Prophet Muhammad but also to his son-in-law and successor Ali b. Abi Talib.

The same saying is found on several other pieces of different shapes, and other pieces bear *hadith*s that can be attributed to Muhammad, Ali or even Musa al-Kazim, the seventh imam of the Twelver Imami Shi'a. A platter in the Museum of Fine Arts, Boston (64.3), is inscribed with

---

[37] Yasser Tabbaa, *The Transformation of Islamic Art During the Sunni Revival* (Seattle, WA, and London, 2001).

[38] Gülru Necipoğlu, *The Topkapi Scroll: Geometry and Ornament in Islamic Architecture* (Santa Monica, CA, 1995).

[39] Caroline Williams, 'The Qur'anic Inscriptions on the *Tabut* of al-Husayn in Cairo', *Islamic Art*, 2 (1987), pp. 3–14.

Figure 11.9 Earthenware bowl, northeastern Iran or Central Asia, 10th century.

the saying, 'There is no youth except Ali; no sword except Dhu'l-Faqar'. A voice is said to have uttered this phrase when Muhammad gave this sword to Ali at the battle of Uhud. The presence in the inscription of four *lam-alif*s, a letter combination that is often said to resemble Dhu'l-Faqar, arranged to form a quadripartite design, might have underscored this interpretation.[40] It is unclear, however, whether the presence of Shi'i *hadith*s on these pieces should be understood as the work of a Shi'i artist, a particularly Shi'i milieu, a more generalised veneration of the Prophet in contemporary society, or simply conventional expressions.

A comparably equivocal example is a teakwood stand for a manuscript of the Quran in the Metropolitan Museum of Art made by Zayn [?] Hasan b. Sulayman Isfahani in 1360 for a *madrasa* near Isfahan. The outer faces of the upper panels are inscribed with the word Allah four

---

[40] Sheila S. Blair, *Text and Image in Medieval Persian Art* (Edinburgh, 2013), pp. 31–32.

Figure 11.10 Wooden stand for a manuscript of the Quran, Isfahan, 1360.

times. On the inner face the stand is inscribed in Arabic *thuluth* script: 'May God bless Muhammad and his family and ... the commander of the faithful Ali b. Abi Talib, may God's good favour be upon all of them. Endowed to the Sadrabad *madrasa* in Anar, may God protect and preserve it from disaster! In the month of Dhu'l-Hijja of the year 761 (October–November 1360).' On the bottom panels, inscriptions in *thuluth* script offer Shiʻi prayers for the Prophet Muhammad and the Twelve imams.

However, an incised inscription on the inner surface of the upper arms originally carried blessings on the Prophet and his immediate successors, but it has been crudely mutilated, probably to remove portions that praised the caliphs Abu Bakr, Umar and Uthman. Only the name and titles of Ali are preserved. The congregational mosque of Ashtarjan near Isfahan, dated 1315, preserves a similar text praising not only the first four caliphs but also the Twelve imams (with the names of the first three caliphs later excised). Although such inscriptions were apparently common in 14th-century Iran, the increasing polarisation of the Sunni

and Shi'i communities in later periods led to the concealment or mutilation of earlier texts.[41] Thus, it is hazardous to state unequivocally that
a stand such as this one in the Metropolitan Museum is an example of
Shi'i art.

A comparable situation is found in contemporary tile decoration. The
early 14th-century shrine of Abd al-Samad at Natanz, like many others
in medieval Iran, was once lavishly decorated with lustre tiles, although
virtually all of them were stripped from the walls in the 19th century
and ended up in European and American museums. Several decades ago
Oliver Watson documented over 100 dated tiles produced between 1203
and 1339. He found that most of the potters were Imami Shi'is belonging
to families claiming descent from Imams Hasan or Husayn, and some
of the inscriptions on tiles included Quranic texts, such as 5:55–59, that
have particular resonance for the Shi'a, as well as sayings by the Prophet
and his family.[42] Watson proposed that the presence of lustre tiles in
medieval Persian buildings, such as the shrines of Fatima at Qumm
or Imam Reza at Mashhad, might be indicative of Shi'i tombs.[43] Sheila
Blair, however, later refuted his suggestion by pointing out that of all
the medieval buildings decorated with lustre tiles, only those associated with Shi'is have survived intact. Those presumably associated
with Sunnis (and abandoned after Shi'ism became the state religion in
Safawid Iran) might have been available for plunder by art collectors in
later centuries since the Shi'a would have continued to venerate shrines
of Shi'i saints. Thus the preservation of lustre tiles in Shi'i shrines is
more an accident of survival than an accurate reflection of a particular
Shi'i taste for luster tiles.[44]

Various kinds of metalware have Shi'i content in the words inscribed
on them. For example, a late 15th or early 16th-century bronze drinking
jug with a dragon handle in the Metropolitan Museum of Art, New York
(91.1.607), is inscribed on the neck with the prayer to Ali b. Abi Talib
known as the *Nad-i Ali:*

> Call upon Ali, the revealer of miracles.
> You will find him a comfort to you in crisis
> Every care and every sorrow will pass
> Through your companionship, O Ali, O Ali, O Ali.

---

[41]   Allan, *Twelver Shi'ism*, p. 47; Maryam Ekhtiar, et al., *Masterpieces from the Department of Islamic Art in The Metropolitan Museum of Art*, introduction by Sheila R. Canby (New Haven, CT, and London, 2011), pp. 107–108.
[42]   Blair, 'Writing About Faith'.
[43]   Oliver Watson, *Persian Lustre Ware* (London, 1985).
[44]   Sheila S. Blair, 'Persian Lustre Ware by Oliver Watson', Review, *Ars Orientalis*, 16 (1986), pp. 176–177.

The poem apparently became popular in the late 15th and early 16th centuries, for it was inscribed on several works from that period, including a nephrite signet ring associated with the Timurid rulers of Khurasan (MMA 12.224.6) and a zoormorphic calligraph,[45] probably designed by Mir Ali Harawi (ca. 1476–1543) in the shape of a lion, for Ali is known as the 'lion of God.'[46] The *Nad-i Ali* was also inscribed on some gold and silver coins issued by Isma'il (r. 1501–1524), the first Safawid shah of Iran. Nevertheless, its popularity transcended the Shi'i milieu, and zoomorphic calligrams of the *Nad-i Ali* were popular not only in Safawid Iran but also in Ottoman Turkey. For example, an Ottoman rendering of the design in cut paper dated 1863–1864 can be associated with the Bektashi Sufi order, which also venerates Ali and, like the Shi'a, personifies him as the lion of God.

*Alam*s, large metal ceremonial standards symbolising the battle standards carried by Husayn and his followers at Karbala, are often shaped like a tear or a hand, whose five fingers the Shi'a claim represent Muhammad, Fatima, Ali, Hasan and Husayn. *Alam*s are carried in Shi'i mourning rituals. In Iran, *alam*s might be made of cut and gilded steel and decorated with inscriptions. A particularly fine example, thought to come from the shrine of Shaykh Safi at Ardabil and now in Stockholm, bears inscriptions naming the figures central to Shi'i piety surrounding a lacy arabesque and enclosed by two dragon heads.[47] In India, *alam*s were normally stored in *ashur khana*s, as at Hyderabad, where some of the mural tile decoration is based on their teardrop design. Surviving Indian *alam*s are normally made of brass, but chronicles mention now-lost examples made of gold studded with jewels. The Fatimid caliphs of Egypt, for example, sent a magnificent emerald and pearl-studded one as a gift to Mecca. The surviving examples are decorated, like other metalwork from the contemporary Deccan, with inscriptions in fine *thuluth* script and dragon heads, as well as symbolic representations of Dhu'l-Faqar (Zulfiqar), Ali's double-edged sword.[48]

An unusual kind of metal object with an Alid association is a wrought steel dervish staff in the David Collection, Copenhagen, once used by an itinerant dervish to keep awake during meditation. The staff, made of steel rod, is ingeniously bent to form the letters *ayn*, *lam* and *ya* spelling out the name Ali and providing a grip for the hand or rest for the arm, chin or forehead. *Kashkul*s, or begging bowls made in the form of a

---

[45] Thomas W. Lentz and Glenn D. Lowry, *Timur and the Princely Vision* (Los Angeles, CA, 1989), no. 142.

[46] Sheila S. Blair, *Islamic Calligraphy* (Edinburgh, 2006), p. 450.

[47] Welch, *Calligraphy*, p. 148.

[48] George Michell and Mark Zebrowski, *Architecture and Arts of the Deccan Sultanate* (Cambridge, 1999), pp. 138, 241–242.

boat (Persian, *kashti*) were normally carried by itinerant dervishes to collect alms. A particularly magnificent example in cast, engraved and tinned bronze, now in the David Collection, is inscribed with religious texts including Quranic verses, the *Nad-i Ali*, and invocations to God, Muhammad, Ali and Fatima. Although the shape reflects Iranian proto-types, the technique suggests that it was made in Qutbshahi Hyderabad. The size and weight of this example, as well as the lack of rings from which it might have been suspended, suggests that it was made for symbolic use in a shrine such as an *ashur khana*.

The Shi'a undoubtedly produced manuscripts with specifically Shi'i content for their own enjoyment, but scholars have not yet identified specifically Shi'i elements in them. The Fatimid libraries are known to have contained hundreds of thousands of manuscripts, but only a handful are known to have survived and they look very much like contemporary manuscripts produced in Sunni contexts. One might expect that manuscripts of the Quran produced by the Shi'a might have some distinctive emphasis, perhaps in the decoration, but again this has not yet been identified. For example, it is widely held that the 'Blue Quran', a dispersed manuscript written in gold leaf on blue parchment, was produced under the auspices of the Fatimid caliphs in 10th-century North Africa; yet specifically Fatimid-Shi'i elements in the text or its embellishment remain to be identified. The famous manuscript of the Quran copied by the noted calligrapher Ibn al-Bawwab at Baghdad in 1000–1001 has a colophon praising God, the Prophet, and his family, and an inscription on one of the illuminated pages states that the text was 'after the counting of the Kufans, on the authority of Ali, the Commander of the Faithful. Greetings upon him and upon our Prophet Muhammad'.[49] In fact, the manuscript does not use the Kufan counting system even though it says it does. Although the manuscript was produced during the period when the Shi'i Buyids held sway in Baghdad and makes several references to Ali, we do not know anything about Ibn al-Bawwab's own religious proclivities, which makes it hard to treat this manuscript as a work of distinctly Shi'i art.

Sometimes explicitly Shi'i elements appear in what might other-wise be considered secular contexts. The *Shahnama*, for example, is the national epic of Iran and, at least from the early 14th century, rulers commissioned illustrated manuscripts of the text. The second Safawid shah, Tahmasp, commissioned an unusually luxurious copy of the *Shahnama* with an astounding 258 illustrations and elaborate illumina-tion on gold-speckled pages. While most of the illustrations show the

---

[49]   D. S. Rice, *The Unique Ibn al-Bawwab Manuscript in the Chester Beatty Library* (Dublin, 1955), pp. 13–15.

narrative episodes of the Persian kings and heroes that are the focus of the *Shahnama*'s text, one unique painting, originally folio 18v, illustrates a parable from Firdausi's introduction to the poem in which he explains his philosophy and religious beliefs.

He envisioned 70 ships bearing representatives of the 70 religions that God launched into a stormy sea. One ship, the largest and fairest, carried the holy family of the Shiʿa – the Prophet, Ali, Hasan and Husayn – who are all depicted in the scene with veiled faces and flaming gold haloes, along with other figures. Aware that all ships will founder in the stormy sea of eternity, Firdausi has booked passage on this ship so that he can clutch the helping hands of the Prophet and his family.[50] A couplet by the poet Saʿdi on the ship's canopy reads, 'Muhammad is here to fortify our inner state! Why heed the waves when Noah is piloting our Ship of State?' Contemporary exegesis likened the family of the Prophet to Noah's ark, for it will safeguard those who choose to ride in it. This particular image clearly has Shiʿi content, though the larger setting – a book of several hundred pages and illustrations by various artists working over ten years – is surely more diffuse.

Conclusion

Throughout this brief survey, we have seen that Shiʿi content in buildings and works of art is primarily manifested less by forms or techniques than by inscriptions, even if they can be equivocal. Monumental inscriptions were sometimes read, understood, and considered to be important, by both Shiʿis and their opponents. Perhaps the most obvious way in which the Shiʿa expressed their beliefs is through their version of the *shahada*, or profession of faith: ('There is no god but God, Muhammad is the prophet of God and Ali is God's friend'), but in other cases references to the Fourteen Immaculate ones or the verses of the *Nad-i Ali* are meant to express Shiʿi beliefs. The most universal were Quranic inscriptions, and we have seen that particular verses were especially popular with the Shiʿa. While most think that the *surat al-fath* (48) refers to the Prophet's conquest of Mecca, the early Imami exegete Ali b. Ibrahim al-Qummi, for example, interpreted it as meaning that help will come from God in this world through the victory of the *qaʾim* (i.e., the return of the Twelfth imam), 'when he will fill the earth with justice just as it is now filled with oppression and darkness'.[51] While Quranic inscriptions were open to multiple readings, in many cases key elements of Shiʿi

---

[50]   Stuart Cary Welch, *A King's Book of Kings* (New York, 1972), p. 84.
[51]   Allan, *Twelver Shiʿism*, p. 64.

inscriptional programmes were the veneration of Ali and the implied downgrading of the four orthodox caliphs.

We have seen that inscriptions praising the first four caliphs as well as the Twelve imams are characteristic of 14th-century Iran and representative of a generalised veneration of the Prophet and his family among Sunnis and the Shi'a alike, but from the 16th century onwards, increasing polarisation of the religious communities led to the concealment or mutilation of earlier texts. Conversely, at the Kali Masjid in Awrangabad in the Deccan, a Nizamshahi building dating from 1600, the mosque has been given a Sunni identity by the removal of the original inscription above the *mihrab* and its replacement by the 'orthodox' *shahada*; the names of the orthodox caliphs have been painted on the walls.[52]

Our desire to find visual expression of Shi'i beliefs should not be confused with more general reverence for the immediate family of the Prophet in virtually all Muslim societies. The veneration of the Prophet, his daughter Fatima, her husband Ali and their sons Hasan and Husayn is often labelled 'Shi'i', but it was a nearly universal phenomenon in the popular religious beliefs and practices in much of the Islamic lands in the Middle Ages. Certainly, there were specifically Shi'i artistic expressions but we see how difficult it is to identify them except through inscriptions, and these inscriptions do not always indicate Shi'ism. The deep devotion that the veneration of the Prophet inspires in people who would normally identify themselves, from a legal standpoint, as Hanafi or Shafi'i points this up. Devotion to the family of the Prophet and belief in the efficacy of the intercession of their descendants can coexist quite easily with adherence to Sunni legal doctrine. As descendants of the family of the Prophet, the imams have spiritual importance for all people, and nominal Sunnis saw no contradiction in pilgrimage to the shrines of such figures as the eighth imam at Mashhad or Ali at Balkh. The Family of the Prophet represented intercession, hope of salvation, a rallying point for public opinion, and consistently the most visible icon in the daily religion of the great bulk of Muslims everywhere.

---

[52] Ibid., p. 63.

Further Reading

Allan, James W. *The Art and Architecture of Twelver Shiʻism: Iraq, Iran, and the Indian Sub-Continent*. London, 2012.

Blair, Sheila S. *Islamic Calligraphy*. Edinburgh, 2006.

—— *Text and Image in Medieval Persian Art*. Edinburgh, 2013.

Bloom, Jonathan M. *Arts of the City Victorious: Islamic Art and Architecture in Fatimid North Africa and Egypt*. London, 2007.

—— 'A Cultural History of the Material World of Islam', in Peter N. Miller, ed., *Cultural Histories of the Material World*. Ann Arbor, MI, 2013, pp. 240–248.

Lentz, Thomas W. and Glenn D. Lowry. *Timur and the Princely Vision*. Los Angeles, CA, 1989.

Michell, George and Mark Zebrowski. *Architecture and Art of the Deccan Sultanates*. Cambridge, 1999.

Mulder, Stephennie. *The Shrines of the ʻAlids in Medieval Syria: Sunnis, Shiʻis and the Architecture of Coexistence*. Edinburgh, 2013.

Suleman, Fahmida, ed. *People of the Prophet's House: Artistic and Ritual Expressions of Shiʻi Islam*. London, 2015.

Taylor, Christopher S. 'Reevaluating the Shiʻi Role in the Development of Monumental Funerary Architecture: The Case of Egypt', *Muqarnas*, 9 (1992), pp. 1–10.

Welch, Stuart Cary. *A King's Book of Kings*. New York, 1972.

Yarshater, Ehsan. 'Contemporary Persian Painting', in Richard Ettinghausen and Ehsan Yarshater, ed., *Highlights of Persian Art*. Boulder, CO, 1979, pp. 362–377.

12

Literature

Eric Ormsby

Introduction: Word and Spirit

At the beginning of his philosophical work *Zad al-musafir* (*The Wayfarer's Provision*), the great Ismaili poet and thinker Nasir-i Khusraw poses a fundamental question. Which is better, he asks, the written word or the spoken word? This might seem a somewhat irrelevant question, especially to us today; we accept whatever is written as final; in our courts, the oral testimony of a witness is transcribed and that transcript serves as the official, legal record of the testimony. But in the Islamic world and indeed, in the ancient world in general, speech was considered superior; an oath or a vow had to be spoken, not written. Plato had argued that oral communication was better than written words. Nasir follows him in this view, though for quite different reasons.

For Nasir, as for many Shi'i authors, the word, like creation itself, is composed of layers; there is an outer and obvious aspect of things but there is also an inner, more hidden side. This is the famous distinction between the *zahir* and the *batin*, Arabic words that mean 'outer' and 'inner', respectively; these terms lie at the heart of much Shi'i literature. The Quran is a prime example. The sacred text has an outward form revealed by the Prophet Muhammad by a process known as *tanzil* ('bringing down'). But its inner meaning can only be revealed by the privileged knowledge of the imam, beginning with Imam Ali, through the process of *ta'wil* ('interpretation'). The revealed text is 'the silent Quran' which must be understood through the imam, 'the speaking Quran'. Nevertheless, it would be wrong to think that the outer face of the sacred scripture is somehow less true, less authentic, than the inner face; both outer and inner make up the truth of revelation.

It would also be a mistake to think that this is a simple conception of reality. The *zahir* may have only a single face but the *batin* is multiple and can be as inexhaustible as creation – or revelation – itself. Thus, Nasir argues that speech is superior to writing. Why? First, because the written word is a material thing; it requires ink, paper and pen. It is like the body but speech is like the soul. Speech is superior because it is closer to the meanings that underlie words. And just as speech serves as the soul of the written word, so too does meaning serve as the soul to speech. What then are words? 'They are ordered letters,' he says, 'that by conventional accord point to one essence among others.' There is a practical side to this view. When we hear a discourse we can question it; we can ask the speaker to explain himself. Not so with writing; we are 'absent' from the speaker when we read. Nasir writes:

> The spirit of the learned man can convey his knowledge to other souls either speaking or by writing; and the soul that has been instructed can receive knowledge from another by the sense of hearing when he speaks or by the sense of sight when he writes. But speaking is nobler and finer than writing because speaking comes from the scholar to those who are present while writing is better for those who are absent.[1]

There is immediacy to spoken language that the written word lacks; it is a living thing, not something fixed within the confines of the written word whose meaning has to be puzzled out. Speech conveys the breath, the spirit, of the meanings that lie beneath words. The distinction that Nasir makes is not unique to the literature of the Shi'a ('The letter kills, the spirit gives life', says a Christian text) but it is characteristic of much Shi'i writing. The sense that words have multiple depths, that their meanings must be discerned and interpreted, and that there is a living spirit underlying them characterises much of the literature that we shall consider in this chapter.

This presents something of a puzzle. After all, are there not thousands upon thousands of written texts in Shi'i literature? It is a learned tradition in which commentary and super-commentary, gloss and super-gloss abound. Yet we must recognise that most of this literature has its origins in oral communication. What is the *hadith* itself but the written record of the living speech of the Prophet and the imams? The commentaries, the textbooks, even didactic verses, were communicated orally and memorised; the great theological treatises retain the traces of their spoken arguments ('If it is said' is followed by 'then I say' again and again). The written literature is constantly seeking to understand and interpret what was originally conveyed orally to 'those who are present', from the Quran itself to the multi-volume works of exegesis and commentary. You might argue that the vast written literature of the Shi'a is one incessant effort to recapture the actual breath, the living impact, of direct verbal discourse.

---

[1]   Nasir-i Khusraw, *Zad al-musafir*, ed. I. Ha'iri (Tehran, 1384/2005), p. 7.

This chapter will not deal with the learned literature of the Shi'a – the great *hadith* collections, the legal and theological treatises, the vast commentary tradition – but instead will look at some manifestations of the Shi'i belletristic achievement in prose as well as in poetry over some five centuries. This is a bit tricky, of course. For the most part, Shi'i authors, whether writing in Arabic or Persian, used the same forms, the same literary devices, as their Sunni counterparts. We will have to look beyond and beneath these superficial aspects, somewhat in the spirit of Nasir-i Khusraw, to discern what is distinctive and characteristic in Shi'i literary art.

Imam Ali and The Path of Eloquence

Ali b. Abi Talib, cousin and son-in-law of the Prophet Muhammad and the earliest convert to Islam, is revered as the first imam of the Shi'a. It was he who, according to tradition, received the Quranic revelation directly from the dictation of the Prophet before his death. But Ali is also celebrated as an outstanding individual in his own right, renowned for his bravery on the battlefield (he is known as 'the Lion of God') as well as for his wisdom and eloquence. He is the fountainhead of all Shi'i literature as well as Shi'i piety.

His fabled eloquence is fully displayed in the book known as *The Path of Eloquence* (*Nahj al-balagha* in Arabic). This is a collection of Ali's sermons, sayings and missives, compiled over three centuries after his death in 661 by the Shi'i poet Sharif al-Radi (d. 1015) of Baghdad. *The Path of Eloquence* is one of the most beautiful works in the Arabic language, a masterpiece acknowledged by Sunnis as well.[2] Its centrality in Shi'i tradition can be gauged by the fact that it has inspired more than 200 commentaries over the centuries, and has been translated into both Persian and Urdu.[3] Moreover, Ali is himself venerated in the Sunni tradition and some of his precepts have become fundamental to intellectual inquiry for Sunnis as well. For example, the Sunni theologian and mystic Abu Hamid al-Ghazali (1058–1111), notorious for his attacks on Shi'i Ismailis, quotes Ali in his spiritual autobiography to explain his own search for truth. Ali's famous statement, 'Do not look at *who* is speaking, rather, look at *what* he says' became Ghazali's guiding

---

[2] Quotations here are from the edition prepared by the great Egyptian Sunni scholar Muhammad Abduh.

[3] See M. Djebli, 'Nahdj al-Balagha', *EI2*, vol. 7, pp. 903–904. See also Farhad Daftary, *A History of Shi'i Islam* (London, 2013), p. 71, which notes that the *Nahj* 'after the Quran and Prophetic Traditions, is regarded by Twelver Shi'is as their most venerated sacred book. Other Shi'i communities also hold this book in high esteem.'

principle when he turned to a consideration of such suspect disciplines as philosophy. Only by looking at what a thinker actually says can we hope to distinguish truth from falsehood; and we do this by the use of the intellect, the human faculty to which Ali accords the highest significance. This is not the intellect in its usual sense of logical reasoning but something more profound. As a contemporary scholar notes, it is 'a spirit that surpasses, while comprising, the activities of the rational mind, as well as encompassing domains not nowadays associated with the intellect, domains such as moral comportment and aesthetic sensibility.'[4] This more comprehensive view of intellect is one shared by many Sunni scholars. It is what gives *The Path of Eloquence* its universality as well as its genuine majesty.

To modern readers it may seem strange that 'eloquence' should play so large a part in this treasury of spiritual wisdom. Isn't eloquence simply the art of speaking well, an ability we associate with orators and after-dinner speakers? But in the Islamic tradition, true eloquence is a spiritual quality. The Quran itself is regarded as supremely eloquent; the beauty of its language is a sign of its divine origin. As a famous tradition (*hadith*) states, 'God is beautiful and He loves beauty'. God's own beauty and His love of beauty are exemplified in the language of His revelation; that very beauty serves as a proof of the Quran's miraculous nature. This is one reason why Muslim theologians declared that the Quran could not be imitated by human effort. The Quran articulates this in the famous 'challenge verses';[5] its truth is embedded in the language in which it was revealed.

The Path of Eloquence is thus not simply a guide to speaking or writing well (though it is that too), but a further instance of the belief that 'truth is beauty, beauty truth'. As a literary work, it is quite remarkable. It is composed in 'rhyming prose', known in Arabic as *saj* (a term that originally meant 'the cooing of a dove'). The sentences rhyme (in this like the Quran itself), but have no fixed measure, no poetic metre. Instead, they are driven by a strong rhythmical beat. The effect is highly musical and can be hypnotic. Those who heard Ali's sermons felt their 'skins shiver, their eyes weep and their hearts tremble'. The work uses other literary devices, such as parallelism, the recasting of a series of thoughts in slightly different ways. Thus, in the first sermon of *The Path of Eloquence*, Ali proclaims:

---

[4]   Reza Shah-Kazemi, *Justice and Remembrance: Introducing the Spirituality of Imam 'Ali* (London, 2006), p. 22.

[5]   For example, Sura 2:23: 'If you doubt what We have revealed to Our servant, produce one chapter comparable to it.'

Praise be to God, whose full praise no articulate beings can express, whose blessings no one counting can count, whose truth even those who strive mightily cannot convey, whose vast designs cannot be grasped, whose fathomless sagacity is unattainable, whose qualities have no fixed limit, nor existing descriptor, nor measurable time, nor computed extent; who brought creatures forth through His power, who diffused spirits through His mercy, who fixed the arena of His earth firmly in place with stony peaks.

Here we move from praise of God to His innumerable blessings, His truth, His designs, His wisdom, all ultimately ungraspable by human beings; and we conclude with God's creation of things in His power and mercy. Each of these phrases reinforces the one that came before and each prepares for the next one; each expresses a different aspect of God's transcendent greatness but with a subtle twist: these divine qualities are utterly real but none of them can be comprehended by human faculties. We stand mute before the grandeur of God. This form of expression (which will later be called 'negative theology') gives terrific intensity to the phrases. Whatever we can say about God falls immeasurably short of Him. Ali ends with a concrete image drawn from the Quran; all the abstract qualities attributed to God are clinched by the mention of the physical creation with 'His earth firmly in place with stony peaks'. This is powerful rhetoric, but rhetoric in the service of a truth: it affirms God's power and wisdom and mercy even while it denies that we can ever truly know them.

Such paradox is characteristic of *The Path of Eloquence*. Paradox expresses a difficult truth in seemingly contradictory terms and Ali is a master of this method. When he states that 'God is with everything but not through association, and other than everything, but not through separation', we are confronted with a brilliant paradoxical expression of the relation of God to His creation, indeed, to ourselves.[6] This could hardly be more succinctly put, for doesn't the Quran declare that nothing 'is in His likeness' and yet that He is, at the same time, closer to a man than 'his own jugular vein'? Through paradox Ali is able to formulate two seemingly incompatible aspects of our relation to God as a single truth; moreover, he does this while preserving the ultimately mysterious nature of that relation.

Another literary aspect of *The Path of Eloquence* is its use of vivid imagery. Much of this imagery alludes to earlier images, especially from

---

[6]   Cited in Shah-Kazemi, *Justice and Remembrance*, p. 147; see also p. 30 for an astute discussion of paradox.

the Quran, as in the image cited above of the earth fixed in place by its mountains; and yet, the imagery in *The Path of Eloquence* possesses its own freshness and originality of effect. For example, in the first sermon, God's creation of the world is described in detail. There, we read that God:

> initiated the splitting of the skies, the cleavage of the zones, the uppermost strata of the winds. He caused water to flow within them whose currents clashed, brimming with massed floods, loading it onto the back of tempest winds and thunderous gales...then He gave the wind mastery over the force of the rains and He bound it to its limit. Then – glory be to Him! – He inaugurated a wind and He made its blustering barren, He fixed its origin forever, He made it gust fiercely and broadened its range, then He commanded it to smite the brimming water and shake the waves of the sea.

Here, the language captures both the tumult of the elements and the power God manifests by ordering them; the language seems to clash like the wind and the water themselves. And he goes on to state that 'the wind churned the sea the way milk is churned'. The image is all the more forceful for being so homely, so domestic, suggesting that God mixed the primordial elements just as we do when we churn fresh milk; the image is startling because it makes something utterly mysterious to us – God's act of creation – as familiar as the labour of a dairyman.

In another sermon he calls the world 'a passing gleam, a vanishing shadow, a tottering column' and then he personifies it: 'It hangs a man on the noose of his fate, hauling him to a narrow couch, a desolate home-coming...' – again using poetic imagery mingled with very down-to-earth touches (the world as a hangman). In a later sermon, he asks, 'Can people plump with youth anticipate anything but the sore cracked ribs of old age?' Elsewhere he describes a dissolute youth as 'dipping into the leather bucket of his passions'.

Throughout the *Nahj al-balagha*, soaring flights of eloquence, exhortations and moral counsel, injunctions to his followers as well as scolding of their lapses, calls to repentance and warnings of the Judgment to come, are delivered in impassioned language that combines the loftiest sentiments with the plainest images – sore cracked ribs and leather buckets – and the imagery drives the message home. To treat *The Path of Eloquence* as a literary masterpiece is not to diminish its spiritual depth; on the contrary, its literary beauty reinforces its profundity.

Literature in the Shi'i Century

A remarkable surge in Shi'i literary production occurred during the 10th and 11th centuries when the major dynastic powers were all controlled by Shi'i rulers. In Iran and Iraq, the traditional areas of the Abbasid caliphate, the Buyids held sway from 934 to 1062. In Egypt, the dynasty of the Fatimids was established under the rule of a succession of imam-caliphs; this was the most enduring of the medieval Shi'i dynasties, lasting from 909 until 1171. A smaller but no less illustrious dynasty was that of the Hamdanids in northern Syria, especially under the reign of Sayf al-Dawla (r. 944–967). All three dynasties were distinguished not only by Shi'i belief in differing forms – the Buyids were originally Zaydi Shi'a, the Fatimids were Ismaili – but by enlightened patronage of the sciences and the arts as well as of traditional Shi'i scholarship.

It was during this period that Shi'i law and theology assumed their definitive shape. Under the Buyids (by then converted to Imami or Twelver Shi'ism), the great canonical collections of *hadith* were compiled and the foundational works of Shi'i theology were formulated. Under the Fatimids, Ismaili law and doctrine were elaborated and disseminated while the imam-caliphs also promoted and sponsored original philosophical and scientific endeavours, especially through such institutions as the Dar al-Ilm, or House of Knowledge, founded by the Imam-caliph al-Hakim in 1005. At the Hamdanid court in Aleppo, a glittering array of thinkers, poets and scholars assembled under the patronage of Sayf al-Dawla. It is hardly surprising that under these circumstances, Shi'i literary culture experienced its most brilliant and creative moment.

The Sincere Brethren of Basra

In Basra, in southern Iraq, a lively intellectual culture had flourished virtually since its founding as a cantonment city in the 7th century. It was here, sometime around the middle of the 10th century, that an obscure brotherhood embarked on a monumental venture: the compilation of an encyclopedia containing all the knowledge of the age, scientific, philosophical, theological and cultural. What resulted was the celebrated 'Epistles' or *Rasa'il* of the 'Sincere Brethren', the Ikhwan al-Safa.

The identity of the members of this 'esoteric coterie'[7] has long remained mysterious, as has their precise affiliation. The scholarly consensus leans

---

[7]   See Nader El-Bizri, ed., *The Ikhwan al-Safa' and Their Rasa'il: An Introduction* (Oxford, 2008), p. 1. For the presumed identity of the group, as reported by the great prose writer al-Tawhidi, their contemporary, and repeated in later sources, see p. 4.

to the likelihood that they were Shi'a and indeed, Ismaili Shi'a; this is supported by the contents of their work. For the Brethren, the Prophet Muhammad was the 'city of knowledge' while Ali was 'its gateway'; we know too that they mourned the murder of Imam Husayn and observed Ashura. During the time of their activity, Basra was under the control of the Qarmatis, a radical utopian Shi'i movement originally affiliated with the Ismailis; presumably the work could not have been carried on without their approbation. Be that as it may, the authors of the *Epistles* appear to have been not only scholars but highly placed functionaries in the Abbasid administration and enjoyed its support. As a modern scholar has observed, 'The Sincere Brethren were a society made up, for the most part, of government secretaries and officials, forming a fraternity (*ukhuwwa*). They met in sessions (*majalis*) in which their esoteric teachings (mainly philosophical in content) were discussed.'[8]

The *Rasa'il* consist of 52 epistles, divided into four parts. The first part deals with mathematics (understood to include not only arithmetic and geometry but astronomy, geography, logic and music); the second part treats of 'natural philosophy'; the third part treats psychology while the final part takes up theology. This summary might make the *Epistles* appear dry. In fact, apart from unavoidable technical passages, they are highly entertaining.

They are written in a lucid and graceful prose – a feature that has given the work the status of a classic of Arabic literature – but they display throughout an unexpectedly friendly and confiding tone; they were addressed to an elite readership of like-minded individuals, and there is chumminess in their tone. Each epistle begins with 'Know, O brother...' and the reader feels drawn into a private conversation with a friend. Then, too, the work draws on an immense diversity of sources and influences; not only Greek science and thought, as we might expect, but Babylonian, Indian and Persian traditions of wisdom. This universalist outlook is confirmed by the Brethren's notion of the ideal human being who is:

> Persian in breeding, Arab in faith, Hanafi in jurisprudence, Iraqi in culture, Hebrew in tradition, Christian in comportment, Syrian in piety, Greek in knowledge, Indian in contemplation and Sufi in intimation and lifestyle.[9]

---

[8]   Joel L. Kraemer, *Humanism in the Renaissance of Islam: The Cultural Revival during the Buyid Age* (Leiden, 1992), pp. 177–178.
[9]   *Rasa'il Ikhwan al-Safa* (Beirut, 1957), vol. 2, p. 376, cited in El-Bizri, p. 13.

This attitude represents something more than simple eclecticism; it expresses an all-embracing worldview. This is consistent with the philosophical orientation of the Brethren. While they may be characterised as 'Neoplatonist' in that they adopt the hierarchical system of the cosmos in which existence emanates from the One along descending levels of being, a system inherited from Late Antiquity, they cannot be so neatly pigeon-holed; the Brethren are far more original than such labels would suggest.

Undoubtedly the most remarkable Epistle in the entire work is the 22nd, entitled 'The Case of the Animals versus Man before the King of the Jinn'. In this amazing fable, a succession of animals – the ram, the horse, the camel, the elephant along with a swarm of birds and insects – charges mankind with intolerable cruelty and mistreatment of the entire animal kingdom and they do this before the dispassionate court of the King of the Jinn (those spirits of 'pure flame' described in the Quran and a third category of creatures, neither human nor angel). Their chief spokesman, and accuser, is Ya'sub, king of the bees. This Epistle, by turns ironic, comical and deeply compassionate, ends with the acquittal of mankind but not before human presumption and arrogance have been savagely arraigned. The Brethren's ability to slip into the skins of their animal characters, to enter the perspective of a bee or a lion or a mule, is at once plausible and moving.[10]

This empathy is characteristic of the Sincere Brethren; it permeates their *Epistles*. Consider Epistle 26 which deals with 'the microcosm', another ancient conception according to which everything in the human body and soul corresponds to other things in the universe, from the farthest stars to the rivers and mountains, down to the ground beneath our feet. Man is 'the little world' in which all that exists in 'the big world' may be found in miniature.

As in the *Nahj al-balagha* earlier, these authors too resort to homely images, in this instance quite literally. Thus, man:

> resembles a house, built for its inhabitant. When he considers the state of his soul and the wonders of its actions within the structure of his body's frame, along with the diffusion of its faculties in the very joints of his body, he is like a resident in his own home with his servants, his family and his children.

---

[10] I have discussed this Epistle in more detail in Amyn B. Sajoo, ed., *A Companion to Muslim Ethics* (London, 2010), at pp. 75–77. For the epistle itself, see *The Case of the Animals versus Man before the King of the Jinn*, ed. and tr. Lenn E. Goodman and Richard McGregor (Oxford, 2012).

Later, we read that:

> The structure of man's body is like the earth; his bones are like
> the mountains and the marrow inside them like minerals. His
> insides are like the ocean; his intestines are like the rivers; his
> veins are like creeks; his flesh like the dust; his hair like the
> plants. His sprouting-place is like good steppe-land and where
> hair does not grow, it is like a marshy earth. From his face to
> his feet he is a populace while his back resembles ruins. His face
> in the front is like the east while the back of his face is like the
> west; his right hand is like the south and his left hand is like the
> north. His breathing is like breezes; his speech is like thunder;
> his voice like thunderbolts; his laughter like the blaze of day;
> his weeping like the rain; his suffering and his sadness are like
> the dark of night. His slumber is like death, his waking like life.

Though very probably of Ismaili Shi'i inspiration, the most diverse
thinkers refer to the *Epistles*. Nasir-i Khusraw derives his scientific
knowledge from it, as does his Sunni contemporary al-Ghazali. They
are only two of the many Muslim thinkers – as well as ordinary readers
– who have turned to it over the centuries, as much for the charm of its
style as for its lore.[11]

Ahmad Ibn Miskawayh: Ethicist and Historian

One of the most engaging authors to emerge under the Buyids in
the 'Shi'i century' was the historian and philosopher Ahmad Ibn
Miskawayh. Born in Rayy near present-day Tehran around 932, he died
at a ripe old age in 1030. Miskawayh was a Shi'i Muslim of Iranian origin
and wrote works in both Arabic and Persian. He was famed as an historian mainly because of his monumental work, *The Experiences of the
Nations (Tajarib al-umam)*, written in Arabic and extending from the
Flood to his own time. But he also wrote philosophical works and Sufi
treatises. More importantly, he was one of the first thinkers to introduce
philosophical ethics into the Muslim tradition.

Miskawayh was close to the centre of Buyid power; he served as a
librarian to the Buyids, no doubt because it gave him access to precious
books. Certainly he benefited from the ongoing translation of Greek

---

[11]   The entire work is now being published in 18 volumes by The Institute of
Ismaili Studies through Oxford University Press (with critical editions of the
Arabic text and definitive translations and annotations). Several volumes have
already appeared on such topics as logic, mathematics, geography, music and the
natural sciences.

works into Arabic, a result of the 'Translation Movement' sponsored by the Abbasid caliphs in their prestigious House of Wisdom (*bayt al-hikma*) in Baghdad. As a result, he was fully conversant with the works of Aristotle who influenced him profoundly. But he was not merely an imitator of Aristotle. He adapted Aristotle within an Islamic context; moreover, he drew on immemorial Persian traditions and practices. His ethical system is synthesised in his delightful treatise entitled *The Refinement of Character* (*Tahdhib al-akhlaq* in Arabic).[12]

There was something revolutionary about Miskawayh's book: this was a work for any intelligent reader, not merely for a privileged elite. He set out to show how a person could be both good and happy in this world without sacrificing his place in the world to come. Instead of holding that character was predetermined, Miskawayh taught that it could be shaped and trained; self-improvement was possible to all. He wrote: 'Our goal in the present work is to secure a moral nature for ourselves, such that all the actions that emanate from us may be good as well as easy for us, requiring neither effort nor pain. This comes about with the help of a science and in accord with a structured teaching.'

What? We are the 'masters of our souls'? Have our characters and our actions not been predetermined by God from all eternity, as Sunni theologians taught? An astonishing claim, based not only on the teachings of Aristotle but no doubt as well, on the formulations of Shi'i theology which held that human beings do possess and exercise free will. It was a claim based also on the power and prestige of the human intellect, God's greatest blessing to mankind. For it is by intellect, Miskawayh taught, that we tame the unruly self and advance in moral perfection.

His treatise is divided into seven chapters, beginning with a discussion of the soul (without knowledge of our souls we cannot hope to progress), continuing through a theory of education to a study of 'the highest good', which is human happiness, and thence to an analysis of the virtues. Miskawayh's fifth chapter is on love; it follows Aristotle's discussion in the *Nicomachean Ethics* very closely but goes well beyond Aristotle; for Miskawayh, the stages of love culminate in a passionate love of God (a love Aristotle considered illogical). His last two chapters discuss 'spiritual medicine', that is, how to heal the soul, and a diagnosis of the illnesses that afflict the soul. It is a complete guide to the good life in the deepest sense.

Miskawayh too can be down to earth. Alongside exalted passages on the ecstatic love of God, he offers advice on the rearing of children. He accepts the old Iranian tradition that a good education inculcates honesty in a child (as well as good horsemanship). But how to accomplish this?

---

12 Translated into English by Constantine Zurayk as *The Refinement of Character* (Chicago, 2003).

He offers several suggestions. First, one must recognise that almost all of a child's acts are bad; they lie, they steal, they disobey. You must begin by telling them stories and poems that illustrate good behaviour. You must always praise them and consider any lapses of conduct as almost unbelievable ('What, you did that? I can't believe it!'). If the child persists, you must reprimand him or her in private; public scolding only makes the child defiant. Table manners are hard to teach but you must tell your child not to 'jump on the food', nor to stare longingly at all the dishes on the table. The child must learn not to eat quickly, not to take huge mouthfuls but rather to chew thoughtfully, and how not to soil one's clothes. Nor must the child watch others as they eat or follow their hands as they lift food to their mouths. Learning how to control one's appetite, and to share one's food, is essential.

Any parent will acknowledge the wisdom of these suggestions. More importantly, they represent the first small stages, the baby-steps, in the refinement of human character and are as indispensable as the stages that lead to the love of God.

Al-Sharif al-Radi, Shi'i Poet of Baghdad

We have already met al-Sharif al-Radi (970–1016) as the compiler of *The Path of Eloquence*, but he was also a celebrated poet, one of the most distinguished not only in Shi'i literature but in the grand classical tradition of Arabic poetry. Born in Baghdad, he and his brother Murtada al-Radi, a major figure in Shi'i theology and also a poet, enjoyed enormous prestige at the Buyid court, both for their writings as well as their impeccable Alid lineage. Al-Sharif al-Radi traced his ancestry to Imam Husayn himself; in one of his poems he addresses Husayn as 'Grandfather'. In certain of his early poems, al-Sharif al-Radi goes so far as to urge the Abbasid caliph to abdicate:

> Return the inheritance of Muhammad, return it!
> For neither the staff nor the Prophet's mantle are yours![13]

And to the Abbasid Caliph al-Qadir he wrote:

> Each of us is of the noblest origins –
> Except for the caliphate: I am deprived of it
> While you are crowned!

---

[13]   Cited in Suzanne Pinckney Stetkevych, 'Al-Sharif al-Radi and the Poetics of Alid Legitimacy: Elegy for al-Husayn ibn 'Ali on "Ashura", 391 A.H.', *Journal of Arabic Literature*, 38 (2007), p. 295.

When his aspirations to the caliphate were thwarted, he turned to literature. One of the most striking and original of al-Sharif al-Radi's poems is the long ode, or *qasida*, he wrote to commemorate the massacre of Husayn and his family at Karbala. This 58-line poem is one of several that the poet wrote on the theme but this particular ode can be dated precisely to Ashura, 10 Muharram in the year of the Hijra 391 (10 December 1000 CE). While the poem uses the traditional elements of a classical ode, it deploys them in an unconventional way, moving from the standard setting of the deserted campsite, so beloved of pre-Islamic poets, to an elegy for Husayn, a denunciation of his Umayyad murderers, praise of the Household of the Prophet and a call for vengeance, ending with a hymn of praise. Thus he writes in mourning for Husayn, addressing the imam directly:

> O Grandfather! May the squadrons of sorrow never cease
> To overwhelm the soul with their charging and pursuit
> Forever over you, nor poured forth tears
> That weeping brings, if not at evening, then at morn.[14]

After sorrow comes praise. In the last lines he again addresses the martyred imam in images suggestive of return and rebirth:

> This is my praise, though I have not reached the finish,
> Rather, my lines are horses gathered at the starting-line
> When the swift steeds' reins are loosed.
> Shall I say, 'May the spring rains pour down upon you',
> To *you* who are the spring rain of every dwelling-place?
> How can one praise the stars when they are high above
> At the farthest distance that the eye can see?
> The rising of the sun defies description
> In its glory, its radiance, and its distant splendour![15]

These images – the impatient horses, the returning rains of spring, the distant stars, the rising of the sun – suggest the presence of the slain imam in the very cycles of nature; he is 'the spring rain of every dwelling-place'. The final tribute to Husayn is triumphant; it is the expression of an unconquerable hope.

---

14   Translation in Stetkevych, p. 317 (slightly modified).
15   Stetkevych, p. 320 (again slightly modified).

Al-Mutanabbi and the Hamdanid Court

At his glittering court in Aleppo, the Hamdanid ruler Sayf al-Dawla gathered about him some of the most distinguished figures of the age. The great philosopher Abu Nasr al-Farabi, a Shi'i and Sufi, spent his last years at that court. There, the Shi'i literary scholar Abu al-Faraj al-Isfahani compiled his massive *Book of Songs*, that vast anthology of Arabic poetry and music (the standard printed version runs to some 33 thick volumes). But the most illustrious – as well as outrageous – character there was certainly the poet Abu Tayyib al-Mutanabbi (915–965), considered the greatest of all Arab poets, the 'Shakespeare of the Arabs'.

The son of a humble water-carrier, al-Mutanabbi rose to prominence in his youth because of his fabulous poetic gifts. Modesty was not one of his virtues; he was a braggart of the first magnitude. As he wrote in an early verse:

> If I'm arrogant, it's the arrogance of a wonder of nature
> Who's never found anyone superior to himself.

His name, which means 'the one who claims to be a prophet', may have been assumed because of his reported affiliation with the radical Qarmati movement. He seems to have been active in his youth as a Qarmati missionary and rabble-rouser. As a poet, however, he functioned as a hired word-slinger, a verbal mercenary available to the highest bidder. His practice was to praise and exalt a patron as long as he remained in favour but when the patron wearied of him, al-Mutanabbi would take his leave in a torrent of abuse.

This was the pattern with Sayf al-Dawla, for whom he wrote some of his most beautiful odes, especially exalting him in his long-drawn-out conflicts with the Byzantines. In a famous ode, al-Mutanabbi praises Sayf al-Dawla as 'the son of Ali' and he includes 'the Fatimids' in his praises, as much for their warrior spirit as for their generosity:

> The Fatimids are sweeter than life restored,
> And more often on our lips than the times of youth.
> You, Ali's son, have succoured Ali with sharp swords
> Of action, unblunted in their striking edges…
> They say that the stars have influence on men,
> So how is it that he himself influences the stars?
> He has mounted the shoulders of the world to reach every goal
> And the world moves with him like a docile beast with its rider.[16]

---

[16] A. J. Arberry, *Poems of al-Mutanabbi: A Selection with Introduction, Translations and Notes* (Cambridge, 1967), pp. 46–47. In his notes, Arberry argues that the

As we saw in al-Sharif al-Radi's ode, nature is evoked in conjunction with Sayf al-Dawla, the 'son of Ali', and by tacit extension, with Ali himself.

Although al-Mutanabbi was a court poet, he bragged of his familiarity with desert life (having in fact spent his youth among the Bedouin); this boasting led to fatal consequences. While travelling from one court to another, in 965, his caravan was attacked by highwaymen. Al-Mutanabbi ran away, at which point his own servant shouted out the lines which had made him famous:

> The horsemen and the night and the desert know me,
> And the sword and the lance, the paper and the pen!

Shamed by his own words for his cowardice, the poet turned and made a last stand but was cut down where he stood.

A Fatimid Ismaili Master: Nasir-i Khusraw

Two of the most influential and brilliant figures of the 'Shi'i century' arrived in the Fatimid capital of Cairo in the same year, 1047. The first was al-Mu'ayyad fi'l-Din al-Shirazi. He had been an Ismaili missionary, or *da'i*, at the Buyid court in Iran, his native land; during the 20 years he spent in Cairo, he rose to the highest position in the Fatimid hierarchy, becoming the chief *da'i*, in charge of the ministry responsible for Ismaili proselytising activities throughout the Islamic world. Al-Mu'ayyad's immense learning, especially in the intricacies of Ismaili doctrine and practice, is reflected in his comprehensive Arabic work, *al-Majalis al-Mu'ayyadiyya* (The Teaching Sessions of al-Mu'ayyad). He was also a poet, composing long odes in Arabic that encapsulate Ismaili belief in vivid form.

The other figure was the poet and philosopher Nasir-i Khusraw, who arrived in Cairo after a long journey in August of 1047 – a journey prompted by a visionary dream in which he was summoned to change his life. Nasir had been born in 1004 in Khurasan (Central Asia), and so he was in middle age when he first came to Cairo; this is not irrelevant, for Nasir would write all the works for which he is renowned in middle or old age, a striking fact given their vigour and freshness of expression. Originally a Shi'a (whether Zaydi or Twelver is not clear), he converted to Ismaili Shi'ism shortly before or during his stay in Cairo. He would develop into one of the most articulate exponents of Ismaili thought,

---

poet does not have the Fatimids of Egypt in mind but rather the Fatimid line; but this is not entirely convincing to me. I have modified the translation somewhat.

writing in both prose and poetry, and always in Persian. He is regarded as one of the four or five greatest poets in the Persian language – an astonishing accomplishment for an ageing man, always on the move in later years and often under serious threat from Sunni persecutors.

In Cairo, Nasir soon came under the tutelage of al-Mu'ayyad, with whom he shared a Persian background, both men being relative newcomers to the Fatimid capital. Moreover, their destinies were curiously parallel. Al-Mu'ayyad had had to flee for his life before coming to Cairo; Nasir would also be compelled later, sometime around 1056, to go into exile in Badakhshan where he spent the rest of his life, far from home (he died there at an unknown date sometime after 1070). Each man had a strong sense of the bitterness of exile. In one of his poems, al-Mu'ayyad writes:

> O, the way of exile, how appalling is your malady!
> Your wealth is poverty and your gifts a torment.

And he adds:

> There was a time when I preyed upon lions in Persia,
> Whereas now it is the sheep who try to kill me.[17]

Through al-Mu'ayyad, Nasir was introduced to the Imam-caliph al-Mustansir who influenced him profoundly. Decades later, in exile in remote Badakhshan, Nasir would continue to assert his allegiance to al-Mustansir. And it was al-Mu'ayyad who instructed Nasir during his five years in Cairo, imparting much of the broad philosophical, theological and scientific knowledge that his work displays.

After leaving Cairo in 1052, newly appointed as an Ismaili *da'i*, and later named overall spiritual leader (*hujja*) for the whole region of Khurasan, Nasir wrote his *Safar-nama* (Book of Travels), a classic of Persian prose and one of the most important books of travel of the entire Middle Ages. Here Nasir gives a detailed factual account of his journey to and from Cairo with all the splendours, and the miseries, it occasioned. His descriptions of Jerusalem and especially, of Fatimid Cairo, are so exact and so vivid that we seem to see those cities rise up before our eyes. No aspect of Cairo appears to have escaped his keen eye: the dwellings, the markets, the mosques, the caliphal palaces and processions, down to the lowliest details – for example, the array of fruits and

---

[17] Al-Mu'ayyad fi'l-Din al-Shirazi, *Mount of Knowledge, Sword of Eloquence: Collected Poems of an Ismaili Muslim Scholar in Fatimid Egypt*, tr. Mohamad Adra, with an Introduction by Kutub Kassam (London, 2011), p. 91.

vegetables the Cairenes grew on their rooftops – are all enumerated and described. Though written in an objective, almost documentary style, the reader can sense Nasir's admiration and excitement, even after the passage of centuries.[18]

Nasir is a poet of many voices. He is a moralist and a metaphysician combined. He can scold his reader: 'Why do you think God gave you a mind? To eat and sleep like a donkey?' he says in one poem and in another, he finds a forceful image for free will: 'Although God creates the mother and the breast and the milk/The children must draw the mother's milk for themselves.' He reinforces this in a famous verse: 'Since you are the author of your own ill-fated star/Don't look up to heaven for some lucky star!' He can write soaring odes in praise of God; he can write startling 'confessional' poems, describing his anguished search for the truth. He is also a fabulist in the line of Aesop, using animals to make a moral point. Here he gives a lesson on pride:

> One day an eagle rose up from his rock
> And full of greed, spread all his plumage out,
> Arranged his wings correctly and spoke thus:
> 'Today the world is all beneath my wings!
> If I fly high the sun no longer sees me
> While I see dust-specks in the ocean's depth;
> And should a gnat be crawling in the dust,
> My eye beholds the insect's movements too!'
> Thus he showed off, not fearing God's decree –
> What happened to him from the cruel sphere?
> For suddenly, from out a hiding place
> An arrow came, shot from a mighty bow.
> The piercing arrow hit the eagle's wing
> And cast him from the cloud onto the dust.
> He wriggled in the dust just like a fish
> And all his plumage fell there left and right.
> 'How strange!' said he, 'this thing is steel and wood?
> How could it be so swift, so piercing sharp?'
> He looked and saw his feathers on the arrow
> And screamed: 'From *me* came what came over me!'
> Cast out your ego and your selfishness!
> Look at the eagle, full of selfish pride![19]

---

[18] The book has been translated, with facing Persian text, by Wheeler M. Thackston as *Naser-e Khosraw's Book of Travels (Safarnama)* (Costa Mesa, CA, 2001).

[19] Annemarie Schimmel in *Make a Shield from Wisdom: Selected Verses from Nasir-i Khusraw's Divan* (London, 2001), pp. 92–93.

In all of Nasir's works, in prose or verse, we hear an individual voice. His theological and philosophical works are rigorous but display the sensibility of the poet. Whether in *The Wayfarer's Provision* or in Nasir's final work, *Twin Wisdoms Reconciled*,[20] he finds a bold image to make subtle matters clear and memorable. The eye for detail that is evident in his *Book of Travels* is constantly at work but now there is a difference. Now he looks at things for their inner meaning; now he looks with 'the eyes of the heart'.

Farid al-Din Attar: A Shi'i Sufi

A century after Nasir, another poet and thinker would practise gazing at the world with 'the eyes of the heart'. This was the Persian Sufi poet and chronicler Farid al-Din Attar, born near Nishapur sometime around 1145. As his name indicates, he was an apothecary, like his father. He lived in a time of terrible upheaval and witnessed the Mongol invasion which destroyed his home town; he himself seems to have perished in that massacre in 1221. Attar was a Sufi though certain of his writings are tinged with Shi'i tones. Indeed, he seems to have become a Shi'i late in life.[21]

Attar's numerous works include his indispensable collection of biographies of earlier Sufis (*The Memorial of the Saints*), and such long poems as *The Book of God*. But it is his great allegorical poem in Persian, titled *Mantiq al-tayr* (The Conference of the Birds), which stands apart as an enduring masterpiece, as charming as it is profound.[22]

The narrative describes the search of 30 birds of all sorts – the parrot, the duck, the goldfinch, the nightingale, among others – for the fabulous bird of birds, the Simurgh. They are led in this quest by the hoopoe, a bird often credited with magic powers. This is no linear narrative. The birds' quest is constantly interrupted by tales and fables of all sorts, recounted by one of the birds or by the poet himself. For Attar is not simply a Sufi but a witty moralist. He uses his birds, as Nasir uses his eagle, to make ethical points. And he often introduces humour to sweeten his counsel. Here, for example, is a little parable about miserliness. I cite the

---

[20] *Jami al-Hikmatayn*, tr. Eric Ormsby as *Between Reason and Revelation: Twin Wisdoms Reconciled* (London, 2012).

[21] This is the view of Hellmut Ritter, the leading authority on Farid al-Din; see his article in *EI2*, vol. 1, pp. 751–755. Ritter's monumental work, *The Ocean of the Soul: Man, the World, and God in the Stories of Farid al-Din 'Attar* (Leiden, 2003), is an unsurpassed study of the poet.

[22] Peter Avery renders it as 'The Speech of the Birds', which is more literal, like his translation. For a brilliant rhyming verse translation of the work, see Dick Davis and Afkham Darbandi, *The Conference of the Birds* (Penguin, 1984).

translation by Edward Fitzgerald, the 19th-century translator of Omar Khayyam:

> A fellow all his life lived hoarding gold,
> And dying, hoarded left it. And behold,
> One night his son saw peering through the house
> A man, with yet the semblance of a mouse,
> Watching a crevice in the wall – and cried,
> 'My Father?' 'Yes', the Musulman replied,
> 'Thy Father!' 'But why watching thus?' 'For fear
> Lest any smell my treasure buried here.'
> 'But wherefore, Sir, so metamousified?'
> 'Because, my Son, such is the true outside
> Of the inner soul by which I lived and died.'[23]

Fitzgerald has caught the humour of the fable by his witty coinage 'metamousified' which exists, needless to say, not in the original Persian but in its inner spirit, its play on outer form and inner being, that *zahir* and *batin* which we met before and which lies at the heart of so many Shi'i (and Sufi) works.

After many difficulties, the birds reach the abode of the Simurgh and are dazzled by its radiance. As in a mirror they see themselves, all 30 birds, reflected:

> In amazement all of them were startled;
> Again, in another way did they become amazed.
> Themselves the complete Simurgh they saw;
> The Simurgh Himself was all the time the *si murgh*!
> When upon the Simurgh they looked,
> These *si murgh* were He, that One in that place;
> But if upon themselves they looked,
> These thirty birds, they were that Other.
> And if they looked at both together,
> Both were the one Simurgh in every way.[24]

It is characteristic both of Sufi perception and of Persian poetry that the culmination of the birds' quest should turn on a play of words. For the name 'Simurgh' may also be read as *si murgh* or '30 birds' in Persian. It is a pun and a paradox: depending upon how they gaze, they are one

---

[23] Edward Fitzgerald, *Selected Works*, ed. Joanna Richardson (London, 1962), pp. 287–288.

[24] As translated by Peter Avery, *The Speech of the Birds* (Cambridge, 2001), p. 378.

with the Simurgh or utterly separate from it. This is the Sufi 'harmony of opposites' given witty and fabulous form.

At the same time, *The Speech of the Birds* is a deeply personal work. We may not know much about Attar's life but we feel that we know him well from his poetry. To God he cries, 'Rescue me and come to my aid/ How long must I wave my hands about my head like a fly?' And sometimes his lines are simply astonishing; in describing the position of the world in space, he writes: 'So what is it all on? On nothing/Nothing being nothing, all of this is nothing but nothing.'[25]

The influence of Attar's work spread among Shi'i readers and was virtually adopted as their own, all the more so as Sufism itself became increasingly popular with the Shi'a, both Twelver and Ismaili, in succeeding centuries. As Attar said, addressing himself:

> Oh Attar, you have over the world been scattering
> The musk-bladder of mysteries, a hundred thousand every moment!
> Because of you the world's horizons are perfume-filled,
> And by you the world's lovers are aroused.[26]

Conclusion

What, then, distinguishes Shi'i literature from that of other Muslim literary traditions? Like their Sunni counterparts, Shi'i poets write long odes, or *qasidas*, as well as short lyrics – the *ghazal* in particular – and prose writers resort to elaborate rhyming prose. Nevertheless, there are distinctive features. For one, a profound reverence for the imams, beginning with Ali, permeates the literature. Ali is at once the model and the mainspring of Shi'i literature. For another, an abiding sense of the contrast between outer and inner truth, the *zahir* and the *batin*, characterises most Shi'i literary works. This is evident not only in explicitly religious texts but in ostensibly 'secular' productions. Such Persian poets as Hafiz constantly draw on a double register: the rose, the nightingale, the lock of the beloved's hair, the moon. These images are at once themselves, real roses and real moons, and symbols of some transcendent beauty and truth hinted at but never completely grasped by the senses. When Hafiz alludes to Joseph (Yusuf) as 'the moon of Canaan', he is simultaneously linking the Quranic Joseph to his scriptural origins and

---

[25] Avery, p. 13. In the Persian the play on 'nothing' (*hich*) has hypnotic effect: *Pas hamah bar chist? bar hich ast o-bas; hich hich-ast in hamah hich-ast o-bas.*

[26] Avery, *Speech of the Birds*, p. 396.

presenting him as a reflection of the divine beauty, just as the moon itself reflects the light of the sun.

Moreover, the underlying impulse of the immemorial oral tradition is discernible throughout the literature of the Shi'a, as I noted at the outset. In this sense, the literary tradition reveals certain affinities with Sufi mystical traditions; both look inward and outward at the same time, both gaze on creation with a respect for its external manifestations which are, however, viewed as 'signs' of a deeper, more hidden truth. Shi'i literature is thus animated throughout by what the great Andalusian mystic Ibn Arabi described as 'the breath of the Merciful', a living breath beneath the fixed form of words.

This chapter has afforded the merest glimpse of Shi'i literary achievement over a span of several centuries. Later, especially under the Safawids, when Twelver Shi'ism was made the official religion of Iran, a great flowering of Shi'i culture occurred in theology, philosophy and literature. The School of Isfahan alone, numbering such towering figures as the philosophers Mir Damad and Mulla Sadra, revived philosophy within the Islamic tradition, infusing it with Sufism and bringing it to new heights of metaphysical speculation.

Then there is the rich popular literature that has existed side-by-side with the great works produced in the 'Shi'i century'. Often oral rather than written, this literature includes folk poetry, song, prayers and meditations from the earliest period to the present day. It has offered spiritual comfort and inspiration to believers for centuries and is often daily on their lips. One of the most renowned of these works is the *Sahifa Sajjadiyya*, or the 'Page of al-Sajjad' (a *sajjad* being one who is constantly prostrate in prayer); this is the reverential title by which the Imam Zayn al-Abidin, to whom the collection of prayers is ascribed, is known. Here is one of his prayers:

> O God, I call You to witness – and You are sufficient witness –
> And I call Your heaven and Your earth to witness
> And Your angels and Your other creatures who inhabit them
> In this my day, this my hour, this my night,
> And this my resting place, that I bear witness
> That You are God, other than whom there is no God,
> Upholding judgment, clement to your servants,
> Master of the kingdom, Compassionate to creatures,
> And that Muhammad is Your servant
> And Your Messenger,
> Your chosen from among Your creatures.[27]

---

[27] Zayn al-Abidin, *The Psalms of Islam: Al-Sahifa al-Sajjadiyya*, tr. William C.

We began with Nasir-i Khusraw's distinction between spoken and written language and so it is perhaps fitting to conclude with the living breath of a spoken, or sung, poem composed in Persian and much loved throughout Tajikistan and Afghanistan. This folk poem, which combines Sufi and Shi'i elements in praise of Ali, has a strong refrain, *Dam Hamah Dam Ali Ali*, or 'with every breath Ali, Ali', that lends itself irresistibly to chant:

> I am the trusted cupbearer:
> With every breath Ali, Ali
> I am a Sufi, pure of heart:
> With every breath, Ali, Ali.
>
> For Ali, dear to God, I burn with love:
> With every breath, Ali, Ali
> I am swept with secret melody:
> With every breath, Ali, Ali...
>
> You are the Law's high lord,
> You are the Master of the Path,
> You are the truth within the Truth:
> With every breath, Ali, Ali...[28]

Chittick (London, 1988), pp. 32–36 (slightly modified).

[28] This is my own version from the transcription of the oral poem.

Further Reading

De Bruijn, J. T. P. and Ehsan Yarshater, ed. *General Introduction to Persian Literature.* London, 2008.

De Callatay, Godefroid. *Ikhwan al-Safaʾ: A Brotherhood of Idealists on the Fringe of Orthodox Islam.* Oxford, 2006.

El-Bizri, Nader, ed. *The Ikhwan al-Safaʾ and Their Rasaʾil: An Introduction.* Oxford, 2008.

Hunsberger, Alice C. *Nasir Khusraw: The Ruby of Badakhshan, a Portrait of the Persian Poet, Traveller and Philosopher.* London, 2000.

Kraemer, Joel L. *Humanism in the Renaissance of Islam.* Leiden, 1992.

Kuiper, Kathleen, ed. *Islamic Art, Literature, and Culture.* New York, 2010.

Mozaffari, Nahid, ed. *Strange Times, My Dear: The PEN Anthology of Contemporary Iranian Literature.* New York, 2005.

al-Mutanabbi, Abu Tayyib. *Poems of al-Mutanabbi: A Selection with Introduction, Translations and Notes,* tr. A. J. Arberry. Cambridge, 1967.

Nasir-i Khusraw. *Jamiʿ al-Hikmatayn,* tr. Eric Ormsby as *Between Reason and Revelation: Twin Wisdoms Reconciled.* London, 2012.

Ritter, Hellmut. *The Ocean of the Soul: Man, the World, and God in the Stories of Farid al-Din ʿAttar.* Leiden, 2003.

13

Music

William Sumits

The ethnic, linguistic and cultural diversity of the Shi'i world is readily apparent in the distinctive musical traditions and practices that have evolved in a broad range of communities. A full account that does justice to these richly varied musical traditions is beyond the scope of the present chapter. Rather, we will highlight the musical diversity of the Shi'i world through a focus on selected repertoires, genres and styles performed by master musicians from two countries that figure prominently in the Shi'i world: Tajikistan and Azerbaijan. We will delve into traditional musical practices in the large Shi'i communities in these countries, in order to explore the delicate dialectic between the spiritual and secular, sectarian and universal, and traditional and contemporary as they are expressed in and through music. As well, we will inquire into how the intentions and beliefs of specific performers influence and interact with their audiences' perceptions in a variety of social settings.

These settings include concert tours and artistic residencies in Western Europe and North America organised under the auspices of the Aga Khan Music Initiative. Since its founding in 2000, this Initiative has played a key role in the preservation, revitalisation, further evolution, and global dissemination of indigenous musical traditions from Central Asia and historically related parts of the Muslim world. As a programme of the Aga Khan Trust for Culture – part of the Aga Khan Development Network, a private endeavour going back nearly half a century – the Music Initiative reifies the Network's principles and strategies in the field of artistic and cultural life. Its activities link exceptionally gifted performers with worldwide audiences, and it is these links that have generated the rich body of performance-related experience discussed and interpreted in this chapter.

It is rare to find the term 'Shi'i music' used as a specific description. Originally a sectarian demarcation that emerged as a result of historical disputes regarding the succession of political and religious authority in the centuries after the death of the Prophet Muhammad, the distinction between Sunni and Shi'i beliefs and practices is most noticeable in the realms of theology, religious statehood and the history of Islamic political authority. Music, along with the fine arts and natural sciences, has largely eluded such a binary classification; hence, one is unlikely to find scholarly discussions of Shi'i astronomy or other secular sciences as such. In music, 'Shi'i' might only be used to describe the recitation of elegiac poetic forms such as *soz* or *marsiya*, which serve to commemorate the martyrdom of Imam Husayn – and are often used in collective mourning rituals associated with Shi'i holy days such as *ashura* or *arba'in*, or in theatrical reenactments depicting the heroic deeds of Husayn at Karbala.

For many listeners, the sung poetry and rhythmic component of mournful recitations such as *soz* and *marsiya* do indeed constitute music; yet this is rarely the case for participating performers and audiences. The reason is quite clear: music has held an ambiguous status throughout the course of Islamic history, at times dismissed by religious scholars as a forbidden profane art that encourages salacious behaviour. It is partly due to the antagonistic stance of certain religious authorities that 'music' has long been officially disassociated from 'religion'.[1] Nevertheless, music has always continued to play a prominent role in the cultural and spiritual life of communities and societies throughout the Islamic world. It comes as no surprise, then, that aspects of Shi'i thought and philosophy have naturally found their way into music performance and theory.

Countless musical genres and repertoires exist across the Shi'i world. These include classical traditions such as Azerbaijani *mugham*, Iranian *dastgah*, Baluchi *zahirig*, and Kurdish and Iraqi *maqam*. There are also many hundreds of folk genres, styles and repertoires scattered across the region. Traditional music everywhere is intimately tied to the life of the community that produces and endorses it. Ingrained in community life, music often serves as a vehicle for expressing the collective ideals of the community or cultural group it represents. At once a creative and artistic expression, traditional music reinforces the cultural identity and moral code of its host society. Passed down from generation to generation, traditional music is also a signifier of cultural history, and, as such, is cared for and maintained by musicians through the support of their own community. As bearers of tradition and transmitters of cultural patrimony, musicians act as teachers and role models as well as harbingers of joy and grief at community events, from births to weddings and funerals.

---

[1]   See, for example, Seyyed Hossein Nasr, 'Islam and Music: The Legal and the Spiritual Dimension', in Lawrence E. Sullivan, ed., *Enchanting Powers: Music in the World's Religions* (Cambridge, MA, 1997), pp. 219–236.

Figure 13.1 Young man sits in a tree playing a lute, with companions, by Abd Allah Shirazi, 1582.

Musical traditions have an innate strength that symbolises the cultural identity, moral worldview and creative heritage of the societies in which they develop. Treasured and nurtured both by musicians and communities of listeners, traditions are nonetheless subject to the vicissitudes of our technology-driven contemporary world and face many challenges to continuing development. Caught between tradition and modernity, preservation and innovation, young generations of music makers and music listeners in our digital age have access to so many options that they may overlook or undervalue their own musical heritage. Time-honoured traditions are left in the shadows of the perceived prestige of modern pop hits emerging from Europe, America, Turkey and Iran. Today's instant access to an all but limitless variety of music-making from around the world is a two-edged sword. On the one hand, it is a positive development with the potential to contribute to the creative development of diverse kinds of music-making; on the other hand, it is a colonising and homogenising force, one that underscores the need for dedicated cultural development programmes to help ensure that traditional music is not overrun by the juggernaut of digitally disseminated commercial pop music.

The Aga Khan Music Initiative

Among organisations devoted to long-term development in the Muslim world, the Aga Khan Development Network occupies a unique niche. Its many agencies and units span the arenas of economic, social and cultural development, the latter being the focus of the Aga Khan Trust for Culture.[2] Founded in 1988 as a private, non-denominational, philanthropic foundation and based in Geneva, Switzerland, the Trust for Culture integrates the work of a half dozen programmes, among the youngest of which is the Aga Khan Music Initiative.

The Music Initiative was created with a remit to collaborate with local traditional musicians in order to preserve, transmit, develop and promote traditional music and musicians in Central Asia. Over time, the Music Initiative has expanded to include programmes in the greater Middle East, North Africa, West Africa and South Asia. Its activities comprise four main areas: music education and mentoring, including the support of key musical tradition bearers; new works, creation and commissioning; music performance and outreach; and artistic production and dissemination. Its objectives are to assist in the revitalisation of important musical repertoires and their transmission by tradition-bearers; build cultural institutions that can be managed and

---

[2]   Available online at: http://www.akdn.org/aktc.

maintained by local organisations and musicians; and support innovative musicians and music educators who are developing new approaches to performing, teaching and disseminating tradition-based music. The musicians discussed in this chapter are all engaged in long-term partnerships with the Initiative. Through its international concert and touring programmes, they have been bringing their musical heritage in contemporary forms to the ears of global audiences.

This partnership has come to create and sustain what is in effect a cosmopolitan musical family. After repeated meetings at international concert performances and festivals, the boundaries of their respective traditions have become eminently permeable, creating auspicious conditions for the birth of new music rooted in multiple traditions. The result has been an ongoing exercise in musical pluralism, fuelled by the virtuosity and innovation of world-class musicians whose talent serves as an incubator for new music. These experiences have had a powerful and long-lasting impact on the participating musicians, and have given them unique opportunities to realise a new potential in collective musical creativity. Such experiences can also produce a long-lasting influence on the development of entire traditions.

Historically, the 'golden' eras of musical creativity have grown out of just such a coalescence of cultures that occurred under the patronage of music-loving rulers. Take, for instance, the cultural efflorescence of 15th-century Herat under the Timurid princes, or the 10th–11th-century 'House of Wisdom' at the Abbasid court in Baghdad, which drew on the erudition of the most talented musicians and music theorists of the Abbasid empire. The cultural development activities of the Aga Khan Music Initiative evoke a similar atmosphere of multicultural musical creativity, and have produced admirable results. While this kind of cultural patronage was once the domain of kings and emirs, the role of patron has more recently come to be fulfilled most prominently by local governments and international cultural development organisations.

The Music Initiative takes a hands-on approach to development initiatives and plays an active role in all of its programmes – not merely as a sponsor, but as strategist, on-the-ground collaborator and facilitator. At the heart of this is education: developing and testing newly created teaching and learning methodologies, setting up teacher-training mechanisms, operating talent-support centres, and presenting performance and artist-in-residence programmes that give students an opportunity to experience the creative challenges of intercultural music-making. Music Initiative residencies and concerts presented at a wide range of academic and cultural institutions in Europe and North America have cultivated three distinct but related approaches to performance. First, performance of traditional repertoires in a style that is itself traditional; second, performance that, while inspired and informed by tradition, is expressed in a contemporary artistic language; and third, performance that draws on the traditions of two or more historically related but distinct regional traditions. The musicians described here, while all strongly rooted in tradition, are also innovators, and have been referred to as 'traditional innovators' or 'innovators in tradition'.

Traditional Innovators in Badakhshan

Among the most accomplished musical collaborators with the Music Initiative is a group from Khorog, Tajikistan called the Badakhshan Ensemble.

The ensemble takes its name from the eponymous region, centred in the Pamir Mountains of eastern Tajikistan and northeastern Afghanistan, often called the 'roof of the world' in old Persian treatises and travelogues. Isolated by some of the world's highest mountain ranges, Badakhshan has preserved languages and cultural traditions that are not found anywhere else in Asia.

Music is often an important vehicle for collective spiritual expression at community events and religious functions in Badakhshan. The population adheres to the Ismaili branch of Shi'i Islam, and preserves a number of distinctive forms of music associated with the community's practices and beliefs. The most important of these are *falak*, *lalai* and *maddoh*. The *maddoh* tradition of Badakhshan is distinct from other traditions

Figure 13.2 The Badakhshan Ensemble.

bearing the same name in the greater Middle East. For example, in much of the Arab world, *madih* refers to a genre of panegyric poetry in praise of the Prophet Muhammad; this is often sung *a cappella* (as well as to the accompaniment of musical instruments at religious gatherings), especially during the *mawlid* celebrations that mark the Prophet's birthday. In Badakhshan, however, the performance of *maddoh* includes prayers interspersed with Quranic verses and poetry in praise of the Prophet and his family and successors, while drawing heavily on the classical heritage of mystical Persian-Tajik poetry. The works of the great Sufi poets of the past such as Shams Tabrizi (d. 1248), Hafiz (ca. 1315–1390), Sa'di (ca. 1210–1292), Jami (1414–1492), Rudaki (858–941), and Hilali (ca. 1470–1529) are commonly sung in *maddoh* performances. The poetry of the great Ismaili saint and scholar Nasir-i Khusraw (1004–after 1070) also forms a vital part of the sung texts, but the majority of the poetry sung in *maddoh* in Badakhshan belongs to Rumi (1207–1273). *Maddoh* also includes many apocryphal poems that are typically attributed to Rumi or Shams Tabrizi, as well as poems by local Ismaili poets whose names can no longer be remembered. The broad variety of lyrical content reflects the spiritual message of music that is capable of rising above sectarian differences, by appealing to universal aspects of the human spiritual experience.

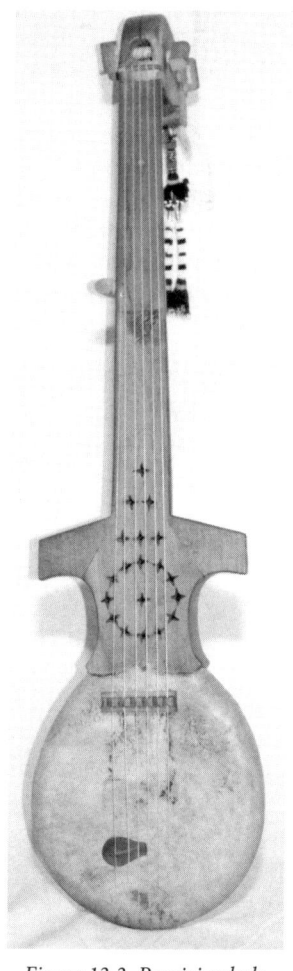

The lyrical content of *maddoh* is complemented by the unique sonorities of the instrumental and rhythmic accompaniment that evoke a contemplative and enigmatic state in the listener. The primary instrument used in *maddoh* is the Pamiri *rubab*, a long-necked fretless lute with gut strings and a thick sheepskin that covers its sound chamber.

According to local beliefs, the *rubab* originated as a Divine gift from heaven, created by God to resemble a human form. The *rubab* is understood as a medium that can help bring human consciousness into a state of perpetual praise and closeness with the divine when used to accompany singers of *maddoh* and other spiritual

Figure 13.3 Pamiri rubab.

genres, such as *falak* or *naat*. Because these forms are so connected to the sacred principles inherent in their spiritual and religious beliefs, they closely adhere to the hierarchy of ethical and aesthetic principles that emanate from those beliefs. In Badakhshan there is a common and sincere belief in the healing properties of music, and it is not unusual for musicians to be invited to perform for those who have fallen ill. Human health is seen as the harmony and balance of physical, mental and spiritual presence, and the audition of *maddoh* has the power to positively reinforce both the mental and spiritual components of health by instilling in the listener the ethical, aesthetic and spiritual worldview conveyed in the music and lyrics of *maddoh*.

One of the most talented and sought-after *maddoh* singers in Badakhshan today is Aqnazar Alovatov (b. 1970). Alovatov is often called upon to sing at religious celebrations and at informal religious gatherings that occur weekly, usually on Thursdays, where *maddoh* performance plays a central role. Alovatov is quick to point out that *maddoh* performance and audition is also a form of moral and spiritual training, both for the performing musicians and for listeners from the community. The moral and spiritual content of *maddoh* is often concealed within mystical allegories and complex symbolism and may be neither apparent nor accessible to all the attendees. Thus, such gatherings are often facilitated by a local religious leader, or *khalifa*, who provides an exegesis explaining the inner meanings of the sung texts.

Alovatov stresses that 'every text used in *maddoh*, whether from Sa'di or Rumi, whether it is about love or about God, has many layers of meaning'. He explains further that 'these layers of inner meaning are educational and can convey important teachings about moral character, right livelihood, empathy, honesty and courage'. The moral qualities of singers who perform *maddoh* must be on a par with their teachings. 'It is also important that the *maddoh* singer be a person of strong moral character,' says Alovatov. 'The stronger the moral code and ethics of the *maddoh* singer, the stronger the message and *baraka* of the *maddoh* performance will be, and the stronger the effect it will have on listeners.'

The significance of inner meaning in music and poetry is a characteristic feature of esoteric tendencies in Sufi and Shi'i philosophy and thought, and is particularly developed in the Ismaili branch of Shi'ism. Scholars have long noted the close connections between Sufism and Shi'ism, and pointed out that mystical and esoteric aspects of Sufism are deeply ingrained in the philosophical and spiritual thought that permeates much of the Shi'i world. Indeed, aspects of esoteric Shi'i theology and philosophy surely comprise the wellspring from which many of the Sufi orders developed. The imams' ability to understand and interpret esoteric meaning, and the concepts of *zahir* and *batin* (apparent versus inner meaning) are all signifiers of the esoteric tendencies of Shi'i

Figure 13.4 Aqnazar Alovatov.

Figure 13.5 Jonboz Dushanbiev.

thought. The sixth imam of Shiʻi Islam, Jaʻfar al-Sadiq, was not only a polymath but is also considered to be the founding figure of the mystical and occult sciences; the famed alchemist Jabir b. Hayyan (d. 804) claimed to have learned everything he knew from Jaʻfar al-Sadiq. Music was usually classified as one of the mathematical sciences, but certain elements of the occult have historically found their way into the 'science' of music, both in the East and the West.[3]

One of the most important treatises on music from the early Islamic period is closely tied to Ismaili Shiʻism. The 'Epistle (*Risala*) on Music' is part of a 10th-century compendium of treatises written by a hermetic brotherhood of philosophers, possibly from Basra, known as the Ikhwan al-Safa, or 'Brethren of Purity'.[4] Their work appears to represent the ideas of the early Ismaili movement, and has been championed by many later Ismaili thinkers as a nascent representation of Ismaili thought. The Ikhwan identify themselves spiritually with *tasawwuf* (mysticism), and the organisation of their brotherhood reflects the structure of many Sufi brotherhoods, but their philosophical ideas are most closely connected with early Shiʻism and Ismailism. Their treatise on music presents a system that is closely tied to early Islamic cosmology, and integrates many Neoplatonic Graeco-Roman elements that were assimilated into Islamic science during the 8th–10th centuries, when there was a flurry of translation activity consolidating all of the knowledge of peoples that had come into the fold of the rapidly expanding Islamic empire.

The Ikhwan al-Safa liken the four strings of the Arabic lute (*ud*) to the four primary elements that make up the cosmos, the four bodily humours that are the basis of human health, the four directions and seasons, and a long list of other quaternaries including colours, scents and precious stones.[5] The Ikhwan claimed to be followers of Pythagoras, and supported ideas about the 'harmony of the spheres'. They tell us that 'the movements of the spheres and stars are clearly notes and melodies'. The Ikhwan also tell us that they 'created music that was used in the hospitals. It relieved the pain of the afflicted, and counteracted their illness, helping to heal the sick'. In this system, music is tied to every

[3] For a historical survey of the influence of mysticism and occult sciences on musical thought, see Joscelyn Godwin, *Harmonies of Heaven and Earth: Mysticism in Music from Antiquity to the Avant-Garde* (Rochester, VT, 1987).
[4] See Nader El-Bizri, ed., *Epistles of the Brethren of Purity: the Ikhwan al-Safa' and Their Rasa'il: An Introduction* (Oxford, 2008).
[5] Henry George Farmer, 'The Influence of Music from Arabic Sources', in Eckhard Neubauer, ed., *The Science of Music in Islam*, vols 1–2: *Studies in Oriental Music* (Frankfurt am Main, 1997).

aspect of the surrounding natural world and has the power to affect human health through its ties to the old system of humoural medicine.[6]

It is informative to compare the musical thought of the Ikhwan al-Safa with the musical thought of modern Ismaili musicians living in Badakhshan. There can be no question that music traditions are in a constant state of evolution, and that today's music surely sounds completely different from what Ismaili musicians were playing and singing in the 10th century. Yet there is certainly a degree of continuity in musical thought from the Ikhwan al-Safa to present-day Ismaili musicians in Badakhshan. The healing properties of music are recognised and continue to be applied in practice in Badakhshan today. According to Ghulomshoh Safarov, a singer and instrumentalist in the Badakhshan Ensemble, 'Music is used for healing, and as a treatment for illness. Often, when someone has fallen ill, the family will invite musicians to come and sing *maddoh* for the afflicted. *Maddoh* can have a positive effect, it relaxes patients and brings happiness to their hearts, allowing them to heal their illness more easily and quickly.'

One could even go so far as to imagine that the Ikhwan's acceptance of the ancient doctrine of the 'harmony of the spheres' has found a distant echo in the Badakhshani vocal genre known as *falak*. The term *falak* literally means 'heavens' or 'firmament', and is another genre of song that is believed to possess healing attributes. It is sung at funerals, as part of *maddoh* performances, or independently as a form of supplication. Its subject often deals with the mutability of fate, reminding the listener that human experience is governed by higher forces that are at work in the universe. *Falak* can convey a wide range of intense feelings that are present in human spiritual and emotional experience, and is often performed as a kind of collective catharsis mediated by musicians. The Ikhwan al-Safa also speak frequently of this emotional power of music, for example, in the following story about an instrumentalist who 'played the strings in a way that made everyone at the gathering laugh from the joy and pleasure that was entering their souls. He then changed the tuning of the strings and played in a different mode that made them all weep from the sadness of the heart. Then he changed the tuning again, and played a melody that caused everyone at the gathering to fall asleep peacefully'. It is music's ability to evoke emotions and to convey meanings cloaked in melodies and metaphors that has imbued it with an inner power to arouse contemplation, wonder, ecstasy or courage in its listeners and performers.

---

[6]   Amnon Shiloah, tr., *The Epistle on Music of the Ikhwan al-Safa (Baghdad, tenth century)* (Tel Aviv, 1978).

Figure 13.6 Soheba Davlatshoeva.

The power of the inner meaning of music to reach even uninitiated listeners has been oft repeated by the Badakhshan Ensemble's founder and director, Soheba Davlatshoeva. An accomplished performer, singer, dancer and instrumentalist, Davlatshoeva joined forces with the Aga Khan Music Initiative more than a decade ago. As the musical director of the Badakhshan Ensemble, she has had many opportunities to share the musical traditions of Badakhshan with audiences across the globe. 'To be a successful performer', Davlatshoeva explained, 'you yourself have to enter the inner form or character of the music and then, through a kind of mimesis, convey this form or character to your listeners.'[7] She elaborated on this saying, 'when we sing, we want to sing so that listeners feel our inner meaning, or *batin*, and understand what we're singing about. This can happen independently of words, through music itself.' Davlatshoeva offered an example of what she meant. 'Once we were giving a concert in Germany, and I sang *lalaik*. *Lalaik* is often about grief. If someone dies, women will lament, and one of them will sing *lalaik*. After the concert, a woman came up to me, and said, "I listened to your song, and I didn't understand the words, but I understood that it was about grief. You sang it for us in a way that came from your heart." What this woman was

---

[7] Conversation with Theodore Levin, 30 November 2013, Dushanbe, Tajikistan.

responding to was the melodic mode I was singing in. As a professional singer, you have to feel this mode and convey it. The mode works almost like words.'

For Soheba Davlatshoeva, musical sound is capable of conveying inner meaning, or *batin*, and it is the duty of performers to understand and transmit this *batin* through their music, regardless of linguistic barriers. This kind of musical *ethos*, which was once common across in the Islamic world, is no longer ubiquitous. But it does appear to have been firmly ingrained in the musical thinking of Ismaili musicians from Badakhshan down to the present day.

Spiritual Audition of Classical Mugham from Azerbaijan

Far from Badakhshan, an audience sat in silent anticipation, absorbed in every sound while an ensemble of instrumentalists gently carved out improvisatory melodic motifs underneath the powerful voices of two singers – an older man and a younger woman, who alternated verses in a vocal antiphony:

> If it is the devil who robs people of their faith by tricking them,
> So why then is it this fairy-faced one who robs my faith from me?
> Oh bow-eyebrowed one, the arrow of your capricious glance has wounded me,
> Press your tresses into my wound, but don't let me bleed to death.
> The heart drags the body to the crossroads to be sacrificed,
> Like Hajis taking a sacrifice to Mina mountain.
> It is love, my friend, that takes religion and faith away from the people.
> It is Sanan,[8] however, who receives the people's pointless blame.
> Said the believer in the One God when he saw that face framed by tresses:
> This is a Hindu child who takes a Quran to school.
> Whoever should wear a shroud at love's gathering place,

---

[8]   Sheikh Sanan was a Sufi disciple famous for falling in love with a Christian girl whom he pursued, hopelessly, as part of his spiritual training. Sanan is mentioned in Farid al-Din Attar's 12th-century Persian epic poem *The Conference of the Birds*, and emerges in Turkic folklore in the 14th-century epic tale 'Shayk Sanan', attributed to Ashik Gulsheri. In Azerbaijani oral and written tradition, Sheikh Sanan is often portrayed as an Azerbaijani who falls in love with a Georgian girl.

The lover from the dawn of time will take him naked to the Day of Judgment
Do not drag Sayyid, who belongs to no sect, towards the tavern,
Just try to find a Muslim who will take this heathen to the Ka'ba.

These verses by the great Azeri poet Seyyid Azim Shirvani (1835–1888) were being sung by the world-renowned Azerbaijani singers Alim Qasimov and his daughter, Fargana Qasimova, to an audience at once enraptured by their virtuosic vocal techniques and surprised by the meaning of the poetry they were singing.

While Azeri audiences may be familiar with the kind of poetic motifs and symbols used by Shirvani, this particular audience consisted primarily of Americans and a diverse mix of other non-Azeri listeners. The venue was a concert that took place within the framework of a North American tour organised by the Aga Khan Music Initiative. During concerts that the Initiative curates, listeners are able to follow the lyrics, sung in Azerbaijani, thanks to the use of supertitled translations projected on a large screen behind the musicians.

The expressions of surprise written on many faces in the audience indicated their unfamiliarity with poetic devices that portend paradoxical symbols and juxtapose seemingly contradictory ideals – for

Figure 13.7 Alim and Fargana Qasimov.

example, as in the work of Shirvani, whose verses pit love against faith as two seemingly incompatible or competing forces. While admitting his own heathen and love-torn state, Shirvani simultaneously expresses longing to escape the vicissitudes of love by returning to faith. It is not unusual for Shirvani to juxtapose Hindu, Christian and specifically Shi'i motifs in the same poem, while professing that his own beliefs are non-sectarian.

To understand the reasons behind these seemingly contradictory expressions, it helps to understand Shirvani's background and upbringing. He was born into a family of Shi'i clerics and was sent to Iraq for his early religious education. He later absconded from the clergy and became a teacher, poet and enlightener. He claimed that he followed in the poetic footsteps of Fuzuli (ca. 1494–1556), one of the greatest poets in the Azerbaijani literary canon, whose best-known work is an extended *masnavi* (a Persian poetic form consisting of rhyming couplets) that tells the classic love story of Layla and Majnun. While Fuzuli is known primarily as a Sufi-inspired poet of love, Shirvani's poetry draws on his religious education and background, and is heavily imbued with the mystical symbolism of multiple spiritual traditions, as well as spiritual love. The intellectual atmosphere that shaped Shirvani's poetic activities pervaded Azerbaijani cultural life in the latter half of the 19th century, a period of vibrant literary and musical activity that is considered by many music connoisseurs and historians to have been a golden age for performance of the classical *mugham* tradition.

Mugham is the tradition of indigenous classical music that Azerbaijanis consider a national art and that is held in high regard by the entire population of Azerbaijan. It consists of a vast repertoire of melodies and songs – a living compendium of the musical heritage of Azerbaijan. The term *mugham* is a derivative of the Arabic word *maqam* that, since the 13th century, has been used in various forms across a wide geographic area to refer to the classical traditions of art music practised in the greater Middle East and Central Asia. A term imbued with multiple meanings and a long period of historical evolution, '*maqam*' in its most basic definition denotes a melodic 'mode' along with the traditional guidelines for its performance, but the term has also come to refer broadly to the domain of classical music and music theory across the Islamic world. In the greater Caucasus region, a *mugham* is at once a musical mode and a non-metred form of vocal improvisation. It also has an extended meaning that denotes a musical suite linking together multiple melodies, songs, and instrumental tunes from the large repertoire of local classical music.

The esteemed writer, teacher and musicologist Mir Mohsun Navvab (1833–1918), a contemporary of the poet Shirvani, was a central figure in musical and literary activities of the greater Caucasus region during the second half of the 19th century. Navvab was a close colleague of the legendary *mugham* singer Haji Husu. During the 1880s, Navvab and Husu organised musical symposia that brought together the finest singers and instrumentalists to discuss musical aesthetics, rhythms, singing techniques and the organisation of the classic *mugham* repertoire. Participants included names today celebrated in Azerbaijani music circles: Meshedi Jamil Amirov, Islam Abdullaev, Seyyid Shushinski, Sadiqjan and others. Many of these musicians are said to have attended Navvab's school and learned the subtleties of *mugham* performance from Navvab himself.[9]

The musicians and poets who contributed to this 19th-century renaissance of music and literature, which was centred in Shusha, the cultural capital of the Qarabagh region, but extended across much of Azerbaijan, continue to be considered the historical progenitors of the modern *mugham* tradition. Their names are often recalled in musical literature today and their rare recordings from the early 20th century are highly sought after. They represent the historical forebears of the contemporary *mugham* tradition – a tradition carried on today by many virtuosic singers and instrumentalists, among whom the most celebrated is the singer Alim Qasimov. In Azerbaijan, it is difficult to have a conversation about *mugham* without mentioning the name of Alim Qasimov as well as, increasingly, the name of his daughter and musical disciple, Fargana Qasimova.

The Qasimovs, however, are not conservators or revivalists of historical forms of *mugham* performance, but rather, musical innovators who have breathed fresh life into the already vibrant living tradition of *mugham*. In their riveting performances, the role of the traditional vocal soloist is split in two, with father and daughter alternating poetic couplets and, at times, joining their voices in an intimate contrapuntal tapestry, as they did in the performance of Shirvani's poetry described above. These vocal lines are in turn interwoven with the melodic lines of a small consort of instruments – spike fiddle (*kamancha*), long-necked lute (*tar*), oboe (*balaban*), double-headed hand drum (*naghara*), and at times, *ud*. This ensemble also represents an innovation, for traditionally, *mugham* singers perform with only a *kamacha* and *tar*, while the singer plays a small frame drum (*daf*). Alim Qasimov has often said that, were it possible, he would perform *mugham* with an entire orchestra so as to express to the fullest a *mugham*'s diverse moods, colours and emotions.

When Alim Qasimov sings the verses of Seyyid Azim Shirvani before an international audience of listeners from diverse backgrounds, he

[9]   Zemfira Safarova, *The 'Vuzuhul Argam'* (Interpretation of Music in Numbers) *of Mir Mohsun Navvab* (Baku, Azerbaijan, 1989), pp. 11–12.

provides a brilliant illustration of *mugham*'s innate power to transcend sectarian differences, offering a universal appeal to the human spirit that can be enjoyed by audiences everywhere. Qasimov is himself a pious Shi'i Muslim, yet in a concert situation, his personal beliefs are not immediately discernable to listeners unfamiliar with his background. It is in large part due to Qasimov's charismatic and universal approach to *mugham* performance that the *mugham* tradition has become accessible to listeners worldwide. In 1999, Qasimov was awarded the title of UNESCO 'Voice of the Universe' for his outstanding contribution to promoting the *mugham* tradition through his virtuosic performances.

Even if Qasimov's personal spiritual beliefs as a Shi'i Muslim are not usually apparent in his demeanour on a concert stage, they inform his performance aesthetic, and may also govern his own experience as a performer of *mugham*. As a versatile master of *mugham* singing, Qasimov adapts his repertoire and choice of poetry to suit the parameters of a specific performance event or occasion. Although Qasimov recognises the universal appeal of *mugham* and its ability to touch the uninitiated, he has often spoken of *mugham* as music for connoisseurs. While *mugham* music may have the power to affect even the uninitiated, he believes that its true meaning can only be comprehended by those who have cultivated a deep and intimate understanding of the *mugham* repertoire and its expressive nuances. Performers and listeners who possess this kind of intimate understanding of *mugham* performance and improvisation, and who themselves have an intrinsically spiritual nature, can reach states of spiritual ecstasy induced by musical performance. Those who are able to reap spiritual benefit from the music are not limited to Azeri *mugham* specialists, but can include any musicians and listeners with a highly refined music aesthetic and musical *ethos*, and an innate spirituality.

Qasimov refers to the states of spiritual rapture induced by performing or listening to *mugham* as *hal*. *Hal* is originally an Arabic word that means 'state of being', but Qasimov uses the term to denote a state of spiritual ecstasy. For him, attaining *hal* is one of the primary goals of music performance and audition, but also one of the most difficult to achieve. In order to reach such a state, performers must embody a musical aesthetic that transcends technical virtuosity, and their understanding must go deeper than musicological expertise. For example, a musician who has attained a high level of technical virtuosity, and who may be comfortable performing the entire classical repertoire of *mugham*, may still not have what it takes to reach or induce states of *hal* through musical performance. This ability arises from a musician's own spiritual understanding and the integration of his or her spiritual beliefs into a unified performance aesthetic and practice.[10] In this way, singing serves as a form of spiritual practice for Qasimov, and as a vehicle for his own personal form of worship. Its capacity to carry him into a high spiritual state, or *hal*, is a way of bringing him closer to God. It is not unusual for him to visit historical and religious sites while travelling internationally on concert tours, and he will often retreat into a corner which has good acoustics and begin to sing, freely improvising on his favourite poetic verses.

Alim Qasimov remains a unique example. His perennial curiosity and charismatic temperament make him appear to be perpetually discovering something new. He can perform the same programme hundreds of times, yet each performance is unique. He has won accolades for his musical innovations while maintaining the deep respect of the most traditional of traditionalists. In an era when the world's most famous singers – whether hailing from the Americas, Europe, Africa or Asia – are almost invariably pop stars, Alim and Fargana Qasimov offers a refreshing counter-example: brilliant innovators in traditional music whose performances have brought them celebrity in Azerbaijan, while at the same time making *mugham* the most celebrated form in the musical repertoire of Azerbaijan.

Despite *mugham*'s status as a central element in the national culture of Azerbaijan, the performance of *mugham* is by no means exclusive to Azerbaijan, or to Azeri musicians. Musical cosmopolitanism has long been an important factor in the development of the region's music, and *mugham* is also performed in other regions of the greater Caucasus, such as Dagestan, Georgia and Armenia. Many connoisseurs of *mugham* consider its homeland to be the disputed region of Qarabagh, which is presently claimed by both Azerbaijan and Armenia – a source of great tension between the two countries. In the 19th and early 20th century, it was common for *mugham* trios to include Azeri, Armenian and Georgian musicians playing together. Alas, this kind of musical cosmopolitanism has become increasingly rare, as nationalist ideas of cultural ownership have permeated musical performance practices as well as state-sponsored cultural activities and music scholarship. In these conditions, the presence of an underlying spirituality in the performance of *mugham*, and in the music and lyrics themselves, becomes even more crucial in preserving the inner meaning of the tradition as it is transmitted to younger generations of performers and audiences.

---

[10] For a parallel with regard to 'authenticity' in Middle Eastern musical performance, see Jonathan Shannon, 'Moving Sounds', in Amyn B. Sajoo, ed., *A Companion to Muslim Cultures* (London, 2012), pp. 165–184, notably at pp. 179–182.

Figure 13.8 Alim Qasimov's ensemble playing at Shirvan Shaz.

Music in the Shiʿi World and Cultural Pluralism

As the programme of a non-sectarian organisation, the Aga Khan Music Initiative has used its resources to bring together musicians from diverse backgrounds to help revitalise traditional repertoires, create new works that transcend geopolitical and religious boundaries, and reunite artistic communities that were once historically tied but have fallen out of touch due to the vicissitudes of history and politics. Under the auspices of the Music Initiative, Shiʿa, Sunnis, Christians, Jews and Hindus, among others, have shared recording studios and concert stages as they strive to convey to worldwide audiences the power of music from Central Asia, the Middle East, North Africa and South Asia. These living heritages share common roots, but have diverged, developing along different cultural paths. The outcome is music that has emerged not only from within the Shiʿi and Sunni worlds, but also from other contexts informed by a tradition of spiritual practice and belief.

Whatever its origin and evolution, music invariably expresses a multitude of meanings linked to the setting of its performance, the intentions of its performers, and the receptiveness of its listeners. While any song, musical work or sacred chant may have a sectarian message in a particular setting for a listener, at another time it may convey a universal spiritual message accessible to anyone from any background. In this way, music can reinforce spiritual and moral ideals in their specific social and cultural milieu – while also leaping over sectarian boundaries by appealing to the universal human experience. This understanding of music seems to have been clear to the late 10th-century Ikhwan al-Safa – the Brethren of Purity, who wrote of music in their Epistle as an 'art which combines the physical and the spiritual,' and that has a 'spiritual effect on souls'.[11] A millennium later, enlightened understandings of music's powers remain much the same. These powers, however, remain tacit until expressed through actual performance. In the end, it is musicians who hold the keys to unlocking music's powers and touching the souls of listeners.

Further Reading and Listening

Alim and Fargana Qasimov: Spiritual Music of Azerbaijan (CD-DVD, booklet notes).

Badakhshan Ensemble: Song and Dance from the Pamir Mountains (CD-DVD, booklet notes), in *The Music of Central Asia*, vol. 5. Smithsonian Folkways Recordings, 2007.

Badakhshan: Mystical Poetry and Songs from the Ismailis of the Pamir Mountains (CD, booklet notes). Pan Records, 1994.

During, Jean. *La Musique traditionnelle de l'Azerbayjan et la science des muqams*. Baden-Baden, 1988.

—— *Musique et extase: L'audition mystique dans la tradition soufie*. Paris, 1988.

—— 'Therapeutic Dimensions of Music in Islamic Culture', in Benjamin Koen, ed., *The Oxford Handbook of Medical Ethnomusicology*. Oxford, 2008.

Koen, Benjamin, 'Music-Prayer-Meditation Dynamics in Healing', in Benjamin Koen, ed., *The Oxford Handbook of Medical Ethnomusicology*. Oxford, 2008.

—— *Beyond the Roof of the World: Music, Prayer, and Healing in the Pamir Mountains*. Oxford, 2008.

Levin, Theodore, Elmira Köchümkulova and Saida Daukeyeva, ed. *The Music of Central Asia*. Bloomington, IN, 2014.

Sullivan, Lawrence E., ed. *Enchanting Powers: Music in the World's Religions*. Cambridge, MA, 1997.

Tomlinson, Gary. *Music in Renaissance Magic: Toward a Historiography of Others*. Chicago, 1994.

Van den Berg, Gabrielle. *Minstrel Poetry from the Pamir Mountains: A Study on the Songs and Poems of the Ismailis of Tajik Badakhshan*. Wiesbaden, 2004.

---

[11] *Epistles of the Brethren of Purity: On Music: An Arabic Critical Edition and English Translation of Epistle 5*, ed. and tr. Owen Wright (Oxford, 2010), pp. 75, 85.

14

Shi'ism in Iranian Cinema

Nacim Pak-Shiraz

The debate over religion and film in Iran can be traced as far back as cinema's public debut in Iran.[1] In a tradition where *shari'a* and *fiqh* (Islamic jurisprudence) as well as *urf* (custom) played an important role, this new Western medium provoked many questions, reactions and heated debates. Some rejected it outright and others argued for its merits. Cinema's position and status in Iran, however, has not been stable and reactions to it have varied. The only time, perhaps, it had been immune to these debates was in its early days, when it remained a private matter of the royal court. The Qajar king, Muzaffar al-Din Shah (r. 1896–1907), was fascinated by cinematography during his trips to Europe and charged his court photographer, Ebrahim Khan Akkasbashi, to bring the first moving camera to Iran in 1900. Akkasbashi's footage, which included royal ceremonies such as circumcision celebrations and religious commemorations, became Iran's first moving images. The earliest films produced in Iran were thus a private enterprise, with screenings confined within the palace walls.

However, the moment moving images were introduced to the public they lost the protection of private space. Instead, they became entangled in a range of socio-political conflicts. While Muzaffar al-Din Shah's memoirs and Akkasbashi's footage provide us with the historical documentation of Iran's first films, there is far less certainty about the dates of the first public cinemas in Iran and the reasons for their closures. In Tehran, the first such movie theatre opened on Cheragh-Gaz Avenue in 1904. However, only a month later, the cinema was forced to shut down. Some argue that this was the result of political disagreements with its founder, and others insist that it was because of the religious pressures

---

[1] This chapter is a summary and update of sections from my book, *Shi'i Islam in Iranian Cinema: Religion and Spirituality in Film* (London, 2011). There are minor changes and alterations to the reprinted sections. The sections on the second period of Ahmadinejad's presidency, recent developments during the first few months of Rouhani's presidency, as well as on diaspora and other cinemas have been specifically written for this publication.

from prominent clerics such as Fazlollah Nuri who condemned its opening during the month of Ramadan.[2] Overall, the clergy and traditionalists harshly opposed the introduction of this new medium, arguing that cinema was morally corrupting and breached Islamic doctrines on visual representation. On the other hand, the educated elite welcomed it as a modernising agent. The subject of Iran's earliest extant film, *Hajj Aqa, the Cinema Actor* (Ovanes Ohanians, 1932) depicted the conflict between religion, tradition and modernity, a dispute that would intensify both in society and on screen.

Cinema was there to stay, however, and it became an important medium in the negotiations of change that took place in Iran. By 1930, the number of theatres across Iran had grown to 33. Ali Issari highlights two main developments between 1930 and 1936 which led cinema to become an important source of communication. In 1932, as part of his modernising policies, Reza Shah Pahlavi banned the performance of the *taziya* (a re-enactment of the events that led to the death of Husayn b. Ali, grandson of the Prophet and early Shi'i Imam), thus forcing the abandonment of major religious gatherings and encouraging instead secular activities and interests. The second development was the banning of the veil in 1936. Although women had attended cinemas before, they were no longer admitted if veiled.[3] Additionally, unlike public ritual gatherings such as at *taziya* and *rowzeh* (sermons about the tragedy of Karbala) where men and women were segregated, in cinemas they were allowed to sit next to each other. Cinema was, therefore, not only a new cultural medium introduced into Iranian Muslim society, but also a social instrument that broke the old social order. Equally, it was not merely that the content of the films and the inappropriate role models offered through the characters posed a threat to the religious classes and their beliefs, but also that by creating a space for mixed-sex entertainment, cinema created a dangerous new 'unIslamic' leisure pastime.

The positions on cinema, however, did not remain static, either amongst the clergy or indeed even among the educated elite. By the 1960s, many Iranian intellectuals had already begun articulating their disenchantment with Western modernity and what it had to offer. This, along with a perceived need to 'return to roots', was also reflected amongst some of the filmmakers. Their films departed from the mainstream, commercial *filmfarsi* genre which comprised tough-guy movies and low-quality melodramas, seeking instead to reflect a nativist 'return to the self'. This trend was referred to as the New Wave Movement. Afterwards,

---

[2]   Negar Mottahedeh, 'Collection and Recollection: On Studying the Early History of Motion Pictures in Iran', *Early Popular Visual Culture*, 6 (2008), p. 114.
[3]   Ali M. Issari, *Cinema in Iran, 1900–1979* (Metuchen, NJ, 1989), p. 71.

during the anti-Shah protests of the late 1970s, some Islamists who had condemned cinema as supportive of the Shah's Westernisation project and US hegemony, burned or demolished 185 cinemas. But Ayatollah Ruhollah Khomeini, who became Iran's supreme leader, reversed his earlier denunciation of cinema as a Western ideological tool detrimental to Islamic values and the development of Iran's youth. Cinema was now cast as a powerful tool that could be put to the service of the Islamic Revolution. In a famous speech at the Behesht-e Zahra cemetery in 1979, he declared:

> Cinema is a modern invention that ought to be used for the sake of educating the people, but as you know, it was used instead to corrupt our youth. It is the misuse of cinema that we are opposed to, a misuse caused by the treacherous policies of our rulers.[4]

Yet it has arguably been one of the most contentious mediums in the Islamic Republic, strictly codified and closely monitored by the Ministry of Culture and Islamic Guidance (MCIG) to ensure its compliance with the Islamic Republic's aspirations. The MCIG codes are not the sole factors controlling which films make it to the screens. There are many cases of post-Revolutionary films that were banned after a short period despite obtaining screening approval from the authorities. For example, even though *The Lizard* (Kamal Tabrizi, 2004), was never officially banned, the clergy's protests resulted in it being removed from the cinemas only a month after its first screening. More recently, in April 2012 the two commercial films *Private Life* (Mohammad-Hosein Farahbakhsh) and *Guidance Patrol* (Saeed Soheili) became other examples of such a ban. The conservatives demonstrated against these two films for what they perceived was a negative depiction of themselves, and the controversies spilt over to the all-important platform of Tehran's Friday prayers. The leader of the Friday prayers admitted he had not seen the films but nonetheless called for the immediate removal of the 'vulgar movies' from the Islamic Republic's screens. However, Ali Janati, President Rouhani's Minister of Culture and Islamic Guidance, announced in late November 2013 that his ministry would be the sole monitor of cultural production in Iran – a welcome development for artists. In the face of competing political powers vying for influence, including on Iran's cultural output, the situation remains in flux.

---

[4]   Ruhollah Khomeini, *Islam and Revolution: Writings and Declarations of Imam Khomeini*, tr. Hamid Algar (Berkeley, CA, 1981), p. 258.

Shi'i Jurisprudents and Intellectuals on Cinema

Once cinema and religion were no longer opposed territories, some traditionalists felt the need to articulate this new relationship within an Islamic discourse. One such attempt was Ayatollah Moravveji's book *Cinema in the Mirror of Fiqh* (1999), divided into various topics ranging from lying, backbiting, and men and women mingling, to playing the roles of the Prophet and the imams, and cross-dressing. Moravveji begins by stating that the book is about the position of Muslim believers and Muslim artists regarding cinema. His analysis, however, does not directly deal with cinema. Instead, it examines various, and occasionally contradictory, *hadith*s on each of the above-listed topics. If any of these are verified as prohibited or approved, then by extension the same applies to those topics within film and acting. The text therefore reads like any other treatise on Islamic jurisprudence.

Considering that Moravveji's work was published two decades after the Revolution, it might strike us as surprising that Moravveji goes to such great lengths solely to approve an already permitted practice. Moreover, from very early on in his text, he makes it clear that he is addressing Iranian audiences. In any case, cinemas already operated throughout the country and Iranians knew that filmmaking was an acceptable profession if practised within the set rules. Thus, Moravveji's assertion that 'Filmmaking and acting by themselves do not necessitate any forbidden act, and as long as they do not include any forbidden intentions and actions, they are unproblematic',[5] might appear a foregone conclusion stated only too obviously. However, his detailed examination of the Quranic verses and *hadith*s can be read in a different light – as an exercise that goes beyond simply attempting to decree cinema as a permitted industry.

For many decades the clergy had strongly condemned cinema and decreed it *haram* (forbidden). Treatises such as Moravveji's provide the space to employ the same religious vocabulary to justify the acceptance of a formerly forbidden activity. Contrary to a common view, then, *fiqh* is not always a closed corpus; it can be a resource that allows for a flexible interpretation of religious law in order to incorporate new circumstances within the life of the believer. Moravveji's writings can thus be seen as an attempt to marry traditional theoretical positions to the laws of the state as well as to current social practices. Cinema's ability to engage seriously with religion and spirituality has remained an important field in which scholars, intellectuals and traditionalists continue to debate.

---

[5]   Ali Moravveji, *Sinema dar ayne-ye fiqh* [Cinema in the Mirror of Jurisprudence] (Tehran, 1999), p. 156.

Of the few treatments of religion and spirituality in Iranian cinema, one can examine Mohammad Maddadpur and Mir-Ahmad Mir-Ehsan's works as examples of serious debates on the topic. Maddadpur (1955–2005) held a doctorate in the Philosophy of Art from the University of Heidelberg, and held various academic positions in Iran. Mir-Ehsan is a literary critic and documentary filmmaker as well as an academic based in Iran. Even though they approach the matter from opposing perspectives, both of them rely heavily on Martin Heidegger's theory of technology in discussing film and religion. Heidegger's influence on Iranian intellectuals goes back to Ahmad Fardid (1912–1994), who introduced his thought to the country's leading philosophers, translators and social thinkers throughout the 1960s, 1970s and even 1980s. Fardid, it appeared, had taken upon himself 'the task of introducing Heidegger's antimodern philosophy into the intellectual circles in Iran'.[6] It was through Heidegger (notably in his understanding of technology and science) that the intellectuals sought to understand and provide a philosophical understanding of their disenchantment with modernity and its rapid implementation throughout the Pahlavi shah's modernisation projects.

Maddadpur examines the incongruities between cinema and religion from various angles.[7] These may be summarised as follows: First, religious narrations and themes possess an otherworldly truth that is discordant with the technical and this-worldly aspect of cinema. Cinema, therefore, can only address the worldly side of human beings, which is carnal, nervous and erotic. Thus, transforming religious narratives and themes into films erodes their divine, sacred and profound characteristics, leaving them as mere entertainment. Secondly, a filmmaker with an impious soul preoccupied with this-worldly life cannot transcend it to achieve an other-worldly status. In fact, individuals looking for perfection do not engage in cinematic presentation as they will subsequently become prisoners of the snare of imagination and illusion by giving to it their hearts and souls and forgetting the truth about themselves. Finally, it is impossible to have an Islamic Cinema, for cinema can be only as Islamic as a camera or machine can be Islamic.

Maddadpur then turns to Iranian cinema, which he refers to as a 'Westoxicated Eastern art'[8] and situates it within the larger history of

---

[6]　Farzin Vahdat, *God and Juggernaut: Iran's Intellectual Encounter with Modernity* (Syracuse, NY, 2002), p. 114.

[7]　Mohammad Maddadpur, *Sayr va suluk-e sinemaʼi* [Cinematic Spiritual Journey] (Tehran, 1997).

[8]　This appellation draws on Jalal Al-e Ahmad's popular nationalist critique in 1962. Like many Iranian intellectuals who had begun articulating their disenchantment with modernity and what it had to offer, he proposed a return

Iran by drawing parallels between Reza Shah's modernising projects and the pioneers of cinema in Iran. He asserts that the first two founders of cinema in Iran – Sepanta, a Zoroastrian, and Ohanians, a Christian – were pursuing the modernising project in much the same way as Reza Shah. Indeed, their eagerness to do so far exceeded that of Reza Shah, evident in the fact that they anticipated him in introducing the unveiling of women. As for post-Revolution cinema, he argues that while cinema during the Pahlavi period was based mostly on 'erotic images', after the Revolution it drew from the heritage of so-called abstract art, resulting in the fruitless efforts of trying to force religious forms onto Western art. Thus, the present avant-garde Iranian cinema, with its semi-religious mysticism and complete lack of a spiritual journey, has in fact replaced the 'roguery' (*lutigari*) and eroticism of pre-Revolutionary cinema.

More recently, Mir-Ehsan also sets out to discuss film and spirituality within a Heideggerian framework of modernity and the technological imagination that dominates the modern world.[9] However, unlike Maddadpur, Mir-Ehsan aims to demonstrate the possibility of overcoming the limits of technology within cinema to support the notion that cinema is able to seriously engage with religion, spirituality, the metaphysical world or the sacred. He argues that cinema is the most essential mirror of modern technology. Thus, when cinema as a technological art turns to a poetic understanding, it overcomes the disjunction between the physical and metaphysical worlds proposed throughout the history of Western philosophy. The Heideggerian method of a poetic approach will liberate cinema from the cul-de-sac created by the scientific approach. Cinema as a technological art can, therefore, have a non-technological essence and remain faithful to the origins of the art. Through cinema, art can overcome technology and, therefore, lead us on a spiritual journey. It is not just any filmmaker, however, who attains this. Rather, it is only an artist who has experienced the Hidden with all his soul and follows the sacred command, who can establish the compound semiotics through the images.

Creating Categories for Film and Religion

In 2005, the Farabi Cinema Foundation, the Ministry of Culture's executive arm, set up the Spiritual Cinema Centre and introduced '*Sinema-ye Maʿnagara*' (translated as 'spiritual cinema') as a category in the country's

---

to the Self against what he defined as Westoxication (*gharbzadegi*, literally 'West-struckness').

[9] Mir Ahmad Mir-Ehsan, *Padidar va maʿna dar sinema-ye Iran* [Phenomenon and Meaning in Iranian Cinema] (Tehran, 2005).

most prestigious festival, the Fajr International Film Festival (FIFF). This represented a clear seal of approval for cinema's ability to deal with religion and spirituality. The festival's inclusion of this new category was also followed by a wave of discussions on the subject in the press, which variously debated, welcomed or rejected this new approach to films. The official website of Farabi defined 'spiritual cinema' as one that 'tries to find its path from "image to meaning", "exterior to interior", "substance to spirit", and "presence to absence"'. The Spiritual Cinema Centre also published and translated many books on the topic in order to clarify and justify the relevance of this newly-introduced category. Debates shifted from the issue of cinema's ability to engage with religion and spirituality, to what constitutes a religious cinema, and more particularly, 'spiritual cinema'.

Alireza Rezadad, director of Farabi and FIFF at the time, described *ma'nagara* cinema as a trend rather than a style or genre. Even though Farabi had translated a number of English titles, which provided an interesting introduction to the field of spiritual cinema, these Western sources obviously focused on Western films with reference to Christianity and Judaism. These works did not, of course, originate in response to the creation of a category within a national film industry; rather, they explored the religious or spiritual elements in films more broadly. The Iranian case was different. There was an indisputable need for an Iranian articulation that drew upon the complex social, cultural and religious fabric of the country.

Numerous authors approached *ma'nagara* cinema from different angles, often offering antithetical views and definitions. The creation and general acceptance of the category of 'spiritual cinema' proved more complicated than Farabi had anticipated. Some proponents of the category laid emphasis on the filmmaker and his/her religious background, others on the engagement of the audience with the film, and yet others on the capabilities of the medium of film itself. It was clear that arriving at a unanimous definition of *ma'nagara* cinema was almost impossible. Opponents did not fare any better. Their articulations, too, were weak and at times contradictory. Where there was a consensus, among both opponents as well as proponents of the *ma'nagara* category, it was that cinema was indeed a proper domain for religious and spiritual discourse.

Amongst critics of *ma'nagara* category, Javad Shamaghdari, then art advisor to President Ahmadinejad, argued in 2006 that since Iran already had religious cinema, there was no need to replace it with *ma'nagara* cinema. For him, the threat was the dilution of religion and infusion of new elements to its understanding. When one hears the term 'religious cinema', he stated, the audience undoubtedly expects films with divine and spiritual concepts. The introduction of the new category of *ma'nagara* had paved the way for various philosophies, ideas, and even inappropriate concepts, to easily be imported in the name of cinema, which was seen as dangerous.[10]

It is perhaps no surprise that with the reorganisation of the new government after the controversial 2009 presidential elections, the *ma'nagara* cinema category proved to be short-lived. It last ran at the 27th Fajr Festival in February 2009. Conceivably, Shamaghdari's criticism of the category had something to do with its removal from the 28th International Festival in 2010, the very first year in which he took up his post as deputy minister of Culture and Islamic Guidance responsible for cinema. Instead, another category, *Sinema-ye Sa'adat*, translated variably as 'cinema of salvation' and 'cinema of felicity', was introduced to the Fajr Festivals in 2012 and 2013. The 32nd FIFF in 2014 still included Salvation Cinema – a category which is not simply a replacement of *ma'nagara* cinema.

Unlike *ma'nagara* cinema, the new category does not appear to have attracted much debate or discussion. This can partly be explained by the clear boundaries that define it. *Ma'nagara* cinema was open to international participation by films that were considered to 'pay attention to the mysterious reality of existence' and reflect the realities of life 'in reference to its esotericism'. A wide range of films were selected and screened as part of *ma'nagara* cinema including American, Greek and Russian productions. Salvation cinema, on the other hand, is advertised as a 'Competition of Islamic World Filmmakers'. Indeed, the publicity materials of the 2013 FIFF positioned its importance squarely within terms of the recent uprisings in the Arab world: 'Given the promising awakening movements in the Islamic countries, this [Salvation Cinema category] will be held to recognise and promote the status of the filmmakers of the Islamic World.'

The election of Hassan Rouhani as president of the Islamic Republic in June 2013 and the subsequent restructuring of government positions, including the MCIG, has at least for the time being, caused new hope to spring up amongst the many disgruntled Iranian filmmakers. So palpable was the discord that on being replaced by Hojjat al-Islam Ayyubi as deputy minister for cinema, Shamaghdari congratulated his opponents. This acknowledged the strong desire for change amongst cineastes and the existing gulf between them and the authorities. It may be too early to judge the consequences of these changes for Iranian

---

[10] Javad Shamaghdari, Interview with Mehr News. 'Jahatgiri-ye barkhi filmha-ye jashnavareh khastgah-e dakheli nadasht: dalili bara-ye jaygozini-ye sinema-ye ma'nagara be ja-ye sinema-ye dini nabud' (1386-11-29 Sh./18 February 2006), available online at: http://www.mehrnews.com/fa/NewsDetail.aspx?NewsID=291358.

cinema, but the stark difference in the tone of Ayyubi's mission statements from those of his predecessor is unmistakable.

Many filmmakers had attacked Shamaghdari's policies over the last
four years as divisive and intent on maintaining a debilitating pressure on those filmmakers who had lost favour with the industry. This
may partly explain Ayyubi's reconciliatory tone, inviting cooperation
based on trust and optimism amongst various groups. While 'Salvation
Cinema' as a category has – for the time being – survived the changes,
the focus has shifted from recognising and promoting Muslim filmmakers to studying 'the increasing utilisation of cinema within the
Islamic world and its role in spreading Islamic values'.[11]

The creation or omission of these official categories, however, is not
the only way through which official narratives of religion in cinema are
endorsed or understood. For instance, the cold reception and subsequent
removal of *ma'nagara* cinema by functionaries of the previous government was not simply a statement about the impossibility of making
films that engaged with religion or spirituality. It was also a political
manoeuvre to assert their divergence from and their disagreement with
their predecessors' judgements and endorsement of cultural productions. Certain productions are referred to as *fakhir* or 'exalted' films,
and this is yet another vague categorisation that has found currency over
the last decade, and includes religious films such as the newly-coined
'Quranic films'.[12] The changes within the cinema industry are in fact a
reflection of a complex political system within which cultural productions are scrutinised and defined. Whilst these changes may affect the
support certain productions receive, they do not depict the full picture
of Iranian cinema's engagement with religion and spirituality.

Even though *ma'nagara* cinema appears to have been sidelined for
now, the various attempts at defining it by Farabi, academics, journalists, filmmakers and others have so widened its scope of interpretation,
that it is clear no one approach could do justice to the numerous possibilities of studying religion or spirituality in film. What is important
is the recognition of cinema's legitimate participation in discourses
on religion and spirituality and more significantly, cinema's ability to
articulate its own religious or spiritual discourse. This has opened up a
new arena for a modern medium: an opportunity to imaginatively retell

---

[11] Iranian Students' News Agency, 'Sinema-garan bara-ye jashnavareh film fajr
fara khandeh shodan' (1392-7-26 Sh./18 October 2013), available online at: http://
isna.ir/fa/news/92072615839.
[12] See Nacim Pak-Shiraz, 'The Divine Word on the Screen: Religious Epics
in Iranian Cinema', in Alessandro Cancian, ed., *Approaches to the Qur'an in
Contemporary Iran* (London, forthcoming).

the beliefs of a 15-centuries-old religious tradition, as well as the many facets of its expression and experiences.

Films Engaging with Religion and Spirituality

The Islamic Republic's initial ambition was to create an 'Islamic cinema'. Within the first decade, however, the project foundered: transforming a national cinema into an all-encompassing genre was ultimately deemed impossible, and maintaining local audiences through one particular approach to film proved impractical. The mushrooming of satellite programmes and the illegal distribution of Western films in the 1990s meant that Islamic cinema faced fierce competition. On the other hand, arriving at a consensus of what constituted 'Islamic cinema' became another insurmountable challenge.

Films labelled as *'erfani'* or mystical in the 1980s were part of the ambition to create an Islamic cinema. The controversy around Saeed Ebrahimifar's *Pomegranate and Reed* (1989) – often labelled as a 'mystical film' – exemplifies the dispute over perceptions. Winner of a number of national and international awards, the film is about the encounter of a photographer with an old man he finds dying on the street. While waiting in the hospital corridor, the photographer finds time and space transformed as he reads the old man's diary, about the simple life he led in Kashan. Many critics read the film as one of Iranian cinema's proudest achievements in both form and content, seeing the depiction of the old man's life as a mystical approach to understanding life and death. Others, however, criticised it as a film void of any cinematic or mystical value and which had in fact not only turned its back on life, but was also a complete failure in delivering the Islamic Republic's aspirations and values. A montage of different sources without identity, the film was dismissed as westoxicated and an insult to Iranian culture, mysticism and the entire East.[13]

What constitutes a serious engagement of religion and spirituality in film remains a contentious topic not only in Iran and Iranian cinema, but also more widely. Within Western academia, various scholars have adopted different frameworks in which to situate their arguments on the study of religion and film, which focus mainly on examining Christian and Judaic elements in Western productions. The small body of litera-ture dedicated to the study of religion and spirituality in Iranian cinema focuses largely on propaganda films exalting the Islamic Republic and its aspirations. It is, however, important to examine ways in which

---

[13] Mas'ud Farasatian, 'Naghdi bar *Nar o Ney*: vay bar maghlub [A critic of *Pomegranate and Reed*: Woe to the defeated]', *Sureh*, 21 (1369 Sh./1990), pp. 54–59.

other films participate and engage with Shi'i expressions of Islam. Thus, having briefly pointed to the dilemmas facing those who have tried to articulate 'religious' and/or 'spiritual' films, I will explore the various ways in which Iranian Shi'i discourses – in various mystical, theological and ritual forms – emerge on the silver screen. These filmic discourses constitute a new addition to the rich corpus of Shi'i religious expressions in literature, poetry, art and architecture.

Shi'ism encompasses modalities of interpretation that range from the communal and public to the highly personal and spiritual. These approaches to religion and spirituality demonstrate the plurality and complexity of Iranian Shi'i identity. Given the breadth of the topic and the numerous expressions of Shi'ism in Iran, I will focus on three main areas within religious discourses, namely the formalist, the mystical and the popular.

The sensitivities surrounding Iranian cinema are complex. An approach to the depiction of religion that deviates from the official stance could result, at the very least, in the banning of a film, and even in the arrest and imprisonment of the filmmaker. Predictably, most of the films that directly refer to religion are those that exalt the Islamic Republic and are, therefore, referred to as propagandist films. However, religious discourse in Iranian films is not limited to this category. Many filmmakers have creatively sought to circumvent censorship and engage in a different approach to religion, which may not necessarily be in line with officially endorsed Shi'i interpretations of Islam.

Films on Formalist Religion

In examining the formalist approach to religion, I have chosen representations of the clergy and their centres of learning. Until recently in post-Revolutionary Iran, there were only deferential references to the clergy in Iranian cinema. Other than leading ritual acts such as prayers, marriages, deaths and sermons, clerics were removed from the daily concerns of ordinary people, and remained largely peripheral to the main characters of the films. This is unsurprising, considering the sensitivity of the topic and the strict codes set down by the MCIG, which bans all films and videos that 'blaspheme against the values and personalities held sacred by Islam and other religions mentioned in the Constitution'.[14] However, the new millennium saw a resurgence of films with the clergy as their protagonists. These included Reza Mirkarimi's

---

[14]   Quoted in Hamid Naficy, 'Islamizing Film Culture in Iran: A Post-Khatami Update', in Richard Tapper, ed., *The New Iranian Cinema: Politics, Representation and Identity* (London, 2002), p. 36.

Under the Moonlight (2001), Kamal Tabrizi's *The Lizard* (2004) and more recently Masud Dehnamaki's *Disgrace* (2013), all of which opened to general release in Iran.

Under the Moonlight and *The Lizard* articulate a discourse that differs from previous cinematic representations of the clergy. They not only propose a different engagement of the clergy with the public but also critically examine the lofty positions they enjoy in society, which in turn serves only to further emphasise their hierarchical relationship with the laity. These filmic narratives provide a space for the articulation of debates on the role of the clergy within society, including some of the more contentious issues that have otherwise been difficult to discuss publicly inside Iran.

A brief examination of the history of clerical influence within the Iranian context reveals a very complex picture. Even though Iran is governed and led by the clerics, one cannot point to a consensus among them about their own social role. Indeed, their diversity of views and understandings on the subject makes it one of the most dynamic and exciting developments in the long history of this institution in Iran. Mirkarimi and Tabrizi have creatively employed film to actively engage in some of these debates. However, their films do not merely reflect these debates, but are themselves part of them and of a larger discourse within society. Whilst the published discourses of intellectuals such as Abdolkarim Soroush are regarded as authoritative both within and outside Iran, these parallel filmic discourses have not yet received such recognition.

This oversight does injustice to the potential of a medium that can often be more effective than its written or oral equivalents, especially in the context of Iran. First, the metaphorical language of film provides a space for discourses that might otherwise face harsh censorship. Even when films are banned, the filmmakers, at least until recently, are not usually punished with the same severity reserved for authors or lecturers propagating similar ideas through their own forms of media. Moreover, a ban on an Iranian film usually turns it into a highly popular commodity, with considerable demand for pirated copies. Secondly, the accessibility of the medium has enabled these films to engage very effectively with a wider audience, even if the level of engagement varies individually.

Under the Moonlight and *The Lizard* function as parables. They not only depict the world of the clergy in its current form within Iranian society, but also include a moral vision of how it ought to be. Through Seyyed's eyes in *Under the Moonlight* and Reza's in *The Lizard*, we enter these two worlds and are at once presented with the contradictions between them. In examining the contemporary role of the clergy, these filmic discourses evoke the debates of intellectuals who have critically engaged with the doctrines that empower the clergy. Interestingly, even though both films discuss many similar issues, *Under the Moonlight* was screened without much controversy whereas *The Lizard* was forced to pull out of cinemas within a month of its release.

Under the Moonlight is the first post-Revolutionary film that critically examines the status of the clergy within society. It begins with a contrast between the life of the clergy and that of the public. Seyyed, a young seminarian who is approaching the end of his studies, appears hesitant to take on the clerical robe. His pursuit of a street urchin who has stolen his vestments leads him to an unfamiliar world of social outcasts in Tehran. The film hints at the hypocrisy of some clerics who act against what they preach and maintain a façade of piety, rather than strive towards the values they preach. The clergy here appear to have forgotten an important part of their duty, to look out for those in need. Many other Iranian films have also highlighted the plight of the underprivileged. However, *Under the Moonlight* differs from them in that the conditions of the destitute are contrasted not with the affluent living in the north of Tehran, but with the clergy in the seminary.

The Lizard is a different film from *Under the Moonlight* in both genre and approach, though the issues it raises are similar. *The Lizard* became the first post-Revolutionary film to position a cleric as the subject of a comedy. Even though it was screened for only a month, it became the biggest box-office hit in the history of Iranian cinema at the time. The real audience of this film, however, exceeded the box-office numbers. Pirated copies were soon in circulation and almost everyone in Iran has seen it. Reza, a convicted thief, steals the robes of a cleric in order to escape prison and finds himself trapped in the role of a cleric far longer than he had intended. The images of an irreligious convict pretending to be a man of God and leading the faithful made for some of the film's most humorous moments. However, the film aroused such fury among the clerics that they refused to acknowledge even its redemptive side, which allowed for a more favourable view of religion. Despite it never being officially banned, the stir it caused was enough for its creators to decide to take it off the screens.

Both *Under the Moonlight* and *The Lizard* critically examine the role and status of the clergy, without accepting or rejecting the religious institutions outright. The discourses are in fact a continuation of an ongoing debate in Iran. Like Soroush, Hasan Yousefi Eshkevari and Mohsen Kadivar, the filmmakers Mirkarimi and Tabrizi invite us to review our understanding of religion and its current role in society. In *Under the Moonlight*, Mirkarimi breaks through the closed quarters of the seminary, and unapologetically examines the relationship of the seminarians with each other and with the outside world, as well as the relevance of their theological understanding to the real world. *The Lizard* highlights the enforcement of one particular interpretation of Islam and contrasts

Figure 14.1 Reza Marmulak, an irreligious convicted thief, escapes from prison by disguising himself as a cleric in The Lizard. *When forced to act out this role for far longer than he had anticipated, he unwittingly succeeds in drawing people back to the mosque. The top image is his first congregation at the village mosque with very few worshippers. But Reza's unconventional sermons and style of engagement make him popular with the villagers, resulting in a gradual increase in attendance. The last image is from the final sequence of the film, when a large congregation waits for Reza to lead the ceremonies.*

it with a pluralistic approach. Both films propose a more fluid relationship between people, the clergy and the Divine, one that is not confined to the rigid boundaries of seminarian debate. Even though the films, particularly *The Lizard*, are subversive in that they question the role of the clergy in society, they remain affirmative of the role of religion in life.

Unlike the two films discussed above, the comedy-drama *Disgrace* is a purely commercial film that takes a very different approach to the depiction of the clergy. Dehnamaki, a conservative and longstanding critic of the reformists, is a latecomer to cinema. Having fought in the Iran-Iraq war in the first decade of the Islamic Republic, and against the reformist policies and student uprisings in the second, he took up the camera as a new weapon with which to fight for justice in the third decade. He rose to fame with his debut feature, the comedy-drama *Outcasts* (2007), which was followed by two further instalments in 2008 and 2010. In the face of increasing pressures on Iranian filmmakers, especially in the second term of Ahmadinejad's presidency, Dehnamaki, a strong ally of the government, enjoyed huge support from the authorities. This included financial backing, the easing off of censorship and widespread advertisements and screenings for his films. This won him both great box-office returns as well as scathing reviews, with some even calling for a boycott of his third instalment of the *Outcasts*. Many of his critics saw the open field he enjoyed as a sign of cinema being yet another medium through which he could attack the reformists. In *Disgrace*, the protagonist is a cleric.

In an unprecedented event, about 300 of the country's Friday-prayer leaders gathered to watch *Disgrace* at the director's invitation. Dehnamaki introduced and positioned his film within the larger discourse of religious teachings. He explained to the clergy that the film was intended for those audiences who did not attend their pulpits in mosques or at Friday prayers and, therefore, he was determined to take the pulpit and sermons to their homes. Since the film did not target the religious or the clergy, he had to calibrate its tone and language to the intended audiences.[15] Dehnamaki was perhaps pre-empting possible criticisms against the film for its heavy reliance on tough-guy dialogues and controversial female depiction. In contrast to the negative responses that Tabrizi received in 2004 when he arranged a special screening of *The Lizard* for a group of clerics, over 90 per cent of the Friday-prayer leaders assessed *Disgrace* as positive. That the film merits such praise is highly contested. Many industry insiders and critics aver that Dehnamaki is ultimately a creator of cheap entertainment with an eye to financial gain

---

[15] ʻDehnamaki *Rosvaʼi* ra bara-ye che kasani sakht', *Alif* (1391-11-12 Sh./1 March 2013), available online at: http://www.alef.ir/prtg7y9qnak9uy4.rpra.html.

and fame – with a zest that has perhaps overtaken his anti-reformist fervour.

Disgrace follows much of the same formula as the *Outcasts* trilogy, with the humour relying mainly on street jokes and roguish phrases reeled off by low social class characters. This time, however, the scoundrel is an attractive young woman who is intent on getting her way even if at the expense of a pious cleric's reputation. The underprivileged here is a cleric who chooses nocturnal hard labour over the religious tax that is due to him. Unlike the critical depictions in *Under the Moonlight* and *The Lizard*, the cleric in *Disgrace* has extraordinary abilities and works hard to enable his charitable acts and simple lifestyle. Despite the threat to his reputation and the loss of his community's trust, he aids an ill-reputed woman in need. His humility and sincerity is contrasted with the greed and hypocrisy of the rich and powerful, in much the same way as in earlier propagandist films. Yet the tone, imagery and narrative used to convey this message are different. They resonate with those of pre-Revolutionary *filmfarsi*s but with a twist[16] – the male saviour of the fallen woman is a cleric. The film provides a model of a spiritually elevated clergy with a worldly life based on simplicity, sacrifice, piety and hardship. More importantly, it conveys the message that the clergy are ultimately people's only hope of gaining salvation.

Mysticism in Film

The formal and institutional approach, however, has never been the sole expression of the beliefs and practices of the Shi'i laity. Indeed, the Sufi and mystical approach has often existed in tandem with, and as an alternative to, the legalistic approach to religion and spirituality in Iran. But those whose personal approach to religion diverged from the public and communal aspects propagated by the establishment and centres of authority, were usually regarded unfavourably and subsequently marginalised by the latter. Yet their rich and varied reading of ways of arriving at spiritual maturity has greatly influenced many facets of

---

[16] A term used to refer to the commercial Iranian films made during the Pahlavi period. Coined in 1953 by the French-educated film critic Amirhushang Kavusi to criticise the poor quality of the local productions, they usually included song and dance items. For a detailed study of the genre see Mohammad Abdi, 'Montaqedan-e Dahe-haye Si va Chehel va Mobarezeh ba Padideh-ye Benam-e Filmfarsi', in *Filmfarsi Chist?*, ed. Hosain Moezezinia (Tehran, 1378/1999), p. 171. For a study of the genre of comedy in Iranian cinema see Nacim Pak-Shiraz, 'Imagining the Diaspora in the New Millennium Comedies of Iranian Cinema', *Iranian Studies*, 46 (2013), pp. 165–184.

Iranian culture and thought. This section will draw on the films of Majid Majidi to show how these mystical approaches find creative expression.

Though modern in form and story, Majidi's films are deeply rooted in medieval Iranian mystical discourse, and especially its poetry. Sufism's early appearance in Islamic history, the vast amount of literature it has produced over the centuries, and its pervasive influence on Muslim culture and society makes it undeniably significant. Persian literature played a major role in the expression of Sufi ideas. Numerous works explore the Sufi states and stations, and the mastery with which many of them have been composed has immortalised their authors. As diverse as these approaches can be, man's spiritual attainment and his proximity to God remain at the core of any Sufi teaching.

Majidi's films demonstrate how the Shiʻi and particularly Iranian Shiʻi expression of religion is deeply rooted not only in sacred texts but also in the cultural expression of the people, especially of the mystical masters. With their poetic language, Majidi's works are filmic discourses on man's journey to spiritual attainment and his proximity to God. The key Sufi postulates – intuition, inward light, going beyond self and love – are all explored in Majidi's films, *The Colour of Paradise* (1999), *Baran* (2001), and *The Willow Tree* (2005). In *The Colour of Paradise*, Mohammad Reza's intuition and inward light despite his physical blindness is contrasted with his father's inward blindness and lack of intuition. They live in different worlds even as they share the same time and space. This leads to the very different ways in which each of them deals with pain and suffering. In *The Willow Tree*, Yusuf's intuition and inward light during the long period of his blindness had allowed him to live in a paradise of peace and happiness, a state which he rapidly loses after the gleam of the outside world blinds his inward light. *Baran* is a filmic discourse on the various Sufi stations and states in which love becomes the guide of the soul on its journey and its ascent to God. *Baran*'s narrative relates the various Sufi stages: drawing back the curtains of ignorance, and stripping off the veils of selfishness and sensuality, to behold the Divine vision. In all these films, spiritual attainment requires no special rank or distinction, and includes the ordinary man. In fact, none of the characters, except for Yusuf, are formally educated in mystical knowledge. Most of the protagonists who undergo these journeys are either children or barely-educated adults from an impoverished social class.

Majidi's works bring these age-old mystical ideas to the screen and apply them to the modern-day lives of ordinary people. Just as Rumi, Attar, Saʻdi and Jami's works are not mere collections of stories and poetry, but imbued and embedded with Sufi teachings and meanings, so Majidi's films are similarly not just stories of destitute or disabled people. They are layered with Sufi notions that let his viewers share the spiritual experiences of his characters. He reifies these notions through the medium of film and draws out their relevance to today's modern world, as much as they were relevant at the time of their articulation many centuries ago. The focus on the Muslim interpretation of self-annihilation is often understood in terms of violent acts of terror and destruction such as suicide attacks. In the Sufi context of Islam, however, it is an arduous process of sacrificing one's desires for the betterment of another, of practising patience, forgiveness and love. What Majidi succeeds in doing is to produce a modern discourse which is rooted in the Persian mystical tradition of Islam. Majidi's stories resonate with the iconic tales of Leyla and Majnun, the Simurgh and the *Mathnawi*, but through the medium of film and with contemporary and ordinary people as his heroes.

Popular Shi'ism in Film

Cinema has provided a new medium of expression for one of the most prominent discourses within Shi'ism. As such it acts as a reservoir for popular, yet threatened traditions such as *taziya* which faces increased pressure from both intellectuals and clerics. *Taziya* is the re-enactment of the events on the plains of Karbala that culminated in the death of the third Shi'i imam, Husayn, in 680. It originates from much older pre-Islamic forms of performance – and it does not always draw its language or facts from official discourses. Rather, these expressions of the laity provide a means for personal and direct engagement with the figure of the imam. They have also led to the creation of religious rituals, many of which have historically met with the disapproval of the clergy and been condemned by them as unIslamic. A few filmmakers such as Bahram Beyzaie have engaged with *taziya* in their films and, through their reinterpretation of this older form of performing art, have reintroduced it to their audiences.

During Nasir al-Din Shah's reign (1848–1896), when *taziya* reached its peak in terms of its artistic and entertainment values, it was divided into two parts: the *pish vaqe-eh* or 'before the incident' and the *vaqe-eh* or 'incident' itself. The *pish vaqe-eh* usually consisted of lighter performances and varied from love stories to satire. This was followed by the *vaqe-eh*, which was three times as long and focused on the tragedy at Karbala.[17] Thus, the *taziya* performance would make people laugh and cry at the same time. It was both a joyous and sad occasion.

Beyzaie's screenplay for *The Day of Incident* (Shahram Asadi, 1994) is set in the 7th century in an unidentified Arab land. Through the love of Rahila, a Muslim girl, a Christian referred to as Abd Allah converts to Islam and his proposal is finally accepted by her family after 37

---

[17] Bahram Beyzaie, *Namayesh dar Iran* (Tehran, 2001), pp. 132–133.

Figure 14.2 Latif in Baran, *is bewildered and overwhelmed when he realises that Rahmat is a girl disguised as a boy. The wind blows back the curtain, revealing her reflection, and therefore her true identity, to Latif. Baran portrays Latif's inner journey, as he matures from a nonchalant boy to a selfless lover.*

rejections. However, on the day of marriage he hears Husayn's call for help and abruptly leaves the ceremonies. Beyzaie employs the techniques of an older performing art to depict an important religious event. The title of the film, *Ruz-e vaqe-eh*, can be read as paying homage to these earlier forms of *taziya*. The film draws from both the *pish vaqe-eh* and *vaqe-eh* portions of the *taziya* performance by starting with a love story. Interestingly, the wedding scenes comprise roughly one third of the entire film (27 out of 95 minutes).

Like *taziya*, the film is not just about the martyrdom of Husayn, but includes the lighter story of the protagonists' love. Similarly, like *pish vaqe-eh* in *taziya*, which provided the space to criticise feudal landlords, the first part of the film provides an opportunity to criticise those who use their privileged social status to inflict injustice on the dispossessed. The film's narrative also emphasises the Shi'i obligation of upholding Husayn's message. Thus, Beyzaie's script is not simply a retelling of the events of Karbala on screen; very little is dedicated to the events of Karbala itself. Instead, he emphasises the impact of Husayn's martyrdom on the lives of the Shi'a and in the formation of their religious identity.

The Travellers (1994) is about a wedding that tragically turns into a mourning ceremony as the bride's sister and her family are killed in an accident. *The Travellers* employs many of the established *taziya* forms of narration. The elements of a lack of suspense, veiled moments of death, the impact and reaction of the bereaved to the tragedy, the circular movements of the camera, the delivery of the dialogue and the cathartic nature of the mourning rituals are all comparable to those of *taziya*. Beyzaie employs these features of *taziya* to narrate a modern tragedy. *The Travellers* also allows Beyzaie, who laments the loss of older Iranian performative art forms, to employ the medium of film to reintroduce and reinterpret these older traditions to his audience.

It is within this evolving context of the Shi'i tradition in Iran that *taziya* has survived its many centuries of eventful history. It has been condemned by some *ulama* as unIslamic and endorsed by some others. *Taziya* flourished under royal patronage but was banned and ignored as being 'backward' during the rule of subsequent monarchs. The tradition has moved from the greatest performance halls in cities to remote rural plateaus. Thus, the lifeblood of *taziya* has historically been held largely in the hands of the religious and ruling authorities and more recently continues to cause concern amongst them as a threat to the reputation of religion, notably of Shi'ism in the wider Sunni-dominated Muslim world.

Films provide *taziya* with a new space that is controlled by the artist rather than those in positions of power. A filmmaker such as Beyzaie employs many of *taziya*'s established modes and motifs, in form and content, when writing and directing his films. *Taziya* informs the narrative structure of *The Day of the Incident*, and its motifs are applied to recount a latter-day tragedy in *The Travellers*. Beyzaie not only revives the old performing art but also demonstrates it relevance to the modern Iranian imagination. Like *taziya*, Beyzaie's films encompass the historical, mythological, national and the religious, as they relate to Iranian society and culture.

Philosophical Approach to Religion

Some films can be read as philosophical texts that, among other things, deliberate on the question of religion. For example, Abbas Kiarostami's films invite viewers to rethink their existing ideas, thoughts and beliefs, be they rooted in scientific or theological approaches to religion. He is a 'poetic philosopher', a term applied to him though not elaborated.[18]

Depicting the sacred through the profane in a medium such as film is a challenge for any director wishing to address the metaphysical without falling into the trap of the dogmatic. Kiarostami is no exception and he counters this challenge with a unique approach. He does not avoid dealing with the religious view, contrary to what many of his critics claim. In fact, he presents an array of religious discourses without trying to prove them true or false before proposing an alternative approach to religion. In Kiarostami's own words, religion and art 'both point to the same direction. Religion points to another world, whereas art points to a better existence. One is an invitation, an offering to a faraway place, the other to a place that is close.'[19] His films are poetic philosophies that contemplate man's existence and its meaning. They are, as Wittgenstein might postulate, one of those 'artistic creations [which] can mediate what is higher'.[20] Even though Kiarostami's films set forth theological or philosophical ideas, his references to the mystical go beyond religious or scientific debate. Human language, as Wittgenstein noted, is incapable of explaining the mystical. The religious, however, are often tempted to make the mistake of explaining it. The moment an explanation is offered, the mystery and wonder of the mystical is destroyed. Kiarostami does not offer an explanation; he points to another way of looking, letting his audience to arrive at a certain understanding themselves. Both Kiarostami and Wittgenstein emphasise showing the viewer/reader a way to see things afresh.

The question of life and death is certainly one of Kiarostami's main philosophical deliberations, evident in his numerous films which deal with the issue. It therefore provides us with an interesting study of how his films are 'philosophy in action' and how they deliberate about religion. In *And Life Goes On* (1992), *Through the Olive Trees* (1994), *Taste*

---

[18] Jared Rapfogel, 'Don't Look at the Camera: Becoming a Woman in Jafar Panahi's Iran' (2001), available online at: http://sensesofcinema.com/2001/jafar-panahi/panahi_jared/.

[19] David Walsh, 'The Compassionate Gaze: Iranian Film-maker Abbas Kiarostami at the San Francisco Film Festival', World Socialist Website (12 June 2000), available online at: http://www.wsws.org/articles/2000/jun2000/sff8-j12.shtml.

[20] Brian R. Clack, *An Introduction to Wittgenstein's Philosophy of Religion* (Edinburgh, 1999), p. 46.

of Cherry (1997) and *The Wind Will Carry Us* (1999), not a single dead body or dying person is actually shown. There are long shots of burial scenes but no close-ups. Like many of Kiarostami's hidden characters whom we never see but get to know, death is present but not staring us in the face. Instead, Kiarostami poetically thinks about the question of life, death and suffering.

This perspective is not argued to the exclusion of others about death and suffering; rather, it finds significance through its contrasts. Many of the religious discourses articulated on life and death seem to fail to respond meaningfully to actual human experience. In a culture that lays great emphasis on mourning rituals and ceremonies, Kiarostami invites us to revisit our understandings of life and death. Like Wittgenstein's silence to 'that of which many are babbling today', Kiarostami, too, refuses to comment on any of the views that he introduces in his films.

After he has presented us with accounts of the religious, the positivist as well as the sceptical, he arrives at a poetic account of death and life. In line with Wittgenstein's thought, Kiarostami's references to the mystical are different from scientific and common-sense statements. His films, therefore, as seen through the example of the theme of life and death, demonstrate a poetic philosophy, an approach that stands out in comparison to the other approaches to religion and spirituality in Iranian films. The world's very existence is seen as mystical. In Kiarostami's films, the beauty of nature provides the backdrop for life that strives to continue in the face of adversity. People dig after an earthquake not in search of bodies, or to bury the dead, but to find the means of living – be it digging for a kettle, a carpet, a pillow, a lamp, or to set up television antennas to follow the World Cup of soccer. The camera does not avoid the destruction that the earthquake has left in its wake, but sees through it: the destroyed shells of windows and doors standing empty in the rubble frame a world of beauty. Instead of focusing his lens on death and suffering, Kiarostami redirects our gaze to man's struggle for life, and the existence of the world itself becomes the object of wonder and mystery.

It should be noted here that the subject of religion and tradition appears in many other Iranian films as a subtext to the themes that these films narrate. These include the work of internationally acclaimed female filmmakers such as Rakhshan Bani-Etemad, Tahmineh Milani, Marziyeh Meshkini and Samira Makhmalbaf, which focus on the challenges that women face in their experience of tradition and patriarchy today.

Figure 14.3 In contrast to the scenes of dead bodies and mourning relatives, which form the main mise-en-scene *of most earthquake films, here the beauty of nature provides a backdrop to life that continues in the face of every adversity, in Kiarostami's* And Life Goes On.

Films of the Iranian Diaspora and Other Cinemas

The greatest emigration of Iranians occurred after the 1979 Revolution, resulting in a numerically and culturally significant diaspora, particularly in the West. Many of the emigrants found themselves between two worlds: of the age-old customs of the homeland and the unfamiliar context of adopted homes. Art and literature became important media for capturing and communicating their exilic and diasporic narratives. Various themes emerged in the diasporic films, ranging from their experiences in the host country to those focusing solely on the country left behind. In the first category, many films focus on the diaspora's overbearing sense of alienation and loneliness, and the difficulties of resisting one or other, or negotiating between the inherited and adopted cultures. However, the second category of films reflects the diaspora's concerns about Iran's destiny and ends up taking strong political positions, with some condemning religion as part of their sceptical view of clerical rule.

The American-Iranian Cyrus Nowrasteh's film, *The Stoning of Soraya M* (2009), is about the brutal stoning of its innocent eponymous character in a remote village in Iran. Its cleric is an untrustworthy, scheming, ex-con who facilitates Soraya's stoning so that her *basiji* (voluntary militia) husband can satisfy his lust and marry a 14-year-old. The particular subject and the harsh rural setting certainly made for a bleak portrayal. Yet in seeking to raise awareness of the injustices against women in Iran, it failed to convey the complexity of the country and the religious tradition that it hurriedly condemns. The film became controversial not just within Iran but also the diaspora, especially among Iranian men who protested against their depiction as savages. Its release around the same time as the contested 2009 Iranian elections not only helped the film's publicity, but also fuelled the international debates and controversies over the stoning sentence of Sekineh Mohammadi Ashtiani who had been convicted of adultery and imprisoned in Tabriz since 2006.

Other films by the diaspora have taken a more nuanced approach to religion in Iran, such as Marjane Satrapi's *Persepolis* (with Vincent Paronnaud, 2008), offering a multilayered picture of Iran and its people's engagement with religion. Most diasporic films that deal with Iran and the Iranian experience, however, are not reflections on religion but are either individual stories of migration or attempts at rewriting official histories.

Growing out as it did from a theocratic state and also enjoying international acclaim, Iranian cinema has become fertile ground for the development of various approaches to film's engagement with Islam, and particularly Shi'ism. This, however, cannot be said of other cinemas in the region, which are mainly Sunni. Much of their commercial cinema is seen as imitations of successful Egyptian films interested purely in providing entertainment. On the other hand, narratives of non-commercial films have been dominated by conflicts in the Middle East, most notably in Palestine, Lebanon and Iraq. Thus, the nation's traumas retold through individual stories tend to take precedence over reflections on religion in these narratives. This is not to say that the questions of religion do not appear; when they do, however, they are often of secondary value to the political conflicts depicted.

Where there is a critical approach to religion, comparison may be drawn between Iranian cinema and Arab films that reflect their own Sunni contexts. Doubts about religious convictions – including the controversial tenet of martyrdom and its employment for ideological gains – are for example explored in the Palestinian-Dutch film *Paradise Now* (Hany Abu-Assad, 2005). The spread of fundamentalism as a response to social alienation, the hypocrisy of men in power and the infliction of injustices on women in the name of Islam are also explored in the Egyptian *The Yacoubian Building* (Marwan Hamed, 2006). There are interesting parallels between Iranian and Israeli cinema, especially in their diverse depictions of the clergy. Illustrative here are the critical approach to an ultra-orthodox rabbi's literal interpretation of scripture in *My Father My Lord* (David Volach, 2007), and the affirming role of the rabbi in the light-hearted comedy *Ushpizin* (Giddi Dar, 2004).

Conclusion

There are different modes of Shi'i interpretation in Iran – from legalistic and formalistic approaches to the more popular and personal interpretations – that make for a rich and complex setting. Each of these modes has evolved over time, finding expression in various forms, with which contemporary Iranian films have engaged. In locating these films within a much larger socio-historical context, this chapter has sought to establish that film is a worthy medium in our understanding of Shi'i expressions; indeed, it is *part* of a much older Iranian discourse on religion and spirituality.

There is a range of views on what constitutes film's engagement with religion and spirituality within the Iranian context. Authorities, academics, religious leaders and critics have all struggled to define the relationship of film to religion and spirituality. However, these various debates reflect a general recognition of cinema's legitimate participation in such discourses. Thus, filmic discourses on the role of the clergy often challenge doctrines that empower it, without denying the clergy's relevance to the believer. Eschewing the debate on a legalistic approach, Majidi instead employs the medium of film to explore key mystical concepts such as love, suffering and mystical annihilation. These films have succeeded in producing a modern discourse that offers an alternative way of understanding religion and spirituality – yet one that has deep roots in medieval Iranian mystical interpretations of Islam. Through their engagement with *taziya* in film, directors such as Beyzaie have reinterpreted this older form of performing art, and reintroduced it to their audiences through a new medium. These films act not only as a cultural reservoir for a threatened tradition, but also more importantly, endow it with new life. Kiarostami's films are poetic philosophies that contemplate man's existence and its meaning; they are 'thinking texts' that employ the lyrical language of Iranian poets, but do not aim to simply illustrate existing philosophies. They invite us rethink our preconceptions and look afresh at life, offering another vision of religion and spirituality today.

Further Reading

Algar, Hamid. *Religion and State in Iran: The Role of the Ulama in the Qajar Period, 1785–1906*. Berkeley, CA, and London, 1980.

Chelkowski, Peter, ed. *Ta'ziyeh: Ritual and Drama in Iran*. New York, 1979.

Dabashi, Hamid. *Close Up: Iranian Cinema, Past, Present and Future*. London and New York, 2001.

Gulger, Josef, ed. *Film in the Middle East and North Africa: Creative Dissidence*. Austin, TX, 2011.

Leaman, Oliver, ed. *Companion Encyclopedia of Middle Eastern and North African Film*. London and New York, 2001.

Litch, Mary M. *Philosophy through Film*. New York, 2002.

Lyden, John. *The Routledge Companion to Religion and Film*. London and New York, 2009.

Naficy, Hamid. *A Social History of Iranian Cinema*. Durham and London, 2011–2012.

Pak-Shiraz, Nacim. *Shi'i Islam in Iranian Cinema: Religion and Spirituality in Film*. London, 2011.

Plate, S. Brent, ed. *Representing Religion in World Cinema: Filmmaking, Mythmaking, Culture Making*. New York, 2003.

Read, Rupert and Jerry Goodenough, eds. *Film as Philosophy: Essays on Cinema after Wittgenstein and Cavell*. New York, 2005.

Tapper, Richard, ed. *The New Iranian Cinema: Politics, Representation and Identity*. London, 2002.

15

Diasporas

Zulfikar Hirji and Karen Ruffle

This chapter surveys the histories, social forms and cultural expressions of Shiʻi diasporas in Asia, Sub-Saharan Africa, Western Europe and North America. We define 'diaspora', a much-debated term, as a community or group that establishes itself outside its place of geographic origin but maintains a connection to that place through various socio-cultural processes. Applied to the Shiʻa, this brings into focus a diverse range of communities that have developed outside the historic heartlands of the Middle East and Iran. One can hardly apply a master narrative to *all* the diverse Shiʻi diasporas. Indeed, if a generalisation were to be made about Shiʻi diasporas, it would relate to the limited scholarship about them today. Hence, this chapter will sketch the historical and contemporary paths of *some* Shiʻi diasporas, across a wide range of geographical regions. For the communities surveyed here, we discuss a number of key features: their ideas about authority and identity, spaces of worship and gathering, rituals, gender, engagements with the state, transnational formations and relations with other Muslim groups.

Asia

Shiʻi communities in Central Asia have received little sustained academic attention. This can be attributed to a number of challenges to conducting research in recent decades in Afghanistan and northern Pakistan – and to the Soviet policy of enforced atheism in Tajikistan. Yet the history and cultural mosaic of Central Asia is characterised by a high degree of linguistic, ethnic and religious pluralism. In Southeast Asia, scholars are becoming increasingly aware of the history, culture and practices of Shiʻi communities, especially because of their precarious political status in countries such as Malaysia.

South Asia

South Asia (the modern nation-states of India and Pakistan) is both a diasporic location for the Shiʻa (particularly the Ithnaʻasharis or

Twelvers); it is also a place of origin and homeland for the contemporary Nizari and Daudi Bohra Ismaili communities. Approximately 116 million and 147 million Shi'is live in Asia, comprising almost 75 per cent of the global Shi'i population.[1] Both India and Pakistan are home to some of the world's largest Shi'i populations, estimated respectively at 16–24 million (9–14 per cent of the global Shi'i population), and 17–26 million (10–15 per cent of the global Shi'i population). Because of South Asia's unique status as a quasi-diaspora for the Twelver Shi'a, and a place of origin for the modern Khoja Nizari Ismaili and Daudi Bohra communities, we have not focused on this region as a site of diasporic Shi'ism. For different Shi'i groups living in the diasporas of East Africa, the Americas, and Europe, South Asia is a *homeland*. The perpetuation of ritual, cultural and literary devotional traditions that find their roots in South Asia reinforce this region's originary status.

Central Asia

Nizari Ismailis live in Tajikistan, primarily in the Gorno-Badakhshan Autonomous *Oblast* (GBAO). In many respects, it is difficult to accurately estimate the Ismaili population of Tajikistan due to more than 50 years of state-sanctioned atheism during the Soviet period (1922–1991), prompting many to practice *taqiyya* in order to avoid punishment and persecution. In the post-Soviet period, of Tajikistan's population of approximately 5.5 million, 93 per cent are Sunni, most of whom follow the Hanafi *madhhab*. Nizari Ismailis comprise the remaining 7 per cent, numbering about 350,000. Included here are the Nizari Ismailis of northern Pakistan – notably the Hunza valley (Gilgit-Baltistan) and Chitral – because of their significant linguistic and cultural difference from the Gujarati-speaking Khoja Nizari Ismailis of Karachi and India. Gilgit-Baltistan is the only Twelver-majority region of Pakistan, where Muharram continues to be celebrated and where Iranian-backed *howzeh*s (religious schools) and offices representing religious scholars have proliferated since the 1979 revolution.

Nizari Ismailism has been present in Central Asia since the 10th century, when a number of *da'i*s (missionaries) were received at the court of the Samanid amir Nasr II (r. 914–943) and achieved a degree of influence. The prestige of the Ismaili *da'i*s at the Samanid court was short-lived; after the overthrow of Nasr II, Ismailis were persecuted throughout the Khurasan and Transoxiana regions. At the start of the

---

[1] The Pew Forum on Religion and Public Life, *Mapping the Global Muslim Population: A Report on the Size and Distribution of the World's Muslim Population* (Washington, DC, 2009), p. 8.

11th century, the *daʿi* Nasir-i Khusraw (1004–after 1070) settled in the Yumgan valley in Badakhshan (Afghanistan), where he continued to practise his calling as a *daʿi* and wrote his theological masterpieces. After Nasir-i Khusraw's death, there is little documentary evidence for the history of the Ismaili communities of Central Asia until the 19th century.

In their quest for domination of 'the roof of the world', both the British and the Russians grasped the need to understand the languages, religious traditions and cultural practices of Central Asia's diverse communities. In 1895, the British and Russians brokered the last of a set of diplomatic agreements between them. These have had long-lasting effects on the Central Asian Shiʿa. For Ismailis in Tajikistan, British and Russian annexations provided a buffer against their Sunni persecutors; yet these borders further isolated Ismaili communities from one another. Studies of Central Asian Nizari Ismailis by Russian and British scholars reveal the extent to which this community had been separated from other Ismailis of the Indian subcontinent. Over the centuries, Central Asian Nizari Ismailis developed their own distinct 'literary tradition, practices, independent leadership and organisational hierarchy, headed by *pirs* and *khalifahs*'.[2]

Following the 1917 Russian Revolution, the Central Asian Ismailis experienced even greater isolation as the Soviet state sought to enforce an official policy of atheism. This was effected through the execution of the *pirs* (spiritual guides) and re-appropriating the role of the *khalifa* (local representatives of the *pir*) to state bureaucracy. In the 1920s, Tajiks living in the mountains of the southeast, who had traditionally worked as small-scale farmers and artisans living in close relationship with the land and its spirits, were resettled on the steppes and forced to farm cotton. In the 1980s, these mountain-dwelling Tajiks began to vocally protest against their decades-long forced migration and diasporic status – and increasingly began returning to their ancestral lands and sacred places. With the fall of the Soviet Union in 1991, Tajikistan became embroiled in a civil war that lasted from 1992–1997, causing significant internal displacement and loss of life, as a result of which tens of thousands of Ismailis sought refuge. The Aga Khan Development Network's (AKDN) initiative in providing humanitarian relief proved critical in providing aid; its charitable and educational activities have since played an important role in integrating both the region and Central Asian Ismailis with the wider world.

---

[2] H. Elnazarov and S. Aksakolov, 'The Nizari Ismailis of Central Asia', in Farhad Daftary, ed., *A Modern History of the Ismailis: Continuity and Change in a Muslim Community* (London, 2011), p. 50.

Afghanistan is home to both Nizari Ismaili and Twelver Shiʻi communities. The Ismailis are concentrated in two regions of Afghanistan – in Badakhshan province in the northeastern part of the country and Hazaristan, where the Ismailis are the second largest religious community after the Twelver Shiʻa. There are no firm numbers for Hazaristan, where the total population is between 5 and 6 million people. Many Ismailis practised *taqiyya* by praying in Sunni mosques. In 1925, the Ismailis of Shughnan and Rushan staged a rebellion to protest against punitive taxation and excessive military conscription. The government swiftly quelled the rebellion and the Ismailis experienced even greater hardship until the establishment of the communist People's Democratic Party of Afghanistan (PDPA), which ruled the country from 1978 to 1992. Aware of their marginalised status, in the 1970s the Ismaili elites argued that socialism was the path to development. Despite the state of war in which most Afghans lived after the Soviet invasion of 1979, the Ismaili community benefited from increased contact with Tajik Ismailis and fresh educational opportunities. With the ascent of the Pashtun Sunni-dominated Taliban in September 1996, the Ismailis were once again extremely vulnerable and many fled to refugee camps in Pakistan.

Hazara Twelver Shiʻism is distinct from the forms practised by Twelvers in the neighbouring South Asian countries of Pakistan and India, as well as Iran. Hazara Shiʻism is not deeply rooted in prescriptive textual traditions. Rather, it is centred on devotion to Imam Ali. Hazara religious life has traditionally operated at the village-level, where small shrines to local saints (*pirs*) and all-purpose religious buildings (*membar*) structure religious and social life. Until the early 1980s, mullahs typically received only a rudimentary religious education, although now young Hazaras study in Iranian *howzeh*s and have returned to their communities preaching a more politicised, reformist ideology.

In recent decades, the observance of Muharram has assumed a more prominent role in Hazara religious life, particularly because of the public nature of its performance and the political message of Imam Husayn's martyrdom. Monsutti notes that Karbala resonates with the Hazaras, who compare their suffering with that of their imam:

For instance, the thirst which tortured the Imam's companions when they were prevented from getting water from the Euphrates is compared with the blockade of the Hazarajat by the Taliban between the summer of 1997 and the fall of 1998, and the profanation of Hosayn's body is compared with the tragic end of Abd-al-Ali Mazari, the Hazara leader captured and killed by the Taliban in March 1995.[3]

The politicisation of the Hazara Twelver Muharram ritual and discourses is also taking place in the Hunza valley of Pakistan's Northern Areas region, where sectarian violence between the Twelver Shiʻa and the Sunni minority has flared since 2000. The Hunza valley is characterised by its ethnic, linguistic and religious diversity. A longstanding centre of Buddhism and rich shamanistic traditions, where Islam was consolidated in the 13th century, the region's religious boundaries have been fluid. The isolation of the region until the 19th century has left us with a limited historical record of the Hunzakut (the inhabitants of the Hunza valley). *Daʻis* from Badakhshan in Afghanistan successfully converted most Twelver Shiʻa to Nizari Ismailism in the 18th and 19th centuries. The Nizaris are also concentrated in the Chitral district, located directly to the west of the Northern Areas. Primarily rural and agricultural, changes have come to the Nizari Ismailis of Chitral and Gilgit-Baltistan only in the past 30 years with the influx of refugees from Afghanistan, the Islamisation of the state in Pakistan, and the infiltration of Taliban elements. Since 1982, the AKDN has been actively involved in rural development programmes to enhance indigenous economic wellbeing.

Esteem for the Aga Khan as the Nizari Imam plays an important role in the Ismaili ritual calendar in Hunza. In his study of the Ismailis of Chitral, Magnus Marsden describes how the Aga Khan visited the region to meet his community of followers, and to give them the opportunity to see him (*deedar korik*). Marsden notes that the traditional ritual encounter of *deedar* had to be performed with discretion, since it may be perceived with hostility by Sunni Muslims.[4]

Southeast Asia

Although the Shiʻi population in Southeast Asia is statistically very small, the history of the Twelver Shiʻa in this region is deep, going back to the 7th century. The Muslim population in Southeast Asia is predominately Sunni. But there are strong traditions of devotion to the Prophet Muhammad's family, signalling the influence of both Shiʻism and Sufism in the region. The Indonesian Shiʻi scholar Jalaluddin Rakhmat has hypothesised that a sort of proto-Shiʻi presence has been present

---

[3] Alessandro Monsutti, 'Hazara iii. Ethnography and Social Organization', *Encyclopaedia Iranica*, 12 (2003), pp. 85–90, available online at: http://www.iranicaonline.org/articles/hazara-3.
[4] Magnus Marsden, *Living Islam: Muslim Religious Experience in Pakistan's North-West Frontier* (Cambridge, 2005), p. 225.

in Southeast Asia since the earliest phases of Islamic history. The term 'Shi'a', Rakhmat argues, 'should not be only used to refer to people who practically follow the Ja'fari school of law but also should refer to those who accepted Shi'i theological doctrines, especially concerning the Imamate.'[5] Musa elaborates on this ambiguous aspect of Shi'i identity, explaining this as being 'Shi'a at heart' and not necessarily adherence to the Ja'fari *madhhab*.[6]

This is especially significant with regard to determining the exact population of the Shi'a in Southeast Asia, where many have practised *taqiyya* both as a way of preserving the interiority of one's faith, while also dissimulating in hostile political contexts, particularly in Malaysia since 1996. In different censuses completed in Malaysia since 2008, the Shi'i population is estimated to be between 200,000 and 331,000, though because of the widespread practice of *taqiyya*, exact numbers are impossible to obtain. Indonesia, Thailand, Vietnam, Cambodia and Singapore's total population is less than 1 per cent Shi'i; no legal constraints apply to religious practice and full rights of citizenship. Indonesia's Shi'i population is the largest in the region, estimated to be between 1 and 3 million, primarily concentrated in Java, Surabaya and Bandung. During the post-Suharto period of democratisation in Indonesia (1998–present), the Shi'i have taken an active role in building civil society. They have been granted the freedom to open their own publishing houses as well as religious schools and colleges.

Despite the long historical presence of Twelver Shi'a in Malaysia, on 5 May 1996, a *fatwa* was issued by the Fatwa Committee of the National Council for Islamic Affairs in Malaysia which effectively outlawed the practice of Shi'ism in the country. The language of this *fatwa* unequivocally labelled Twelver Shi'ism as a 'deviant teaching' (*ajaran menyimpang*). State repression has been justified through fear mongering about the spread of Shi'ism and violence in the post–1979 Iranian revolution context. The majority of Malaysian Shi'a practice *taqiyya*, avoid praying in the state-run Sunni mosques and gather at privately run *husayniyya*s. Even practising in secret does not shield the community from State action. On 15 December 2010, a group of 200 Malaysian Shi'a was arrested during a private *majlis* commemorating the martyrdom of Imam Husayn. Invoked here was section 12(c) of the Enactment 9 1995 Sharia Criminal Enactment (Selangor), which makes the practice of Shi'ism illegal in Malaysia.

---

[5] Jalaluddin Rakhmat quoted in Mohd Faizal Musa, 'The Malaysian Shi'a: A Preliminary Study of their History, Oppression, and Denied Rights', *Journal of Shi'a Islamic Studies*, 6 (2013), p. 415.

[6] Musa, 'The Malaysian Shi'a', pp. 415, 417.

Despite the community's precarious status in much of this region, Shi'i influence is visible in Muslim ritual, in literature and the martial arts. For instance, the *dabus* dance traditionally practised in the Malaysian states of Perak and Selangor uses sharp metallic objects to strike the body – akin to the Muharram ritual of *qameh zani*, or striking the head with a sharp object to express grief for Imam Husayn's martyrdom. Practitioners of the martial arts (*silat*) in Malaysia take Imam Ali as the model of chivalric behaviour (*futuwwa*) and bravery.

In the Malay literary tradition, devotion to the Prophet Muhammad and his family (*ahl al-bayt*) is clearly pronounced. A body of stories (*hikayat*) written in the *jawi* script is devoted to Fatima al-Zahra, Imam Ali, Imam Hasan, Imam Husayn, the Prophet Muhammad and Ali's son Muhammad b. al-Hanafiyya. One group of these texts, known as the 'Fatima Admonitions', are short stories that recount lessons imparted by the Prophet to his daughter about piety and married life. The *hikayat* have circulated from at least the 16th century. By the early-20th century with the proliferation of print technology coupled with what Wendy Mukherjee has called a 'long process of "de-Shi'ization"', these narratives are no longer in circulation; however, they now receive increased scholarly attention.[7]

Sub-Saharan Africa

The Shi'a in this region are primarily comprised of migrants who came from South Asia between the 19th and 20th centuries and settled in East Africa, migrants who came from Lebanon and settled in West Africa as early as the 1880s and later, and indigenous communities who converted to Shi'ism through different forms of proselytisation. Studies are extremely limited with regard to the Shi'a across Sub-Saharan Africa. This section will focus on diasporic communities in West Africa, particularly Senegal and Nigeria, and on East Africa, notably Kenya, Uganda and Tanzania.

West Africa

Muslims in West Africa are mostly Sunni. Many belong to Sufi *tariqa*s. Owing to economic decline in the Levant, small numbers of Twelver Shi'a from Lebanon began arriving in the 1880s, through France, en

---

[7]   Wendy Mukherjee, 'Fatimah in Nusantara', *Sari*, 23 (2005), p. 146. See also Ronit Ricci, 'Perfect Wedding, Penniless Life: Ali and Fatima in a Sri Lankan Malay Text', *South Asian History and Culture*, 4 (2013), pp. 266–277; and Majid Daneshgar et al., 'A Study on the Notions of Ali ibn Abi Talib in Malay Popular Culture', *Journal of Shi'a Islamic Studies*, 6 (2013), pp. 465–479.

route to the United States and South America. Upon arrival at the French colonial capital at Dakar, Senegal, some migrants decided to remain. In the 1920s, fleeing continued troubles in Lebanon and the Franco-Syrian War, more Lebanese Shi'a arrived in West Africa. The French colonial government, which held power over large sections of West Africa, did not support these migrants. However, upon the region's independence in the 1960s, the Lebanese Shi'a acquired good social and economic status and remained, spreading to other countries in the region. Today, Lebanese migrants make up most of the Shi'i communities in the region.

As of 2010, there were some 15,000–30,000 Lebanese settled in Senegal, the vast majority of them Shi'i.[8] These communities have prospered in various businesses and professions. Many once saw themselves as temporary migrants, but with the continued conflicts in Lebanon in contrast to Senegal's political stability, as well as their relative prosperity, the prospect of returning 'home' has become less attractive. Some feel discriminated against by the Sunni majority community, however.

Senegal's Lebanese Shi'is regularly revert to Lebanon for their religious needs. Having visited Senegal in 1967, the well-known Lebanese cleric Musa al-Sadr (1928–1978?) sent another Lebanese cleric, Shaykh Abdul Munam al-Zayn, to Dakar to help with the community's religious affairs. Al-Zayn, who still lives in Senegal, is its most prominent Shi'i leader. He has opened Islamic schools and an Islamic Institute with a *husayniyya*. These facilities are used to conduct religious affairs including Ashura. Community members sustain their identity as 'Lebanese Shi'a' through the somewhat exclusive use of these facilities and by maintaining their connections to their diasporic home. There are regular visits of religious personnel from Lebanon, as well as visits from groups who represent Lebanese Islamic political parties and causes.

The recent availability of satellite television with 24-hour Middle East news stations in Senegal brings Lebanon's issues even closer to Senegal's Lebanese Shi'a. An index of this change is the community's political reaction to Lebanon's 2006 July War that took the form of public protests on the streets of Dakar and calls for Senegal's government to respond. It is increasingly 'difficult to separate Lebanese religious and political transnationalisms', according to one observer.[9]

---

[8] Mara A. Leichtman, 'Migration, War, and the Making of a Transnational Lebanese Shi'i community in Senegal', *International Journal of Middle Eastern Studies*, 42 (2010), pp. 269–290, and her article, 'The Legacy of Transnational Lives: Beyond the First Generation of Lebanese in Senegal', *Ethnic and Racial Studies*, 28 (2005), pp. 663–686.

[9] Leichtman, 'Migration, War', p. 285.

The Lebanese Shi'a have actively supported the 'Senegalese Shi'a'.[10] Originally, Sunni Muslims associated with Sufi *tariqa*s, members of this group have been converting to Twelver Shi'ism since the 1980s. Among the factors that have motivated these conversions are the influence of Iranian literature circulated in Senegal since the 1970s, and the attraction of Ayatollah Khomeini as a social reformer; a rejection of Sufi *maraboutic* authority and also of Salafism (as 'Arab-dominated Islam'); religious instruction from Shaykh al-Zayn; and financial support from the Lebanese Shi'a. Converts often retain connections to their Sunni–Sufi *tariqa*s; looking both ways makes their Shi'ism especially 'Senegalese'. Indeed, they have developed unique 'Africanised Ashura' celebrations and forms of piety.[11] The community now has a *masjid* whose sheikh is Senegalese, with *khutba*s in Wolof – and where Sunnis are welcomed.

East Africa

Historically, the majority of East Africa's Muslims have been Sunnis, of the Shafi'i *madhhab*. The region has also had influential minorities of Ibadi Muslims with ties to Oman, and Sufi *tariqa*s with connections to Yemen. Before the 19th century, the number of Shi'a in East Africa was likely to have been quite small. Their histories and influences in the region remain unascertained.

There was a significant migration of Shi'i Muslims to colonial East Africa in the 1800s, mainly from the Indian provinces of Gujarat and Maharashtra. They included members of the Daudi Bohra, Tayyibi Ismaili Shi'a, Nizari Ismaili Shi'a Khoja and Twelver Shi'a Khoja communities, whose ancestors had by and large embraced Shi'ism in South Asia. Their appellations – 'Bohra' and 'Khoja' – are forms of 'caste' identification that are indicative of their complex conversion histories. They remain the most prominent Shi'i communities in East Africa today.

The migration of Shi'i communities to East Africa was occasioned by an admixture of push and pull factors. These included: encouragement from the Omani Sultanate and its promise of religious tolerance; the British hegemony over the region and the increase of commercial trading networks; labour demands for colonial infrastructure projects;

---

[10] Mara A. Leichtman, 'The Authentication of a Discursive Islam: Shi'a Alternatives to Sufi Orders', in Mamadou Diouf and Mara A. Leichtman, ed., *New Perspectives on Islam in Senegal* (New York, 2009), pp. 111–138; Mara A. Leichtman, 'Revolution, Modernity and (Trans)National Shi'i Islam: Rethinking Religious Conversion in Senegal', *Journal of Religion in Africa*, 39 (2009), pp. 319–351.
[11] Mara A. Leichtman, 'The Africanisation of 'Ashura in Senegal', in Lloyd Ridgeon, ed., *Shi'i Islam and Identity* (London, 2012), pp. 144–169.

and uncertain economic prospects in India owing to crippling famines and social unrest. Taking advantage of these social and economic transformations, Shi'i groups quickly established themselves in the region. By the 1900s, the Bohras and Khoja Nizaris in East Africa were fully-fledged diasporas of their home communities in India, while the Khoja Twelvers had established themselves as a new community.

In 1750, the Bohras had a single settlement in East Africa in Madagascar.[12] There was also a Bohra community in Zanzibar in the mid-1800s of about 300 men, women and children. By the end of 1800s, they began to spread out along the East African coast. Engaging in commerce with small shops and businesses, they settled in urban areas, residing in close proximity to each other and forming cohesive, bounded communities. They established Bohra *masjid*s that included a prayer hall for religious observances and communal gathering spaces. *Masjid*s catered to men and women of all ages, and were used exclusively by the community. It is likely that Lamu is the site of East Africa's first Bohra *masjid*.[13]

East Africa's Bohras regarded themselves members of the greater Bohra community and gave allegiance to the *da'i mutlaq* based in India. From the 1800s to 1915, the Bohras had a series of nine successive *da'i*s. The succession of Sayyidna Tahir Sayf al-Din (1915–1965), the 51st *da'i mutlaq*, coincided with a time when Bohra settlers developed stronger East African roots. His succession also ignited a series of inter-communal disputes amongst Bohras on both sides of the western Indian Ocean. In 1917, disputants from India and East Africa accused the *da'i* of financial mismanagement and blocking educational reforms. They launched a case against him in the High Court of Bombay – which was won by the *da'i*, who retained full authority over the community. In 1944, reformists mounted another challenge; they were again defeated and excommunicated. These disputes brought a rift between the majority of traditional-minded Bohras who continued to follow the *da'i* and his successors, and a minority of reform-minded Bohras.

Cognisant of these intra-communal tensions, between 1951 and 1955 the *da'i* allowed East Africa's Bohras to develop their own constitution. The resulting document brought in democratically elected councils with fixed terms to govern the community's affairs, and entrusted the community's property such as *masjid*s and schools to five local trustees. However, in 1965, when Sayyidna Mohammed Burhanuddin (1915–2014) became

---

[12] Hatim Amiji, 'The Bohras of East Africa', *Journal of Religion in Africa*, 7 (1975), pp. 34ff.
[13] Cynthia Salvadori, *Through Open Doors: A View of Asian Cultures in Kenya* (Nairobi, 1983), p. 258.

the 52nd *daʿi*, the East African Bohra constitution was annulled. The *daʿi* provided them with an alternative constitution that reasserted his absolute power over the community's governance and their communal property and reserved his right to expel community members. Tensions resurfaced between the traditionalists and the reformers, resulting in ostracisation of the reformists. Acrimony between the two groups continues today.

The number of East African Bohra reformists remains small. In the early 1980s, the total population of Bohras in Kenya was 8,000 whereas the reformists numbered 180. In 2009, there were around 150 reformists in Kenya.[14] These reformists are part of a transnational network of 'progressive Dawoodi Bohras' who reside in India, Kuwait, Britain, Canada and the USA, and continue to fight for social reform.[15] They have their own constitution, central board and a Mumbai-based headquarters. They accept the *daʿi*'s authority but allege that the 'bureaucracy of the priestly class' that surrounds him unduly 'taxes and controls the community "from womb to tomb"'.[16] Most East African Bohras continue to acknowledge the *daʿi*'s authority in spiritual and secular matters and his institutions. The 52nd *daʿi*, who retained his headquarters in Mumbai, visited East Africa on numerous occasions. During his 1980 visit, the *daʿi* established the Burhani Foundation in Nairobi to benefit poor Kenyans of all backgrounds and establish a clinic. The East African Bohras, while remaining a locally bounded diasporic community, are engaging with the non-Bohra East Africans amongst whom they live.

East Africa's Khoja Ismailis and Khoja Twelvers have intertwined histories. Community members from both migrated to East Africa from India in the 1800s. The Twelvers emerged in India in the mid-1800s in the wake of disputes they had with the Khoja Ismaili community (of which they were initially part) and their imam, Aga Khan I (1804–1881). In India, the two groups identified as a single Khoja community whose religious practices and communal life drew upon common religious ideas and cultural traditions. When the Aga Khans established themselves in India in the 1840s, they asserted their authority over the Khojas as their imams, defining them as 'Khoja Nizari Ismaili Shiʿa'. Some Khojas disputed this and lodged a case against Aga Khan I in 1866 at the High Court in Bombay. The case was firmly settled in the Aga Khan's favour. Nevertheless, some dissidents broke away and variously self-identified as Khoja Sunnis or Khoja Twelver Shiʿa. Dewji Jamal and Allarakhiyya Vali, influential traders based between Bombay and Zanzibar, were among

---

[14] Available online at: http://www.dawoodi-bohras.com/news/299/66/Quran-lays-foundation-of-global-ethics/d,news_detail/.

[15] Jonah Blank, *Mullahs on the Mainframe* (Chicago, 2001), pp. 229ff.

[16] Available online at: http://dawoodi-bohras.com/about_us/our-mission/.

those who claimed Twelver identity.[17] In the late 1800s, they founded the Khoja Twelver community in East Africa, setting up in Zanzibar their first *masjid* (Quwwat ul-Islam) in 1880, followed by an *imambara*.

The Khoja Twelvers in East Africa continued to secede from the Khoja Nizaris. For example, in Zanzibar, Khojas from both communities had continued to pray in the same *jamatkhana* (albeit adopting different ritual postures and liturgies), intermarried and feasted together during religious festivals. In 1899, on his inaugural visit to East Africa, Aga Khan III (1877–1957), who had succeed to the imamate in 1885, advised his followers to make a clean break with the Khoja Twelvers. Lingering disputes were eventually resolved in the courts and by 1905 the two communities had parted ways.

As such, the Khoja Twelvers of East Africa were not strictly a 'diaspora' from South Asia, but rather a community that largely arose within the region. They came together on the bases of their religious conviction, the common experience of having split from the Nizaris, common business interests and family ties. Dewji Jamal's son, Nasir, built a Khoja Twelver *masjid*, *imambara* and *musafirkhana* at Lamu between 1890 and 1905. Fanning out along the East African coast and the interior in the 1900s, the community established places of worship as well as schools and volunteer associations, as their numbers grew and diversified. By 1945, Twelver Khoja communities dispersed as widely as Burundi, Madagascar, Mauritius, Rwanda and Somalia were consolidated with the East African ones into a 'federation' for Africa. Eventually, with the region's shifting political tides in the postcolonial era, there occurred a significant migration of the community to other parts of the globe, including North America and Europe. By 1976, Khoja Twelvers had formed a United Kingdom-based 'World Federation' – which today works with congregations and regional bodies to support the community's social and economic development and religious formation.[18]

Efforts have been made to proselytise amongst indigenous African communities. Early on, locally produced magazines were used to spread their faith. In 1964, the Khoja Twelvers established the Bilal Muslim Mission (BMM) for the explicit purpose of propagating the faith to indigenous Africans.[19] Today, the BMM has missions in Kenya and Tanzania, running bookshops and schools and public events. The BMM

---

[17] Hatim Amiji, 'Some Notes on Religious Dissent in Nineteenth-Century East Africa', *African Historical Studies*, 4 (1971), p. 611.
[18] Available online at: http://www.world-federation.org/default.htm.
[19] Available online at: http://www.world federation.org/Secretariat/Articles/ Archive/From_Afed_archives_ Recollections_over_5decades.htm; http://www. bilaltz.org/about-us/.

claims that over the years it has converted more than 100,000 indigenous Africans.[20]

Since the 1800s, the community has regularly sought religious guidance from *mujtahids* in India, Iraq and Iran, and invited clerics to come to East Africa.[21] Pilgrimages to Iraq and Iran have also served to forge ties between the Khoja and Shiʿi Twelvers elsewhere. Presently, scholars based and trained in Iran support religious formations in Kenya and Tanzania.[22] At the same time, Khoja Twelver religious and social rituals and customs, such as marriage, retain aspects of their South Asian origins. But the community also shows other influences. For example, women are increasingly adopting the Iranian style *chador*. Interestingly, their specific form of *matam*, which involves 'mourners chanting hymns and refrains while linking with one another in a large circle, treading in a swaying fashion around the *imambara*, and beating their breasts', has received criticism for looking too much like secular dancing and singing.[23]

Most Khoja Nizari Ismailis arrived in East Africa after the 1840s, preceded by a handful of pioneering merchants. Although united in terms of their core religious beliefs, particularly the singular authority of a living imam, the migrants had different linguistic, cultural and occupational backgrounds. Some spoke Gujarati, while others spoke Katchi or Sindhi. Some were business-minded and able to set up shops. Others were farmers who took up jobs as labourers. By the late 19th century, East Africa's Khoja Nizaris constituted a trans-oceanic diaspora of their Indian home community with which they had retained business relationships, kinship networks and religious associations. From the 19th century to the first half of the 20th century, the Ismaili imams, Shah Khalil Allah (d. 1817), Hasan Ali Shah, Aga Khan I (1804–1881), Aqa Ali Shah, Aga Khan II (1830–1885), and Sultan Muhammad (Mahomed) Shah, Aga Khan III (1877–1957), were based in India for significant periods of time.

Aga Khan I and Aga Khan II oversaw the initial migrations of community members to East Africa, whereas Aga Khan III oversaw the community's settlement in the region. In 1899, Aga Khan III travelled to East Africa to meet his followers and attend to their affairs. He

---

[20] Abbas Jaffer, 'Conversion to Shiʿism in Africa', *Journal of Shiʿa Islamic Studies*, 6 (2013), p. 137.

[21] Seyyid Saeed Akhtar Rizvi and Noel Q. King, 'Some East African Ithna-Asheri Jamaats (1840–1967)', *Journal of Religion in Africa*, 5 (1973), p. 15.

[22] Available online at: http://www.bilaltz.org/2013/02/14/sayyid-muhammad-rizvi-visits-bilal-muslim-mission-head-office-and-bilal-comprehensive-school-temeke-in-tanzania/.

[23] Salvadori, *Through Open Doors*, pp. 252–253.

returned in 1905 to inaugurate the first written Ismaili 'constitution', a two-part document issued in Gujarati and published in Zanzibar. Allegiance to the imam was a central tenet. Concurrently, he established the Supreme Council for Africa. These instruments provided East Africa's Khoja Nizaris with an organisational structure and rules for governance. In addition, the imam issued *firman*s, guidance for the community's spiritual and secular wellbeing, including both social and religious reforms.

During his 1905 visit, Aga Khan III also opened the region's first principal *jamatkhana* at Zanzibar, which had spaces for prayer and communal gathering. As is the case today, *jamatkhana*s were reserved for prayer and the devotional activities of the community's men, women and children, presided over by local representatives of the imam. Many of the original *jamatkhana*s built in the first half of the 20th century in Kenya, Tanzania and Uganda remain in use today.

After World War I, Khoja Nizaris established firmer roots in East Africa. In 1918 and 1919 respectively, the community with the imam's assistance established their first schools for boys and girls at Mombasa. Subsequently, the imamate established other institutions to support the community. East Africa's local councils grew into territorial councils, and by 1945, an institution to deal with religious formation. Volunteers have run virtually all community organisations.

The institutions established by Aga Khan III were expanded and developed by his grandson and successor, Aga Khan IV, the present and 49th Nizari Ismaili Imam. Now headquartered in France, Aga Khan IV was familiar with East Africa after spending his early childhood in Nairobi. When he became imam in 1957, the East African Khoja Nizaris faced rapid and intense socio-political change. European colonialism in East Africa had given way to African nationalism; non-African origin communities were especially challenged in this differently racialised context. The Khoja Nizaris, identified as an 'Asian' community, were frequently the target of prejudice and scapegoating – most evident in Idi Amin's 1972 expulsion of Ugandan Asians, including many Khoja Nizaris. In this turbulent political context, East Africa's Khoja Nizaris began emigrating to other parts of the world, particularly Europe and North America. These migrants soon formed diasporas of East African Khoja Nizaris, their forebears having less than a century ago been diasporas of South Asian communities. In recent years, there have been new influxes of Nizari Ismailis from India and Pakistan in East Africa, who like previous generations seek economic opportunities in the region.

Steadily over recent decades, the Khoja Nizaris have also begun to identify themselves as part of a wider global community of Nizari Ismaili Shi'a. Indeed, this was already evident in 1925, when their constitution deleted 'Khoja' from its title and was entitled *Rules of the Shi'a Imami Ismailia of the Continent of Africa*. In 1986, Aga Khan IV issued the *Constitution of the Shi'a Imami Ismailis*, a single document governing the global community. In keeping with a pluralist ethos, however, Nizaris from diverse regions maintain aspects of their particular religious expressions and social customs. For East Africa's Nizaris, a composite South Asian-African heritage is reflected in their supererogatory devotional practices, life-cycle rituals and food culture.

Aga Khan IV also responded to the global changes taking place in the world by establishing the AKDN, mentioned earlier in this chapter. This non-governmental organisation works primarily in Asia and Africa through a range of agencies that support the economic, social and cultural development of communities around the world – far beyond Nizari, Shi'i or Muslim bounds.[24] East Africa is home to numerous AKDN projects including schools, hospitals, heritage preservation and infrastructure projects.

Western Europe

Western Europe is home to a range of Shi'i communities. They have various migration histories and points of origin including East Africa, Iran, Iraq, Lebanon and South Asia. Like other Muslims, the Shi'a began travelling to the region in significant numbers in the late 19th century from South Asia and other regions under European colonial rule. Some stayed and settled. Small numbers of Muslims continued to migrate to Europe into the 1960s – and some Shi'i groups established religious spaces and organisations. The Nizaris set up their first *jamatkhana* in London in 1951.[25] A group of Twelver Shi'i traders from Iran initiated a project for establishing a *masjid* and Islamic centre in Hamburg in 1953. In the 1970s, significant numbers of both Khoja Nizaris and Khoja Twelvers arrived in Europe as political refugees from Uganda, followed by migrants from conflicts in Lebanon, Iran, Iraq and Afghanistan into the 1980s.[26] Economic opportunity has also fuelled the migration of Shi'i groups. Ireland's Shi'i population, for example, largely comprises economic migrants from Iraq, the Gulf, Saudi Arabia and Pakistan.[27] However, scholarship on European Muslims tends to focus primarily on

---

[24] Available online at: http://www.akdn.org/about_akdn.asp.
[25] Available online at: http://www.theismaili.org/cms/831/menu.
[26] Matthijs van den Bos, 'European Shi'ism? Counterpoints from Shi'ites' organization in Britain and the Netherlands', *Ethnicities*, 12 (2011), pp. 556–580.
[27] Oliver Scharbrodt, 'Shaping the Public Image of Islam: The Shi'is of Ireland as "Moderate" Muslims', *Journal of Muslim Minority Affairs*, 13 (2011), pp. 518–533.

Sunni groups, or use 'ethnic' categories such as 'Pakistani' and 'Iranian'.[28] This section focuses on studies of Shi'i communities in Britain, Ireland, Denmark and the Netherlands.

As with Europe's Muslims as a whole, questions of 'identity', 'integration' and 'networks' dominate studies about the Shi'a. Illustrative is the 'identity-seeking' in the sacred narratives of refugee Iraqi Shi'i women in the Netherlands, retold in the ritual context of the *majlis al-qiraya*, a mournful gathering in remembrance of the Prophet's family.[29] Personal and religious stories are often fused in these settings, where the women create a diasporic network that helps them overcome the trauma associated with migration and settlement. Again, Iranian local and transnational networks in Britain during the 1990s provided a specific setting for the forming of female identity. Women living in various parts of London, for instance, generated multiple and contested discourses about their religiosity in the context of *sofreh*, a ritual of food offerings and prayer to Shi'i holy figures. Such women-only gatherings are 'used by some Iranian women as an identity-building vehicle in the process of emigration', and also serve as private spaces where Shi'i Iranian women from different backgrounds debate what it means to be 'an Iranian Muslim outside Iran'.[30] By comparison, an 'Iranian intra-diasporic secular' identity has also emerged in London through 'culturalising or neutralizing the specifically Islamic religious character of religious practices'.[31] Festivals such as *nawruz* or greetings and naming of children, are given an 'Iranian' gloss and allow a distancing from official Iran without giving up on 'Iranianness' and deeply-felt connections to the homeland. In these ways, community members make a place for themselves in Britain.

'Place-making' is also a critical concern for Iraqi Shi'i women in Denmark, many of whom arrived as refugees after the first Gulf War.[32]

[28] See, for example, Humayun Ansari, *Muslims in Britain since 1800* (London, 2004); Tahir Abbas, ed., *Muslim Britain: Communities under Pressure* (London, 2005); Jørgen S. Nielsen, *Muslims in Western Europe* (Edinburgh, 2004); and Shireen Hunter, ed., *Islam, Europe's Second Religion: The New Social, Cultural, and Political Landscape* (Westport, CT, 2002).
[29] Tayba Hassan Al Khalifa Sharif, 'Sacred Narratives Linking Iraqi Shi'ite Women', in Miriam Cooke and Bruce B. Lawrence, ed., *Muslim Networks from Hajj to Hip Hop* (Chapel Hill, NC, 2005), pp. 132ff.
[30] Kathryn Spellman, *Religion and Nation* (New York, 2004), pp. 59–102; quote at pp. 96–97.
[31] Reza Gholami, '"Is this Islamic Enough?" Intra-diasporic Secularism and Religious Experience in the Shi'a Iranian Diaspora in London', *Journal of Ethnic and Migration Studies*, 40 (2014), pp. 62–64.
[32] Marianne Holm Pederson, 'Going on a Class Journey: The Inclusion and Exclusion of Iraqi Refugees in Denmark', *Journal of Ethnic and Migration Studies*,

In fostering a sense of belonging to a new home, networks have once again played an important role, evolving in response to the women's need to create social ties with members of their host community during their settlement processes. By contrast, Twelver Shi'i groups in Ireland – many of whom originated in Iraq, the Gulf and Saudi Arabia – have sought to make a place for themselves in Irish society by representing themselves as 'moderate Muslims'.[33] Through conferences, publications and civic engagement, members of these communities present themselves as 'a double minority' espousing a 'moderate and integrationist understanding of Islam' – distancing themselves from 'radical and militant expressions of Sunni Islam' that permeate Europe's public space.

The Irish example above also shows how community-based organisations and religious authorities shape Shi'i group identity, discourses among diverse ethnic Shi'i groups, and between these groups and the state. One aspect of this, in common with Muslim diasporas at large, is 'national and ethnic fragmentation ... where most Shi'is prefer to socialise with fellow Shi'is from their countries of origin and of the same cultural and linguistic backgrounds'.[34] Van den Bos's study of Twelver Shi'i organisations in Britain and the Netherlands, looking at the extent to which Shi'i organisations are transnational, transethnic and European, found the majority to be ethnically oriented.[35] Their representatives, boards and users may be Afghan, Khoja East African, Iranian, Iraqi, Pakistani or Turkish Shi'a. He concludes that these groups are defined *both* by ethnicity or place of origin and their Shi'ism. However, Twelver Shi'i organisations in Britain and the Netherlands did not much associate with each other on a trans-ethnic or transnational level; and they had yet to operate as a European community.

North America

The study of Shi'i diasporic communities here is a burgeoning field. Much of this scholarship focuses on issues of identity, cultural and religious, in relation to living in a non-Muslim, secular context. Ritual practice, relations with a community's ancestral homeland, and gender roles are also areas of research that have garnered significant scholarly attention. In the context of the Caribbean, one of the greatest challenges to studying the Shi'i diaspora is that active secularisation of the community by Christian churches and the British colonial government

---

38 (2012), pp. 1105–1106.
33 Scharbrodt, 'The Shi'is of Ireland', pp. 519ff.
34 Ibid., p. 521.
35 Van den Bos, 'European Shi'ism?', pp. 556ff.

in the 19th and early 20th century means that the Indo-Caribbean diaspora no longer maintains a distinctive (Twelver) Shi'i identity. In the United States, future research might focus more on ritual and literary devotional practices, especially in second and third generation communities. The well-established Nizari Ismaili diaspora in Canada presents a number of possibilities for further research, including institutional structures and networks, and religious practice – as do the sizeable and growing Twelver and Daudi Bohra communities.

The Caribbean

In 1838, the first wave of indentured labourers was brought from India to Guyana, and in 1845, a second wave arrived in Trinidad and Jamaica to work on the sugar cane plantations. Most of these labourers came from North India, especially Bihar, and what is today Uttar Pradesh. With the abolition of slavery in Great Britain and its colonies in 1833, indentured labour took its place as a way of preserving the plantation economy. Most of the Indians were to settle, establishing deep roots and influencing the local Afro-Caribbean culture. By the end of the 19th century, locally born 'Creole Indians' came to outnumber their forebears.[36] In the 1990 *Census of Trinidad and Tobago*, Muslims comprised 15 per cent of the Indo-Trinidadian community, and 6 per cent of the overall population. From the beginning of South Asian labour migration to the Caribbean, Sunni and Shi'i Muslims have not been distinguished. Since the *Census* has not counted Muslims according to sectarian identity, we have no precise sense of how many Shi'is migrated to the Caribbean. Furthermore, it is likely that Shi'is who did migrate to the Caribbean practised *taqiyya*.

For Indo-Caribbeans, Muharram was the exclusive domain of the Shi'a. In the 19th century, Muharram was observed in accord with the Islamic lunar calendar, and *panchayats* (councils of five members) oversaw the planning and schedule of events. On the first day of Muharram, *taziya*s were built using bamboo and brightly coloured paper. In the evenings, people would attend *majlis* where men and women would sing *marsiya*s (songs of mourning) through the night. On Ashura, the *taziya*s were brought out in procession accompanied by drummers, while men would perform acrobatic stick fighting (*gutka*). Over time, Muharram was 'creolised' and transformed into 'Hosay'. Afro-Caribbean religion and culture has gradually transformed

---

[36] Frank Korom, *Hosay Trinidad: Muharram Performances in an Indo-Caribbean Diaspora* (Philadelphia, PA, 2003), pp. 98–99.

Muharram into a festive, carnivalesque event, now much devoid of its religious origins and meaning.

The United States and Canada

The first Shiʻa arrived in the United States in the late 19th and early 20th centuries, primarily from the Ottoman Empire, notably Lebanon, Syria and Iraq. A small group settled in the early 1900s in Michigan City, Indiana, where they worked for the railways and steel factories. Another centre for Shiʻi migration – notably from Lebanon's Bekaa valley – was Dearborn, Michigan. As in their homeland, these immigrants occupied a lower socioeconomic status and worked primarily as labourers, peddlers and small business owners.[37] From 1924 to 1965 the United States government imposed strict quotas for non-West European immigrants, drastically reducing Muslim immigration. The Hart-Celler Act signed by President Lyndon Johnson repealed the quotas, opening the door for Asian and African migrants. Muslims from South Asia immigrated to the United States in record numbers.[38]

American Shiʻism has been shaped by a complex array of elements, many of them external when it comes to the Twelver community.[39] In the religious realm, the institution of the *marja-i taqlid* – the supreme living authority on Jaʻfari jurisprudence and doctrine – is a key factor. In this regard, both Ayatollah Ali Sistani (b. 1930) and Ayatollah Muhammad Husain Fadlallah (1935–2010) are highly influential. The latter is especially popular among American Shiʻi youth for his relatively liberal perspective and the pragmatic tone of his religious opinions (*fatawa*). When it comes to politics, events in the Middle East have had repercussions on the community in the United States. Until the 1970s, Sunnis and Shiʻis for the most part, interacted closely with each other under the banner of their collective Muslim identity. In 1963, the first Muslim Student Association was established at the University of Illinois at Urbana-Champaign, with Sunnis and Shiʻis actively participating in the organisation as it acquired a national profile. The 1979 Iranian revolution reinvigorated many Twelver Americans; pictures of Ayatollah Khomeini appeared in mosques and cultural centres across the country, and women were encouraged to dress more conservatively. Not surprisingly, this had a varied impact on Twelver-Sunni relations, just as in the Middle East itself.

---

[37] Liyakat Takim, *Shiʻism in America* (New York, 2009), p. 14.
[38] Pew Forum, *Mapping the Global Muslim Population*, p. 10.
[39] Liyakat Takim, 'Foreign Influences on American Shiʻism', *The Muslim World*, 90 (2000), p. 459.

Cultural difference has also played a major role. The linguistic, ethnic and cultural diversity of the American Shi'a, Twelver and otherwise, is expressed in terms of ritual practice during Muharram, in domestic rituals, and in ethical and social norms. Predictably, language plays a key part in the alignment of mosques, religious centres and schools along particular lines. Even when a religious centre is shared by different ethnic or national groups, events such as the Muharram *majlis* are often performed separately and in the language of each – such as Urdu for South Asians, Arabic for Iraqis and Lebanese, and Persian for Iranian Shi'a. Linguistic fragmentation makes it difficult for different Shi'i national groups to come together in the North American diaspora.

In many respects, the history of Shi'i migration to Canada follows that of the United States from the 19th until the mid-20th century. In the late 1800s, immigrants from the Ottoman Empire, especially Syria, settled on Canada's western frontier. Most of these immigrants were Christian rather than Muslim. Until 1951, Canada's Muslim population remained low, when post-World War II economic development compelled the liberalisation of immigration laws in order to aid the growth of the economy. Canada's Muslim population is approximately 940,000 or 2.8 per cent of the country's population.[40] Of this, the Shi'i population is estimated to be about 141,000 or 15 per cent. With the decolonisation of Africa in the 1960s, a new wave of Muslim immigrants settled in Canada, a significant number of whom were Ismaili and Twelver Shi'a. Most came from East Africa after Idi Amin expelled all Asians from Uganda in 1972. Through the diplomatic efforts of Aga Khan IV, Uganda's Ismailis were resettled, with Canada accepting the largest proportion.

Canada's 1988 Multiculturalism Act – which guaranteed minority groups the freedom to participate in and express their religious and cultural identities – has contributed to a significant body of scholarship that has focused on Nizari Ismaili women in Canadian society. One study observes that *The Constitution of the Shi'a Imami Ismaili Muslims* of 1986 serves not only as a unitary document of governance, but also has 'provided a degree of continuity and a means of balancing past values with…those of the new independent nations, whose personal laws they also complemented'.[41] This has had a major effect on the reor-

---

[40] Pew Forum on Religion in Public Life, 'The Future of the Global Muslim Population' (2011), available online at: http://features.pewforum.org/muslim-population/?sort=Pop2010.

[41] Fariyal Ross-Sheriff and Azim Nanji, 'Islamic Identity, Family, and Community: The Case of the Nizari Ismaili Community', in Earle H. Waugh, Sharon McIrvin Abu-Laban and Regula Burkhardt-Qureshi, ed., *Muslim Families*

ganisation of gender relations, providing women with more of a public role in the *jamatkhana*.

Indeed, scholarship on the perception and performance of gender roles by Ismaili men and women has been the subject of a number of studies.[42] Mamodaly and Fakirani posit that the 'ethical framework of the Imamat Institutions, inspired by the Quran itself, places importance on universal values of equality, tolerance, and service to humanity, regardless of gender, race or religion, thereby enabling women to envision their role in meaningful ways'.[43] Many of these studies focus on the compatibility of Ismaili teachings with the values of gender equality and multiculturalism that are central to Canadian national identity. Women take an active role in the professions, volunteering for Ismaili institutions and charitable organisations, as well as in their faith and family. On the other hand, when Ismaili women settled with their families in Canada in the 1970s, the majority worked outside the home were working a 'double-shift', also at home serving as the family's primary caretaker. For many Ismaili women, the integration of these multiple aspects of identity and the social, religious and familial responsibilities were unequally engendered.[44] At least for immigrant middle-aged Ismaili women, the challenges of juggling careers and family life were only partly abated by their husbands providing merely some assistance rather than fully sharing responsibility. However, this was a reflection of wider societal trends regarding the gendering of domestic labour in the nuclear, patriarchal family – rather than something unique to the Ismaili community.

Conclusion

This chapter highlights the diversity of the Shi'i diaspora, its global diffusion, and adaptation in different cultural, religious, social, political and historical contexts. It is rather vexing to apply the term 'diaspora' to these communities at a time when movement between places

---

in North America (Edmonton, 1991), p. 103.

[42] Tasleem Damji and Catherine M. Lee, 'Gender Role Identity and Perceptions of Ismaili Muslim Men and Women', *The Journal of Social Psychology*, 135 (1995), pp. 215–223; Ross-Sheriff and Nanji, 'Islamic Identity, Family, and Community', pp. 101–117; Adil Mamodaly and Alim Fakirani, 'Voices from Shi'a Ismaili Nizari Muslim Women: Reflections from Canada on Past and Present Gendered Roles in Islam', in Terence Lovat, ed., *Women in Islam: Reflections on Historical and Contemporary Research* (New York, 2012), pp. 213–236.

[43] Mamodaly and Fakirani, 'Voices', p. 214.

[44] Parin A. Dossa, '(Re)imagining Aging Lives: Ethnographic Narratives of Muslim Women in Diaspora', *Journal of Cross-Cultural Gerontology*, 14 (1999), pp. 245–272.

– either physically (as a result of voluntary or forced migration) or virtually (through the circulation of texts and images in the forms of print or digital media) – is more a norm more than an exception. Indeed, 'home' is a constantly reconfigured and contested category: one generation's 'diaspora' is the next generation's 'homeland', and vice versa. Our survey also suggests that some Shi'a struggle within their host countries to articulate and assert their Muslim identity and, more particularly, their Shi'i identity. This is achieved through distinctive ritual expressions, institutional formations and various forms of dialogue. However, articulations of and associations with gender, ethnicity, race, nationality, often compound these struggles and lead to fragmentation and isolation. Historic ruptures such as the Iranian revolution and the events of 11 September 2001 add a greater complexity to these struggles. For all the challenges, it is evident that many Shi'i diaspora communities have flourished in the global age. Drawing on the opportunities provided by new forms of communication and transnational networks, they navigate expertly between the far-flung localities in which their members live, and today constitute globalised communities.

Further Reading

Asani, Ali. 'The Khojahs of Indo-Pakistan: The Quest for an Islamic Identity', *Journal of Muslim Minority Affairs*, 8 (1987), pp. 31–41.

Hirji, Zulfikar. 'The Socio-Legal Formation of the Nizari Ismailis of East Africa, 1800–1950', in Farhad Daftary, ed., *A Modern History of the Ismailis*. London, 2011, pp. 129–159.

Leichtman, Mara A. 'Migration, War, and the Making of a Transnational Lebanese Shi'i Community in Senegal', *International Journal of Middle Eastern Studies*, 42 (2010), pp. 269–290.

MacLean, Derryl N. 'Religion, Ethnicity, and the Double Diaspora of Asian Muslims', in L. DeVries, D. Baker and D. Overmyer, ed., *Asian Religions in British Columbia*. Vancouver and Toronto, 2010, pp. 64–84.

Marcinkowski, Christoph. 'Aspects of Shi'ism in Contemporary Southeast Asia', *The Muslim World*, 98 (2008), pp. 36–71.

Mir, Raza A. 'Religion as a Coping Mechanism for Global Labor: Lessons from the South Asian Shi'a Muslim Diaspora in the US', *Equality, Diversity and Inclusion: An International Journal*, 32 (2013), pp. 325–337.

Salvadori, Cynthia. *Through Open Doors: A View of Asian Cultures in Kenya*. Nairobi, 1983.

Sharif, Tayba Hassan Al Khalifa. 'Sacred Narratives Linking Iraqi Shi'ite Women', in Miriam Cooke and Bruce B. Lawrence, ed., *Muslim Networks from Hajj to Hip Hop* (Chapel Hill, NC, 2005), pp. 132–154.

Spellman, Kathryn. *Religion and Nation*. Berghahn, NY, 2004.

Sulaiman, Muhammad Dahiru. 'Shi'ism and the Islamic Movement in Nigeria – 1979–1981', in Ousmane Kane, ed., *Islam et islamismes au sud du Sahara* (Paris, 1998), pp. 183–196.

Takim, Liyakat. *Shi'ism in America*. New York, 2009.

Walbridge, Linda. *Without Forgetting the Imam: Lebanese Shi'ism in an American Community*. Detroit, MI, 1997.

16

Modernity: The Ethics of Identity

Amyn B. Sajoo

Of my two eyes, one is Shi'a and the other is Sunni.
Wajid Ali Shah, last (Shi'i) Nawab of Awadh, India
(r. 1847–1856)[1]

Faith is an act of choosing, a fateful act. The ideal society for faith and the faithful is one in which this choice is most widely available ... the forsaking of imitated faith and adoption of conscious faith.
Mojtahed Shabestari, Senior Iranian Shi'i Theologian[2]

In the process of nurturing a healthy sense of identity, we must resist the temptation to normatise any particular culture, to demonise 'the other', and to turn healthy diversity into dangerous discord.
Karim Aga Khan, Imam of the Shi'a Nizari Ismailis[3]

In their assembly hall in the London borough of Harrow, the young Twelver Shi'a who organise this community's affairs are happy to welcome Sunni worshippers, and have male and female congregants mingle on the carpeted floor. Most of the men are clean shaven. Only for the evening *salat* do unveiled women don hijabs from a 'prayer garments' box, and the genders separate. They mingle for the lively programme of talks – which has featured the social philosophy of Michael Sandel, and speakers such as the leading Shi'i intellectuals Abdolkarim Soroush and Abdulaziz Sachedina. English is the community's formal medium.

[1]   Quoted in A. Halim Sharar, *Lucknow: The Last Phase of an Oriental Culture*, ed. and tr. E. S. Harcourt and F. Hussain (London, 1975), pp. 74–75.
[2]   *Hermenutik, Ketab va Sunnat: Farayand-e Tafsir-e Vahy* (Tehran, 1996), pp. 184–185.
[3]   Foundation Ceremony, The Aga Khan Academy (Dhaka, Bangladesh), 20 May 2008, available online at: http://www.akdn.org/Content/661/ Foundation-Stone-Laying-Ceremony-of-the-Aga-Khan-Academy-Dhaka.

Whom do congregants regard as their *marja* (designated guide) in accord with Twelver custom? There is no uniform choice: older congregants have followed Lebanese, Iraqi and Iranian *marja*, while the younger ones tend to consult websites run by various scholars, and email them if necessary.[4]

Memory, it is often observed, is a vibrant feature of Shi'i identity. This is manifest especially in the remembrance of episodes in the lives of Muhammad and his closest companion, Ali b. Abi Talib – including the affirmation of the latter's stewardship of the *umma* after the Prophet's passing – coupled with Imam Husayn's martyrdom at Karbala. Yet a more immediate narrative has effectively shaped this particular Harrow community. It is that of students arriving from East Africa in the 1960s, with a larger influx triggered by that region's political turmoil in the 1970s, and a journey from modest prayer gatherings and Ramadan *iftar*s in private homes to the acquisition from the borough of the North Harrow Assembly Hall where they congregate today. These collective experiences inform the outlook of a community which is now ethno-culturally diverse, and clearly values its traditions in pluralist fashion – within a host society that is robustly secular in its modernity. Far from being unique, this pattern in the negotiation of religious identity is pervasive, whether the outcome turns out to be 'progressive' or 'illiberal'.

Previous chapters in this volume have drawn out specific legacies of and their implications for the Shi'a into the contemporary era, down to the engendering of far-flung diaspora communities. Varieties of Shi'i traditions and identities evidently have been deeply sculpted by, and in turn sought to shape, the social environments which they inhabit. This interface is increasingly framed by scholars as the manner in which individuals and societies experience and perceive modernity in all its complexity. Charles Taylor traces the historical unfolding of such processes via 'social imaginaries' – shared maps of social and moral order – in which religion, secularism, individual autonomy and political life take forms that we now regard as modern.[5] Inevitably, this leads us to an appreciation of the global *varieties* of social imaginaries, of multiple

---

4   See I. Bowen, *Medina in Birmingham, Najaf in Brent* (London, 2014), pp. 152–154; and the community's website at http://www.sicm.org.uk/index. php?page=about_sicm.

5   *A Secular Age* (Cambridge, MA, 2008), especially at pp. 159–211. The socio-logical idea of 'nomos' – as the habitus in which individuals and communities situate themselves in the world – is not dissimilar: P. Berger, *The Sacred Canopy: Elements of a Sociology of Religion* (New York, 1967). Indeed, nomos is reminis-cent of the Muslim idea of *maslak* as an ethical pathway that captures one's core theological commitments, though some narrow it down to one's particular school of law (*madhhab*).

ways of being modern.[6] It also enables us to grasp the changing and successive *phases* of modernity: social imaginaries can hardly be fixed amid the shifts in economic, cultural and political realities, abetted by new global communications networks. Both the evolving 'Arab Spring' of 2011 and the 1979 Iranian Revolution can be understood in terms of phases, with much back and forth movement, of how societies expect their quests for modern democratic life and human rights to find practical expression.

In this final chapter, key features in the historical experience of Shi'i Islam are situated within the context of a dominantly secular but contested modernity, underscored in our time by the forces of globalisation and the responses which they inspire. We will consider how civic as well as theological identities play out and test old boundaries ('who is Shi'i'?) – amid the rise of sectarianism ('who is Muslim'?) as a challenge to pluralist and cosmopolitan tendencies. Insofar as civil society is vital in fostering quests for change and reform, not the least with regard to gender equity, we will consider Shi'i intellectual and social ventures that effectively signal the stakes and the prospects at hand. In all this, the approach will be to draw upon illustrative examples which highlight the foregoing themes, while also recalling the sheer diversity of communities of interpretation, particularly those that range beyond the more familiar locales and modes of Shi'ism.

'Defining' Shi'i Identities

Modernity and its social imaginaries make fresh demands on the *particulars* of identity. While the Twelvers, Ismailis and Zaydis have long been quite well recognised as Shi'i, communities such as the Turkish Alevi are less amenable to firm categorisation. They certainly share core aspects of Shi'ism such as the elevated theological place accorded to the Prophet's Family, and especially to Imam Ali; esotericism and spirituality run strong in their outlook, as they do for the Shi'a at large. Yet their various beliefs and practices can include Christian, folkloric and sometimes Sunni traditions, in settings which are not predominantly Shi'i – notably Turkey, Syria, the Balkans and Lebanon. There have long been political and religious debates about the orientation of these communities; the Syrian Alawites were deemed to be infidels in the 14th century by the Sunni jurist Ibn Taymiyya. Similar

---

[6]   A. B. Sajoo, ed., *Muslim Modernities: Expressions of the Civil Imagination* (London, 2008); D. Jung, M. J. Petersen and S. L. Sparre, *Politics of Modern Muslim Subjectivities: Islam, Youth and Social Activism in the Middle East* (New York, 2014).

attacks were often levelled at all Shi'a, but some of them were greater targets, on occasion even within the Shi'i fold itself. These debates can be extremely intense today, both in political and scholarly quarters.[7] The perceived need to articulate a coherent and appropriate theology – whether in response to the wider social environment, or the internal drives of selfhood – is conspicuous.

Since the Alevi are the most numerous and widespread of such communities, estimated within Turkey alone at between 15 and 20 million, with sizable Austrian and German diasporas, debates around their identity offer useful insights into how contemporary Shi'ism is understood.[8] An array of ethno-cultural groups, spread over the centuries across the Balkans and Turkey, with significant variations in theology, is today collectively referred to as 'Alevi'. Their Central Asian ancestors were the Qızılbaş and the Bektashi, whose Shi'i leanings and settlement in Anatolia evolved in an expanding Ottoman domain. Hacı Bektaş Veli, originally from Iran, remains an overarching figure in this narrative: a charismatic 13th-century contemporary of Jalal al-Din Rumi, whose celebrated legacy was the Bektashi Sufi order which came to be embraced by the Sunni rulers of the Ottoman Empire until the 19th century. Modern Turkey's onslaught against expressions of Sufism did not spare the Bektashi order, which had already fallen on hard times.

Yet the increasingly urbanised Alevi – now the preferred name for the Qızılbaş/Bektashi – were among the strongest supporters of Atatürk's Republic, seeing its secular ideals as potentially favourable to the well-being of a minority. This became a more complicated affair amid the nationalist narrowing of 'Turkishness', especially for Kurdish Alevis. Among the Alevi themselves, a range of opinions on their identity came to the fore in the second half of the 20th century, with vital political implications in an often stridently secular environment. For many, the central issue was the nature of Alevism as a faith tradition, whether in

---

[7] See M. Cook, *Ancient Religions, Modern Politics: The Islamic Case in Modern Perspective* (Princeton, NJ, 2014); D. Sila-Khan, *Crossing the Threshold: Understanding Religious Identities in South Asia* (London, 2005); L. Ridgeon, ed., *Shi'i Islam and Identity: Religion, Politics and Change in the Global Community* (London, 2012); T. Olsson, E. Özdalga and C. Raudvere, ed. *Alevi Identity: Cultural, Religious and Social Perspectives* (2nd ed., London, 2005) (includes essays on the Druze and Syrian Alawites).

[8] The account here and in the next paragraph draws on M. Dressler, 'Religio-Secular Metamorphoses: The Re-Making of Modern Alevism', *Journal of the American Academy of Religion*, 76 (2008), pp. 280–311; *Alevi Identity: Cultural Religious and Social Perspectives*; and M. Dressler, 'Alevis', *Encyclopaedia of Islam*, 3rd ed. (Leiden, 2014), available online at: http://referenceworks.brillonline.com/entries/encyclopaedia-of-islam-3/alevi-s-COM_0167.

its mystical versions, or a more Twelver-centric one; for others, they were primarily a cultural community with a 'liberation theology' that supported Kurdish and other aspirations for a modernist autonomy. Such key traditional elements, then, as the supreme status accorded to Imam Ali, the emphasis on love above formal piety and orthodoxy, the *cem* assembly for prayer, hymns, music and socials in a *cemevi* (house of assembly), and bonds of socio-spiritual companionship or *musahiplik*, lend themselves to secular *and* confessional Alevi revivalism.

In drawing attention to how theology and ideology are kin responses here to modern political contexts – including for migrants in the large German diaspora – a leading social anthropologist asks whether the Alevi should be regarded as Shi'i, and concludes that they should not. The very question, he argues, assumes that an 'inescapable underlying partition within Islamic societies' must accommodate the 'overflow of spirituality' among the Alevi.[9] Indeed, many Turkish Alevis within the spectrum of opinion noted above share this view; some go as far as to insist they are Sunni. Now a scholarly resistance to a forced Shi'i-Sunni dichotomy is surely admirable; and Alevi pragmatism in identifying with official Turkish proclivities (including about links to the Twelver Shi'ism of post-revolutionary Iran) is perhaps understandable. But this appears to raise a more profound query: are we to reduce Shi'ism to a particular orthodoxy, or to the preferences of one or another national culture?

Ironically where states, like the empires of old, press for a politicised answer to the question of religious affiliation, communities may choose to 'religionise' their civic identity, where this is seen as a promising way of belonging. Until the recent past, 'civic' identity was wrapped up in most societies with religious affiliation; the Ottoman *millet* system was exemplary, with its creation of civil-religious spaces for minorities. Modern citizenship is secular and, if also liberal, may accommodate diverse religious affiliations; yet this can hardly preclude tensions between the different senses of belonging. Markus Dressler captures the negotiation of Alevi identity as part of their modern journey:

> The debates on Alevism circle around questions of origin and essence, and are articulated through a language which is based on the dichotomy of the secular-religious. In that sense, they are radically modernist. While critical discourse on religion has reached its post-secular turn as an act of emancipation from the modernist paradigm, the case of Alevism's religionisation is

---

[9]   D. Shankland, 'Are the Alevis Shi'ite', in *Shi'i Islam and Identity*, pp. 210–228, at pp. 225–226.

a compelling example for the continuous thriving of modernist semantics in public discourses on religion.[10]

A fine illustration of this negotiation stemmed from the challenge by Hasan Zengin, an Istanbul Alevi, to the state's insistence that his daughter, Eylem, attend a school course on 'religion and ethics'.[11] Seeing the course as Hanafi-Sunni oriented, he asked for her to be granted an exemption, to which Christian and Jewish students were formally entitled; this was refused. On appeal to the European Court of Human Rights, the course was indeed judged to be Sunni-centred rather than inclusive or neutral. Alevi faith was 'distinct from the Sunni understanding of Islam', the court observed, and imposing the course on Eylem was a violation of religious freedom. While the purported intent of the course to foster tolerant religious understanding was not rejected, it was found to have fallen far short of pluralist standards: 'Pupils receive no teaching on the confessional or ritual specificities of the Alevi faith, although the proportion of the Turkish population belonging to is very large.' In response, the education authorities have embarked on a process of revising the syllabus, in consultation with Alevi community leaders, theologians and intellectuals.[12]

However, it is not only the language of secular politics and human rights that enables a modernist negotiation of identity. Refashioning old practices into forms with contemporary appeal, while preserving a measure of 'authenticity', is a familiar recourse. For Alevis keen to situate traditional practices in a 'progressive' present that includes gender equality, much rethinking is directed at how to re-channel the 'overflow of spirituality' in rituals and institutions such as the *cem* and the *dedelik* (office of the elder). This occurs in the shadow of the politics of assimilation vis-à-vis mainstream Turkish Islam, which Alevis frequently cast as a regressive orthodoxy. At the same time, 'it is the grammar of Turkish laicism that renders the question of the legitimate

---

[10] Dressler, 'Religio-secular metamorphoses', p. 304.

[11] *Hasan and Eylem Zengin vs. Turkey*, European Court of Human Rights, Judgment of 9 October 2007, available online at: http://hudoc.echr.coe.int/sites/eng/pages/search.aspx?i=001-82580.

[12] Execution of the Judgment of Hasan ve Eylem Zengin/Turkey, Monitoring Report (Ankara, 2013), available online at: http://aihmiz.org.tr/files/01_Hasan_ve_Eylem_Zengin_Report_EN.pdf. The report notes that the revisions process has been tardy, with a growing demand for exemptions from the course. A larger trust-deficit has prevailed in regard to what is seen as educational indoctrination into 'national Sunni' Islam: Faruk Bilici, 'The Function of Alevi-Bektashi Theology in Modern Turkey', in *Alevi Identity*, pp. 59–73, at pp. 68–70.

place of Alevism a religious one', argues Dressler – which surely is no less true in the avowedly secular settings of the European diaspora.[13]

A remarkably imaginative case of refashioning old practices, with regard to a 'core' facet of Shi'i tradition, is offered at a distant remove from the Middle East and Europe, in Senegal. In the midst of an overwhelmingly Sunni Muslim community with robust Sufi traditions, Senegalese converts to Shi'ism have in recent decades formed a community quite distinct from the established local Lebanese Shi'a (discussed in the 'Diasporas' chapter in this volume). The converts have indigenised their understandings of Shi'a theology as acquired from Lebanese and Iranian sources, to foster a specifically 'Senegalese Shi'i' identity. This is best exemplified in their framing of Ashura. For many Shi'i communities across the world, the annual Ashura rituals that mark Imam Husayn's martyrdom, observed on the 10th day of the Muslim month of Muharram, are an iconic observance. Lament for the tragic events at Karbala in 680 is expressed not only in special prayers and formal mourning but also other acts of symbolic remembrance, often with great poignancy.[14] For the Senegalese Shi'a – that is the community of converts, excluding the Lebanese Shi'a in Senegal – the 'traditional' Ashura rituals reflect Middle Eastern cultural practices; these are not seen as determinative for other Shi'a, like themselves.[15]

Here the observance overlaps with and merges into Tamkharit, an important Senegalese Sufi holiday that begins with a daytime fast and culminates in much festivity. Shi'i-led Ashura gatherings also involve a large Sunni presence with colourful garments, music and singing, where participants are reminded of the Prophet's Family and the events at Karbala. While there are the black banners of mourning commonly seen elsewhere at Ashura, common public acts of grief, self-flagellation (*matam*) and 'martyrdom theatre' (*taziya*) are entirely absent. There is much discussion in the community about the precise theology of a merged Tamkharit/Ashura observance, along with initiatives to educate Senegalese Muslims about the legacy of Karbala, including through electronic media. Yet the overriding objective for the Shi'a is to locate their identity within the 'geographies of religious ceremonies' *and* to

---

[13] 'Religio-Secular Metamorphosis', pp. 294 (quote), 299. In Germany, where Turkish Alevis enjoy official recognition as a religious community, they have chosen to develop a school curriculum entirely distinctive from that of Turkish Sunnis, with an 'alternative' presentation of Islam in which Alevism is situated.

[14] K. S. Aghaie, *The Martyrs of Karbala: Shi'i Symbols and Rituals in Modern Iran* (Seattle, WA, 2004); A. R. Norton, 'Ritual, Blood, and Shi'ite Identity: Ashura in Nabatiyya, Lebanon', *The Drama Review*, 49 (2005), pp. 140–155; S. A. Hyder, *Reliving Karbala: Martyrdom in South Asian Memory* (Oxford, 2006).

[15] M. Leichtman, 'The Africanisation of 'Ashura in Senegal', in *Shi'i Islam and Identity*, pp. 144–169, which is the basis of my account in this paragraph.

'claim their belonging to Senegalese religious space',[16] even if this means appropriating what many regard as pagan rituals. The upshot is that a thoroughly modern Shi'i identity may rest its integrity on a hybrid of *traditions*, in all their familiarity and continuity.

One recalls a parallel in diasporic Trinidad, where the most vivid observance of Ashura is the lively, multicultural 'Hosay', a derivative of Husayn. The admixture of raucous Caribbean festivity and solemn commemoration has been assailed by Sunni Trinidadians as violating Muslim orthodoxy – and is defended by its Shi'i protagonists in the name of preserving tradition, even if localised in provocative ways. Frank Korom points out in *Hosay Trinidad: Muharram Performances in an Indo-Caribbean Diaspora* (2003) that public 'creolisation' of the observance is only decisive 'if we ignore the esoteric dimension, which is so crucial' (p. 230). In private yards and other spaces safe from the sectarian prejudices and bacchanalian tenor of the public domain, the solemnity of the *batin* (esoteric) facet finds proper expression. Elements of this are likewise visible in Senegal: Tamkharit offers the outer shell in a non-Shi'i setting, while the spirituality of Ashura can be captured more privately in communal and individual ways alike. This is not to suggest that 'authentic' religion only happens in private; *zahir* and *batin* both matter in most faith traditions. Their effective balancing that seems vital to the process of reinventing tradition in the negotiation of Shi'i identities, if modernity is not to simply mean discontinuity.

The Right and the Good: Law's Empire

Memory has always been essential to the sustenance of communities, since identity can hardly thrive on collective amnesia. The ruptures of modernity – where 'all that is solid melts into air' in both physical and social environments – put a further premium on remembering.[17] This is commonly cast as the burden of 'tradition', in tension with the constant upheavals of the modern. For monotheistic communities, 'orthodoxy' with its emphasis on right belief and practice is a favoured repository of tradition and memory, for this captures the continuities of tradition.[18]

---

[16] Leichtman, 'The Africanisation', p. 151.

[17] The title of Marshall Berman's *All that is Solid Melts into Air: The Experience of Modernity* (New York, 1982) borrows from Karl Marx and Friedrich Engel's critique of capitalism in the 1848 *Communist Manifesto*. Michel Foucault sees this as 'consciousness of the discontinuity of time: a break with tradition' – as I have discussed in *Muslim Modernities* (London, 2008), at pp. 3–13.

[18] One may technically distinguish between orthodoxy as pertaining to belief and orthopraxy to practice; but in the context of the discussion here, the distinction is not particularly useful.

Muslims and Jews generally associate orthodoxy with a complex *legal culture*, which is felt to capture vital features of the 'original intent' of the faith. Specific religious law may, of course, change in many respects over time; but principles that are deemed to be foundational, along with the idea of taking the law seriously, are what orthodoxy is about. And in the midst of modernity's upheavals, the stability of orthodoxy's rules can offer a sheltering tradition – with the risk that this might turn into a stubborn resistance to change. 'Tradition is the living faith of the dead; traditionalism is the dead faith of the living', in Jaroslav Pelikan's apt formulation.[19]

This is not to say that orthodoxy's rules are perforce unbending, shutting out any measure of moral reasoning in pursuit of the good. On the contrary, the *shari'a* and its derivative body of rules, the *fiqh*, which sit at the heart of any Islamic conception of 'right belief and practice', mark what the Quran (5:48, 45:18) presents as a 'path' (*shar*) – an *ethical* compass. The privileging today of juridical over ethical norms may echo phases of Muslim history; but it is far more about a modernity where law enjoys special prestige.[20] This is part of the political narrative of the rise of the state since the 17th century, coupled with constitutionalism and the rule of law. Often the privileging of rules entails a collision with the ideals of justice; clearly, the perils are far greater where the rules lay claim to sacred sanction. Yet in contests that involve religious identities, such claims are all too common. They are only enhanced in the face of perceived secularist assaults on faith and faith-based identity. And the dance of the secular and sacred can take on a particularly sharp twist when claims of justice in the form of basic human rights are deemed also to be Western impositions. Here is an illustrative episode.

In July 2009, Afghanistan adopted its first 'Shi'a Personal Status Law' (SPSL) which governs matters of marriage, divorce and inheritance. Distinct laws in this regard for the country's 6 million Shi'a, about 15 per cent of the population, were envisaged under the new 2004 constitution as an exception to the Sunni Hanafi personal laws of the majority. The SPSL imposed severe constraints on a Shi'i woman – such as requiring that she 'submit to her husband's reasonable sexual enjoyment' on pain of punishment, seek permission to leave the house except for urgent matters, and have vastly inferior custodial rights to children – despite

---

[19]   *The Vindication of Tradition* (New Haven, CT, and London, 1984), p. 65.

[20]   See N. Calder, 'The Limits of Islamic Orthodoxy', in F. Daftary, ed., *Intellectual Traditions in Islam* (London, 2000), pp. 66–85. For a Jewish perspective on 'modern orthodoxy', see J. Lefkovitz, 'The Rise of Social Orthodoxy: A Personal Account', *Commentary*, April 2014, available online at: http://www.commentary-magazine.com/article/the-rise-of-social-orthodoxy-a-personal-account/.

the constitution's firm guarantee of gender equality, in keeping with international legal commitments. An even more restrictive version of the SPSL approved earlier that year by President Hamid Karzai was revised after a storm of local and global protest about legitimising marital rape and backsliding into Taliban-era gender repression. What explains the success of the SPSL initiative? Why would its main constituency, the minority Hazara ethnic community that had suffered appallingly under the Taliban's misogynist rule, not seek to reverse that legacy?

For the conservative, non-Hazara Shi'i cleric who spearheaded the SPSL, Asif Mohseni, the legislation affirmed the *shari'a* in its shared Shi'i-Sunni principles (mindful of the hegemonial Sunni context) as well as Afghan custom, and opponents were 'meddlers'.[21] The Afghan Shi'i women and men who disagreed, such as Zareen Taj, saw it as identity politics wrapped up in legalised orthodoxy:

> First, there are those who feel this law ... provides recognition of their Shi'a religion in Afghanistan, which gives them pride and identity. They support this law because it is a Shi'a law, without knowing the entire law or the consequences of this law. Second, there are those who feel the law reinforces the classic patriarchal boundaries on women that have been eroding with their new found freedoms. Third, there are those who wish to advance their political agendas under the guise of 'Shi'a Family law'. To challenge a religious law brings immediate condemnation and accusations of blasphemy and infidel.
>
> Fourth, there are those who feel that this law will silence any modern, progressive thinking and advancement. People are afraid and intimidated to speak out publically for fear of all kinds of retribution. This law will silence those individuals.[22]

---

[21] 'Mohsini Backs "Rape Law", Muhaqiq terms Offence to Hazaras, if not amended', *Hazaristan Times*, 13 April 2009; R. Faiez and H. Vogt, 'Afghan cleric defends "rape" law', *Toronto Star*, 12 April 2009; L. Oates, 'A Closer Look: The Policy and Law-Making Process behind the Shi'ite Personal Status Law', Afghanistan Research and Evaluation Unit, September 2009. For the original draft text, see 'Shi'ite Personal Law', USAID (2009), available online at: http://www.refworld.org/docid/4a24ed5b2.html.

[22] Z. Taj, 'Why Afghanistan's Family Shi'a Status Law Must Be Changed', *Kabul Press*, 4 May 2009, available online at: http://kabulpress.org/my/spip.php?article3418; Minority Rights Group International, 'Fakhria Ibrahimi' [conversation with 'a Hazara woman who has high hopes'], October 2009; H. Vogt, 'Afghan activists still oppose new marriage law', *Associated Press*, 13 July 2009; Human Rights Watch, 'Afghanistan: Law Curbing Women's Rights Takes Effect', 13 August 2009.

The resulting empowerment of traditionalism in the guise of tradition, to recall Pelikan's adage, is evident.

As in many parts of the world, Muslim and otherwise, religious identity remains a vital part of both formal and customary legal systems – and gender is no small aspect of identity among the monotheisms. Over 70 per cent of Afghanistan's population sees the *shari'a* as embodying the sacred, an overwhelming majority favour enshrining it as official law, and most believe that it is only open to a single interpretation; all this while holding that women are subordinate to men in all family matters.[23] Not surprisingly, appeals to the *shari'a*'s authority in shaping public discourse can be decisive, as was the case with the SPSL: the Shi'a-Hazara milieu could not be taken out of its larger Afghan setting. Nor could it be a consolation to Shi'i women that as recently as the 1970s the world's most 'advanced' legal systems had yet to act against marital rape, or that dozens of countries have yet to do so.

It is scarcely a coincidence, however, that an insistently traditionalist view of the *shari'a* and of gender roles prevails most strongly where national legal systems are fragile and have limited social legitimacy. Where formal justice systems are well established, the state is expected to deliver credible justice – which is mostly not the case in Afghanistan's painfully gradual transition from customary law, especially outside the urban centres. An ethos of human rights and gender equity cannot be rooted in formal law-making if the latter is itself marginal to most of society.[24] Nevertheless, the fact that conservative clerics like Mohseni sought to have their understanding of the *shari'a* legitimated by the formal provisions of the SPSL is instructive. There are competing religious and secular voices and they succeeded in having the original version amended, even though it was the conservative clerical one that Karzai's government endorsed. Increasingly the formal legal system does matter; the stakes in contesting how the *shari'a* is interpreted will escalate both there *and* in the customary realm.

This contest has unfolded since modernity's earliest phases, when colonial governments and declining local rulers vied for legitimacy with new communal voices. Consider, for example, the dramatic outcome of the British vanquishing of Awadh in the 1860s, a once powerful Shi'i Nawabi domain centred on the city of Lucknow in northeast India. A fresh cast of players began to articulate competing Shi'i identities in

---

[23] Pew Research Centre Survey, 'The World's Muslims: Religion, Politics, and Society' (April 2013), pp. 41–58 (on the *shari'a*), pp. 91–99 (on gender roles).

[24] T. Barfield, 'Culture and Custom in Nation-Building: Law in Afghanistan', *Maine Law Review*, 60 (2008), p. 348; L. Smith, 'Implementing International Human Rights Law in Post Conflict Settings – Backlash without Buy-In: Lessons from Afghanistan', *Muslim World Journal of Human Rights*, 5 (2008) [online].

the late 19th and early 20th centuries, against the shaky cultural legitimacy of old aristocratic and new British claims to authority. Lucknow's leading scholars enjoyed a following independent of the Twelver centres of Najaf in Iraq and Qumm in Iran – and along with diverse lay actors, effectively reinvented Shi'i tradition in Urdu, always mindful of their double-minority status as Muslims and Shi'a in India. The result was a post-Awadh florescence well into the early 20th century:

> The *ulama* strengthened their social roles and profile, and formed the educational infrastructure to sustain themselves as a professionalised group. Meanwhile, the lay Shi'a were engaged with their religion as active agents through new and active cultures of exuberant ritualism, personal piety, public propagation and creative debating. Equally, a whole range of activities was employed in the name of Shi'a communal solidarity: public charity, social action and, ultimately, political mobilisation.[25]

Sectarian tendencies were part of this activism with the prominence of clerical figures such as Sayyid Ghulam Hasnain Kintori, Nasir Hussain and Muhammad Naseer – even as the Aligarh movement strived for a unified Muslim modernist outlook, in which the Shi'a Ismaili Imam Sultan Muhammad Shah Aga Khan III played a crucial part. As Jones sees it, even the sectarian discourses were quintessentially modern in using theology as part of the jostling for state recognition and standing, *within and beyond* the diverse Shi'i fold. 'Orthodoxy', then, was entirely malleable as a response to the prevailing social and political environment. Such contests were to become ever fiercer in Pakistan, where the growing frailty of the formal legal-political system has been accompanied by hardline stances on the *shari'a*, reminiscent of Afghanistan.[26]

Yet the malleability of orthodoxy and the shifting understanding of the *shari'a* as an ethical compass have also served to advance progressive ends in the Shi'i world. On matters ranging from access to education and gender equity to public health, environmental stewardship and nuclear weapons, appeals to established ethico-legal principles have challenged

---

[25] J. Jones, *Shi'a Islam in Colonial India: Religion, Community and Sectarianism* (New York, 2012), at p. 225. For an account of the community's fostering of historical memory – notably through sermons and lamentations – in shaping a distinctive identity in northern India see T. Howarth, *The Twelver Shi'a as a Muslim Minority in India* (London, 2004).

[26] The Pew Survey results cited above for Afghanistan are not much different for Pakistan: over 80 per cent regard the *shari'a* as sacred and favour its adoption as national law, over 60 per cent believe that only a single interpretation must prevail; attitudes towards gender roles are only slightly less patriarchal.

traditionalism and patriarchy. Such activism is especially robust in the context of civil society, which will be addressed in the next section. However, what deserves a fuller appreciation in the present discussion of how orthodoxy and the *shari'a* play out as modern concepts is the role of Shi'i thinkers in grappling with modernity's implications for core aspects of tradition. Since the 1950s, but more intensely in the Iranian world in the aftermath of the 1979 revolution, influential theologians and philosophers – known as *rowshanfekran* in the Persianate-Shi'i milieu – have engaged in penetrating debates that seek to reframe the very basis of Shi'i identity and faith, including the question of legitimate authority.

Among the contemporary luminaries in these debates are Hasan Eshkavari, Mohsen Kadivar, Abdolkarim Soroush, Reza Davani Ardakani, Mojtahed Shabestari and Akbar Ganji – in the wake of an earlier constellation that included Ali Shariati, Jalal Al-e Ahmad, Allama Tabatabai, Morteza Motahari and the Iraqi Mohammad Baqir al-Sadr. The implications of their critiques are not only theological but also social and political, whether explicitly or more subtly. At their philosophical heart is the nature of human subjectivity in modernity: here, the scope of individual autonomy and agency is 'mediated' by its dependence on the Divine. This mediated subjectivity involves, nonetheless, a great deal of choice about religious belief and practice itself, as reflected in the epigraphic quote from Shabestari. Communal and individual virtue alike are determined not by dogmatic frameworks but by ethical orientation, in Shabestari's view; a theocratic state is neither here nor there on this score. In this latter regard he is at odds with Ardakani who defends the idea of 'moral guardianship', while at the opposite end Soroush favours private religion, and Ganji is a passionate secularist.[27] These perspectives are a long way from Jalal Al-e Ahmad's focus in the 1960s on *gharbzadegi* or 'westoxication' that impelled a nativist 'return to the self', even if the summons still finds an echo in nationalist rhetoric.

There are parallels here with the discourses of modern Catholic theological and lay figures wrestling with the hegemonial claims of secular liberalism – from Karl Barth, Hans Küng and Alasdair MacIntyre to Charles Taylor, William Cavanaugh and Richard Neuhaus.[28] In the

---

[27] F. Vahdat, 'Post-Revolutionary Islamic Modernity in Iran: The Intersubjective Hermeneutics of Mohamad Mojtahed Shabestari', in S. Taji-Farouki, ed., *Modern Muslim Intellectuals and the Qur'an* (Oxford, 2004), pp. 193–224; A. Soroush, *Reason, Freedom, and Democracy in Islam*, ed. M. Sadri and A. Sadri (Oxford, 2000); M. Kamrava, *Iran's Intellectual Revolution* (New York, 2008); and A. Mirsepassi, *Intellectual Discourse and the Politics of Modernization: Negotiating Modernity in Iran* (Cambridge, 2000).

[28] T. E. Woods, *The Church Confronts Modernity: Catholic Intellectuals and the*

shared concern with post-Enlightenment reason and faith, Catholic thinkers have also found it necessary to revisit foundational tenets in ways that are informed by rationalist as well as spiritual pathways. Where the Vatican had denounced the entire venture of modernity in a 'Syllabus of Errors' in the mid-19th century, 'Vatican II' sought to fully engage and come to terms with the implications of an all-pervasive secular public sphere in the 1960s. On both sides of the Atlantic, and eventually in the global south, critiques emerged across the ideological spectrum both of the Church's doctrinal stance and, distinctly, of the dominant influence of American secular liberalism. In the Muslim world, the legacy of European colonialism forced people to respond to what their *particular* encounter with the bearers of occidental modernity entailed on a daily basis, since colonial regimes were governing ones – even as individual figures and institutions such as Cairo's al-Azhar sought to articulate a broader vision of the terms of engagement with that modernity. In the highly institutionalised Roman Catholic world, the Church sought to do both: articulate a universal doctrine and also present fresh liturgical and pastoral observances.

Yet the fragmentation of authority, religious and secular, is one of modernity's hard truths: official voices, even statist ones, compete with many others in this fractured landscape, which extends to cyberspace. For many Catholics and Shi'a, orthodoxy and its empire of rules provide a refuge from the perceived assaults on traditional identity. But it is the new ethical critiques both of modernity and consensual tradition that make the new discourses relevant in a secular age. Increasingly, the stakes are recognised as being about the texture of public space, where individuals and communities can thrive in solidarity rather than alienated from society and state alike. In effect, the mediated subjectivity of Shabestari and his fellow *rowshanfekran* channels into the socially 'situated self' of Taylor and his fellow critics of liberal individualism (or atomism). What gives meaning to autonomy here is its embedded character in a web of relationships and affinities, from the social/civic to the communal/kin and spiritual. It is this modern social imaginary that is seen as capturing what 'belonging' means for selfhood today.

Progressive Era (New York, 2004); C. Taylor, *A Catholic Modernity?* (Oxford, 1999); and D. Jodock, ed., *Catholicism Contending with Modernity* (Cambridge, 2000).

Beyond State and Territory:
Faith in Civil Society

Early in 2005, Iraqis began to discuss a constitution that would enable a democratic transition from the fraught authoritarianism of Saddam Hussein, and the United States-led occupation of the country after the invasion that had toppled him in 2003. A violent insurgency by remnants of Saddam's Ba'ath Party, in alliance with disaffected members of the Sunni minority (less than 20 per cent of the population) which had enjoyed political dominance in Iraq's postcolonial history, raged all the while. This in turn had sparked a sectarian Shi'i militancy – ironically one that also shared in the general Sunni disaffection with the political direction of the occupation. Under these conditions, the representatives of the assortment of Shi'a, Kurds, Sunnis and other minority groups were given less than eight months after the January elections to draft a new constitution.

The outcome was a constitution with no real participation on behalf of most Sunnis and many Shi'a, various minority religious groups, and women's organisations. According to Jonathan Morrow of the United States Institute for Peace, a federal nonpartisan institution that provided expert support for the constitutional process, responsibility for its effective failure lay squarely with the United States itself. Rather than recognise that an inclusive process was a precondition for success, the fateful decision was made not to exercise the available option of extending the deadline for consultations. Above all, even though 'some of the most promising initiatives in the post-election period came from civil society leaders who wanted to form umbrella organisations to represent civil society in constitutional discussions', they were hobbled by the limited timeframe in which they had to mobilise and to advance the goals of a nonsectarian approach to building democracy. Even faith-based actors that sought to act civically were forestalled:

> Thaqalayn Research Institute, an independent Shi'a religious NGO, started up a 'Civil Constitutional Forum' of NGOs working on the constitution under the leadership of Dr. Sallama al-Khafaji and Sheikh Fateh al-Ghitta. The Forum was designed to educate religious Shi'a communities on the value of constitutionalism, the separation between church and state, and to bring consolidated civil society views to the Committee ... [The] organisation, however, was [unable] to realise its goal of creating the institutions necessary to strengthen civil society's

influence on the draft ... Sheikh Fateh al-Ghitta pointed to the lack of time as the primary reason for failure.[29]

Likewise, a Constitutional Outreach Unit formed by the National Assembly to publicise details about the process and assess public responses was given eight weeks to accomplish this task, clearly an unrealistic expectation. After an impaired consultative process overseen by the United States, Morrow then observed that the 'damage has already been done' to the constitutional future, with the alienation of Sunni Arabs now 'amplified'.[30] The judgement was all too prescient in view of what was to transpire, with the local ascendancy of al-Qaeda and then its offshoot, the self-styled Islamic State in Iraq and Syria (ISIS), fed by Sunni and Ba'athist resentment. There is an abundance of responsibility to be apportioned for the blunting of civic identities in the post-Saddam phase when sectarianism began to flourish – abetted by theologies that gave voice to political grievances *and* also to puritanical impulses. Conservative religious organisations, both Shi'i and Sunni, certainly played their part in narrowing the civic space. However, a substantial share of the blame clearly rests with an occupation that not only lacked any legal legitimacy, but whose persistent ineptitude included knowing virtually nothing about the Shi'i and Sunni Muslims over whom it was imposed. The legacy of this failure – and of the historical privileging of Sunni Iraqis – is not readily undone.[31]

Indeed, recognising the theological stakes in the post-September 11 era, some 180 Sunni and Shi'i scholars from 45 countries converged in Amman (Jordan) in 2005 to affirm the plurality of Muslim traditions of law and worship.[32] Recalling the longstanding stance that 'variance in

---

[29]   J. Morrow, 'Iraq's Constitutional Process II: An Opportunity Lost', Special Report 155, United States Institute of Peace, Washington, DC, November 2005, p. 16. Morrow was no armchair expert, but worked directly with Iraqi and international participants/experts in Baghdad in the constitutional process.

[30]   'Iraq's Constitutional Process', p. 22. For the wider historical context in this regard, see K. Osman, *Sectarianism in Iraq: The Making of State and Nation Since 1920* (London, 2015).

[31]   J. Stein, 'Can You Tell a Sunni from a Shi'ite?', *New York Times*, 17 October 2006, A21 (even the head of the FBI was unsure whether *Iran* was Shi'i); Osman, *Sectarianism in Iraq*, pp. 219–279; A. B. Sajoo, 'It's Theology, Not Baseball: Misunderstanding Iraq's Sectarian Conflicts', *Religion Dispatches*, August 2014, available online at: http://religiondispatches.org/its-theology-not-baseball-misunderstanding-iraqs-sectarian-conflicts/. In 2014, while admitting that it had failed to grasp the threat posed by militant Sunni radicalism in the form of ISIS, the Obama administration accepted no US responsibility for its appearance in Iraq: P. Baker and E. Schmitt, 'Many Missteps in Assessment of ISIS Threat', *New York Times*, 29 September 2014.

[32]   For the full text and accompanying documentary resources, see the official

opinion among the *'ulama'* (scholars) "is a good affair"', the assembly firmly rejected declarations about the apostasy of fellow Muslims, and urged interfaith dialogue 'not simply to promote tolerance, but to establish full acceptance'. Major Islamic centres the world over were represented in what was clearly a global initiative, with the Jordanian hosts striving for a fully inclusive institutional basis for future action. Yet if this ecumenism is to find any resonance beyond elite scholars and emissaries, surely its message requires carriers beyond 'officialdom' and the religious domain. Again, a much-publicised scholarly rebuttal of the theological claims of ISIS in September 2014, while arguing for tolerance, failed to engage in any direct way with the Shi'a, a particular target of Sunni radicalism in many of the countries from which the signatories themselves hailed.[33] 'Religious' voices, of the kind noted in Morrow's report above on Iraq, can only find resonance on the ground if they are *integral* to civic realities.

Consider, for example, the situation since the brutal 2011 crackdown on Bahrain's Shi'i majority by the Sunni-dominated ruling establishment – with the support of Saudi military units – in a conflict that is rooted in autocracy, socio-economic marginalisation, and institutionalised discrimination.[34] From the outset, the pro-democracy unrest amid the uprisings of the 'Arab Spring' was officially cast as sectarian and allegedly driven by Iran, claims which were clearly aimed at garnering Western strategic concern and support. The United States, with its Fifth Fleet stationed in Bahrain, neither opposed the Saudi intervention nor supported the majoritarian demands for accountable governance. What is remarkable is the extent to which Bahrain's leading Shi'i activists have sought resolutely to frame their grievances in civic terms. Figures such as Nabil Rajab, Abdulhadi al-Khawaja, Munira Fakhro, Zainab al-Khawaja and her sister Maryam al-Khawaja, director of the Beirut/Copenhagen-based Gulf Centre for Human Rights, are household names in global civil society quarters. Regime loyalists, on the other hand, have formed what amounts to an anti-democratic 'Sunni bloc' under the umbrella of

---

website at: http://ammanmessage com/index.php?option=com_contentandtask= viewandid=20andItemid=34.

[33] 'Open Letter to Al-Baghdadi' (the self-declared ISIS 'caliph'), 24 September 2014, available online at: http://www.lettertobaghdadi.com/; T. Heneghan, 'Muslim Scholars Present Religious Rebuttal to Islamic State', *Reuters*, 25 September 2014. Some 126 eminent Muslim scholars signed the letter, with their diverse nationalities and affiliations duly provided; none were identified as Shi'i, or from Iran.

[34] Report of the Bahrain Independent Commission of Inquiry, Manama, Bahrain, 23 November 2011 (chaired by the noted jurist M. Cherif Bassiouni); International Crisis Group, 'Popular Protest in North Africa and the Middle East (VIII): Bahrain's Rocky Road to Reform', Report of 28 July 2011.

the Saudi-dominated Gulf Co-operation Council.[35] The reinforcement of a sectarian divide is obvious, given that Bahrain's Shiʻa and Sunni are both Arab.

The resilience of civic actors – with transnational solidarities, aided by new media platforms – has surely contributed to the capacity of a polarised Bahrain to mitigate the risks of outright civil war while in transition. In this respect it shares the experience today of Tunisia, in contrast to Iraq, Libya, Somalia, Syria and Yemen. For civic ventures to ripen into enduring institutions of civil society, rootedness in indigenous cultural and faith traditions has proved indispensable across much of the world. In Muslim-majority locales, an insistence on purely secular civic identities carries scant weight. No less essential is an openness to public cultures if civic pluralism, rather than exclusivism, is to be sustained. The mix of 'bonding' and 'bridging' capital finds robust support within Muslim tradition with its manifold networks of solidarity across time and space; scholars such as Bruce Lawrence and Carl Ernst regard such networks as a defining feature of Muslim history.[36] True, such solidarities can be anti-pluralist, as with radical movements and patriarchal enclaves; hence the constant need here for 'civil' society as more than a purely social, value-neutral phenomenon.[37] Potent resources in this regard, including an energetic civic cosmopolitanism, are to be found

---

[35] D. Kirkpatrick, 'Power Struggles in Middle East Exploit Islam's Ancient Sectarian Rift', *New York Times*, 5 July 2014; International Crisis Group, 'Bahrain's Sectarian Challenge', Report of 9 May 2005; S. Aziz and A. Musalem, 'Citizens, Not Subjects: Debunking the Sectarian Narrative', Report of the Institute for Social Policy and Understanding, July 2011. Broadly on the Saudi role see European Council on Foreign Relations, 'The Gulf and Sectarianism', London, November 2013; R. Ismail, 'The Saudi Ulema and the Shiʻa of Saudi Arabia', *Journal of Shiʻa Islamic Studies*, 5 (2012), pp. 403–422; D. Kirkpatrick, 'ISIS' Harsh Brand of Islam Is Rooted in Austere Saudi Creed', *New York Times*, 24 September 2014.

[36] M. Cooke and B. Lawrence, ed., *Muslim Networks: From Hajj to Hip Hop* (Chapel Hill, NC, 2005). This fits into William Connolly's observation that an embedded pluralism requires a diverse social and political culture supported by 'civic virtues' and a robust 'commitment to justice': *Pluralism* (Durham, NC, 2005), p. 43. In other words, pluralism as an ethos cannot be about formal institutional life alone.

[37] A. B. Sajoo, ed., *Civil Society in the Muslim World: Contemporary Perspectives* (London, 2002); N. J. Demerath III, 'Civil Society and Civil Religion as Mutually Dependent', in M. Dillon, ed., *Handbook of the Sociology of Religion* (Cambridge, 2003), pp. 348–358; B. Turner, ed., *Religious Diversity and Civil Society: A Comparative Analysis* (Oxford, 2008). On the importance of linking theology and public culture see O. Roy, *Holy Ignorance: When Religion and Culture Part Ways*, trans. R. Schwartz (New York, 2010); A. Sajoo, 'Faith in Rights: Ethics of the Public Square', *Open Democracy*, 14 May 2014, available online at: https://www.opendemocracy.net/openglobalrights/amyn-b-sajoo/faith-in-rights-ethics-of-public-square.

within Islam's diverse heritage. Pluralism is no more inherently secular than exclusivism is religious.

A notable Shi'i example of institutionalised ethico-civic action is the cluster of socio-economic entities of the Aga Khan Development Network (AKDN). This transnational initiative is avowedly non-denominational yet ascribes to the 'social conscience of Islam' and headed by the Shi'a Ismaili Imam, Aga Khan IV, who sees it thus:

> The engagement of the Imamat in development is guided by the ethics of Islam which bridge faith and society, a premise on which I established the Aga Khan Development Network. Its cultural, social and economic development agencies seek to improve opportunities and living conditions of the weakest in society, without regard to their origin, gender or faith.[38]

From poverty alleviation and education to health, urban development and heritage preservation, the Network spans 30 countries. Its approach reflects what Katherine Marshall notes is a feature among faith-inspired actors: an 'integrated' rather than sectoral view of human well-being, in this instance with a remarkable track record.[39] Most of AKDN's beneficiaries – located mainly in South and Central Asia and Sub-Saharan Africa, but also parts of the Middle East, Europe and North America – are neither Ismaili nor Shi'a, and include large numbers of Sunni Muslims.

In essence, the welfare of the Shi'i community which the imam leads is regarded as inseparable from that of fellow Muslims and non-Muslims alike. Further evidence of this is the lead taken by him in launching the Global Centre for Pluralism (GCP) in 2006, located in Ottawa in partnership with Canada. Sensitive to the challenges of 'civic cohesion' in which valuing diversity is regarded as 'a global proposition', the GCP has sought to address contexts as disparate as Kyrgyzstan, Kenya and

---

[38] The Aga Khan, *Where Hope Takes Root: Democracy and Pluralism in an Interdependent World* (Vancouver, 2008), pp. 57–69 (Address to German Ambassadors, Berlin, 6 September 2004). AKDN's personnel at all levels are likewise multinational, including Jews and Christians. See generally the official website at http://www.akdn.org/; M. Ruthven, 'The Aga Khan Development Network and Institutions', in F. Daftary, ed., *A Modern History of the Ismailis* (London, 2011), pp. 189–220; D. Mohammad Poor, *Authority without Territory: The Aga Khan Development Network and the Ismaili Imamate* (New York, 2014).

[39] K. Marshall, *Global Institutions of Religion: Ancient Movers, Modern Shakers* (London, 2013), pp. 165–168, especially at pp. 174–175; AKDN specifically is covered at pp. 165–166. See also C. Lynch, 'Religious Humanitarianism and the Global Politics of Secularism', in C. Calhoun, M. Juergensmeyer and J. Van Antwerpen, ed., *Rethinking Secularism* (Oxford, 2011), pp. 204–224.

Canada.[40] This orientation on the part of the Imamat might be perceived by some as undercutting the particulars of Muslim and/or Shi'i identity, especially in the midst of cultural globalisation. Still others may be disappointed by a quite different undercutting – of the insistent claim about an unbridgeable gulf between the ostensibly distinct worlds of Islam and the West. The notion that identities can or ought to flourish in splendid isolation rests on a conflation of the 'distinctive' and the 'exclusive'; while the former may be laudable in favouring a positive sense of selfhood, the latter will most likely favour chauvinism.

*   *   *

A striking pair of portraits from Safawid Iran (1501–1732), depicting elegantly-attired male and female figures, are once thought to have graced the walls either of the royal palace in Isfahan or a residence in the city's Armenian quarter [Figures 16.1 and 16.2]. Now as part of the Aga Khan Museum's collection the portraits are accessible globally on its website.[41] In their compositional technique, the modelling of the figures, and the overall presentational style, European and especially Dutch influences are obvious. Yet the portraits also firmly partake of an established Persianate mode of pictorial representation, wherein gifted artists shaped aesthetic sensibilities as far afield as Mughal India and Central Asia. That this intertwining of occidental and oriental modes occurred during the Safawid period – when numerous such works were sponsored – is instructive. For it coincides with Shi'ism's establishment as the official Iranian religion (beginning in 1501–1512), in the making of a distinctive identity at the dawn of the modern era. At the height of their success during the 16th and 17th centuries, the Safawids cultivated a robust cosmopolitanism to which countless foreign visitors attested, hand-in-hand with the development of fresh Shi'i theologies and institutions. The portraits here are a reminder of the creative energies of that age within the larger narratives of Iran and Shi'ism.

The paradox of religion, Ali Shariati observed, is that it 'can destroy or revitalise, put to sleep or awaken, enslave or emancipate';[42] this alongside

---

[40] Official website at http://www.pluralism.ca/index.php?lang=en.

[41] Official website at https://www.agakhanmuseum.org, with commentary on the portraits. See generally A. J. Newman, *Safawid Iran: Rebirth of a Persian Empire* (London, 2009); S. Blair and J. Bloom, 'The Arts in Iran Under the Safawids and Zands', in *The Art and Architecture of Islam, 1250–1800* (New Haven, CT, 1994), pp. 165–181.

[42] *What Is to Be Done: The Enlightened Thinkers and an Islamic Renaissance*, trans. F. Rajaee (Houston, TX, 1986), p. 48. See generally R. S. Appleby, *The Ambivalence of the Sacred: Religion, Violence, and Reconciliation* (Oxford, 2000).

Figure 16.1 Portrait of a Safawid nobleman, 17th century.

Figure 16.2 Portrait of a Safawid noblewoman, 17th century.

teaching that balance is a key virtue. As a counterweight to the nativist positions that colonial as well as postcolonial history have witnessed in the Muslim world and elsewhere (the West included), the pluralist outlook sketched here is more than a civically desirable strategy. Its justification is grounded both in secular welfare/pragmatism as well as in theological conviction, neither of which is static. This dual grounding is not peculiar to the Shiʿi world; it is found in rich veins of interpretation past and present across faith traditions. For their part, the Shiʿa can draw upon a potent legacy of rationalist theological discourse, discussed by several authors in this volume as well as in this chapter, which lends support to a progressive civic ethos. Modernity's offspring, it would seem, are fated to grapple with identities that are inextricably secular as well as religious – and resisting this reality is as much part of our social imaginaries as embracing it.

Further Reading

Asad, Talal. *Formations of the Secular: Christianity, Islam, Modernity.* Stanford, CA, 2003.

Dabashi, Hamid. *Shi'ism: A Religion of Protest.* Cambridge, MA, 2011.

Deeb, Lara and Mona Harb. *Leisurely Islam: Negotiating Geography and Morality in Shi'ite South Beirut.* Princeton, NJ, 2013.

Korom, Frank J. *Hosay Trinidad: Muharram Performances in an Indo-Caribbean Diaspora.* Philadelphia, PA, 2003.

Machlis, Elisheva. *Shi'i Sectarianism in the Middle East: Modernization and the Quest for Islamic Universalism.* London, 2014.

Marcinkowski, Christoph. *Shi'ite Identities: Community and Culture in Changing Social Contexts.* Zurich, 2010.

Mavani, Hamid. *Religious Authority and Political Thought in Twelver Shi'ism: From Ali to Post-Khomeini.* London and New York, 2013.

Mohammad Poor, Daryoush. *Authority Without Territory: The Aga Khan Development Network and the Ismaili Imamate.* New York, 2014.

Monsutti, Alessandro, S. Naef, Silvia and F. Sabahi, ed. *The Other Shi'ites: From the Mediterranean to Central Asia.* Bern, 2007.

Ridgeon, Lloyd, ed. *Shi'i Islam and Identity: Religion, Politics and Change in the Global Muslim Community.* London, 2012.

Sajoo, Amyn B. *Muslim Modernities: Expressions of the Civil Imagination.* London, 2008.

Vahdat, Farzin. *God and Juggernaut: Iran's Encounter with Modernity.* Syracuse, NY, 2002.

Glossary

ʿAbbāsids: (Banu'l-ʿAbbās); descendants of al-ʿAbbās, the uncle of the Prophet, they took the caliphate from the Umayyads in 750, established their capital at Baghdad and ruled most of the Islamic world until 1258 when Baghdad was captured and the last caliph was killed by the Mongols. Thereafter they existed as a shadow-caliphate in Egypt under the control of the Mamluk sultanate until 1517.

ahl al-bayt: lit., the 'people of the house'; members of the household of the Prophet, including especially Muḥammad, ʿAlī, Fāṭima, al-Ḥasan, al-Ḥusayn and their progeny. The Prophet's family is also designated as *āl Muḥammad*.

ahl al-kisa: lit., the 'people of the cloak', the holy pentad identified in the tradition known as the *ḥadīth al-kisā* as the Prophet himself, ʿAlī, Fāṭima, al-Ḥasan and al-Ḥusayn. The *ḥadīth* recounts how the Prophet cast a cloak around his son-in-law, his daughter and their two sons and said, 'O God, these are my family whom I have chosen; take the pollution from them and purify them thoroughly.'

ʿAlids: descendants of ʿAlī b. Abī Ṭālib, cousin and son-in-law of the Prophet, and also the fourth caliph and the first Shiʿi imam (q.v.). The Shiʿis believed certain ʿAlids should be imams, and they acknowledged ʿAlī as the first among their imams. ʿAlī's first spouse was Fāṭima, the Prophet's daughter, and ʿAlī's descendants by Fāṭima (the only descendants of the Prophet) are in particular called Fāṭimids (q.v.). Descendants of ʿAlī and Fāṭima through their sons al-Ḥasan and al-Ḥusayn are also called Ḥasanids and Ḥusaynids. Descendants of al-Ḥasan and al-Ḥusayn are often also designated, respectively, as *sharīf*s and *sayyid*s.

ʿālim (pl. *ʿulamā*'): a learned man; specifically a scholar in Islamic religious sciences.

ʿaql: intellect, intelligence, reason.

ʿashūra: Derived from *ʿashara*, meaning ten, and referring to the tenth day of the Muslim month of Muḥarram 60/680, when the Prophet's grandson al-Ḥusayn was martyred; a day of mourning and ritual commemoration particularly sacred to Shiʿi communities around the world.

bāṭin/bāṭinī: the inward, hidden or esoteric meaning behind the literal wording of sacred texts and religious prescriptions, notably the Quran and the *sharīʿa* (q.v.), as distinct from the *ẓāhir* (q.v.); hence,

Bāṭinis, Bāṭiniyya and the groups associated with such ideas. Most of these groups were Shiʿi, particularly Ismaili.

caliph (Arabic, *khalīfa*):   lit., deputy, vicegerent, thus Deputy of the Prophet of God; the title of the leaders of the Muslim community after the death of the Prophet including most prominently, in Sunni tradition, the four 'rightly-guided' caliphs who came after the Prophet, and the Umayyad and the ʿAbbāsid dynasties, as well as the Fāṭimid Shiʿi dynasty of Imam-caliphs.

dāʿī: lit., he who summons; a religious propagandist or missionary of various Muslim groups, especially amongst the Ismaili and Zaydī Shiʿis. The term *dāʿī* came to be used generically from early on by the Ismailis in reference to any authorised representative of their *daʿwa* (q.v.); a propagandist responsible for spreading the Ismaili religious teachings and for winning suitable converts. The Zaydī Shiʿis used the term in reference to their spiritual leaders who were not qualified to be recognised as full imams (q.v.).

daʿwa: mission or propaganda; in the religio-political sense, *daʿwa* is the invitation or call to adopt the cause of an individual or family claiming the right to the imamate; it also refers to the entire hierarchy of ranks within the particular religious organisation developed for this purpose, especially amongst the Ismailis. The Ismailis often referred to their movement simply as *al-daʿwa* or more formally as *al-daʿwa al-hādiya*, the 'rightly guiding mission'. Any qualified person aspiring to the imamate of the Zaydīs also needed to launch an open *daʿwa*, inviting the faithful to accept his leadership.

faqīh (pl. *fuqahā*):   in its technical meaning it denotes an exponent of *fiqh* (q.v.); a specialist in Islamic jurisprudence; a Muslim jurist in general.

Fāṭimids: descendants of ʿAlī b. Abī Ṭālib and the Prophet's daughter Fāṭima, corresponding to Fāṭimid ʿAlids (q.v.); also the name of the Ismaili dynasty of Imam-caliphs, claiming Fāṭimid descent, reigning from 909 to 1171.

fiqh: the technical term for Islamic jurisprudence; the science of law in Islam; the discipline of elucidating the *sharīʿa* (q.v.).

Ghadīr Khumm: name of a pool between Mecca and Medina. On 16 March 632 the Prophet halted here on returning from the *ḥajj* with his followers and in the course of a sermon, according to Shiʿi tradition, designated his cousin and son-in-law ʿAlī as his successor with the words: *man kuntū mawlāhu fā ʿAlī mawlāhu* (whomsoever I am the master of, ʿAlī is also his master).

ghayba: lit., absence; the word has been used in a technical sense for the condition of anyone who has been withdrawn by God from the eyes of men and whose life during that period of occultation (called his *ghayba*) may be miraculously prolonged. In this sense, a number of Shiʿi groups have recognised the *ghayba* of a particular imam (q.v.), with the implication that no further imam was to succeed him and he was to return at a foreordained time before the Day of Resurrection, *qiyāma* (q.v.), as the *mahdī* (q.v.). The twelfth imam of the Twelver Shiʿis has remained in *ghayba* since 874.

ghulāt (sing. *ghālī*): exaggerator, extremist; a term of disapproval for individuals accused of exaggeration (*ghuluww*) in religion and in respect of imams (q.v.); it was applied particularly to those Shiʿi personalities and groups whose doctrines were offensive to the Twelver Shiʿis.

ḥadīth: a report, sometimes translated as Tradition, relating an action or saying of the Prophet, or the corpus of such reports collectively, constituting one of the major sources of Islamic law, second in importance only to the Quran. For the Shiʿi communities, it generally also refers to the deeds and sayings of the imams (q.v.). The Shiʿis accept those *ḥadīths* related from the Prophet which had been handed down or sanctioned by their imams in conjunction with those *ḥadīths* related from the imams recognised by them. The Shiʿis also use the terms *riwāyāt* and *akhbār* as synonyms of *ḥadīth*.

Ḥasanids: see ʿAlids.

Ḥusaynids: see ʿAlids.

Ḥusayniyya: also called *takiya*, a permanent Shiʿi ritual-oriented building, also known as an *ʿashūrkhāna* or *imāmbārā* in India, serving as a place for collective mourning rituals, for instance *taʿziya* (q.v.), the departure and arrival point for processions, and as the repository for *ʿashūra* related ceremonial objects.

ijtihād: independent legal decision or judgment arrived at by knowledge and reasoning, *ʿaql*, particularly in matters pertaining to the *sharīʿa* (q.v.); one who practises *ijtihād* is called a *mujtahid*.

ʿilm: knowledge, more specifically religious knowledge. Amongst the Shiʿis, it was held that every imam (q.v.) possessed a special secret knowledge, *ʿilm*, which was divinely inspired and transmitted through the *naṣṣ* (q.v.) of the preceding imam.

imam (Arabic, *imām*; pl. *aʾimma*): leader of a group of Muslims in prayer, *ṣalāt*; the supreme leader of the Muslim community. The titles was used particularly by the Shiʿis in reference to the persons recognised by them as the heads of the Muslim community after the Prophet. The Shiʿis regard ʿAlī b. Abī Ṭālib and certain of his descendants as such leaders or imams, the legitimate successors to the Prophet. The imams are held to be *maʿṣūm*, fully immune from sin and error; they are generally held to be also divinely appointed, and divinely guided in the discharge of the special spiritual functions. Amongst the Sunnis, the term is used in reference to any great *'ālim* (q.v.), especially the founder of a legal *madhhab* (q.v.). The office of imam is called imamate (Arabic, *imāma*).

īmān: faith; belief; from the same root derives *mu'min*, believer.

'irfān: gnosis or the way of knowledge which is the heart of Sufi (q.v.) teachings, and the means whereby man is led to the realisation of the divine through illuminative knowledge.

'iṣma: inerrancy, infallibility; a quality attributed to prophets and, in Shi'i Islam, to imams (q.v.). One who is endowed with *'iṣma* is called *ma'ṣūm*.

isnād (sing. *sanad*):   lit., supports, authorities; refers to a 'chain of authorities' that stands as verification for a *ḥadīth* (q.v.) and thus to the record of the oral transfer of the *ḥadīth* from individual to individual.

khuṭba: an address or sermon delivered by a *khāṭib* at the Friday midday public prayers in the mosque; since it includes a prayer for the ruler, mention in the *khuṭba* is a mark of sovereignty in Islam.

madhhab (pl. *madhāhib*):   a system or school of religious law in Islam; in particular it is applied to the four main systems of *fiqh* (q.v.) that arose among the Sunni Muslims, namely, Ḥanafī, Mālikī, Shāfi'ī and Ḥanbalī, named after the jurists who founded them. Different Shi'i communities have had their own *madhāhib*; the Twelver Imami Shi'i *madhhab* is known as Ja'farī, named after Imam Ja'far al-Ṣādiq. In Persian, the word *madhhab* is also used to mean religion, a synonym of *dīn*.

mahdī: 'the rightly-guided one'; a name applied to the restorer of true religion and justice who, according to a widely held Muslim belief, will appear and rule before the end of the world. This name with its various messianic connotations has been applied to different individuals by Shi'i and Sunni Muslims in the course of the centuries. Belief in the coming of the *mahdī* of the family of the Prophet, the *ahl al-bayt* (q.v.), became a central aspect of the faith in Shi'i Islam, in contrast to Sunnism. Also distinctively Shi'i was the common belief in a temporary absence or occultation, *ghayba* (q.v.), of the *mahdī* and his eventual return, *raj'a* (q.v.), in glory. In Shi'i terminology at least from the 8th century CE, the *mahdī* was commonly given the epithet *al-qā'im* (q.v.), 'riser', also called *qā'im āl Muḥammad*, denoting a member of the Prophet's family who would rise and restore justice on earth. Various early Shi'i groups expected the return of the last imam (q.v.) recognised by them in the role of the *qāʾim*. The majority of the early Ismailis, including especially the Qarmaṭīs, recognised their seventh imam, Muḥammad b. Ismāʿīl, as the Mahdī. The Twelver Shiʿis have acknowledged their twelfth imam as their hidden Mahdī. The Zaydīs did not generally recognise any of their imams as the *mahdī*.

marjaʿ al-taqlīd (Persian, *marjaʿ-i taqlīd*):   the 'source of emulation', or the 'supreme exemplar'; as a technical term it refers to that Shiʿi religious scholar who through his learning and probity is qualified to be followed in all points of religious practice and law by the generality of the Twelver Shiʿi Muslims.

mujtahid: see *ijtihād*.

muqallid: see *taqlīd*.

murīd: disciple; specifically disciple of a Sufi (q.v.) master; member of a Sufi order in general; also frequently used in reference to an ordinary Nizārī Ismaili in Persia and elsewhere during the post-Alamūt phase of Nizārī history.

murshid: guide, Sufi (q.v.) master; also used in reference to the imam (q.v.) of the Nizārī Ismailis during the post-Alamūt phase of their history.

naṣṣ   explicit designation of a successor by his predecessor, particularly relating to the Shiʿi view of succession to the imamate, whereby each imam (q.v.), under divine guidance, designates his successor. One who receives the *naṣṣ* is called *manṣūṣ*.

nāṭiq (pl. *nuṭaqāʾ*):   lit., speaker, one gifted with speech; in Ismaili thought, a speaking or law-announcing prophet who brings a new religious law, *sharīʿa* (q.v.), abrogating the previous law and hence initiating a new era in the sacred history of humankind.

panj tān-i pak: see *ahl al-kisa*.

pīr: the Persian equivalent of the Arabic word *shaykh* in the sense of a spiritual guide, Sufi (q.v.) master or *murshid* (q.v.), qualified to lead disciples, *murīd*s (q.v.), on the mystical path, *ṭarīqa* (q.v.), to truth (*ḥaqīqa*); also used loosely in reference to the imam (q.v.) and the holders of the highest ranks in the *daʿwa* (q.v.) hierarchy of the post-Alamūt Nizārī Ismailis.

qāḍī (pl. *quḍāt*):   a religious judge administering Islamic law, the *sharīʿa* (q.v.).

qāʾim: 'riser'; the eschatological *mahdī* (q.v.)

qiyāma: Resurrection and the Last Day, when mankind will be judged and committed forever to either Paradise or Hell.

rajʿa: lit., return; the word has been used in a technical sense to denote the return or reappearance of a messianic personality, specifically one considered as the *mahdī* (q.v.). A number of early Shi'i groups awaited the return of one or another imam (q.v.) as the *mahdī*, often together with many of his supporters, from the dead or from occultation, *ghayba* (q.v.), before the Day of Resurrection, *qiyāma* (q.v.).

Ṣafawids:　dynasty that ruled Persia as sovereigns from 1501 to 1722, as puppet monarchs from 1729 to 1736 and as pretenders to the throne up to 1773. The first Ṣafawid monarch, Shah Ismā'īl declared Twelver Shi'ism the official religion of the new state.

sharī'a:　the whole body of rules guiding the life of a Muslim. The provisions of the *sharī'a* are worked out through the discipline of *fiqh* (q.v.).

Sufi:　an exponent of Sufism (*taṣawwuf*), the commonest term for that aspect of Islam which is based on the mystical life; hence it denotes a Muslim mystic; more specifically, a member of an organised Sufi order, *ṭarīqa* (q.v.).

sunna:　custom; practice; particularly that associated with the exemplary life of the Prophet, comprising his deeds, utterances and his unspoken approval; it is embodied in *ḥadīth* (q.v.).

tafsīr (pl. *tafāsir*):　lit., explanation, commentary; particularly the commentaries on the Quran; the external, philological exegesis of the Quran, as distinct from *ta'wīl* (q.v.). A Quran commentator is called *mufasir* (pl. *mufasirūn*).

taqiyya:　precautionary dissimulation of one's true religious beliefs, especially in times of danger, used in particular by Twelvers (Ithnā'asharīs) and Ismailis. It is the equivalent of the Persian word *kitmān*.

taqlīd:　lit., emulation, imitation or following; it denotes the following of the authoritative guidance of a qualified *mujtahid*; one who practises *taqlīd* is know as *muqallid*; the opposite of *ijtihād* (q.v.).

ṭarīqa:　way, path; the mystical spiritual path followed by Sufis (q.v.); any one of the organised Sufi orders. It is also used by the Nizārī Ismailis in reference to their interpretation of Islam.

ta'wīl:　the educing of the inner meaning from the literal wording or apparent meaning of a text or a ritual, religious prescription; as a technical term among the Shi'i Muslims, particularly the Ismailis, it denotes the method of educing the *bāṭin* (q.v.) from the *ẓāhir* (q.v.). Translated also as spiritual or hermeneutic exegesis, *ta'wīl* may be distinguished from *tafsīr* (q.v.).

ta'ziya:　from the Arabic *'azza* (to mourn or to console); in Iran *ta'ziya* denotes a theatrical production of a Shi'i passion play focusing on the martyrdom of Imam al-Ḥusayn and his companions at Karbala.

The term can also refer to any ritual devoted to commemorating the suffering of Imam Ḥusayn.

'ulamā': see *'ālim.*

Umayyads: (Banū Umayya); a dynasty that ruled the Islamic empire from 661 to 750. The first caliph of the Umayyad dynasty was Mu'āwiya b. Abī Sufyān, governor of Syria and member of a family of Meccan notables. He established himself as caliph after the murder of the fourth rightly-guided caliph of the Sunnis and first Imam of the Shi'is, 'Alī b. Abī Ṭālib.

umma: community, any people as followers of a particular religion or prophet; in particular, the Muslims as forming a religious community.

uṣūl (pl. of *aṣl*): lit., roots; as a technical term it refers to primary principles, either of religion, *uṣūl al-dīn*, or of jurisprudence, *uṣūl al-fiqh.*

walāya: devotion; devoted love; in Shi'i usage *walāya* denotes the loyalty, devotion and love that is due to the imam (q.v.) from his followers because of his *wilāya* (q.v.) or authority. *Walāya* is regarded as one of the main principles of Islam for the Shi'is.

walī: friend; possessor of authority. In the Shi'i tradition 'Alī is the *walī Allāh* (the guardian of the Muslim community and the friend of God).

wilāya: authority; for the Shi'is *wilāya* applies to the position of 'Alī b. Abī Ṭālib as the single, explicitly designated heir and successor to the Prophet in whom all responsibility for the guidance of the Muslims was subsequently vested. See *walāya.*

waṣī (pl. *awṣiyā'*): legatee, executor of a will; the immediate successor to a prophet; in this sense, it was the function of *awṣiyā'* to interpret and explain the messages brought by prophets, *anbiyā'*; see *nāṭiq.*

ẓāhir/ẓāhirī: the outward, literal, or exoteric meaning of sacred texts and religious prescriptions, notably the Quran and the *sharī'a* (q.v.), as distinct from the *bāṭin* (q.v.).

Index

Page numbers in italics refer to illustrations